European Security Policy and Strategic Culture

With the Lisbon Treaty in place and the European Union increasingly involved in international crisis management and stabilization operations in places near and far, this volume revisits the trajectory of a European strategic culture. Specifically, it studies the usefulness of its application in a variety of circumstances, including the EU's operations in Africa and the Balkans as well as joint operations with NATO and the United Nations.

The contributors find that strategic culture is a useful tool to explain and understand the EU's civilian *and* military operations, not in the sense of a 'cause', but as a European normative framework of preferences and constraints. Accordingly, classical notions of strategic culture in the field of international security must be adapted to highlight the specific character of Europe's strategic culture, especially by taking the interaction with the United Nations and NATO into account. Though at variance over the extent to which security and defence missions have demonstrated or promoted a shared strategic culture in Europe, the authors reveal a growing sense that a cohesive strategic culture is critical in the EU's ambition of being a global actor. Should Europe fail to nurture a shared strategic culture, its actions will be based much more on flexibility than on cohesion.

This book was published as a special issue of *Contemporary Security Policy*.

Peter Schmidt is Academic Director of the newly founded Deutsches Institut für Demokratieentwicklung und Sicherheit (Berlin) and Honorary Professor at the University of Mannheim. Until 2008 he was a senior fellow of the Stiftung Wissenschaft und Politik in Berlin.

Benjamin Zyla, Ph.D. is Assistant Professor (tenure-track) in the School of International Development and Global Studies at the University of Ottawa, and recently was a visiting professor at the École Normale Supérieure de Lyon. He also held the prestigious Social Sciences and Humanities Research Council of Canada (SSHRC) Postdoctoral Fellowship, and was a fellow at the Europe Center at Stanford University, the Centre for International Relations at Queen's University and the Centre for International Policy Studies at the University of Ottawa. His research interests include global governance, regional organizations, international peace-operations, strategic culture, and European foreign and security policy.

European Security Policy and Strategic Culture

Edited by
Peter Schmidt and Benjamin Zyla

LONDON AND NEW YORK

First published 2013
by Routledge
2 Park Square, Milton Park, Abingdon, Oxfordshire OX14 4RN

Simultaneously published in the USA and Canada
by Routledge
711 Third Avenue, New York, NY 10017

First issued in paperback 2015

Routledge is an imprint of the Taylor & Francis Group, an informa business

© 2013 Taylor & Francis

This book is a reproduction of *Contemporary Security Policy*, vol. 32, issue 3. The Publisher requests to those authors who may be citing this book to state, also, the bibliographical details of the special issue on which the book was based.

All rights reserved. No part of this book may be reprinted or reproduced or utilised in any form or by any electronic, mechanical, or other means, now known or hereafter invented, including photocopying and recording, or in any information storage or retrieval system, without permission in writing from the publishers.

Trademark notice: Product or corporate names may be trademarks or registered trademarks, and are used only for identification and explanation without intent to infringe.

British Library Cataloguing in Publication Data
A catalogue record for this book is available from the British Library

ISBN13: 978-1-138-94430-5 (pbk)
ISBN13: 978-0-415-63838-8 (hbk)

Typeset in Times New Roman
by Taylor & Francis Books

Publisher's Note
The publisher would like to make readers aware that the chapters in this book may be referred to as articles as they are identical to the articles published in the special issue. The publisher accepts responsibility for any inconsistencies that may have arisen in the course of preparing this volume for print

Contents

Citation Information	vii
Notes on Contributors	ix
Abstracts of Articles	xi
Preface	xvii
Acronyms	xix

1. European Security Policy: Strategic Culture in Operation?
   Peter Schmidt and Benjamin Zyla   1

EUROPEAN STRATEGIC CULTURE

2. 'Let's Call the Whole Thing Off'? Security Culture as Strategic Culture
   David G. Haglund   11

3. EU Strategic Culture: When the Means Becomes the End
   Per M. Norheim-Martinsen   34

4. Strategic Culture and the Common Security and Defence Policy – A Classical Realist Assessment and Critique
   Sten Rynning   52

TESTING STRATEGIC CULTURE: MILITARY OPERATIONS

5. From Words to Deeds: Strategic Culture and the European Union's Balkan Military Missions
   Charles C. Pentland   68

6. The EU's Military Involvement in the Democratic Republic of Congo: Security Culture, Interests and Games
   Peter Schmidt   84

7. The Failure of a European Strategic Culture – EUFOR CHAD: The Last of its Kind?
   Jean Yves Haine   99

CONTENTS

TESTING STRATEGIC CULTURE: CIVILIAN OPERATIONS

8. In Search of a Trademark: EU Civilian Operations in Africa
   Reinhardt Rummel 121

9. Putting Ideas into Action: EU Civilian Crisis Management in the Western Balkans
   Arnold H. Kammel 142

CONNECTING: THE EU, UN AND NATO

10. Strategic Culture and Multilateralism: The Interplay of the EU and the UN in Conflict and Crisis Management
    Ingo Peters 161

11. Overlap or Opposition? EU and NATO's Strategic (Sub-)Culture
    Benjamin Zyla 184

    Index 205

Citation Information

The chapters in this book were originally published in *Contemporary Security Policy*, volume 32, issue 3 (December 2011). When citing this material, please use the original page numbering for each article, as follows:

Chapter 1
European Security Policy: Strategic Culture in Operation?
Peter Schmidt and Benjamin Zyla
Contemporary Security Policy, volume 32, issue 3 (December 2011)
pp. 484-493

Chapter 2
'Let's Call the Whole Thing Off'? Security Culture as Strategic Culture
David G. Haglund
Contemporary Security Policy, volume 32, issue 3 (December 2011)
pp. 494-516

Chapter 3
EU Strategic Culture: When the Means Becomes the End
Per M. Norheim-Martinsen
Contemporary Security Policy, volume 32, issue 3 (December 2011)
pp. 517-534

Chapter 4
Strategic Culture and the Common Security and Defence Policy – A Classical Realist Assessment and Critique
Sten Rynning
Contemporary Security Policy, volume 32, issue 3 (December 2011)
pp. 535-550

Chapter 5
From Words to Deeds: Strategic Culture and the European Union's Balkan Military Missions
Charles C. Pentland

Chapter 6
The EU's Military Involvement in the Democratic Republic of Congo: Security Culture, Interests and Games
Peter Schmidt

Chapter 7
The Failure of a European Strategic Culture – EUFOR CHAD: The Last of its Kind?
Jean Yves Haine

Chapter 8
In Search of a Trademark: EU Civilian Operations in Africa
Reinhardt Rummel

Chapter 9
Putting Ideas into Action: EU Civilian Crisis Management in the Western Balkans
Arnold H. Kammel

Chapter 10
Strategic Culture and Multilateralism: The Interplay of the EU and the UN in Conflict and Crisis Management
Ingo Peters

Chapter 11
Overlap or Opposition? EU and NATO's Strategic (Sub-)Culture
Benjamin Zyla

Notes on Contributors

David G. Haglund is a Professor of Political Studies at Queen's University, in Kingston, Ontario, Canada. He concentrates on transatlantic and North American security relations, and is currently writing a monograph on ethnic diasporas and the North American security community. He is co-editor of the *International Journal*.

Jean Yves Haine is a Professor at the Department of Political Science, University of Toronto, and an Associate at the Trudeau Centre for Peace and Conflict Studies. He writes on International and Atlantic security, European integration, US foreign policy and the use of force. His book *Les Etats-Unis ont-ils besoin d'alliés?* (Payot 2004) received the France-Amérique Prize, 2004.

Arnold H. Kammel holds a Doctor of Law degree from the University of Graz. In 2004 he became a research fellow at the Austrian Institute for European and Security Policy (AIES). Since 2007, he has been Secretary General of the AIES. Before joining the AIES he was a research fellow at the Institute of Austrian, European and Comparative Public Law and Political Science at the Karl-Franzens-University of Graz. His research covers European integration (focusing on European Union foreign, security and defence policy) as well as European Union governance.

Per M. Norheim-Martinsen is a Senior Research Fellow at the Fafo Institute for Applied International Studies in Oslo. His recent publications include 'Beyond Intergovernmentalism: European Security and Defence Policy and the Governance Approach' (*Journal of Common Market Studies*, 48/5, 2010) and *The European Union and Military Force* (Cambridge University Press, 2013).

Charles C. Pentland is a Professor of Political Studies at Queen's University, in Kingston, Ontario, Canada, where he teaches courses on international organization and global governance. He served as Director of Queen's University's Centre for International Relations from 2002 to 2010. In recent years his research has focused on the external relations of the

European Union, especially its eastward enlargement, its role in the Balkans, its relations with the former Soviet Union, and its Common Foreign and Security Policy.

Ingo Peters is Associate Professor of Political Science, Freie Universität Berlin, and Executive Director of the Center for Transnational Relations, Foreign and Security Policy at the Otto-Suhr-Institut of Political Science. His major research interests are European security policy, German foreign policy and transatlantic relations. His recent publications include *Transatlantic Tug-of-War: Prospects for US-European Cooperation* (Lit Verlag, 2006) and *20 Years since the Fall of the Berlin Wall. Transitions, State Break-Up and Democratic Politics in Central Europe and Germany* which was edited with Elizabeth Bakke (Berliner Wissenschafts-Verlag/Intersentia, 2011).

Reinhardt Rummel is a former Senior Fellow of the Stiftung Wissenschaft und Politik in Berlin, and currently a Senior Scholar at the Center for Applied Policy Research, Ludwig-Maximilians-University Munich. His teaching, research, and publications concentrate on contemporary foreign, security, and defence policies of the European Union.

Sten Rynning is Professor of Political Science as well as Head of the Center for War Studies, the University of Southern Denmark. His books include *The Liberal Disconnect: NATO and Afghanistan, 2001–2012* (Stanford University Press, 2012) and *NATO Renewed: The Power and Purpose of Transatlantic Cooperation* (Palgrave-MacMillan, 2005).

Peter Schmidt is Academic Director of the newly founded Deutsches Institut für Demokratieentwicklung und Sicherheit (Berlin) and Honorary Professor at the University of Mannheim. Until 2008 he was a senior fellow of the Stiftung Wissenschaft und Politik in Berlin. He regularly organizes international crisis management simulations and scenario workshops on an international scale and has published widely on issues of European security, transatlantic relations, regional crisis management, and sustainability questions of the armed forces.

Benjamin Zyla, Ph.D. is Assistant Professor (tenure-track) in the School of International Development and Global Studies at the University of Ottawa, and recently was a visiting professor at the École Normale Supérieure de Lyon. He also held the prestigious Social Sciences and Humanities Research Council of Canada (SSHRC) Postdoctoral Fellowship, and was a fellow at the Europe Center at Stanford University, the Centre for International Relations at Queen's University and the Centre for International Policy Studies at the University of Ottawa. His research interests include global governance, regional organizations, international peace-operations, strategic culture, and European foreign and security policy.

Abstracts of Articles

European Security Policy: Strategic Culture in Operation?
by Peter Schmidt and Benjamin Zyla

With the Lisbon Treaty in place and the European Union increasingly involved in crisis management and stabilization in places near and far, this Special Issue examines whether European security behaviour is evidence of an actual *strategic culture*. Contrary to prevailing scholarship on the subject, this volume demonstrates that strategic culture, as an analytical tool and force on European strategic goals and conduct, is far from conclusive. Ostensibly, the development of a security culture was a major lever by which the European Union's principal planning document, the European Security Strategy of 2003, tried to guide the European Union's role in international security. This volume revisits the trajectory of the concept of strategic culture and examines its application in a variety of circumstances, especially operations in Africa and the Balkans, including joint operations with NATO and the United Nations. The contributors to this Special Issue find that strategic culture is a useful tool to understand EU's operations, not in the sense of a 'cause', but as a uniquely European normative framework of preferences and constraints. Classical notions of strategic culture must be adapted to highlight the specific evolution of Europe's strategic culture. Though at variance over the extent to which security and defense missions have promoted a shared strategic culture in Europe, the authors in this Special Issue reveal a growing sense that a strategic culture is critical for European ambition as a global actor. Should Europe fail to nurture a shared strategic culture, its ambitions and the normative framework that underpins it will unravel.

'Let's Call the Whole Thing Off'? Security Culture as Strategic Culture
by David G. Haglund

Scholars interested in contemporary security and defence policy, in Europe as elsewhere, often seek refuge in conceptual havens, and the articles in this special issue are no exceptions. One of those sheltering spots has been dubbed *security culture*, while another fashionable resting place carries the label, 'strategic culture'. This article argues that attempts to draw a distinction between the two categories are superfluous, not to say meaningless, and that insofar as what we should call our concept, it really is a case of Tweedledum and Tweedledee. More important is the task of attempting to abstract policy significance from the complexity and definitional vagueness of the more 'senior' of the two concepts, namely strategic culture. This complexity and vagueness to the contrary notwithstanding, this article claims that strategic culture can be of some analytical use in highlighting the ways in which both context and character have played, and continue to play, a part in shaping states' orientation toward security and defence policy.

EU Strategic Culture: When the Means Becomes the End
by Per M. Norheim-Martinsen

After being debated in academic circles for years, the idea of a common European Union strategic culture was elevated to a policy objective in the 2003 European Security Strategy. However, whether the European Union has a strategic culture or not is still up for debate. By drawing on developments in strategic culture theory, this article demonstrates that the idea of strategic culture is not only compatible with the European Union, but may be a particularly useful conceptual tool for studying actors for which cultural factors can make up for the lack of more material ones, such as borders, language, political structure, national history, and so on. Offering a fresh perspective on the European Security Strategy, it shows that a specific strategic culture has evolved in the EU, in which consensus on a comprehensive approach to security as a unique European asset has become a focal point for the fledgling European Security and Defense Policy (ESDP). However, the article concludes that this does not provide for a robust strategic culture. The repeated emphasis on the EU's unique potentials as a comprehensive security actor will also invite criticism if the EU fails to mount operations that reflect its own success formula.

Strategic Culture and the Common Security and Defence Policy – A Classical Realist Assessment and Critique
by Sten Rynning

The European Union has for the better part of a decade been in possession of a Common Security and Defence Policy (CSDP) that promises to place a missing but crucial arrow in the European Union quiver, namely an instrument of hard power. It is no wonder that many observers see in the CSDP a power ambition wrapped in a particular European view of the world – or, an emerging European strategic culture. The European Union mostly communicates this culture in benevolent terms, promising a policy of tolerance and international legitimacy and the employment of power for the sake of development and good governance. All this is misleading, however, if we follow the classical study of power, namely classical realism. It tells us that the CSDP is not about balancing or projecting power internationally: the European Union is simply too weak for this. It tells us that the CSDP instead is primarily about maintaining restraint within Europe where the shadow of great power rivalry and war still looms. It is about the institutionalization of the weakness of the European nation-state. This leads classical realism to caution about how far the EU should reach in external affairs and thus how progressive the EU should want to be. The European Union should be wary of strong claims to strategic culture and European purpose. Because prudence defines the CSDP's roots and rationale, classical realism argues, the EU is better off with modest goals integrated into an Atlantic framework. According to classical realism it is therefore in the American interest to remain engaged in Europe to promote this type of development.

From Words to Deeds: Strategic Culture and the European Union's Balkan Military Missions
by Charles C. Pentland

Evidence that the European Union has acquired a distinctive strategic culture must be sought in the realms both of ideas and of action. Elements of a declaratory European Union strategic culture are to be found in the 2003 European Security Strategy and the subsequent reflections of officials and academics. A supplementary but perhaps more reliable guide to its central features may lie in how the European Union has conducted itself in the 24 European Security and Defence Policy missions, both military and civilian, that it has created since 2003. Overviews of these missions reveal some consistent themes and patterns of behaviour roughly congruent with the discourse of EU strategic culture. A closer analysis of the two Balkan military operations – Concordia in the Former Yugoslav Republic of Macedonia and Althea in Bosnia-Herzegovina – gives a richer and more nuanced picture of the relationship between words and deeds. The aim in studying strategic culture should be not to reveal causality as much as to explore consistency between ideas and action.

EU's Military Involvement in the Democratic Republic of Congo: Security Culture, Interests and Games
by Peter Schmidt

The following exploratory case study analyses European Union's military involvement in the Democratic Republic of Congo in the framework of two operations: Artemis (2003) and EUFOR (2006). The European Union in this context is not regarded as a 'single actor' but as part of a system, including the member states and the United Nations. In order to bridge the gap between strategic culture and behaviour, it is proposed to broaden the scope of the strategic culture approach by taking specific interests and 'games' played by the actors across these levels into consideration. The analysis also suggests that two background features of the multi-level 'game' as part of the European Union's strategic culture should be especially recognized: the 'barrack yard syndrome' as a principle of behaviour influencing the question who of participates in the operation, and 'multilateral Caesarism' as a feature of the 'multilevel game' which limits parliamentarian control of decisions and may also have a major impact on decisions to launch a military operation in the framework of the EU.

The Failure of a European Strategic Culture – EUFOR CHAD: The Last of its Kind?
by Jean Yves Haine

The Common Security and Defence Policy (CSDP) is in crisis. The concept of strategic culture is controversial, even more so at the European level. Yet as a historical context and as a grouping of shared beliefs and practices, it helps us to better understand how and why the promises of Saint-Malo were not met. A specific set of

European *political* and *security* beliefs that should not be confused with a *strategic* culture were developed at the European level. The EU's misunderstanding of human security, combined with a widespread risk aversion, has transformed CSDP missions into political exercises, more focused on Europe's own image, posture and legitimacy than on the strategic requirements necessary to their success. The EUFOR Chad mission, the longest and most complex CSDP mission so far, was a good illustration of this problem. Moreover, this operation played a significant role in the French disillusion and estrangement from CSDP itself. The credibility and legitimacy of the Union in security and defence are now in doubt.

In Search of a Trademark: EU Civilian Operations in Africa
by Reinhardt Rummel

Is the European Union about to develop a strategic culture? Analysis of past and present civilian missions under the European Security and Defence Policy in Africa and the assessment of the corresponding institutional setup in Brussels, including the Lisbon Treaty, does not deliver evidence for such a geopolitical quality. Most of the European Union member states continue to be preoccupied with the practical puzzle of the EU's internal build-up. At best the former colonial powers, especially Paris and London, seem to have an idea of a more far-reaching role of the EU on the African continent (see Libya). In the security field the European Union remains a collection of states with no common defence and not much collective, let alone unified, political will. It also lacks the ability to mount the resources for its declared international ambitions. Without these prerequisites for any development of a strategic culture Brussels is condemned to stay at the margin of an increasingly competitive multipolar world and to simply hope for some influence in individual cases of intervention.

Putting ideas into action: EU Civilian Crisis Management in the Western Balkans
by Arnold H. Kammel

Since the early days of the Common Foreign and Security Policy and the European Security and Defence Policy, the EU has always paid special attention to developments in the Western Balkans and therefore declared them a strategic priority for European external action. Thus, it is not surprising that the first missions in the framework of ESDP were deployed to this region. Considering the deployment of civilian crisis management missions to the Western Balkans a first step in the shaping of a strategic culture and based on the assumption that the European Union clearly possesses the prerequisites to form such a strategic culture, the following chapter will analyse the development of civilian crisis management and chronologically describe and evaluate the four civilian missions carried out in the Western Balkans. The conclusion is that despite the fact that ESDP is still a work in progress, the engagement in civilian crisis management missions already provides a marker for the existence of an emerging European strategic culture in the process of formation.

Strategic Culture and Multilateralism: The interplay of the EU and the UN in conflict and crisis management
by Ingo Peters

This analysis aims to identify the relative significance of strategic culture for inter-organizational cooperation problems, here of the European Union and United Nations in the realm of conflict and crisis management. First, the respective strategic cultures are identified and compared in order to formulate expectations (hypotheses) for co-operation problems. Second, the practice of inter-organizational co-operation is investigated by using illustrative examples from three European Union operations conducted in collaboration with the United Nations: Operation Artemis, DR Congo 2003, EU EUFOR DR Congo 2006, and EUFOR Chad 2008. Different types of material and institutional factors hampering cooperation are identified. Third, empirical findings are interpreted and evaluated in terms of evidence for strategic culture as a causal factor influencing co-operation. This analysis suggests that in this case strategic culture is apparently a comparatively marginal factor hampering inter-organizational co-operation.

Overlap or Opposition? EU and NATO's Strategic (Sub-)Culture
by Benjamin Zyla

This paper discusses the inter-organizational relationship of the two leading security organizations in Europe: the European Union and the North Atlantic Treaty Organization. Rather than discussing the two organizations' material overlaps, the paper discusses their quest for organizational identity and role in the domain of foreign and defence policy, as well as the ideational structures that affect both institutions' social behaviour and their behaviour toward each other. It aims first to tease out how structures of meaning in the form of norms, values, and beliefs have affected the two organizations' behaviour toward each other; and second to introduce explanatory arguments about their subcultural relationship that can help explain their attitudinal divergences.

The article makes two arguments: First, there is a significant normative overlap between the two institutions, especially with regards to future challenges and threats and the role of third parties and international organizations. Second, I introduce a preliminary argument by holding that the best way to make sense of the ideational divergences between the two organizations is to conceptualize NATO's strategic culture as a subculture of the European Union's strategic culture.

Preface

This special issue would not have been possible without the gracious help, assistance, and wisdom of a number of people and institutions. To start with, some of the papers within originate from the annual conference of the Centre for International Relations at Queen's University held in 2008, which assessed the progress and prospects of the European Security and Defence Policy ten years after the seminal Franco-British summit meeting at Saint-Malo. A total of 17 specialists in matters of European security and defence came together for two days of discussion to examine the twenty-plus military and civilian operations that the EU has conducted under ESDP since 2003. Thanks, therefore, go to the Centre for International Relations at Queen's University, Canada (QCIR), and in particular Charles Pentland and Maureen Bartram for their tireless work organizing and running it.

We would also like to thank the authors of the papers that follow. Without them, this special issue may not have been possible, would certainly look much different, and possibly would not even have materialized. Some joined at a very short notice, while another laboured from his sickbed while recovering from a heart attack and a ligament rupture. We are very grateful for all of their contributions.

Above all, however, this special issue would not have been possible without Regina and Aaron Karp, the two editors of *Contemporary Security Policy*. Special thanks goes to them for their wisdom, enthusiasm, and encouragement from the first moment that we proposed this project. It has been wonderful working with you – thank you!

Peter Schmidt
Benjamin Zyla

The managing editors extend their appreciation to the guest editors of this special issue, Peter Schmidt and Benjamin Zyla, for their vision, engagement and camaraderie, and to the European Union and *AccessEU*, an EU-funded project at Old Dominion University, for making the publication of this issue possible.

Acronyms

AMIS	African Unions missions in Sudan
AMISON	African Union Mission in Somalia
APF	African Peace Facility
APSA	African Peace and Security Architecture
ASF	African Standby Force
BiH	Bosnia and Herzegovina
CARDS	Community Assistance for Reconstruction, Development and Stabilisation
CFSP	Common Foreign and Security Policy
CIVCOM	Civilian Aspects of Crisis Management
CMCO	Civil–Military Cooperation
CMPD	Crisis Management and Planning Directorate
CPCC	Civilian Planning and Conduct Capability
CRCT	Crisis Response Coordinating Team
CRTC	Crisis Response Co-ordination Team
CSDP	Common Security and Defence Policy
DITF	Darfur Integrated Task Force
DPKO	UN Department of Peacekeeping Operations
DRC	Democratic Republic of Congo
EC	European Communities
EDA	European Defence Agency
EEAS	European External Action Service
EMP	Euro–Mediterranean Partnership
ENP	European Neighbourhood Policy
ESDI	European Security and Defence Identity
ESDP	European Security and Defence Policy
ESS	European Security Strategy
EU	European Union
EUFOR	European Force
EUISS	European Institute for Security Studies
EUPAT	European Police Advisory Team
EUPM	European Police Mission
EUPT	EU Planning Team
EUSR	European Special Representative
FYROM	Former Yugoslav Republic of Macedonia
HR	High Representative
IFOR	Implementation Force
IMF	International Monetary Fund
IMTF	Integrated Mission Task Forces
IPU	Integrated Police Unit

ACRONYMS

ISF	Integrated Strategic Framework
ISG	Integration Steering Group
JAES	Joint Africa–EU Strategy
MAD	Mutually Assured Destruction
MÍNURCAT	UN Mission to Central Africa and Chad
MS	Member States
NATO	North Atlantic Treaty Organization
NSS	US National Security Strategy
OHQ	Operational Headquarters
OSCE	Organization for Security and Cooperation in Europe
PSC	Political and Security Committee
QDR	Quadrennial Defence Review
RFC	Rassemblement des Forces pour le Changement
RRM	Rapid Reaction Mechanism
SACEUR	Supreme Allied Commander Europe
SFOR	Stabilization Force
SHAPE	Supreme Headquarters Allies Powers Europe
SRSG	Special Representative of the Secretary-General
SSR	Security Sector Reform
UN	United Nations
UNCT	UN Country Team
UNHCR	UN High Commission for Refugees
UNMIBH	United Nations Mission in Bosnia and Herzegovina
UNMIK	UN Mission in Kosovo
UNPREDEP	United Nations Preventive Deployment
WMD	Weapons of Mass Destruction
WTO	World Trade Organization

European Security Policy: Strategic Culture in Operation?

PETER SCHMIDT AND BENJAMIN ZYLA

The recent disagreement among EU member states with regard to the air campaign against Muammar Gaddafi's authoritarian regime in Libya has raised questions about the EU's strategic culture and role in international security policy. On the one hand the project of European security cooperation advanced rapidly with the turn of the new century, on the other there re-occurred – after the split on the Iraqi issue in 2003 – a major disagreement among member states with regard to an important security issue in the EU's southern neighborhood. In the end, NATO took on the task of carrying out air operations because the EU was not able to come to a decision. Against this backdrop, policy makers and scholars alike face ever more serious questions: What kind of security actor is the EU? What substance does it bring to the world stage? How is it different from other security actors? This special issue examines these questions from a strategic culture (SC) perspective. This suggests itself because the development of a strategic culture was the major lever by which the European Union's principal planning document, the European Security Strategy (ESS), tried to guide its Common Security and Defence Policy (CSDP), and by this the EU's role in the world in security matters.[1]

Why are these questions important? In the late 1990s, the European Union started to become a truly internationally operating security actor with operations ranging from southern Europe to Africa, the Middle East, and South-East Asia. Europe's presence in the world advanced rather rapidly, from concentrating on creating a pool of 60,000 rapidly available troops (the so-called Helsinki headline goals) to be deployed to global hot-spots, to the first signs of strategic thinking and planning by the formulation of a European Security Strategy in 2003, and finally to the formation of European Union battle groups in 2004.[2] These capacity-building efforts included the necessary institution-building – that is, putting in place governance mechanisms that could oversee the planning, deployment, and evaluation of European Union operations abroad – as well as the establishment of formal coordination mechanisms with the United Nations (UN) and NATO. All these efforts materialized in some twenty-plus missions on three continents.[3]

Why Strategic Culture?

This volume aims to respond to a flagrant lacuna in the literature on assessing the EU's operations by using a well-known analytical concept in the field of international relations, the strategic culture approach. In doing so, it provides one of the rare analyses where many of the EU's military and civilian crisis management operations are used as case studies to gain access to larger cultural developments and predispositions of the actors involved. Existing studies on this topic mostly concentrate on one particular operation rather than setting their single case in a larger analytical context, which makes generalizations resulting from the case studies more difficult.

Many scholars regard the SC approach, notwithstanding some major criticism, as something which is worth to be examined and further advanced. This accepted wisdom led us to take a closer look at both sides of the coin: the operational side of CSDP (including cooperation with the UN and NATO)[4] and the theoretical efforts to use SC as a tool for the understanding of states' behaviour in the area of foreign and security policy. Furthermore, we found that the strategic culture approach is an ideal starting point for analysing CSDP operations for two additional reasons:

Firstly, it allows conceptual and theoretical elasticity, and thus promises to be inclusive of a variety of scholars and theoretical traditions in international relations. It thus holds the prospect of 'bridging' the gap between two dominant streams of IR theory that seldom cross-fertilize, namely the orthodox 'rationalist' approaches most prominently advocated by realists and neo-institutionalists on the one hand, and 'reflectivist' theories (i.e., constructivism) on the other.[5] Because the strategic culture approach is not automatically associated with one particular theoretical paradigm in the field of international relations, it promises to produce novel empirical, theoretical, and possibly interdisciplinary insights into cultural studies in general, and international relations theory in particular. While being relatively new in the literature (see further below for details), the strategic culture concept promises to provide insights into the exogenous as well as endogenous material and non-material predispositions of nation states' behaviour.

Secondly, the placing of cultural studies in the context of an evolving European foreign and security policy is in itself new, and thus holds great promise not only for a better understanding of the EU's external actions, but also to refine the strategic culture concept as an analytical tool.

Trajectory of the strategic culture paradigm

While subscribing to theoretical pluralism in this special issue, it is useful to revisit the trajectory of the strategic culture concept. Whereas each chapter individually refers to and builds upon the strategic culture paradigm, none of the chapters that follow gives historical significance to the concept itself or discusses its intellectual evolution in greater detail. Reviewing the history as well as the ontological underpinnings of the strategic culture concept thus lets us appreciate the origins and theoretical refinements of this approach over time. It also provides a better grounding of the discussions that follow in this special issue as the authors engage with the analytical concept rather selectively.

The literature, broadly speaking, clusters the scholarship on strategic cultures into three 'generations'.[6] The first generation preferred to use the term 'national character' rather than 'strategic culture' to explain national behaviours and to link political attitudes to personalities.[7] Scholars of this generation were interested in examining how forms of language, religion, beliefs, and values shaped, for example, the German and

Japanese 'national character' in World War II that led them to fight in the ways they did (such as by employing kamikaze fighters in the case of Japan). In other words, scholars studied what we would now call the political culture, which was defined as a 'subset of beliefs and values of a society that relate to the political system'.[8]

This national character scholarship was further developed in the 1970s by Jack Snyder, who is often credited with being the first to 'export' the concept of political culture into the domain of security studies. He was interested in looking at how the behaviour of the Soviet Union could be explained by examining the organizational, historical, and political contexts in which those decisions were made. Snyder's work was to a great extent applied and designed for government officials in order to predict the behaviour of America's pivotal enemy. Political elites, in his mind, articulate a 'unique strategic culture related to security-military affairs that is a wider manifestation of public opinion, socialized into a distinctive mode of strategic thinking'.[9] Snyder defined culture as 'symbolic vehicles of meaning, including beliefs, ritual, practices, art forums, and ceremonies, as well as informal culture practices such as language, gossips, stories, and the rituals of life'[10]. A few years later, Colin Gray refined Snyder's work and argued that distinctive national styles with 'deep roots within a particular stream of historical experience'[11] can influence the foreign policy behaviour of states. They provide a milieu in which decisions regarding national security issues are made. In short, this first generation of scholarship defined strategic culture as 'context' that bridges the epistemological divide between both cause and effect. David Haglund's paper in this volume partially speaks to this generation. It is a tool that helps us to understand rather than explain the behaviour of states.

The second generation of strategic culture scholars questioned the first generation's epistemological claims and developed testable hypotheses.[12] Their objective was to apply a rigorous scientific approach to the study of strategic culture(s) by constructing a falsifiable methodology that would lead to a cumulative research programme, and one that could be used to predict the future behaviour of states.[13] Such behaviour was conceptualized as being detached from political culture in order to isolate strategic culture as the independent variable and the former as the dependent variable, and to avoid tautological arguments. The consistency of the independent variable over time determined the coherence of a strategic culture.

The third generation of strategic culture scholarship emerged in the early 1990s and, again, questioned the epistemological assumptions of the earlier generations. Inspired by the evolving constructivist school of international relations, scholars began to theorize about identity formations and norms that were shaped by the interplay of history, tradition, and culture. Similar to the second generation, strategic culture was conceptualized as an independent or intervening variable affecting state behaviour.[14] However, it is a metaconcept that goes beyond representing a singular process of cause and effect.[15] It informs social actors normatively of what they are supposed to do and how to behave in particular situations, as well as in the cultural and social contexts in which they operate. Along those lines, national identities and interests are not simply the product of the so-called international system but are socially constructed and shaped by practices of interaction among social actors. In turn, this reasoning implies that collective units (that is, society) play an integral part in shaping and defining national identities and interests, and that society holds normative elements that are in need of interpretation and understanding.[16] To put it in other words: social actors reproduce norms and structure and base their actions on their acquired knowledge, habits, and routines. It is precisely in this sense that strategic cultures are able to provide an insight into the 'reasons' for state actions.[17]

A brief look at the theoretical chapters and case studies

The volume starts off with three theoretical chapters, all of which speak to and discuss the above mentioned first and third generation of strategic culture research. The second generation is missing from this discussion because, as already stated, we did not conceptualize the empirical part as a test case, as envisaged by the second generation of SC research, but rather as a process of inferring insights of elements of a SC and the explanatory power of the strategic culture approach in general.

David Haglund's paper, rooted in the realist research design, seeks to further develop the first generation of strategic culture research. After an extensive discussion of the methodological snags of the concept, he defends SC in a moderate fashion as being useful as 'context' and even more as 'cognition'.

Per Norheim-Martinsen, taking as his starting point the last wave of strategic culture research – the constructivist angle – argues that the European Union's strategic culture is not so much about common interests than it is about 'preferred means' of action, with the concept of cohesion as the major focal point.

Sten Rynning examines strategic culture from the vantage point of classical realism. It is very interesting to see that despite his taking a very different theoretical approach than Norheim-Martinsen's, he comes to a similar conclusion in arguing that CSDP can only produce moderate results because it is primarily 'about maintaining restraint within Europe, where the shadow of great power rivalry and war still looms'.

As we see, these theoretical approaches have different foci: Haglund discusses the methodological question of *Verstehen* versus *Erklären*, Norheim-Martinsen analyses the European Union's narrative on SC and Rynning determines the 'real function' of CSDP from the perspective of classical realism and on this basis the limits of the strategic culture concept.

Military operations

The theoretical discussion is followed by an analysis of ESDP's military operations. The section starts off with Charles Pentland's discussion of the deployment of European Union forces in the Balkans (Operation Concordia in Macedonia and EUFOR Althea in Bosnia-Herzegovina). He uses Jack Snyder's early definition of strategic culture, taking ideas, emotions and habits that the members of a strategic community have shared over time as a reference point, and argues that – regardless of the limitations of analysing two cases only – it is possible to identify at least rudiments of a 'distinctive strategic culture' beyond the world of words: the missions were aimed at responding to major threats as indicated in the ESS, the member states shared the same interests in this case, the Balkans are a regional priority for all member states, there was an attempt to install a system of 'effective multilateralism', and 'soft power' is the EU's primary mode of influence. Pentland sees SC not as a cause, but as the 'context' of behaviour, allowing observers 'to detect intimations' of the central ideas in EU strategic culture.

Analysing Europe's two Congo missions (Artemis and EUFOR Congo), Peter Schmidt proposes to extend the scope of strategic culture to make it a more meaningful concept in analysing the European Union's military operations. By this, he looks to advance the concept of SC in a multi-level decision-making context. He focuses not only on strategic preferences, but also on specific interests in a certain situation and the 'games' played across three decision-making levels. He identifies at least two types of 'game' which have a substantial impact on the configuration and mandate of the mission: the 'barrack yard syndrome', which has an effect on the way countries take part in operations, and 'multilateral Caesarism' as a feature which threatens the role of parliamentarian control and in this way can have a substantial impact on the formulation of the mandate of the mission.

Jean Y. Haine's analysis of the Chad operation transcends the traditional theoretical and political debate on strategic culture by assessing the SC 'in practice' through the classical definition of 'strategy'. For Haine, strategy aims at 'setting the conditions and objectives to influence the adversary's will'. Against this background, he considers the Chad operation not as a strategic undertaking but as the appliance of a 'specific set of European *political* and *security* beliefs that should not be confused with a *strategic* culture'.

Civilian operations

Reinhardt Rummel and Arnold Kammel investigate the CSDP's civilian missions in the Balkans, Democratic Republic of Congo, Guinea Basso and, via the African Union, in Sudan, and ask if some sort of European strategic culture can be found in these cases, which span two continents.

Rummel sets the bar high by taking 'geopolitical quality' as a reference point. Against this background, he assesses that the European Union is not about to create a SC, because it lacks a serious civilian–military nexus which is, in his view, a prerequisite of a factual SC. On the civilian side, he observes also that the EU limits its actions to the handling of a series of individual cases of intervention which lack a strategic focus and grand design. He realizes that only France and the United Kingdom see themselves as having a far-reaching role in a multipolar world. In a moderate sense, he admits, however, that Brussels can take pride in its civil–military comprehensive approach and its policy of assistance to the African Union. What is missing in general terms is a cohesive political framework for the European Union's actions.

Kammel makes this political point more explicit. He agrees that the four Balkan missions 'already provide [...] a marker for the existence of an emerging European strategic culture in the process of formation', but he identifies one decisive hampering factor – a real Common Foreign and Security Policy, or in other words, a cohesive political framework.

Institutional outreach

Ingo Peters scrutinizes the European Union/United Nations relationship from the standpoint of asking how much differences with regard to strategic culture hamper inter-organizational cooperation, and by this the EU's goal of establishing a system of 'effective multilateralism'. He comes to the conclusion that more than any differences with regard to SCs, 'material factors such as budgetary interests, institutional factors and operational practices, for example decision-making rules, or standard operational procedures for conduction of missions and operations' create obstacles to effective cooperation.

Benjamin Zyla unpacks the prevalent strategic cultures of the European Union and NATO into their normative, ideational, and behavioural components and detects a significant normative overlap between the two institutions, with the exception of 'the use of force, the sanctioned range and type of missions, and the resources justified to carry them out'. He tries to explain this cultural overlap by considering NATO's strategic culture as a subculture of the EU's.

The gist of the subject

Indeed, our focus on the European Union's operations and cooperation with NATO and United Nations did not disclose picture-perfect links among the case studies and between the case studies and the theoretical aspect of SC. However, a number of interesting findings across the empirical part and the theoretical articles surfaced.

First, it does not come as a surprise that the answer to the question of whether the European Union possesses a certain strategic culture or not depends on the reference point and definition of the terms employed. When you take a 'geopolitical quality' or the influence on 'the adversary's will' as a benchmark, the European Union has no real strategic culture. Nonetheless, there are many indications that there exists a cluster of ideational and cultural preferences that guide Europe's civilian and military operations or at least have the potential to do so. This divergence of definitions, however, discloses a certain tension between – at least some – national SCs and the European Union's SC, because the above mentioned high benchmarks refer to traditional national understandings of strategy. In this regard, the European Union's SC is more than just the aggregate of national SCs: it transcends them.

Second, there is an interesting link between Norheim-Martinsen's constructivist and Rynning's neoclassical realist analysis with regard to the European Union's constraints of being a global actor. Both authors emphasize the limitations of the EU's strategic culture: Norheim-Martinsen argues that there is agreement only on the means and not on the interests; Rynning identifies similar constraints but sees these constraints as being rooted in still ongoing power struggles among member states. This bears witness to the above mentioned potential for the SC approach 'to bridge gaps' between streams of IR theories.

Third, the convergence of the European Union's and United Nations' strategic cultures, as documented above all by Ingo Peters, suggests two points: first, despite the fact that the SCs of both organizations are very similar, the realization of 'effective multilateralism' knows other factors that can obstruct cooperation. Indeed, 'effective multilateralism' seems much harder to achieve than is envisaged by the ESS.

Much of the United Nations' culture is about impartiality and neutrality. It is shown that the European Union and the UN's predispositions are very similar in this regard. This explains why the European Union does not fit into Haine's notion of strategy aiming to influence an 'adversary's will'. It also, however, raises the question of whether the European Union–United Nations relationship will always be a complementary one or will also develop competitive features, because both are acting on the basis of a similar SC in the same field. And indeed, some of the operations which are not investigated here – for example, the European Union's observation mission in Georgia or the mission on the Palestinian–Egyptian border – are operations which have been undertaken by the UN.

Fourth, the picture is, nonetheless, not crystal clear. On the Balkans, the European Union member states not only agree on the appropriate means, as Norheim-Martinsen emphasizes, but also on some interests, regardless of their disagreement with regard to the recognition of Kosovo as a sovereign state. These interests become increasingly differentiated when the question of a military operation is on the negotiation table and the targeted region is further away. Decisions on whether such operations take place originate from the interest of a member state but are heavily constrained by the European Union's strategic culture (as in the operations in Chad and DR Congo). Against this background, it appears more appropriate to speak in these cases of the European Union's SC as a 'system of constraints' for national approaches, rather than a 'system of preferences'. This provides some support for Sten Rynning's neoclassical realist approach to CSDP as a system of inner-EU constraints.

Fifth, this state of affairs is closely related to the convergences and differences between NATO's and the European Union's strategic culture as analysed by Benjamin Zyla. NATO places far fewer constraints on the use of military force than the European Union does. This is also exemplified by the Libyan air strikes against Gaddafi's Libya: it was not the European Union but NATO which was able to run the air campaign. In this regard one can argue that the existence of NATO still prevents the European Union from further developing its SC and becoming a competent military actor. However, the opposite view also has a lot to commend it: NATO provides more flexibility and is able to overcome political deadlocks inside the European Union.

Sixth, the similarities between the European Union's and the UN's strategic cultures, as well as the important role of member states when it comes to the deployment of military force, suggests that the scope of strategic culture should be extended to specific interests of member states and especially to the games played by international organizations and member states at the various levels. In order to bridge the gap between SC and behaviour, the traditional SC approach must adapt to the fact that there is a multi-level system. In this regard the European Union should not be regarded as an autonomous actor with a single SC: the decision-making system includes member states and the United Nations in a way that enables one to speak of a common 'cultural space'.

Seventh, one can assume that there is some sort of system of preferences – or constraints – which has an influence on the European Union's general approach to the role of civilian and military means in international politics, as well as the EU's operations. The relationship still exists, but is not such a close one when it comes to civilian operations – this is even more true with regard to military operations. From a methodological point of view, the relationship between these preferences and specific operations, however, cannot be seen as a cause, and only to a certain extent as a context, for the European Union's campaigns. In this regard, use of the SC concept to explain specific EU security operations is more limited than in the case of fully-fledged nation states' operations. The reason for this is the lack of political cohesion among the 27 member states, which makes the EU a rather fluctuating actor. Specific interests and the behaviour of actors during the 'games' on the various political levels leading to military operations are highly influential factors. In other words, flexibility governs the European Union's military decision-making process in particular and, in turn, explains the variable force composition of the EU's military expeditionary undertakings.

Eighth, flexibility is the enemy of causal explanations. In the case of the multi-level decision-making processes of the European Union, the strategic culture approach appears less able to establish a link between the European Union's SC and behaviour than in the case of nation states. Including specific interests and 'games' to close the gap is useful – but not in the sense of causal thinking; only in order to develop a more meaningful framework for the interpretation of specific decisions.

Finally, a cautionary point for integration processes in regions beyond Europe. The European Union's principle of flexibility carries, from the point of view of an 'ever closer Union', a negative connotation. In spite of this, it is only through this flexibility that the EU is able to act, especially in the military sphere. It seems that processes of integration always face the question 'how much is too much'? The current Euro crisis embodies a negative example in this regard: the abolition of exchange rate flexibility, regardless of the major economic and political discrepancies among Euro member states, has made the system too inflexible. The result is severe turmoil. The European Union's CSDP has escaped this deadlock until now. This limits its outreach on the one hand, but at the same time provides many opportunities to act on the world stage.

What does this all imply for the utility of the SC concept, the EU's role in the world and the future of European cooperation in security matters?

There is evidence that the SC approach is a useful concept through which to understand the EU's actions with regard to security operations. However, it has to be adapted to the multi-level character of EU decision-making in order to provide a full-blown understanding of the evolution and composition of the EU's strategic culture. The problem is that these extensions, such as special national interests and the SCs of member states, as well as political games across the various levels of decision-making, seem to bridge the gap between the EU's SC and behaviour on the supranational level less convincingly than in the case of consolidated nation states. This is also due to the fact that other organizations, like the UN or even NATO, are able to take actions which could also be undertaken by the EU. European states have some choice with regard to the actions to be taken. To make the SC concept more compelling, it is therefore suggested in the discussions on EU's SC to focus not too much on the EU itself, but to also include the UN and even NATO and to understand these IOs as a 'cultural space'. The case of Libya provides evidence for this approach: while the air campaign was undertaken by NATO, the EU indeed has – together with the UN – a greater role to play in the aftermath of the war.

The EU's Chad operation and the Libyan case also shed light on the EU's role in the world. Indeed, it has a role to play on the world's stage (not in the sense of classic strategic approaches, but in the sense of a set of political and security beliefs), which is quite similar to the UN's approach. More precisely, the role is based on a comprehensive understanding of security and is quite often symbolic, in the sense that specific operations are meant less to solve the security problem at hand than to promote and support the further building up of European instruments in security matters. The EU will also try to establish a system of 'effective multilateralism'. This, however, is easier said than done, even in the case of the 'similar-minded' UN. It is likely that the more the EU takes on actions which were previously typical UN operations (such as the European Monitory Mission in Georgia or the EU mission in Rafah at the crossing point between Gaza and Egypt, currently on standby), the more not only organizational obstacles but also elements of competition will play a role in downgrading the effectiveness of cooperation.

Regardless of all ambitions for greater jointness and cohesion, the future of the European Union's SC will still be based on the principle of 'flexibility' rather than bringing the combined power of all member states and EU bodies to bear. NATO plays a contradictory role in the future development of the EU's SC: on the one hand it allows, as shown recently in the Libyan case, for deadlocks among EU member states to be overcome; on the other, its involvement can also be understood as a stumbling block to the further development of CSDP and thus the EU's strategic culture. In that sense, to borrow William Wallace's words, the EU's strategic culture is 'so far, not very far'.

NOTES

1. With the entry into force of the Lisbon Treaty, the European Security and Defence Policy (ESDP) became the Common Security and Defence Policy (CSDP).
2. See stock-taking of the first five years see Nicole Gnesotto (ed.), *EU Security and Defence Policy. The First Five Years (1999-2004)* (Institute for Security Studies, European Union: Paris, 2004).
3. See http://consilium.europa.eu/media/1232545/map_en0711.pdf
4. It is necessary to raise two points here. First, from our point of view, operations, which can be considered practices of CSDP policies, reveal more about a strategic culture than the building up of sheer military and civilian capacities. They are in a way practices of sometimes stiff policy, which often is nothing more than rhetoric. This is especially true for the multi-level decision-making process of the EU, which is based on decisions by 27 member states. In this complex decision-making environment the agreement on building up capacities easily becomes an 'empty promise' that has little impact on real behaviour. Second, the European Union's outreach to other IOs also

has a theoretical dimension, in the sense that it can answer the question of whether the European Union disposes over a unique and separate strategic culture and whether and – if at all – how it is interwoven with NATO and the United Nations. There is the hope that this outreach provides a contribution to the further development of SC approaches in general, and the EU's SC in particular.

5. Robert O. Keohane, 'International Institutions: Two Approaches', *International Studies Quarterly*, Vol. 32, No. 4 (1988), pp. 382.
6. It should be noted, though, that not all scholars agree with this clustering. For a different approach see Alastair Iain Johnston, *Cultural Realism: Strategic Culture and Grand Strategy in Chinese History* (Princeton, NJ: Princeton University Press, 1995), pp. 5–22.
7. See, for example, Ruth Benedict, *The Chrysanthemum and the Sword: Patterns of Japanese Culture* (Boston, MA: Houghton Mifflin, 1946).
8. Gabriel A. Almond and Sidney Verba, *The Civic Culture: Political Attitudes and Democracy in Five Nations* (Princeton, NJ: Princeton University Press, 1965), p.11.
9. Quoted in Jeffrey S. Lantis and Darryl Howlett, 'Strategic Culture', in John Baylis, Steve Smith, and Eliot Cohen (eds), *Strategy in the Contemporary World: An Introduction to Strategic Studies* (Oxford/New York: Oxford University Press, 2007), p.85.
10. Jack L. Snyder, *The Soviet Strategic Culture: Implications for Limited Nuclear Operations* (Santa Monica, CA: RAND Corporation, 1977), p.8.
11. Colin S. Gray, 'Comparative Strategic Culture', *Parameters*, Vol. XIV, No. 4 (1984), p.28; see also Colin S. Gray, 'National Style in Strategy: The American Example', *International Security*, Vol. 6, No. 2 (1981), pp. 35–37.
12. A rebuttal of the first generation arrived promptly: Colin Gray, 'Strategic Culture as Context: the First Generation of Theory Strikes Back', *Review of International Studies*, Vol. 25, No. 1 (1999), pp. 49–69.
13. Alastair Iain Johnston, 'Thinking about Strategic Culture', *International Security*, Vol. 19, No. 4 (1995), pp. 32–64.
14. John S. Duffield, *World Power Forsaken: Political Culture, International Institutions, and German Security Policy after Unification* (Stanford, CA: Stanford University Press, 1998); Theo Farrell and Terry Terriff, *The Sources of Military Change: Culture, Politics, Technology* (Boulder, CO: Lynne Rienner Publishers, 2002); Gray, 'Strategic Culture as Context' (note 12); Peter J. Katzenstein, *The Culture of National Security: Norms and Identity in World Politics* (New York: Columbia University Press, 1996).
15. Ronald L. Jepperson and Ann Swidler, 'What Properties of Culture do we Measure?', *Poetics*, Vol. 22, No. 4 (1994), p. 360.
16. John Gerard Ruggie, 'Continuity and Transformation in the World Polity: Towards a Neo-Realist Synthesis', *World Politics*, Vol. 35, No. 2 (1983), pp. 261–285; John Gerard Ruggie, 'What Makes the World Hang Together? Neo-Utilitarianism and the Social Constructivist Challenge', *International Organization*, Vol. 52, No. 4 (1998), pp. 855–885.
17. Martha Finnemore, *The Purpose of Intervention: Changing Beliefs about the Use of Force* (Ithaca, NY: Cornell University Press, 2003), p.15.

'Let's Call the Whole Thing Off'? Security Culture as Strategic Culture

DAVID G. HAGLUND

You Like Potato and I Like Potahto

A constant theme of scholarly inquiry into international security matters, and indeed a constant theme of cultural inquiry in general – whether of the 'high' culture of literature or the 'low' culture of popular film and song – concerns how we should define our core concepts. The articles published in this special theme issue constitute no exception to the rule, for some argue that it matters a great deal not only how we define 'security culture' but also that in defining it we take care to distinguish this concept from another conceptual staple of contemporary discourse, namely 'strategic culture'. The difference, for those who take it to exist and to be meaningful, is said to reside less in the ends than in the means of diplomatic endeavours, with 'Europe' being held to evince a greater preference for multilateralism and non-military policy assets, while its significant other, the United States, is said to lean toward self-help (at times, 'unilateralism') and to betray a willingness and, to some, eagerness to employ military force.

The argument that I will make in this article is that the attempt to distinguish between security culture and strategic culture is itself a fool's errand, and if pursued strenuously is more likely to confuse than to elucidate. I am going to argue that the distinction, if there is one, between our two modified variants of culture resembles nothing so much as the 'distinction' about which Fred Astaire sang in the 1937 musical 'Shall We Dance?' – namely an *ersatz* definitional distinction that turned out only to be a matter of pronunciation and not signification. The business of deciphering the meaning of 'strategic culture' is complicated enough without adding the additional wrinkle of 'security culture', and in what follows I will be undertaking a lengthy interrogation into what, if any, usable definitional content might be gleaned from the debate about the former. Illustratively, I will start by referring to one particular transatlantic security relationship – the one between France and the United States – in a bid to introduce some ways in which 'culture' might be imported into that bilateral setting. Following this, I expand the inquiry so as to include, in subsequent subsections of the article, epistemological and conceptual matters of importance related to the evolving debate over strategic culture. I conclude with a few suggestions as to how students of contemporary European security might operationalize the notion of culture.

A Matter of Temperament?

In Year XIII of the French Republic (1805), François Marie Perrin du Lac published an account of his recent trip into the North American heartland under the title *Voyage dans les deux Louisianes et chez les régions sauvages du Missouri.* Not for the first time, and certainly not for the last, would an accomplished French observer travel in the New World to get a first-hand look at the American people. Already the signs of tension between the two 'first allies' were too manifest to be ignored, and what Perrin detected at the onset of the 19th century – to wit, divergent behavioural patterns – would become a dominant characteristic of the bilateral relationship throughout the ensuing decades; so much so that one prominent NATO-watcher from France could be excused for observing, toward the end of the 20th century, that the 'most acute transatlantic antagonisms' had been and still were those between the French and the Americans.[1] (In fact, it would be better to qualify those genuine 'transatlantic antagonisms' as chronic, because the most *acute* tensions in transatlantic relations, certainly during the 20th century, involved crises not in Franco-American but in German-American relations.)[2]

From his coign of vantage at the start of the 19th century, Perrin understood the source of the problem to be cultural in nature, and summed things up with the pithy observation that '[t]he guiding principle of Americans seems to be never to do anything as we do'.[3] More than a hundred years later, André Tardieu would second that cultural diagnosis when, taking the measure of the bilateral relationship shortly after the ending of the First World War, he insisted that 'instinct' had kept, and would continue to keep, the two 'sister republics' locked into a chronically dysfunctional embrace. Things could never be improved, Tardieu cautioned, until such time as policy elites in both countries abandoned the destructive fiction that common republican institutions somehow enshrined healthy bilateral cooperation between putative like-minded entities, and recognized the obvious – namely, that the two societies were fundamentally dissimilar, and were so for reasons rooted in their respective *cultures.*

As he saw matters, nothing could be better guaranteed to ensure continued turmoil in the relationship than the mistaken belief that the two countries somehow shared in an institution-based collective identity. 'Sister Democracies, both equally Republics – as the parrot-like exponents of the alleged identity of French and American institutions keep on repeating' – these qualities had next to nothing to do with the underlying reality of the bilateral relationship. 'If we rely on alleged identity for ease of mutual understanding, surely we rely in vain!' Instead, it was and would remain the *temperament* of two fundamentally distinct societies, reflective of basal cultural divergence, which would set the tone of bilateral relations in the future, just as it had assuredly done in the past.[4] Only after accepting that their two countries were not really alike could leaders in both begin to take the steps necessary to set the relationship on a more mature footing.

It has been a long time since analysts of international relations and foreign policy have made of either 'instinct' or 'temperament' a leading explanatory category, or at least have explicitly done so under either of those labels. This does not mean that they have been averse to exploring the social-psychological phenomena that might be said to result in a national orientation toward a particular course of action on the part of any country. It simply means that they have other words, and other conceptual tools, at their disposal as they seek to establish connections between culturally conditioned social attributes and state behaviour. An earlier generation of social scientists, around the time of the Second World War, expended enormous intellectual resources attempting to discern the 'national character' that underpinned state behaviour. Today, such behaviour, especially when it involves matters of national security and 'grand strategy', often gets garbed in the conceptual raiment of an analytical approach that has come to be called 'strategic culture'. But what, exactly, is this supposed to mean, and of what possible use can it be to scholars interested in understanding how countries, whether European or not, conceptualize and promote their strategic interests?

A Conceptual Conundrum[5]

What Oscar Wilde once said about fox-hunting – namely that it represented the 'unspeakable in pursuit of the inedible' – might also, *mutatis mutandis*, be remarked of those who are tempted to analyse political developments through the prism of strategic culture. Do we not resemble the unintelligible in pursuit of the incomprehensible, as we speed off in quest of our conceptual quarry? For sure, the problem of how to define the terms we rely upon is hardly limited to those who take as their point of departure strategic culture; the problem is endemic throughout the social (or human) sciences. But recognizing the widespread nature of the problem provides no reason to absent those who would utilize strategic culture from the task, and obligation, of saying what they think the concept means, and how it might be put to the analysis of foreign policy.

An article by Jeffrey Lantis highlights both the potential and the pitfalls of reliance upon strategic culture for policy insight (in his case, into the manner in which America's adversaries think about weapons of mass destruction, or WMD). Lantis, whose research is part of a broader WMD-related project conducted under the aegis of the Defense Threat Reduction Agency in Washington DC,[6] laments not only weapons proliferation but also the proliferation of definitions of strategic culture; withal, he expresses the hope that given enough time, scholars will be able to develop 'a common definition of strategic culture [so as] to build theoretically progressive models', which in turn can be put to the service of guiding policy makers.[7] The goal is admirable. The likelihood of its being attained, however, is slender. Colin Gray is almost certainly correct in suspecting that 'scholarship on strategic culture ... is bound to fail when it ventures far beyond our culture-bound common sense and positivistically seeks a certain general wisdom'.[8]

Why is this? It is because no matter how achingly compelling the need to render our concepts sharp tools for analysis, we unfailingly get entangled in constant wrangling over their very definition, with the result being that the passage of time usually results in spreading confusion instead of enlightenment. This is so notwithstanding the expressed hope of many that the same passage of time might reasonably be expected to generate a 'literature' capable of penetrating and dispelling the conceptual fog, by speaking definitional truth to us. But if the literature on strategic culture is to resemble that on every other political concept, it will become apparent that not only is the body of writing on our topic often bereft of literary merit, but will also inevitably produce noteworthy, unavoidable and ongoing dissension in the analytical ranks: truths perhaps, when taken singly and contemplatively, but no overarching truth – especially if the *sine qua non* of the latter is held to be the production of useful predictions. Still, our failure to come to agreement over the term's meaning and applicability should be neither surprising nor particularly discouraging; it simply illustrates we are dealing with an interesting concept that – as with all such concepts – can be used to advantage if used carefully, as a means of organizing our knowledge about those matters over which we can claim to know a thing or two, instead of as a device for supplying reliable insight into that about which we know nothing; that is, the future.

Strategic culture might not be a meta-concept in the way that, say, 'power' is, but there is utility in the comparison. Consider that power is supposed to be one of the key notions at our disposal when we wax theoretical about international relations and foreign policy, and yet what strikes the student of power analysis is how much basic disagreement there can be over this word's meaning. If power is nothing other than aggregate capability, as many structural realists insist it is,[9] then it becomes possible to make certain claims about the 'structure' of the international system. Among the most important of such claims is the one that permits us to discern a systemic pecking order predicated upon 'relative capability', enabling us in turn to develop such other important concepts as unipolarity, bipolarity, or multipolarity in a bid to *describe* and comprehend that system. But if you follow the injunction of others, and regard power as simply being another way of saying 'influence', then all descriptive bets are off and theories about how and why states act become increasingly complicated, because they are dependent upon a myriad of situationally specific contexts.[10]

The point is not that there is something abnormal about the way the debate rages over the meta-concept of power; to the contrary, the debate is completely normal and, indeed, necessary, for unless there is healthy and substantial scholarly divisiveness about concepts, there can be no advance of theoretical knowledge in social science.[11] And while it is perhaps possible to imagine consensual understanding enveloping some political concepts, the cases when such occurs must be rare, and a concept about which we can say there exists basal agreement is probably not a very important tool for anyone's use.

Thus, if the normal trajectory of political concepts is to be followed by strategic culture – which, it bears noting, is still in its relative infancy, having been apparently first employed *under that name* only in the late 1970s[12] – then we can expect not only that debates about its meaning will be ceaseless, but that it will be prone, as are all concepts, to expansion. Churchill's quip about democracy being the worst form of government except for all the rest serves as a useful reminder about how unexceptional conceptual discord really is. And no less exceptional, even though one might wish it to be otherwise, is conceptual expansion.[13] This is so not only because of the very ambiguity of the concepts we deploy (no mean consideration in itself), but also because of the impact of changing conditions on the words we use to describe and understand those conditions. One political philosopher, T.D. Weldon, insists that because circumstances change, we must continually adjust the manner in which we express them. The adjustment can take two forms: we can either invent a new concept, or we can expand a familiar word or concept. 'Usually', says Weldon, 'the second method is preferred, partly because it avoids more confusion than it creates, indeed it seldom confuses anybody but political philosophers, and partly because the extended use has often come to be adopted uncritically in the natural course of events'.[14]

Actually, our concept may just be in the early stages of expansion, given its relative youth, but its two 'parent' elements are considerably older, and have probably spent more time than was good for them on the stretching rack. Thus, its nominal infancy to the contrary notwithstanding, strategic culture comes to us with a family history of conceptual confusion – one that has left its mark.

Towards a Definition of Strategic Culture?

Ample foretaste of the debate about what strategic culture is to signify has been provided by earlier discussions over 'culture' as a social variable, for – as Raymond Williams has noted – the word ranks as one of the two or three most difficult in the English language (and, he could have added, in any other language).[15] If things were not murky enough as a result of the nominative half of our concept, what shall we say of its modifier, 'strategic'? Put this adjective and this noun together, and you get a sense of why Alastair Iain Johnston should have complained about how 'remarkably undefined' our concept is.[16]

How could it be otherwise, in view of the parental elements' own definitional promiscuity? Let us take for starters the modifier, 'strategic', as it is probably the less unruly parent. Although many seem to think that the root formation of strategic, 'strategy', must be about things martial – and by extension, so too must strategic culture[17] – this does not have to be the case. Strategy can be about military matters, and often is, but those who insist it must *always* be called to the colours do it, and us, a disservice. The term actually connotes much more: used most commonly (as in the 'strategic planning' that is all the rage in academic, and other, administrative circles these days), it simply seeks to establish a 'rational' link between ends and means. Thinking or acting strategically stands for the attempt to correlate, in a manner that can pass basic cost-benefit muster, one's goals with the resources at one's disposal to meet those goals, and vice versa. As John Lewis Gaddis explains, 'by "strategy," I mean quite simply the process by which ends are related to means, intentions to capabilities, objectives to resources'.[18]

Things begin to get more complex when we couple the adjective with its noun, for unless we know what is meant by 'culture', we are at a complete loss to determine its relationship to strategy. To be sure, culture has become a very popular notion in the human (or social) sciences, never more so than over the past fifteen or so years, for reasons I relate in the section that follows. It has been nearly twenty years since two sociologists told us that now that culture's ship had come in, the time was ripe for social scientists to do an 'inventory of its cargo'.[19] But before we could take a peek inside the cargo hold, we had first to locate its hatch, meaning that we needed to come to some understanding of the basic structure of this vessel called culture. This was all the more necessary because the concept's earlier career had been such as to lead to its being branded, with reason, a 'semantic monstrosity'.[20]

If it had stood for anything consistently since Giovanni Andres introduced it, back in 1782, under the name *coltura* (by which he meant to imply the conditions of human attainment preserved in writing), it was the notion of extension, or growth.[21] And grow it did: in less than a century it was expanded from the written to all other forms of registering the achievements of humanity, so that the anthropologist Edward B. Tylor could conceive of it in a seminal 1865 work as 'that complex whole which includes knowledge, belief, art, morals, law, custom, and any other capabilities and habits acquired by man as a member of society'.[22]

Culture did not only possess importance as a register of civilization's noblest accomplishments (its 'high', or big-C, variant); it was also beginning to take on an epistemological function, helping those who engaged in studying collective life to develop ways of thinking about what was important in group cognition. One early discipline to feel the effects of culture's epistemological role would be history, where the 'new history' of the late 19th and early 20th century (old history, actually, from today's standpoint) stood out against dominant perspectives associated with Leopold von Ranke's 'scientific' approach to history and Edward Freeman's notion of history as merely being the record of 'past politics'.[23]

That 'new history' faced an uphill climb in the early decades of the 20th century – especially in America, where it seemed downright antediluvian to argue against a hard-headed economic interpretation of history propagated by the Progressive (or Wisconsin) school, for whom class interests provided the most elegant and satisfactory answer to the large questions about America's past. But following the Second World War, it became not just possible but well nigh obligatory for American history and politics to be examined under a new, cultural, lamp – one that shone light into such heretofore overlooked collective categories as ethnicity and socialpsychological propensities toward irrationality and antinomy.[24] And though it might not have been easy at mid-century to identify what culture *was*, it was more than possible to signal two areas of enquiry that properly belonged to the new cultural history. The first was *ideas*, such that generically culture could come to stand, as one student of US foreign policy explains, for 'any set of interlocking values, beliefs, and assumptions that are held collectively by a given group and passed on through socialization'.[25] The second was *ethnicity*. Thus intellectual history and ethnocultural studies began to emerge as important subdisciplines in their own right, each subsumed under the broader, cultural, rubric.[26]

What was occurring in history was also taking place in most of the other human sciences, with anthropologists among the most noteworthy contributors. And even if no one could define culture to everyone's satisfaction, the name of one anthropologist in particular was becoming a consensus repeater on most lists of authorial 'must reads'. This was Clifford Geertz, whose 1973 collection of essays, *The Interpretation of Cultures*,[27] quickly established itself as the *locus classicus* in the field of cultural studies. What Geertz did in this book, which has rightly been adjudged 'phenomenally influential',[28] was to propose that we regard culture as consisting in 'socially established structures of meaning in terms of which people do ... things'.[29]

By so proposing, Geertz not only contributed to culture's growing popularity in social sciences beyond anthropology (with economics and psychology being notable holdouts); he also provided the opportunity for analysts of international security with a fascination for the emerging notion of strategic culture to contemplate actually *defining* their concept. Now, definitional consensus would, in the nature of things, remain elusive, but some analysts began taking their cues from the cognitive instructions implicit in Geertz's work. More and more, and again following Geertz, culture was being conceived as a system of symbols by which collectivities transmit knowledge across time and space. As William Sewell put it, culture was nothing other than the 'semiotic dimension of human social practice in general'.[30]

It was this recognition of the *symbolic* content of culture that Alastair Iain Johnston seized upon in offering what is, to date, the most ambitious and sophisticated attempt at defining strategic culture. Its Geertzian pedigree is obvious, for as Johnston defines it, strategic culture consists in:

> an integrated system of symbols (i.e., argumentation structures, languages, analogies, metaphors, etc.) that acts to establish pervasive and long-lasting grand strategic preferences by formulating concepts of the role and efficacy of military force in interstate political affairs, and by clothing these conceptions with such an aura of factuality that the strategic preferences seem uniquely realistic and efficacious.[31]

Lest it be thought that his reference above to 'military force' makes his construe a narrowly bounded one, Johnston goes on to stipulate that the 'grand strategic preferences' at whose service strategic culture must be placed entail more than purely military considerations, and include *all* those economic and political, as well as military, aspects of national power that must be brought to bear upon the task of accomplishing 'national goals'.[32]

It may not be particularly easy to put into application Johnston's definition of our concept (notwithstanding that it may be the most elegant one going); still, it is not so difficult to detect what he had in mind in choosing to argue that strategic culture deserves to be taken seriously. First on his target list are those who minimize, or dismiss outright, ideational factors when they theorize 'explanatory' variables in international security. Most visible in his cross hairs is the group he calls the 'neorealists', that is, the structural realists who he says are oblivious of the role of culture and history when they conceive the basis of state action. There is clearly something to the allegation, and even if it was Kenneth Waltz who primarily served to inspire his critique, Johnston's admonition could apply equally well to Robert Kagan's more recent invocation of strategic culture as a quintessentially 'dependent variable' (my words, not Kagan's) in international security matters. To Kagan, strategic culture certainly may exist, but it stands for effect not cause, being entirely explicable in terms of something else – relative capability. This accounts for America's being 'from Mars' and quick to countenance martial solutions to security challenges, while Europe is (mainly) 'from Venus', and reluctant to frame responses in the same way as its whilom friend across the Atlantic.[33]

The structural realists may be Johnston's principal objects of pursuit, but they are not his only quarry. He is also concerned with improving upon the work of two prior 'generations' of strategic culturalists. In particular, he chides 1. the 'first generation' of strategic culturalists, chiefly area-studies specialists of the Cold War period with an interest in the Soviet Union, for their indifference to specifying their variables; and 2. the 'second generation', Gramscians of the late Cold War/early post-Cold War period, for their laziness in tracing the manner in which they would link their causes and effects.[34]

In the end, and despite his criticism of 'positivists', Johnston remains at one with them on the importance of establishing reliable causality, though he recognizes the complexity of the challenge. Accordingly, he makes a determined effort to demonstrate how it is that the past continues to influence contemporary strategic choices (in his case, of the Chinese leadership) in such a way as to constrain, or bound, rationality in state decision-making.[35] The irony is that Johnston's methodological rigour aligns him with his principal theoretical foes, the structural realists, with whom he shares a conviction that a certain kind of causal 'explanation' is possible and therefore desirable, and distances him from so many of those who have otherwise themselves taken the cultural 'turn' in international security, and who see it as their primary task to 'understand' strategic reality, rather than to 'explain' it in any reliably causal manner.

Turn, Turn, Turn: The Re-Emergence of Culture in Security Studies

What has been called the cultural (also sociological, as well as historical) 'turn' in the human sciences was primarily a result of forces internal to the various disciplines and fields of inquiry involved, and reflected nothing so much as the latest phase in a continuous agreement to disagree over the very purpose of those sciences.[36] But in international security studies there was also an important external stimulus at work, which did much to ratify the recent re-emergence of culture as a category of importance. In this section I address these two sources of change, starting with the explanation/ understanding debate, which was itself a legacy of the earlier 'turn' at the end of the 19th century that resulted in the aforementioned 'new' (that is, cultural) history – a turn that witnessed, and was a manifestation of, the emergence of the hermeneutical tradition associated with Wilhelm Dilthey, who had an enormous influence upon the thinking of Max Weber.[37]

When Alastair Iain Johnston criticized what he termed the first generation's inability or unwillingness, or both, to distinguish between cause and effect, he touched an epistemological nerve. Colin Gray's rebuttal of the charge constituted something of a *tu quoque*, for Gray presumed to tar Johnston with the same 'positivist' allegation Johnston had brought to bear against those 'ahistorical, aculturalist' structuralists who had spurred him to action. Gray's rejoinder made two significant points: 1) not all realists (in whose ranks Gray included himself) were ahistorical or aculturalist; and 2) it was wrong to assume that strategic culture could be a causal variable; the best that could be hoped for being to regard it as 'context', a category transcending both cause and effect. Gray essayed his own concise definition of the concept: 'Strategic culture is the world of mind, feeling, and *habit in behaviour.*'[38]

In his response to Johnston, Gray staked out his own position on the explanation/understanding debate, one that put him close to the interpretivist side of the house and at some philosophical distance from the alleged 'positivism' of his fellow-travelling realists. (Not only this, but Gray, who had developed a reputation during the Cold War as an anti-Soviet hawk, also found reason to heap praise upon the leading Marxian scholar of culture, Raymond Williams!). Ultimately, however, there remained an ineradicable Forrest Gump aspect to Gray's use of strategic culture as context rather than causality, his insistence that 'culture is as culture does'[39] sounding more than vaguely reminiscent of Tom Hanks' film recitation, 'stupid is as stupid does'.

Perhaps strategic-culture-as-context underspecifies *too* much, but there really need be nothing stupid about denying, as does Gray, that the search for reliable causality must be the *sine qua non* of social science, nor can the rejection of such causality be taken to be synonymous with the rejection of theory; indeed, what Gray was chiefly articulating was a case for an hermeneutical approach to strategic culture. In so doing, he made explicit appeal to the contributions of two theorists of international relations, Martin Hollis and Steve Smith. (In the event, he would have been better off relying upon only half of the tandem, as the two authors end up on different pages when it comes to assessing the relative merits of a Weberian *Verstehen*, whose earmark is the attempt to understand action from the perspective of the intentional actor, and a more structural *Erklären*, predicated upon the kind of causal explanations from without that one finds – or expects to find – in the natural sciences; Hollis plumps for the former, Smith for the latter.)[40]

Be that as it may, the debate between enthusiasts of *Verstehen* and advocates of *Erklären* is an old one in the history of ideas, with echoes going back far longer than a century, and detectable even today in the manner in which the concept of strategic culture is used. *Erklären* is associated with a Galilean approach to causal explanation in science (as in, 'this took place because *that* did'), while *Verstehen* makes appeal to an Aristotelian approach, stressing teleological accounts (as in, 'this happened so that *that* should occur') – that is, it is suffused with intentionality. But it was only in the late nineteenth century that the social sciences experienced their own 'great awakening', with the emergence of a 'positivism' displaying clear affinities to the Galilean tradition. Opposed to this would surface an antipositivism – a philosophy of science at times labelled 'idealism', but one that would be better remembered as 'hermeneutics'. It was the German philosopher Johann Gustav Droysen who coined the distinction between *Verstehen* and *Erklären*, with the former being said (by him) to be the method of the historical sciences, and the latter that of the natural sciences.[41]

The battle begun a century ago continues today, and the Johnston-Gray tussle over the definition of strategic culture reflects a more general split among social scientists, who cannot seem to decide whether they should follow Émile Durkheim down the path of positivism, or Max Weber along the road to interpretivism. This debate has possibly outlived its usefulness, as more than one philosopher of science is prepared to accept that the distinction between explanation and

19

understanding can be overdrawn[42] and perhaps should be laid to rest in favour of agreement that what we are really trying to generate, or must at least content ourselves with, is some modicum of 'explicative understanding'.[43] If this is so, then both Durkheim and Weber are after the same thing, and the path of positivism turns out to be a wide one indeed.[44]

In the two sections that follow, I am going to advert to this debate in illustrating what I take to be the two principal ways in which strategic culture might be invoked in the analysis of foreign policy, both for European and non-European countries. But in what remains of this section, I want to say something about that other relevant feature of the recent cultural turn in international security, namely the structural earthquake set off by the ending of the Cold War, disappearance of the Soviet Union, and collapse of the bipolar era.

The ending of bipolarity obviously made life more complicated for those who had assimilated what Kenneth Waltz had to say about the basic stability of bipolarity.[45] Not that everyone was in agreement with Waltz during the Cold War – not even all realists were –[46] but at least there was for a time a certain *descriptive* merit in taking as seriously as Waltz did the implications of the bipolar world – implications that ceased to be worth thinking about once their structural precondition disappeared. Many assumed that the (temporary?) derailing of structural realism à la Waltz meant the end of an assumed realist hegemony over international relations theory;[47] hence the emphasis upon the 'turn' the discipline was ostensibly in the process of making, away from realism and toward some other body of theory, constructivism to be precise, with adherents of this startlingly popular new approach insisting that only it could account for the phenomenon of *change* in international relations.[48]

So the turn was argued to be very much a constructivist one, in which cultural variables were increasingly going to make themselves felt in states' decision-making post-bipolarity. And with culture's (re)appearance as a variable to reckon with came another concept that was bound to be important: 'identity'.[49] This latter concept would be elevated to a central position in constructivist accounts of international outcomes, occupying for these theorists a position as central as that held by 'power' for a certain kind of realist theoretician; identity would be the core organizing concept for realism's challenger, imparting meaning to both cognition and 'interests'.[50] If some might have raised the quibble that this new core concept was itself riddled with ambiguity,[51] the rejoinder came quickly that power's ambiguity had never stopped structural realists from placing *it* upon their theoretical pedestal.

Must Culture be at Odds with 'Science'?

Lost sight of as a result of the brouhaha attending the constructivist challenge to realist primacy were three matters that have implications for the way in which we might employ strategic culture. First, culture was not a particularly novel variable in international security. Second, not all constructivists could be said to be antipositivists.[52] And third, not all realists could be accused of being 'aculturalists'.

Regarding the first of these matters, it cannot even be maintained that *strategic* culture, albeit under some other label, had been unexplored theoretically prior to the decade in which it received its name, the 1970s. We can accept that culture and conflict have been intermeshed for as long as there has been strife among social groupings, but the systematic, scientific study of the relationship between culture and conflict really began to take off during the Second World War, stimulated by funding provided by an American government eager to acquire operational insight into the national (strategic-cultural) 'character' of its German and Japanese enemies. To this end, theory was essential. Johnston's three generations might be accurately enumerated insofar as concerns discussions of strategic culturalists so *named*, but it is apparent, as Michael Desch has shown, that there was at least one significant previous generation of 'culturalists' who sought to demonstrate how and to what effect culture and strategic outcomes could be interrelated. Like Molière's M. Jourdain, this generation was speaking prose – the prose of strategic culture – without realizing it. Thus, the *real* first-generationers in the field of security studies were those cultural anthropologists motivated in the 1940s to demonstrate how 'national character' had an impact upon a state's development of strategic will.[53]

Desch's other two generational cohorts, the second and third, correspond roughly to Johnston's first and third generations, and what is particularly worthy of note is Desch's contention that what he calls the third (that is, post-Cold War) generation is, by dint of the emphasis it places upon 'ideational' variables, less attached to positivist approaches to the study of security than are competing paradigms within the field, such as realism. However, if what Desch intends to demonstrate is that realism 'explains' strategic outcomes better than cultural accounts, then it must be because of something other than realism's positivist epistemology (if it indeed has such an epistemology). What I think Desch really meant to suggest is that *structural* realist, not *all* realist, accounts trump culturalist ones, with the latter able, at best, to supplement realism: 'In short, the new strategic culturalist theories will not supplant realist theories in national security studies because, by themselves, they have very limited explanatory power.'[54]

Two things need to be said about this. First, it simply is not correct to argue that constructivist accounts that elevate ideational factors to the role of 'explanatory' (or 'independent') variables must be antipositivist. Not all constructivists deserve to be placed outside the positivist pale, even if they might themselves insist upon the relegation. What is at issue here, as was demonstrated by the rejoinders Desch's article attracted,[55] is not necessarily whether causal explanation is desirable (or possible), but rather what sorts of explanation have greater persuasiveness: those derived from assessments of relative capability, or those embedded in national and international norms and discourses? While it would be wrong to argue all constructivists are positivists, it is equally fallacious to claim none (or at most, only a few) are.

At the very least, those constructivists who insist upon the autonomous, causal prowess of ideas and discourse can be taken as positivists even within a restrictive understanding of positivism that emphasizes a nomothetic (or 'covering-law') conception of explanation. But if David Dessler is to be believed, the positivist strain in constructivism extends more broadly to include those favouring, as did Weber, a 'particularistic' and narrative-dependent rendering of causation. Whether or not we are prepared to include even Weber in the ranks of the positivists (a companionship that would have surprised him probably as much as Durkheim), it still can be said that constructivism *per se* need not be antithetical to the quest for reliable causality.[56]

By the very same token, Colin Gray is right to object to the dismissal of realists as 'acultural, ahistorical' automatons. It is ironic enough to find constructivist tents pitched inside positivist epistemological campgrounds; even more ironic is the discovery of realists grazing in the pastures of interpretivism. For what else can this variety of realist be said to be doing when state action is ascribed to endogenous, identity-derived categories, rather than deduced from assessments of a systemic structure revealed through relative capability? Adrian Hyde-Price and Lisbeth Aggestam were on the mark when they noted that realists of a non-structural kidney have been enjoying 'a renewed burst of life, particularly as the limitations of Waltzian parsimony become ever clearer'.[57] Some have seen fit to label this more reflective theoretical orientation 'neoclassical' realism.[58] It is usually a bad idea to attach the prefix 'neo-' to otherwise serviceable concepts, as witnessed by the tortured semantic career of 'neorealism', which not only never *was* required as a means of conveying the meaning amply supplied by 'structural' realism, but which completely reversed the original sense that some proposed to attach to the 'neorealism' that first appeared on the scene in the early 1980s, as an inventory of the accoutrements of sound policy in an era of 'complex interdependence' – that is, an inventory that *denied* the utility of an aggregate construe of power![59]

Strategic Culture as Context: History, Identity, Character

Whether the above mentioned variant of realism actually requires being called 'neoclassical' need not distract us from pondering how the relative demise of structuralism should have stimulated a resurgence of interesting work on the part of traditional (or 'classical') realists. This is not to say that constructivists were themselves absent from the renewal process; quite the contrary, it is simply to claim that they did not *own* the process, and to remark a (generally unappreciated) synthesis of constructivism and classicalism.[60] And even if Gideon Rose might be scolded for abetting the neologists, he certainly deserves praise for drawing to our attention the preferred methodology of this genre of non-structural realists, who, he instructs us, place a premium upon 'theoretically informed narratives, ideally supplemented by explicit counterfactual analysis, that trace the ways different factors combine to yield particular foreign policies'.[61]

Here, then, is a clue to the first of two ways in which strategic culture conceived as *context* can be put to work. What culture-as-context analysts seek to do is explicate foreign policies in terms either of 1. how particular states have acted in the past (that is, their previous behaviour is argued to have great bearing on their current and future options), or 2. how states are thought by their own and other peoples as being likely to act based on the 'way they are' (that is, their identity, or character, is said to predispose them toward certain policies). Analysts who employ strategic culture as a means of accounting for behaviour's impact often turn to *historical sociology* for guidance; those who prefer to put the emphasis upon conceptions attending identity also avail themselves of approaches with a long-established pedigree, subsumed under the rubric *national character*. If both approaches are similar in dating from the first half of the 20th century, a difference worth noting is that historical sociology has regained scholarly respectability after having been in eclipse for some years,[62] while national character studies, under that name, remain controversial – though when repackaged under the label 'national identity' they become not just respectable, but voguish.[63]

Whatever else might divide them, strategic culturalists are all dissatisfied with structuralist accounts of foreign policy behaviour; they may or may not be in agreement as to the attainability of reliable causality, but they do accept that cultural context, and therefore history, should 'matter'. *How* history should matter, no one can say exactly, but many analysts have been turning to narrative to supply explicative energy, via an approach sometimes called 'narrative positivism'.[64] The turn to narrative has led many of them to focus on the process (or phenomenon) known as 'path dependence'. Path dependence, as Paul Pierson observes, stands in contradistinction to certain assumptions of rational-choice theory that claim 'large' causes should result in 'large' outcomes.[65] As such, path dependence will have an ever more congenial ring in the ears of some strategic culturalists, whose anti-structuralist epistemology, coupled with their conviction that patterns of behaviour are 'culturally' significant variables, will entice them to search for the cultural origins and character of path-dependent foreign policy choices.

It is, of course, one thing to invoke path dependence as the mechanism by which history can be said to continue to matter in the shaping of foreign (including security) policy, for instance in the general, and commonsensical, observation that choices made long in the past can go on limiting policy options in the future.[66] Yet it is quite another thing actually to tease out, or 'trace',[67] the process(es) by which path dependence manages to yield the context called strategic culture. Strategic culturalists exploring the behavioural component of context will find themselves being drawn ever closer to historical sociology, and will as a result have to come to grips with concepts closely related to path dependence. Among these latter, two stand out: temporal sequencing and contingency. Path dependence cannot mean sensitive dependence upon 'initial conditions'; rather, it must suggest a break point after which the ability of those initial conditions to shape the future altered substantially.[68] Some will label that break point 'contingency', by which they will mean the development required to have set in train a new inertia – one in which the 'path' led either to the efficient reproduction of cooperation (sometimes called 'self-reinforcing sequences') or the reverse, the efficient reproduction of conflict and discord (called 'reactive sequences').[69] Which it is to be, and why, can be expected to provide work for strategic culturalists who take their concept to mean the 'context' revealed by behaviour, and who understand strategic culture as virtually indistinguishable from a country's historical record.

But as I said above, other strategic culturalists have taken contextual clues from elsewhere, and have not relied upon the behavioural record as evidenced in history. Not that they hold the past per se to lack instructive merit; rather they prefer to delve into 'national character' as the source of whatever is deemed to be cultural in foreign policy. This is, of course, the conceptual terrain upon which Perrin du Lac trod so long ago, with his insights into the clashing 'temperaments' of the Americans and the French. As noted above, no one likes these days to make explicit reference to temperament a part of their contemporary theory building, although policymakers have been known even in recent years to avail themselves of the concept – the most notable perhaps being Richard Nixon, who a year and a half before the collapse of his presidency was recorded on tape as denying he harboured any prejudices against national collectivities, while at the same time insisting to his adviser, Charles W. Colson, that all peoples possessed certain temperamental attributes (he called these 'traits'), and then by way of illustration proceeding to disparage the Jews, the Irish, the Italians, and the African-Americans.[70] More typically, however, recourse is had to another, and less controversial, word when specifying the object of one's intellectual curiosity. That word is identity, a category that is held by constructivist and classical realist alike to endow meaning to 'interest' – including and especially the 'national interest'.[71]

To be sure, there is nothing about identity that requires that its group, or societal, referent be the state or nation; collective identity accounts of international security phenomena are certainly not rare, or insignificant, and they might feature, *inter alia*, such transnational variables as religion or liberal democracy, to take just two common referents. But when it comes to the strategic culture of any particular country, the group referent reduces to the state or nation, and even to subnational identity groupings.[72]

Interestingly, for all the attention accorded these days to identity – even and especially the 'national' variant thereof – there is a marked reluctance of scholars openly to embrace the erstwhile concept of 'national character', held by some to be a retrogressive notion that smacks of 'essentialist' or 'primordialist' categories.[73] If what is being alleged is that national character has been found guilty by prior association with 'hereditarian' or racist assumptions about international relations, then one can easily see why it should have fallen out of favour; but if it is being avoided in name (though not in practice) because it is, as are most political concepts, ambiguous and even self-contradictory, then the shunning becomes less easy to justify, given the generic problems associated with political concepts – and especially given that national character's replacement by national identity merely substitutes one essentially contested category for another, in the process violating Ockham's razor.[74]

It can come as no surprise that even those social scientists who continue to employ the concept by its name disagree over its definition. Indeed, some will willingly concede that it resists defining – but is nevertheless too important to discard! One such scholar was Arthur Schlesinger, Jr., for whom national character raised important questions about the ability of America's creedal (constitutional) identity to withstand the challenge of a contemporary ethnic politics subsumed under the name 'multiculturalism'.[75] Although Schlesinger's pessimism on this score may not have been justified, he was certainly correct in noting the important part played by ethnicity in discussions about national character. What this implies for analysts who interpret strategic culture as context is, or should be, apparent: the impact of ethnicity as a conditioning element in foreign policy making is a worthy object for their scholarly attentions. They might not think of themselves in this connection, but analysts who attempt to come to grips with the impact of ethnic diasporas in liberal-pluralist (or other kinds of) societies can be said to be working in the field of strategic culture.[76]

Attempts to assess the impact of a country's ethnic mix on its grand strategy do not exhaust the category of national character, of course.[77] A major alternative manner in which the category is applied relates to the social-psychological variable known as 'modal personality'. Unlike ethnicity-based approaches to national character, studies that rely upon modal personality (that is, a statistical notion for expressing personalities that appear with great frequency among members of a particular society) concentrate upon three major sources of evidence of a national character: personality assessments of individuals, psychological analyses of collective phenomena (especially 'nationalism'), and psychological assessments of child-rearing practices.[78]

Then there are, of course, those 'non-ethnic' attributes of identity/character that can and do attest to how countries see themselves and others. As I argue below, these too form part of the strategic-cultural approach to foreign policy, for they go to the very means by which collective cognition is enshrined and transmitted.

Strategic Culture as Cognition: Symbolism, Myth, Metaphor

There are enough similarities between strategic culture as context and strategic culture as cognition for anyone to make too big a fuss about their analytical separability;[79] nevertheless, there is at least one difference worth noting, and it speaks to the very core of the explicative enterprise. Recall the thrust of Johnston's criticism of Gray, namely that his use of strategic culture was hopelessly muddled, as it so blurred the distinction between independent and dependent variables as to eliminate any prospect of strategic culture being of anyone's use in trying to sort cause from effect. I have hinted that this criticism has merit only to the extent one is committed to the notion of reliable causality; the more Laodicean the analyst is regarding the attainability of such causality, the less problematical becomes strategic culture as context. After all, and heretical though it might sound to some, if taxonomy and the kind of systematic understanding conveyed through interpretation are themselves part of the explicative enterprise, then even culture as context can serve us profitably, by helping us see things in foreign policy we might otherwise have missed.

Some are unhappy with this thought, which seems to them to be defeatist, going as it does against the grain of aspiring to the kind of knowledge that presumably can only be ours if we distinguish our 'variables' in a credible manner.[80] And it is in this respect that the *second* major category of strategic culture comes into play. It is no coincidence that the causal ambitiousness of Alistair Iain Johnston should have led him to a Geertzian approach to his topic (even though many will tell you, perhaps wrongly, that Geertz himself was agnostic on the issue of reliable causality).[81] But it is not just, or even perhaps chiefly, to Geertz that Johnston is indebted, for his approach to the subdisciplinary derivative, strategic culture, puts it squarely into alignment with an earlier tradition that had arisen in the main body of the discipline of political science – the tradition of 'political culture', which as we are about to see has remarkable affinities with our category in this section, strategic culture as cognition.

If the basic problem with culture as context is definitional fuzziness,[82] culture as cognition holds out the promise of definitional clarity. Once the definition has been sufficiently 'precised', why not envision using it as an independent variable? And what could be better than *political* culture to blaze the trail for *strategic* culture, for did not the career of the former concept demonstrate that it slew the very same definitional dragon whose breath has been heating up the debate over the latter concept? Why not turn to political culture as a means of 'operationalizing' strategic culture?

The argument, on the surface, is not a bad one: for just as strategic culture is, political culture itself used to be subject to a variety of definitions; indeed, one critic observed that there were almost as many different meanings of political culture as there were political scientists professing an interest in it.[83] When it first burst on the scene in political science, during the 1930s and 1940s, it was as a result of the same interdisciplinary transfusion process that would bring culture into the purview of those who contemplated strategy, and it was again the anthropologists who were making the initial running. What happened in the subfield of strategy also occurred in the discipline more broadly: culture was often equated with 'character' in the early days, but the more the latter was dissected the more it grew suspect as a useful category. By 1956, some two decades earlier than in the case of strategic culture, political culture got its name; yet even though Gabriel Almond might have told us what we should call it, he could not decree what it meant. Debate continued as to whether it was to signify the 'generalized personality' of a people, or the collectivity's history, or something else altogether. By the late 1960s, political culture was well on the way to the conceptual dust heap.[84]

Political culture's rebound owed a bit to changes in the international system attending the Cold War's end, but it was primarily some analysts' discontent with rational-choice modelling and game theory that gave the concept a new lease of life in the 1980s and 1990s.[85] For while the concept might have taken a nose-dive in the late 1960s and early 1970s, its core question – namely how to tap the subjective orientations of societies' members so as to account for political differences cross-nationally – had never gone out of fashion.[86] What had changed in the period between the decline and re-emergence of political culture was that a new element had been injected into the discussions of political scientists when they pondered how to assess 'culture'. That element was symbolism.

Symbolism helped resuscitate political culture in two ways. First, it solved the level-of-analysis problem hobbling political culture, for much of the early work by Almond and his associates relied upon survey data that, while indicating much of value about the perceptions and psychological state of *individuals*, seemed incapable of generating usable knowledge about the cognitive patterns of *collectivities*. Individuals, after all, had personalities, but only collectivities could be said to possess cultures, and the trick was to find a way to go from the individual to the collective level of analysis if culture was to mean anything. Symbolism provided the answer, enabling theorists to explore the *social* ideas of individuals.[87]

Symbolism could do this because of its second major contribution, which was to draw us to the cognitive devices that social groupings rely upon, as Lowell Dittmer nicely phrased it, to 'transmit meanings from person to person despite vast distances of space and time'. Dittmer invited us to think of those devices, which include but are not limited to imagery and metaphor, as being identical to what the poet T.S. Eliot called 'objective correlatives', namely mechanisms for the efficient expression of feelings. In this regard, symbols become a 'depository of widespread interest and feeling'; and for Dittmer, the task of those who would employ political culture must be nothing other than the systematic, *scientific* analysis of society's key symbols.[88] For, as Michael Walzer eloquently put the same thought, symbols and images tell us 'more than we can easily repeat'.[89]

From the above, it will be apparent how strategic culture as cognition might assist in shaping a research agenda, and this is so whether or not one believes in reliable causality. What I mean is that even if this category of strategic culture proves incapable of serving as anyone's independent variable, it can still do valuable scientific duty as a 'specifying' or conditioning element in explicative understandings of strategy, just as political culture supplies a conditioning element in political choice.[90] Analysts whose interest in strategic culture is situated primarily in the cognitive category might, for instance, be drawn to efforts at explicating strategic choice through the study of such nonliteral forms of communication as myth and metaphor, to take just the two most obvious such examples.[91]

Conclusion: What's Culture Got to do with it?

So what does all of the above have to do with this special issue's inquiry into the historic record and future prospects of European security? Perhaps not as much as would be thought if 'culture' is invoked as an omnibus explanation for whatever is said to be worthy of mention when thoughts turn to the current shape of European security cooperation (or lack thereof); yet more than might be apparent at first glance to those who would be tempted to minimize the utility of culture, if not to dismiss it altogether. The current NATO intervention in Libya is perhaps an instructive one, making the point that it is unwise to lay too much emphasis upon our concept's serving as the 'dependent variable', even if it is easy – perhaps too tempting – for scholars to wish to derive inferences from relative capability. For too long, too many observers have been tempted to prate on about the Europeans having a strategy (or security) characterized by a preference for 'soft' power assets over 'hard' power ones. Whatever else the Libyan episode might show, it certainly demonstrates that it is time to lay this cliché to rest. Since the tools being used against the Gaddafi regime are fairly hard ones, the only 'soft' thing in the Europeans' response concerns their resolve to fund defence and security operations – a point that America's outgoing Secretary of Defense, Robert Gates, took pains to highlight in his valedictory speech in Brussels in June 2011.[92]

This article has consisted of an effort to make a modest defence of strategic culture as a potentially useful construct for organizing the manner in which we address empirical and policy issues in international relations. Some who would employ the rubric might have more ambitious aims, including developing an explanatory framework within which could be effected reliable causality, and therefore a capability to make predictions. Others might even see in the strategic-culture rubric redemptive qualities, enabling the analyst to be freed from the constraints of 'realism', said by many to be the source of much if not all that goes wrong in the world of theory, as well as of policy.

Many writers can and do proclaim an interest in culture because of a dissatisfaction with realism, but I am not one of them. Instead, I have employed strategic culture to illuminate patterns of interaction that are hardly antithetical to classical realist expectations about states' behaviour in the international system. My argument has been a modest one. I have claimed that there is not much of a distinction worth making between security culture and strategic culture, for the latter category contains enough suggestive elements to satisfy the intellectual curiosity of those who would seek to link culture with European security policies and outcomes. I have further claimed that strategic culture does have an analytical payoff, one that inheres in the related, but only partly overlapping, categories I label *context* and *cognition*. To date, much of the scholarly inquiry into European strategic culture centres on the former (as in the frequent recourse had to historical learning as a cultural game-changer, obviously mostly in respect of Germany but also relating to other European states). But cognition can also surrender its yield of relevant policy ideas, as sustained and systematic inquiry turns more and more to the analysis of the key symbols of European security in the early 21st century.

NOTES

1. Alfred Grosser, *The Western Alliance* (New York: Continuum, 1980), p. xv.
2. See Jörg Nagler, 'From *Culture* to Kultur: Changing American Perceptions of Imperial Germany, 1870–1914', in David E. Barclay and Elisabeth Glaser-Schmidt (eds), *Transatlantic Images and Perceptions: Germany and America Since 1776* (Cambridge: Cambridge University Press, 1997), pp. 131–54 and Michaela Hönicke, '"Know Your Enemy": American Wartime Images of Germany, 1942-1943', in Ragnhild Fiebig-von Hase and Ursula Lehmkuhl (eds), *Enemy Images in American History* (Providence, RI: Berghahn, 1997), pp. 232–278.
3. Quoted in André Tardieu, *France and America: Some Experiences in Cooperation* (Boston, MA: Houghton Mifflin, 1927), p. 64. Perrin du Lac was a French colonial administrator who, for reasons both political and geopolitical, found himself stranded in the New World from 1789 until 1803, when he was finally able to return to France.
4. *Ibid.*, pp. 50–51.
5. Parts of this and the following sections have been based on my article 'What Good Is Strategic Culture? A Modest Defence of an Immodest Concept', *International Journal*, Vol. 59 (Summer 2004), pp. 479–502.
6. For the results of that project, see Jeannie L. Johnson, Kerry M. Kartchner, and Jeffrey A. Larsen (eds), *Strategic Culture and Weapons of Mass Destruction: Culturally Based Insights into Comparative National Security Policymaking* (New York: Palgrave Macmillan, 2009).
7. Jeffrey S. Lantis, 'Strategic Culture: From Clausewitz to Constructivism', Paper prepared for the Advanced Systems and Concepts Office, Defense Threat Reduction Agency, Washington, DC, 31 October 2006, p. 13.
8. Colin S. Gray, 'Out of the Wilderness: Prime Time for Strategic Culture', *Comparative Strategy*, Vol. 26 (January–March 2007), pp. 1–20.
9. On the necessity for structural realists to conceive of power as 'aggregate capability', see John J. Mearsheimer, *The Tragedy of Great Power Politics* (New York: W.W. Norton, 2001), p. 60.
10. For a vigorous rejection of the understanding of power as aggregate capability, see David A. Baldwin, *Paradoxes of Power* (Oxford: Basil Blackwell, 1989), especially chapter 4.

11. Some would object, and insist instead that unless we can come to agreed-upon working definitions, we can never assign a value to our terms, thus cannot hope to measure them 'scientifically'. This insistence strikes me as being in its own way unscientific, if by the term science we simply mean the systematic organization and use of knowledge in a given area of inquiry. For a refreshingly catholic view of such a way to organize thinking about foreign policy, see James N. Rosenau, *The Scientific Study of Foreign Policy*, rev. and enl. edn. (London: Frances Pinter, 1980).
12. Jack Snyder is often credited with being the first writer explicitly to employ the rubric, in his *The Soviet Strategic Culture: Implications for Nuclear Options* (Santa Monica: RAND Corporation, 1977).
13. For a cautionary reminder, see Giovanni Sartori, 'Concept Misformation in Comparative Politics', *American Political Science Review*, Vol. 64 (December 1970), pp. 1033–1053. But for a tacit recognition that the problem may be immune to resolution, see David Collier and James E. Mahon, '"Conceptual Stretching" Revisited: Adapting Categories in Comparative Analysis', *American Political Science Review*, Vol. 87 (December 1999), pp,845–855.
14. T.D. Weldon, *The Vocabulary of Politics* (Harmondsworth: Penguin Books, 1953), pp. 26–27.
15. Williams, cited by William H. Sewell, Jr., 'The Concept(s) of Culture', in Victoria E. Bonnell and Lynn Hunt (eds), *Beyond the Cultural Turn: New Directions in the Study of Society and Culture* (Berkeley: University of California Press, 1999), pp. 35–61. For an extensive catalogue of culture's many, and at times contradictory, meanings, see A.L. Kroeber and Clyde Kluckhohn, *Culture: A Critical Review of Concepts and Definitions* (New York: Vintage Books, 1963).
16. Alastair Iain Johnston, *Cultural Realism: Strategic Culture and Grand Strategy in Chinese History* (Princeton, NJ: Princeton University Press, 1995), p. 1.
17. For such a bounded application of strategic culture, see Yitzhak Klein, 'A Theory of Strategic Culture', *Comparative Strategy*, Vol. 10 (January–March 1991), pp. 3–23. Sometimes a modifier even more limiting than 'strategic' is chosen, as in the case of the debate over France's and other states' *military* culture. For that debate see Elizabeth Kier, 'Culture and Military Doctrine: France between the Wars', *International Security*, 19 (Spring 1995), pp. 65–93; Elizabeth Kier, *Imagining War: French Military Doctrine between the Wars* (Princeton: Princeton University Press, 1997); Douglas Porch, 'Military "Culture" and the Fall of France in 1940: A Review Essay', *International Security*, 24 (Spring 2000), pp. 157–180; and Isabel V. Hull, *Absolute Destruction: Military Culture and the Practices of War in Imperial Germany* (Ithaca: Cornell University Press, 2006).
18. John Lewis Gaddis, *Strategies of Containment: A Critical Appraisal of Postwar American National Security Policy* (Oxford: Oxford University Press, 1982), p. viii.
19. Ronald Jepperson and Ann Swidler, 'What Properties of Culture Should we Measure?' *Poetics*, 22 (1994), pp. 359–371.
20. Donald R. Kelley, 'The Old Cultural History', *History of the Human Sciences*, Vol. 9 (August 1996), pp. 101–126.
21. In the first of his seven-volume magnum opus; see Giovanni Andres, *Dell'origine, progressi e stato attuale d'ogni letteratura*, 7 vols. (Parma: Stamperia reale, 1782-99).
22. Kelley, 'Old Cultural History' (note 20), p. 109. Tylor's book was entitled *Early History of Mankind and the Development of Civilization*.
23. *Ibid.*, pp. 114–116.
24. See David Brion Davis, 'Some Recent Directions in American Cultural History', *American Historical Review*, Vol. 73 (February 1968), pp. 696–707.
25. Colin Dueck, *Reluctant Crusaders: Power, Culture, and Change in American Grand Strategy* (Princeton, NJ: Princeton University Press, 2006), pp. 14–15.
26. Robert Kelley, *The Cultural Pattern in American Politics: The First Century* (New York: Alfred A. Knopf, 1979), pp. 6–9. For an early attempt to associate culture with ethno-nationalism, through the concept of national 'genius' (or, as it would subsequently be rendered, 'national character'), see Edward Sapir, 'Culture, Genuine and Spurious', *American Journal of Sociology*, Vol. 29 (January 1924), pp. 401–429.
27. (New York: Basic Books, 1973).
28. Victoria E. Bonnell and Lynn Hunt, 'Introduction', in *Beyond the Cultural Turn* (note 15), pp. 1–32.
29. Quoted in Kelley, *Cultural Pattern in American Politics* (note 26), p. 12.
30. Sewell, 'Concept(s) of Culture' (note 15), p. 48.
31. Johnston, *Cultural Realism* (note 16), pp. 36–37. Also see his 'Thinking about Strategic Culture', *International Security*, Vol. 19 (Spring 1995), pp. 32–64.
32. Johnston, *Cultural Realism*, pp. 36–37.
33. Robert Kagan, *Of Paradise and Power: America and the New World Order* (New York: Alfred A. Knopf, 2003).

34. Examples, respectively, of first- and second-generationers, as Johnston interprets them, are Colin S. Gray, 'Strategic Culture as Context: The First Generation of Theory Strikes Back', *Review of International Studies*, 25 (January 1999), pp. 49–69; and Bradley Klein, 'Hegemony and Strategic Culture: American Power Projection and Alliance Defence Politics', *Review of International Studies*, Vol. 14 (April 1988), pp. 133–148.
35. Johnston, *Cultural Realism* (note 16), pp. 1–2, 37–39.
36. Terrence J. McDonald (ed.), *The Historic Turn in the Human Sciences* (Ann Arbor: University of Michigan Press, 1996). Also see Mark M. Blyth, '"Any More Bright Ideas?" The Ideational Turn of Comparative Political Economy', *Comparative Politics*, 29 (January 1997), pp. 229–50; and David Chaney, *The Cultural Turn: Scene-Setting Essays on Contemporary Cultural History* (London: Routledge, 1994).
37. Kelley, 'Old Cultural History' (note 20), p. 117.
38. Gray, 'Strategic Culture as Context' (note 34), p. 58 (emphasis in original). In this regard, Gray's understanding of strategic culture is similar to the way in which Fukuyama defines culture, as 'inherited ethical habit'. See Francis Fukuyama, *Trust: The Social Virtues and the Creation of Prosperity* (New York: Free Press, 1995), p. 34. Also see, for this distinction, Stuart Poore, 'What is the Context? A Reply to the Gray-Johnston Debate on Strategic Culture', *Review of International Studies*, Vol. 29 (April 2003), pp. 279–284.
39. Gray, 'Strategic Culture as Context' (note 34), p. 69.
40. Martin Hollis and Steve Smith, *Explaining and Understanding International Relations* (Oxford: Clarendon Press, 1990), pp. 72–74, 206–15.
41. Georg Henrik von Wright, *Explanation and Understanding* (Ithaca, NY: Cornell University Press, 1971), pp. 4–6.
42. For one claim that historical explanation is possible, but requires taking the 'inside view' – that is, getting into the heads of sentient decisionmakers so as to comprehend how *they* understood reality – see Isaiah Berlin, 'History and Theory: The Concept of Scientific History', *History and Theory*, Vol. 1, No. 1 (1961), pp. 1–31.
43. Von Wright, *Explanation and Understanding* (note 43), pp. 134–135. Also see Richard Biernacki, 'Method and Metaphor after the New Cultural History', in *Beyond the Cultural Turn* (note 15), pp. 62–92; Patrick L. Gardiner, *The Nature of Historical Explanation* (Oxford: Oxford University Press, 1952); and Marc Trachtenberg, *The Craft of International History: A Guide to Method* (Princeton, NJ: Princeton University Press, 2006).
44. As is argued in Michael Nicholson, 'What's the Use of International Relations?', *Review of International Studies*, Vol. 26 (April 2000), pp. 183–198.
45. Kenneth N. Waltz, *Theory of International Politics* (Reading, MA: Addison-Wesley, 1979).
46. See Robert Gilpin, *War and Change in World Politics* (Cambridge: Cambridge University Press, 1981), for a reminder that bipolarity might just be unstable and very dangerous.
47. Illustratively, a survey of IR practitioners in North American universities found only 15 per cent of Canadian professors self-identified as working within the 'realist' paradigm, as against a somewhat larger minority (25 per cent) in the US. See Michael Lipson, Daniel Maliniak, Amy Oakes, Susan Peterson, and Michael J. Tierney, 'Divided Discipline? Comparing Views of US and Canadian IR Scholars', *International Journal*, Vol. 62 (Spring 2007), pp. 327–343.
48. For one realist's assessment of constructivism, see Stephen M. Walt, 'International Relations: One World, Many Theories', *Foreign Policy*, No. 110 (Spring 1998), pp. 29–46.
49. Jeffrey Checkel, 'The Constructivist Turn in International Relations Theory', *World Politics*, 50 (January 1998), pp. 324–348; Sujata Chakrabarti Pasic, 'Culturing International Relations Theory: A Call for Extension', in Yosef Lapid and Friedrich Kratochwil (eds), *The Return of Culture and Identity in IR Theory* (Boulder, CO: Lynne Rienner, 1997), pp. 85–104.
50. Ted Hopf, 'The Promise of Constructivism in International Relations Theory', *International Security*, 23 (Summer 1998), pp. 171–200.
51. For the argument that 'identity' is simply too loose and self-contradictory a category to provide guidance for serious analysis, see Rogers Brubaker and Frederick Cooper, 'Beyond "Identity"', *Theory and Society*, Vol. 29 (February 2000), pp. 1–47.
52. In the words of two scholars, 'both constructivism and rationalism are broadly positivistic in orientation'. David Dessler and John Owen, 'Constructivism and the Problem of Explanation: A Review Article', *Perspectives on Politics*, Vol. 3 (September 2005), pp. 597–610.
53. On the prominence of anthropologists among this pioneering generation of strategic culturalists, see E. Adamson Hoebel, 'Anthropological Perspectives on National Character', *Annals of the American Academy of Political and Social Science*, Vol. 370 (March 1967), pp. 1–7.

54. Michael C. Desch, 'Culture Clash: Assessing the Importance of Ideas in Security Studies', *International Security*, Vol. 23 (Summer 1998), pp. 141–170.
55. For some examples of the criticisms unleashed in his direction, see the separate contributions of John S. Duffield, Theo Farrell, and Richard Price, under the heading 'Isms and Schisms: Culturalism versus Realism in Security Studies', *International Security*, Vol. 24 (Summer 1999), pp. 156–172.
56. See David Dessler, 'Constructivism within a Positivist Social Science', *Review of International Studies*, Vol. 25 (January 1999), pp. 123–37.
57. Adrian Hyde-Price and Lisbeth Aggestam, 'Conclusion: Exploring the New Agenda', in Lisbeth Aggestam and Adrian Hyde-Price (eds), *Security and Identity in Europe: Exploring the New Agenda* (New York: St. Martin's, 2000), pp. 234–262.
58. Gideon Rose, 'Neoclassical Realism and Theories of Foreign Policy', *World Politics*, Vol. 51 (October 1998), pp. 144–172.
59. In what has to be the best example of the international relations conceptual equivalent of Gresham's Law, neorealism was debased to such an extent that it would soon come to stand for the virtual opposite of what it had originally been intended to represent. That the debasing was in some large measure the doing of Robert Keohane, one of the pioneers of 'complex interdependence' theory, only adds to the curiosity. For early applications of neorealism as a means of assessing the relative merits of a variety of 'power assets' (including 'soft power' ones) in an era in which *aggregate* capability was said to have lost relevance, see Robert Lieber, *No Common Power* (Glenview, IL: Scott Foresman, 1988); Richard Feinberg, *The Intemperate Zone: The Third World Challenge to US Foreign Policy* (New York: W.W. Norton, 1983); and David B. Dewitt and John J. Kirton, *Canada as a Principal Power* (Toronto: John Wiley and Sons, 1983). The work most often associated with the transformation of the concept was Robert Keohane (ed.), *Neorealism and its Critics* (New York: Columbia University Press, 1986), which was really a debate about the pros and cons of structural realism, the label Kenneth Waltz chose for his theory.
60. It is unappreciated in large measure due to the mistaken assumption of so many that realism must be all about either 'security' (as those structuralists sometimes labelled 'defensive realists'' stress) or 'power' (said to be the stellar variable for structuralists called 'offensive realists'). But as Randall Schweller reminds us, structural realists, whether defensive or offensive, seem to have forgotten classical realism's roots, which reveal myriad objects of states' desire – including prestige, status, leadership, and market share (objects, he goes on to note, that probably ensure states will be more predisposed to competition than to cooperation). See Randall L. Schweller, 'Realism and the Present Great Power System: Growth and Positional Conflict Over Scarce Resources', in Ethan B. Kapstein and Michael Mastanduno (eds), *Unipolar Politics: Realism and State Strategies After the Cold War* (New York: Columbia University Press, 1999), pp. 28–68. On the synthesis of classicalism and constructivism, see J. Samuel Barkin, 'Realist Constructivism', *International Studies Review*, Vol. 5 (September 2003), pp. 325–342; and Patrick Thaddeus Jackson and Daniel H. Nexon, 'Constructivist Realism or Realist-Constructivism?' *International Studies Review*, Vol. 6 (Summer 2004), pp. 337–341.
61. Rose, 'Neoclassical Realism' (note 58), pp. 152–153.
62. On the rise, decline, and re-emergence of historical sociology, see Harry Elmer Barnes, *Historical Sociology: Its Origins and Development* (New York: Philosophical Library, 1948) and Dennis Smith, *The Rise of Historical Sociology* (Cambridge: Polity Press, 1991).
63. On the arrival of identity as an element of conceptual high-fashion, see Glenn Chafetz, Michael Spirtas, and Benjamin Frankel, 'Introduction: Tracing the Influence of Identity on Foreign Policy', *Security Studies*, Vol. 8 (Winter 1998/99–Spring 1999), pp. vii–xxii.
64. See Andrew Abbott, 'From Causes to Events: Notes on Narrative Positivism', *Sociological Methods and Research*, Vol. 20 (May 1992), pp. 428–455. Also relevant here are John Gerard Ruggie, 'Peace In Our Time? Causality, Social Facts and Narrative Knowing', *American Society of International Law: Proceedings 89th Annual Meeting* (1995), pp. 93–100; Lawrence Stone, 'The Revival of the Narrative: Reflections on a New Old History', *Past and Present*, Vol. 85 (November 1979), pp. 3–24; and Ian Lustick, 'History, Historiography, and Political Science: Multiple Historical Records and the Problem of Selection Bias', *American Political Science Review*, Vol. 90 (September 1996), pp. 605–618.
65. Paul Pierson, 'Increasing Returns, Path Dependence, and the Study of Politics', *American Political Science Review*, Vol. 94 (June 2000), pp. 251–268. Also see Margaret R. Somers, '"We're No Angels": Realism, Rational Choice, and Relationality in Social Science', *American Journal of Sociology*, Vol. 104 (November 1998), pp. 722–784.
66. See Theda Skocpol, 'Sociology's Historical Imagination', in Skocpol (ed.), *Vision and Method in Historical Sociology* (Cambridge: Cambridge University Press, 1984), pp. 1–21.

67. On the methodological bona fides of 'process tracing', see Stephen Van Evera, *Guide to Methods for Students of Political Science* (Ithaca, NY: Cornell University Press, 1997), pp. 64–67.
68. See Jack A. Goldstone, 'Initial Conditions, General Laws, Path Dependence, and Explanation in Historical Sociology', *American Journal of Sociology*, Vol. 104 (November 1998), pp. 829–845.
69. James Mahoney, 'Path Dependence in Historical Sociology', *Theory and Society*, Vol. 29 (August 2000), pp. 507–548.
70. Adam Nagourney, 'In Tapes, Nixon Rails About Jews and Blacks', *New York Times*, 10 December 2010 (online edition), http://www.nytimes.com (accessed 11 December 2010).
71. See Christina Rowley and Jutta Weldes, 'Identities and US Foreign Policy', in Michael Cox and Doug Stokes (eds.), *US Foreign Policy* (Oxford: Oxford University Press, 2008), pp. 183–209.
72. See Rodney Bruce Hall, *National Collective Identity: Social Constructs and International Systems* (New York: Columbia University Press, 1999) and William Bloom, *Personal Identity, National Identity and International Relations* (Cambridge: Cambridge University Press, 1990).
73. This critique is made by Paul A. Kowert in 'National Identity: Inside and Out', *Security Studies*, Vol. 8 (Winter 1998/99–Spring 1999), pp. 1–34. But for a rebuttal, see Francisco Gil-White, 'How Thick is Blood? The Plot Thickens...: If Ethnic Actors Are Primordialists, What Remains of the Circumstantialis/Primordialist Controversy?' *Ethnic and Racial Studies*, Vol. 22 (September 1999), pp. 789–820.
74. For a sharp critique of those who would steer clear of national character while embracing other vague categories (for example 'class'), see Dean Peabody, *National Characteristics* (Cambridge: Cambridge University Press, 1985).
75. Arthur M. Schlesinger, Jr., *The Disuniting of America: Reflections on a Multicultural Society*, new and rev. edn (New York: W.W. Norton, 1998), p. 169. Also see, on this theme, Samuel P. Huntington, 'The Hispanic Challenge', *Foreign Policy*, No. 141 (March/April 2004), pp. 30–45.
76. For an example, see Tony Smith, *Foreign Attachments: The Power of Ethnic Groups in the Making of American Foreign Policy* (Cambridge, MA: Harvard University Press, 2000).
77. A point that is sometimes missed by writers who seem to think that national character has to be synonymous with ethnicity. For such a conflation of terms, see Victor T. Le Vine, 'Conceptualizing "Ethnicity" and "Ethnic Conflict": A Controversy Revisited', *Studies in Comparative International Development*, Vol. 32 (Summer 1997), pp. 47–75.
78. See Alex Inkeles and Daniel J. Levinson, 'National Character: The Study of Modal Personality and Sociocultural Systems', in Gardner Lindzey and Elliot Aronson (eds), *The Handbook of Social Psychology* (2nd edn): *Group Psychology and Phenomena of Interaction* (Reading, MA: Addison-Wesley, 1969), pp. 418–506. Also see Geoffrey Gorer, *The American People: A Study in National Character* (New York: W.W. Norton, 1948).
79. For instance, see Yaacov Y.I. Vertzberger, *The World in Their Minds: Information Processing, Cognition, and Perception in Foreign Policy Decisionmaking* (Stanford, CA: Stanford University Press, 1990), pp. 270–273, where a country's strategic culture is held to be a function of both context (that is, its historical experience and geopolitical setting) and cognition, with the latter paying heed to the manner in which decisionmakers utilize myth, metaphor, analogy, and extrapolation in order to comprehend reality.
80. One such critic is Christopher P. Twomey in 'Lacunae in the Study of Culture in International Security', *Contemporary Security Policy*, Vol. 29 (August 2008), pp. 338–357.
81. Geertz is often associated with the argument that the best we can hope for is 'thick description' of social reality, but one writer claims he nevertheless often strayed into the realm of implicit causality. Says this writer, the 'riddle of what constitutes an adequate explication and how to distinguish causal claims from interpretive ones has vexed the best minds in philosophy for more than a century'. Biernacki, 'Method and Metaphor' (note 43), pp. 72–73. A similar argument is made in James Mahoney and Dietrich Rueschemeyer, 'Comparative Historical Analysis: Achievements and Agendas', in Mahoney and Rueschemeyer (eds), *Comparative Historical Analysis in the Social Sciences* (Cambridge: Cambridge University Press, 2003), pp. 3–38.
82. As one analyst puts it, '[y]ou know you are in trouble when our culture specialists, the cultural anthropologists and sociologists, cannot agree on a definition'. Gray, 'Out of the Wilderness' (note 8), p. 7.
83. William M. Reisinger, 'The Renaissance of a Rubric: Political Culture as Concept and Theory', *International Journal of Public Opinion Research*, Vol. 7 (Winter 1995), pp. 328–352.
84. Lucian Pye, 'Political Culture Revisited', *Political Psychology*, Vol. 12 (September 1991), pp. 487–508.
85. Ronald Inglehart, 'The Renaissance of Political Culture', *American Political Science Review*, Vol. 82 (December 1988), pp. 1203–1230.
86. Reisinger, 'Renaissance of a Rubric' (note 83), p. 331.

87. See, for the level-of-analysis problem, David J. Elkins and Richard E.B. Simeon, 'A Cause in Search of Its Effect, or What Does Political Culture Explain?' *Comparative Politics*, Vol. 11 (July 1979), pp. 127–145 and Ruth Lane, 'Political Culture: Residual Category or General Theory?' *Comparative Political Studies*, Vol. 25 (October 1992), pp. 362–387.
88. Lowell Dittmer, 'Political Culture and Political Symbolism', *World Politics*, Vol. 29 (July 1977), pp. 552–583.
89. Michael Walzer, 'On the Role of Symbolism in Political Thought', *Political Science Quarterly*, Vol. 82 (June 1967), pp. 191–204.
90. As argued by Edward W. Lehman, 'On the Concept of Political Culture: A Theoretical Reassessment', *Social Forces*, Vol. 50 (March 1972), pp. 361–370.
91. See Charles Hill, *Grand Strategies: Literature, Statecraft, and World Order* (New Haven, CT: Yale University Press, 2010).
92. Thom Shanker and Steven Erlanger, 'Gates Delivers a Blunt Warning on NATO Future', *New York Times*, 11 June 2001, pp. A1, A6.

EU Strategic Culture: When the Means Becomes the End

PER M. NORHEIM-MARTINSEN

Going back some thirty years, the strategic culture debate has evolved in step with scholarly developments and changes in the security environment, proving its endurance with the recent revival of the concept as part of the contemporary European security debate.[1] The appeal of the concept rests in its inherent potential for incorporating a range of more or less elusive ideational factors, such as history, norms, identity, values and ideas, in explanations of why certain states – and, more recently, institutions – act the way they do. Herein we also find strategic culture's weak spot: the term means different things to different people. Or, as Colin Gray remarks: 'The ability of scholars to make a necessarily opaque concept like strategic culture even less penetrable is truly amazing'.[2] Indeed, to some the idea of a European Union strategic culture represents something of a contradiction in terms, because the persistence of heavily ingrained *national* strategic cultures would seem to render it impossible.[3] To others, the idea that national strategic cultures may coexist with a European one seems wholly uncontroversial.[4] However, this article starts with the assumption that when the EU uses military force or other instruments of power, it does so *de facto* within some notion of a strategic culture.[5] That is, strategic culture should be seen as a constitutive factor that facilitates and/or constrains strategic actorness. From this point of departure, the article moves on to show that, since the adoption of the European Security Strategy (ESS) in 2003, a specific strategic culture has in fact evolved, in which consensus on a comprehensive approach to security as a unique European Union asset, rather than on a broad set of shared security interests amongst its Member States, has become the focal point for the fledgling ESDP.[6]

The end of the Cold War spurred some essential changes to the European security environment that together pushed in the direction of a heavier security role for the European Union. At the same time, the EU carried forward a strong awareness of its origin as a project for peace, having risen from the ashes of two world wars. This necessarily put some constraints on the way that defence aspects were to be accommodated in the European Union framework. Moreover, after having been subject to debate in academic circles for some time, the idea of a common EU strategic culture 'that fosters early, rapid and when necessary, robust intervention' was also elevated to a policy objective in the European Security Strategy.[7] Seven years on, it is still too early to judge if this objective has been met – if, indeed, a culture is something that can be purposely created or shaped as one sees fit. However, the document itself soon became a source of ambition and a benchmark against which the Union's security policy was to be measured.[8] But the almost routine comparisons with its American counterpart, the 2002 National Security Strategy (NSS), initially obscured the wider role that the ESS was to play in consolidating a common European strategic narrative.[9] A fresh look at the ESS reveals that the EU need not be very different from a state in the way that it uses strategic narratives as a way to legitimize, expand or restrict the scope of its actions. As such, the document had a reach far beyond the short-term political context in which it was conceived. It was in itself a significant step in the constant reaffirmation and incremental evolution of an EU strategic culture.

This article, therefore, approaches the European Security Strategy as a key expression of a nascent strategic narrative, and a readily observable social mechanism through which an EU strategic culture reveals itself. This implies an interpretative approach, in which the European Security Strategy is analysed in the context of how ESDP has evolved over the last years. The article argues that the notion of a comprehensive approach to security stands out as a natural – or culturally conditioned – focal point around which ESDP was to be shaped. It concludes that acting comprehensively has become an end in itself for the EU, and a rather successful way to frame EU actions under ESDP. However, before moving on, it is necessary to revisit briefly both the recent academic debate on an EU strategic culture and the overall strategic culture research agenda, to avoid some of the loopholes and conceptual difficulties that studies of culture tend to entail.

Strategic Culture Revisited

The strategic culture research agenda has, since the term was first coined by Jack Snyder in 1977, evolved in step with scholarly trends and changes in the security environment. Snyder himself held that strategic cultures are the product of each state's unique historical experience, which is reaffirmed and sustained as new generations of policy-makers are socialized into a particular way of thinking.[10] Criticizing the rational actor models of the time, Snyder questioned the predominant assumption that the Soviet Union and the United States would share nuclear strategic thinking, which among other truisms had laid the basis for the MAD (Mutually Assured Destruction) strategy. This shift of focus 'from rational man to national man' was immediately picked up by a number of scholars in the late 1970s and early 1980s who agreed that factors such as historical experience, political culture and geography can and often do act as constraints on strategic thinking.[11] However, as Snyder later summed up: '... some of the early American literature on strategic culture exaggerated past US-Soviet differences, and exaggerated the likelihood that such differences would persist in the future'.[12] Incidentally, similar criticisms can be launched against the persistent propensity to make comparisons across the Atlantic, this time between western Europe – with the EU as the most pertinent expression of what is typically European – and the United States.[13] The resulting stereotyping of Europe as weak and the United States as strong has helped obscure questions such as whether comparisons between two such vastly different entities are even feasible, whether US standards represent sensible yardsticks against which to measure European power, or whether transatlantic differences are rooted merely in material preconditions or in more fundamental differences of identity and culture. As a timely reminder, therefore, one should bear in mind that strategic culture, despite some of its later uses, was originally intended as a tool to explain the persistence of the way that a given strategic community thinks and behaves; it was not intended as a comparative tool.

As a reaction to the inherent danger of ending up with 'caricatures of culture', a second generation of strategic culture scholars, having observed the differences between what policy-makers say and what they actually do, voiced a general scepticism towards the feasibility of studying culture at all.[14] According to them, strategic culture was not expected to have much effect on strategic behaviour. Again, similar sentiments are mirrored in the recent debate about a European Union strategic culture. Some scholars remain sceptical of the actual impact of an EU strategic culture, since it seems to them to be reflected mostly in rhetoric.[15] And whereas some tend to downplay the role of 'symbolic victories' such as the 2001 Laeken Council, at which the ESDP was declared operational,[16] others conclude more favourably.[17] The point is that there might be a considerable gap between the usually upbeat tone of EU declarations and actual improvements, material or otherwise, in strategic capacity, as perhaps best conceptualized in Christopher Hill's 'capability-expectations gap'.[18]

Some of these apparent inconsistencies were picked up by a third generation of scholars, who essentially parted ways on the question of whether or not *behaviour* was to be defined inside or outside of the term. If behaviour was separated from culture, as Iain Alistair Johnston argued, one would be able to draw up a falsifiable theory of strategic culture, which could be pitted against other alternative explanations.[19] Yet Johnston's attack on previous strategic culture scholars resulted in a protracted discussion with Colin Gray, who argued that strategic behaviour must irrevocably be part of strategic culture, since culture represents the context for *all* things strategic.[20] In a more recent paper Gray also rather tellingly deems the failure to agree on a definition of strategic culture 'rather foolish since there is general agreement on the content of the subject and, roughly, on how it functions'. Including or excluding behaviour from the definition is, he goes on, 'a burning issue for theory builders but otherwise not really of any great significance'.[21] However, while one could be tempted to sympathize with Gray's conclusion, it seems worthwhile to try to pursue some level of scholarly agreement on the relationship between strategic culture and actorness. One way to conceptualize this relationship that would also incorporate the more contextual quality of the concept of culture is to look at it as a *constitutive* one. While traditional causal theorizing involves asking whether x causes y, and then measures correlation between the independent and dependent variable(s) and the corresponding causal effects, students of strategic culture are more interested in the conditions that constrain or make y possible. According to its main proponent, Alexander Wendt, constitutive theorizing involves asking 'how possible' and 'what' questions in order to reveal 'conceptually necessitating' conditions for a phenomenon to take place; for example, the existence of the rules and norms of diplomacy can be seen as constitutive for interstate bargaining.[22] Similarly, strategic culture can be seen as constitutive for strategic actorness. Yet for Wendt, rules, discourses and social structures are constitutive of objects, agents or actions.

Constitutive theorizing is, therefore, cautiously presented as explicitly non-causal, and as a scientifically valid alternative to causal explanations. However, others have argued that constitution is not just conceptual

> but also ontological, that is, conceptual relations that define meanings play themselves out in the (materially embodied) world outside of language. Constitutive theorising, then, is not just about inquiring into how they play themselves out in the social world, giving rise to certain practices and social relations.[23]

The key point is that constitutive theorizing is a valid part of scientific inquiry that arguably offers a useful understanding of the perceived epistemological relationship between strategic culture and actorness.

From this understanding, we can move on to pinpoint the social mechanisms through which strategic culture reveals itself. Strategic culture is, after all, a notoriously elusive concept, the appeal *and* curse of which rests in its inherent inclusiveness and all-encompassing nature. However, it can be argued that some elements of a strategic culture can be studied with more precision than others. Going beyond the Johnston/Gray debate, Kerry Longhurst, for example, offers a distinction between unobservable and observable components of strategic culture.[24] In the first category we find the 'foundational elements' of strategic culture, or the core values that give it 'its basal quality and characteristics'.[25] As unobservables, or *a priori* qualities, these are the factors that seem prone to the kind of caricatures of culture for which earlier strategic culture studies have been criticized. Ole Waever raises a similar concern with regard to analyses of Europe as a security community. He argues that the origins of peaceful Europe seem 'terribly over-determined', and that 'thus, a study of "security communities" should not focus on origins but try to grasp the clashing social forces that uphold and undermine "expectations of non-war"'.[26] These clashing social forces parallel, in turn, what Longhurst refers to as the 'actual *observable* manifestations of the strategic culture – the "self-regulating *policies* and *practices*" which give active meaning to the foundational elements by relating and promoting them to the external environment'.[27]

In a similar vein, Iver B. Neumann and Henrikki Heikka approach strategic culture as the product of the dynamic interplay between *discourse* and *practice*.[28] Drawing on sociological studies of culture, they argue that discourse is the vehicle through which strategic culture reveals itself, while practice is the socially recognized form of behaviour that stems from it and ultimately defines the strategic culture in question.[29] This discursive turn in strategic culture studies can, in turn, be related to a growing interest in the role of *strategic narratives*.[30] Lawrence Freedman contends, for example, that

> Culture, and the cognition which it influences, is rarely fixed but in a process of development and adaptation... It is in this context that the concept of narratives – compelling story lines which can explain convincingly and from which inferences can be drawn – becomes relevant. Narratives are designed or nurtured with the intention of structuring the responses of others to developing events. They are strategic because they do not arise spontaneously but are deliberately

constructed or reinforced out of ideas and thoughts that are already current... Narratives are about the ways that issues are framed and responses suggested.[31]

In a contemporary security environment, Freedman goes on, the role of strategic narratives has become even more salient, since the wars of ideas that take place in the media and the public domain are often as important as the ones on the ground. Security strategies, strategy papers, Defence White Papers and the like, as the most deliberate expressions of strategic narratives, represent not merely, or perhaps even primarily, strategic guidelines, but documents for public consumption, deliberate efforts to legitimize future actions and reconcile with or signal difference to the 'other' as part of shaping one's own strategic identity. In his book *Writing Security*, David Campbell, for example, shows how the United States has continuously and actively used narrative descriptions of 'the other' to consolidate an American 'self' that needs to be kept secure.[32]

Strategic narratives are, as such, not merely rhetorical, but represent 'speech acts' – that is sentences or locutions with a certain force.[33] Sometimes they even contain the power to change, insofar as by saying something, or performing a speech act, an option that was not there before is created. Repeating the statement can, in turn, reinforce an idea, build up a sense of common identity or cause, or even command certain actions by way of rhetorical entrapment. Strategic narratives represent, as such, a key mechanism through which strategic cultures reproduce, expand or limit the cultural boundaries for what a strategic actor can or is expected to do.

This does *not* imply that an actor is in a position to use narratives freely to change or create a certain strategic culture, which seems to be indicated by the ESS' call for one that specifically 'fosters early, rapid and when necessary, robust intervention'. Strategic narratives are essentially conservative, since they need to be constructed out of ideas that are recognizable to and considered legitimate by their recipients. Nevertheless, the European Union is – perhaps more than most states, upon which centuries of history and traditions weigh heavily – in a position to shape its strategic narrative. Or as Martin Ortega claims, since it was created in a benign environment, it could be constructive rather than responsive.[34] However, insofar as (strategic) narratives are 'compelling storylines' and not 'the truth', they may be challenged by competing narratives if or when the EU were to 'lose its aura of progressivism', as Mark Gilbert warns in his excellent analysis of how a commonly shared progressive conception of the European integration project has produced an over-simplified, unhistorical and somewhat teleological version of contemporary European history.[35] A strategic narrative, as any narrative, is ultimately reliant on its credibility and legitimacy as such.

With this in mind, we shall now move on to revisit the European Security Strategy as essentially a strategic narrative intended to 'sell' the burgeoning ESDP as an inherent and natural part of an evolving EU. Accordingly, attention is predominantly directed to the overall storyline that the document conveys and its implications for ESDP, rather than to the more historically dependent details of a document which is now more than seven years old.

The European Security Strategy in Context: Going beyond Constructive Ambiguity

Until 2003, ESDP had been successfully clouded by 'constructive ambiguity'.[36] The relatively loose shape and direction of the project, as reflected in the, to some, irreconcilable goals of European autonomy *and* the strengthening of the Atlantic Alliance, gave ample room for coordinative narratives at the national level that supported the fleeting ESDP but still agreed with the rather different aspirations of what Jolyon Howorth has labelled French Europeanism, British Atlanticism and German federalism respectively.[37] However, as the evolving crisis in Iraq made it obvious just how fragile the political unity on which ESDP rested was, it eventually became clear that 'constructive ambiguity was no longer an option'.[38] Therefore, although the need for a firmer policy platform on which to base ESDP had been obvious for some time, it was the Iraq crisis that triggered the process that led to the adoption of the document titled *A Secure Europe in a Better World: European Security Strategy* at the Brussels European Council on 12 December 2003.

The European Security Strategy thus served the specific purpose of mending relations between US Secretary of Defense Donald Rumsfeld's infamously branded 'old' and 'new' Europe, and the rift that had emerged between Europe and the United States. However, in hindsight it can be seen also, in the words of Alyson Bayles, as a 'conceptual and procedural turning point [and] an important stage in the developing self-awareness and ambition of the EU as a player in the global arena'.[39] In the end, the ESS was drafted and adopted in less than seven months, truly a remarkable feat in light of the cumbersome intergovernmental procedures that formally underpin ESDP. This was made possible by a combination of a favourable political climate at the time, a sense of urgency, and the fact that Solana and his team were there to pick up the task and carry it through efficiently without breaking the trust of the Member States.

As became clear in 2007, when President Sarkozy signalled a major revision of the ESS as part of his plans for the upcoming French Council Presidency (in the second half of 2008), this combination of factors was something that could not easily be reproduced.[40] Instead, the European Union Member States mandated a *review* of the implementation of the ESS in December 2007. This resulted in a round of high-level seminars, which gave a small group of senior academics and practitioners the opportunity to offer their views on the future parameters of the EU's security and defence policy. The method was, as such, not dissimilar to the one that produced the ESS in 2003, but this time the impact was more sobering. Rather than resulting in the bold new security strategy that President Sarkozy had signalled, the December 2008 European Council adopted a rather more modest *Report on the Implementation of the European Security Strategy*. Apart from adding some threats to the list, the document essentially reaffirmed the key elements of the 2003 ESS, making clear that it 'remains fully relevant' and that the report 'does not replace the ESS, but reinforces it'.[41] In any case, the document was almost immediately forgotten and never received a fraction of the comments and analysis that the 2003 ESS attracted. That the latter did receive so much attention is probably also the main reason why it has proved so enduring in the minds of both academics and practitioners.

Because of the special political circumstances in which it came about, the European Security Strategy was followed by a trail of analyses that compared it with the US National Security Strategy (NSS) issued by the Bush Administration the year before.[42] Whether the two documents – one issued by an ageing superpower and the other by a regional security institution with newfound military ambitions – are, in fact, comparable is certainly questionable: some would argue that this amounts to comparing apples and oranges. Nevertheless, Christoph Heusgen, then Director of the Policy Planning and Early Warning Unit, is reported to have said that the title and acronym of the ESS was chosen deliberately because comparisons with the US version were not only inevitable but also what the Member States intended.[43] Consequently, as Simon Duke points out, the existence of the NSS was exploited in the ESS, which used, in the words of Alyson Bayles, 'the concomitant language to signal subtle differences as well as togetherness'.[44] On the other hand, whereas the NSS served as 'a reference and justification for action policy choices', the ESS served as a reference and justification for having a common security and defence policy in the first place.[45] Also, whereas the publication of the NSS is a more or less frequent enterprise, allowing the reader to assess the evolution of a national strategy, the ESS was a first, though obviously not appearing in a strategic void. At the same time, it was 'too late' in the sense that the ESDP was already well under way. As such, the European Security Strategy had not only to define where the ESDP was going, but also its status as of 2003. That is, it had to reconstruct the rationale for ESDP, until then based on 'constructive ambiguity', a notion that simply did not hold water as the project was taking shape.

The European Security Strategy as Strategic Narrative: Creating a Purpose for ESDP

A strategy paper ought to define actual goals and set up priorities to achieve policy objectives, while describing which means can be used, and under what conditions, to fulfil those objectives.[46] However, it also serves as a premeditated justification or rationale for situations where ultimately external use of force can be used. It is a tool for building preparedness for and acceptance of these situations in the minds of constituents as well as the outside world. Accordingly, a strategy paper typically starts with a general description of the security environment, which in turn sets the pace and direction for the rest of the document; that is, a paper that starts from the assumption that one is at war will necessarily invoke a greater sense of urgency than one that places itself in a less threatening security environment. As part of this exercise, a strategy paper typically offers an interpretation of how the status quo has emerged and the role that the state or organization has played in getting there.

Whereas the American National Security Strategy took as its point of departure the end of the Cold War, 'a decisive victory for the forces of freedom', the European Security Strategy – somewhat surprisingly, given the centrality of this event for the creation of ESDP – virtually leapfrogs over the Cold War. Instead, it goes back to what Frank Schimmelfenning refers to as the 'founding myth' of European integration, the historical responsibility for creating lasting peace among democratic European states.[47] As such, the ESS essentially restored an idea that had played a minor role in the integration process during the Cold War, by placing it at the heart of the forces that had 'transformed relations between our states, and the lives of our citizens', with the result that Europe had never been 'so prosperous, secure or free'.[48] Having successfully escaped the legacy of two devastating world wars, the logic goes, Europe should now 'be ready to share in the responsibility for global security and in building a better world'.[49]

The reference to the founding myth can be seen as an attempt at pinning ESDP to the one uniting experience that the European states have in common, while offering an alternative to national strategic cultures. However, a question that has been frequently asked is whether it represents a strong enough rationale on which to build a shared and strong European strategic culture. Adrian Hyde-Price argues that the unprecedented effect that the experience of war has traditionally had on national strategic cultures is exactly why such a common European strategic culture is unlikely to emerge.[50] In a similar vein, Peter van Ham argues that the founding myth 'breaks a pattern since historically war and violence have played a major part in state-formation'.[51] Or, as he goes on to state: 'Without war "we" hardly know who "we" are'. Consequently, the absence of robust EU military operations may help us appreciate 'why the EU lacks confidence and status in the military arena'.[52] The National Security Strategy, again offering a striking contrast, described a state at war again, only ten years after declaring victory in the Cold War.[53] The war references are toned down in later versions of the NSS, but the typical NSS rhetoric nevertheless signifies a strikingly different strategic outlook to that of the ESS.[54] While the United States continues to see a world replete with dangers, the EU rather sees security challenges that need to be taken seriously in order to avoid a situation where Europe '*could* be confronted with a very radical threat indeed'.[55]

In fact, the European Security Strategy presented a rather different rationale for a security strategy. Insofar as an important function of such a document is to preserve or strengthen a strategic culture, the peaceful starting point for the ESS represented a less solid cultural building block, so to speak, when compared with the role that the experience of war has traditionally played in the shaping of national strategic cultures. In other words, the EU founding myth, regardless of the unprecedented role that it had played in the transformation of a Europe never 'so prosperous, secure or free', represented an inevitably weak platform on which to base the use of force, which is what a security strategy – or at least the more controversial parts of it – is mainly about. Nevertheless, the European option clearly has its appeal, as reflected, for example, in the re-education of the German public and Europe at large over the course of the 1990s, leading to the general acceptance and even encouragement of German armed forces being used for purposes other than territorial defence, even as it challenged supposedly deep-rooted national strategic cultures built on the experience of suffering two world wars.[56] However, the success and prominence granted to the European integration project in the shaping of the status quo inevitably leaves an obligation, whether moral or instrumental, upon the EU to continue the enlargement process, thus 'making a reality of the vision of a united and peaceful continent'.[57] This has made it progressively harder to identify an 'other' that may serve as a reference point for the European 'we', a concern that has been raised at every juncture in the integration process.

Despite the obvious tacit awareness of a set of common values that constitute a European epistemic community, the European Security Strategy also lacks references to core European values or beliefs (such as Christianity or liberal democracy), as well as the more moral tone that the American National Security Strategy tends to display. While the latter, underpinned by the unique position of the United States, describes a global responsibility for spreading moral principles revolving around the central ideas of freedom and liberalism, the ESS, in contrast, restricts the European Union's primary role to the maintenance of regional stability, while recognizing that the EU 'should be ready to share in the responsibility for global security'.[58] Only in its own neighbourhood does the ESS explicitly identify a responsibility for promoting certain values, since 'it is in the European interest that countries on our borders are well governed'.[59] The ESS also lacks the NSS' unambiguous will to use military force to protect core values when under threat.

In fact, it is notable how few pointers the European Security Strategy offers on the use of military force, at least when judging by the amount of comment that the EU's move into the military realm has attracted. The absence of military references in the document can, of course, be attributed to the continual lack of agreement amongst the Member States on this particular issue.[60] Yet the apparent preference given to non-military instruments in the ESS is also, as indicated above, rooted in distinctive features of an EU strategic culture, and represents thus at least partly a conscious or path-dependent European choice.

A Reluctant Military Actor: Acting *European* as an End in Itself

The only place where the use of military force is explicitly mentioned in the European Security Strategy is in connection with failed states in which 'military instruments may be needed to restore order'.[61] The use of the term 'restore' seems, in turn, to restrict military means to the post-conflict phase, and then only in concert with other reconstruction tools.[62] At the same time, the ESS does recognize a need for a stronger focus on military instruments, and even proactive military engagement, as reflected in the call for a strategic culture that fosters 'early and robust intervention' and the recognition of the need for 'the full spectrum of instruments' to be available for the European Union.[63] In fact, the somewhat ambiguous treatment of the issue of military force, and the apparent cautious downplaying of any references to such, seem to counteract previous and current steps toward a stronger military role for the EU. In light of other developments, therefore, the strategic narrative conveyed by the ESS seems somewhat out of touch with the way that ESDP has evolved in practice.

This perceived disparity is best explained with recourse to the peaceful rationale from which the European Security Strategy started out, which from the outset resonates badly with a strong military focus. On the one hand, most Member States do seem to appreciate that military power is necessary for increasing the EU's weight on the world stage, and that engaging in military operations is a rational way to boost its hard power. Yet, on the other hand, they are well aware of the fact that the move into the military realm in certain respects conflicts with the very image of the EU and the ideas, values and norms that uphold it.[64] In that sense, acting militarily, but well within the overarching conflict-preventive (read: more benign) parameters, has become an end in itself and a way to legitimize military force as an inherent and natural part of an EU strategic culture.

When read as a traditional security strategy, the European Security Strategy does not immediately or principally lend itself to the usual ends/means teleology.[65] In looking at how the military dimension has been incorporated into the EU, therefore, it is arguably better understood as the product of a logic of *appropriateness* rather than of a logic of *consequences*.[66] ESDP is, indeed, a pertinent example of how culture binds rationality. We could thus add a notion to the 30-year-old strategic culture dichotomy of *rational* man vs. *national* man, namely that of *supranational* man: that is, when acting within the auspices of ESDP, all actors are induced or compelled to do so in a way that falls within certain premeditated conceptions of how the EU as a collective should behave. In other words, the way in which to act has become a source of a European 'self'. The 'other', as the omnipresent contrast against which an identity needs to be shaped, is in this logic to be found in the United States.[67]

Despite the reconciliatory motive of the European Security Strategy, which predominantly came to the fore in a general convergence on the interpretation of threats (terrorism, proliferation of weapons of mass destruction [WMDs], and 'rogue' or 'failed' states),[68] a gap was evident in the particular approaches to countering or managing the threats. A central point of the subsequent debate was the real and perceived difference between the ESS' *preventive engagement* and the NSS' *pre-emptive action*. The latter, referred to as the Bush doctrine, signalled that the US would be willing not only to prevent but also forestall an adversary from attacking vital US interests by way of a pre-emptive military attack.[69] However, Solana, speaking on behalf of the EU, made it clear that preventive engagement stops at the 'mainstreaming of conflict prevention without implying any obligation to undertake pre-emptive military strikes either by the EU or by individual member states'.[70] The message was further underlined by the change of wording, reportedly due to German insistence, away from 'pre-emptive engagement' after the first version of the ESS was presented in Thessaloniki in June 2003. However, some of the more striking differences were gradually toned down after the initial shock of the 11 September attacks faded. The 2006 version of the NSS gave, for example, a more sobering account of the terrorist threat and the 'protracted struggle' (as opposed to 'war'; see above) against it.

Yet beyond the more obvious differences, the European Security Strategy was at its core a confirmation of a broad, multidimensional or *comprehensive* notion of security that had emerged over the years.[71] At the heart of this approach is the integration of all dimensions of foreign policy, from aid and trade to diplomacy and the military, and a preference for conflict prevention through dialogue, cooperation and partnership rather than armed intervention. However, the idea of a holistic approach was, as Sven Biscop points out, certainly not new.[72] Organizations such as the UN and the CSCE/OSCE had been promoting comprehensive security during the Cold

War, while the EC/EU mostly played the part of the follower, at least when it came to actively promoting the idea – although peace through cooperation had, of course, been the central rationale for the European integration project from the start. However, in the mid-1990s the EU also started to reform its structures for conflict prevention and crisis management, joining the 'comprehensive trend' that gained momentum in the first decade after the Cold War.[73] Eventually a comprehensive security logic received something of an omnipresence in EU documents, as reflected, for example, in the *Stability Pact for Central and Eastern Europe*, as well as in actual policies, such as the Stability and Association Process(es) in the Balkans and the Euro-Mediterranean Partnership programme (EMP).[74] The acknowledgement of the *need* for comprehensive approaches was, in turn, gradually translated into a potential *asset* for the EU – that is, something that Europeans are 'particularly well equipped' to do.[75]

This created a strong, almost teleological drive to highlight integrated civil–military concepts as a way to legitimize and take ESDP forward. This was also duly reflected in the ESS, which stated that 'none of the new threats is purely military; nor can be tackled by purely military means [but] each requires a mixture of instruments'.[76] Incidentally, the lack of preparedness of the US-led coalition in Iraq for dealing with the massive challenges that emerged in the wake of the war, and the dawning of the fact that a 'war' on terror could not be won militarily, placed the EU firmly in the driver's seat of the ongoing comprehensive trend. As Sven Biscop remarks:

> From being absent in the Iraq debate, the European Union thus became a trendsetter, or perhaps more accurately, helped to clear the obstacles for the already existing trend towards a holistic approach to continue after the low point of the Iraq crisis.[77]

Eventually, the European Union also warmly endorsed (or perhaps *hijacked* is a better word) the *Comprehensive Approach* – a term that in its abbreviated, conceptual form was initially associated with NATO civil–military operations – and started to refer to it as a success factor for its policies and operations.[78] In that sense, it has successfully been 'written into' the EU's strategic narrative and accepted as an inherent part of its strategic culture. This was possible because the idea of a comprehensive approach to security fitted well into the conventional narrative of the European integration process as a project for peace by underlining the military dimension's secondary nature. That is, the EU prefers to act using its traditional strengths as a non-military power – and has successfully done so in the past, 'making a reality of the vision of a united and peaceful continent' – but must also be able to use force to tackle emerging crises in its neighbourhood and beyond.[79] It has a stated non-aggressive purpose and has allowed the EU, at least until recently, to portray itself as a 'benign interventionist' perhaps not devoid of, but somewhere above the national interest.[80] Moreover, the idea of a comprehensive approach to security represents a source of a strategic 'self' for a peaceful Europe without clearly defined enemies. As such, a contrasting 'other' is typically found in the United States, but without having to resort to the kind of negative stereotype imaging of an adversary that has often dominated national strategic cultures in the past.

Finally, the comprehensive approach underlines that ESDP represents something different and that it does not duplicate NATO. This was a precondition for ESDP in the first place, as reflected perhaps most explicitly in US Secretary of State Madeleine Albright's famous three Ds – no diminution of NATO, no discrimination and no duplication – formulated in her speech to the 1998 NATO summit. That the term 'Comprehensive Approach', albeit as a concept and not an idea, originated in NATO was then perhaps somewhat ironic, but the way in which the EU has taken ownership of the term suggests that the EU may be inherently and intuitively better equipped to carry it through. As such, it also represented a potential comparative advantage for the EU, or a European *way of warfare* that has suddenly come into fashion with the need for post-conflict stabilization and reconstruction in places such as the Balkans, Central Africa, Iraq and Afghanistan.

Concluding Remarks

The purpose of this article was to show that the concept of strategic culture can be usefully applied to a non-state actor like the European Union. By drawing on recent developments in strategic culture theory, it has shown that the idea of strategic culture is not only compatible with the European Union, but may be a particularly useful conceptual tool for studying actors for which cultural factors can make up for the lack of more material ones, such as borders, language, political structure, national history, and so on. It seems that students of strategic culture have for too long been preoccupied with the national interest, as reflected in the repeated claims that an EU strategic culture is impossible due to the inherent differences between its 27 Member States. At the same time, *how* to act has become all the more important in the modern world – as reflected, for example, in the massive opposition against some of the excesses of the American war on terror in the wake of 11 September, at a time when moral support should never have been higher. Focusing on discourses or strategic narratives as an inherent part of a strategic culture thus opens up avenues for further research, including more fruitful comparisons between the United States and the European Union than the traditional strong/weak dichotomy.[81]

From this point of departure, this article has shown that, since the adoption of the ESS, a quite specific strategic culture has in fact evolved in the European Union, in which consensus on a comprehensive approach to security as a unique European asset, rather than on a broad set of shared security interests amongst its Member States, has become a focal point for the fledgling ESDP. This is important because it shows that the EU may be capable of strategic action even in the absence of clear agreement on a pre-identified set of collective security interests that could replace the national interest. That is, behaving like Europeans, or within the boundaries of a shared strategic culture, becomes an end in itself when acting as a collective under the ESDP label. In other words, an EU strategic culture does not replace national strategic cultures, but rather supplements them.

However, one problem seems to be that this does not provide for a particularly strong or robust strategic culture. Indeed, European Union assertiveness tends to crumble in the face of competing political agendas, as can be observed currently in the slump in EU operational activities following the enduring economic crisis that continues to preoccupy European state leaders. This has also left Germany firmly in the driver's seat. It is no secret that Berlin has been sceptical towards expanding the ESDP agenda in Africa, for example, which until recently has been a key area of operations for the EU. In the case of Libya it also made its objections obvious to the rest of the world by abstaining from the vote on UN Security Council Resolution 1473. At the moment, an EU strategic culture does not appear robust enough to trump these and other concerns. This could change following the prospective withdrawal of European troops from Afghanistan in 2015. The Libya campaign may point towards a renewed Franco-British push for Western intervention in this region. The question is whether the EU will be chosen as the vehicle through which to channel new operations.

If the slump in European Union operational activities continues, the danger is that the EU's own strategic narrative, as described in this article, will be challenged by competing, less appealing narratives as the institution fails to produce ways, means and results that fall within the inevitable constraints and expectations that come with the narrative.[82] Strategic culture is, after all, not a one-way street, but the product of the *dynamic interplay* between discourses or narratives, on the one hand, and practices on the other. A strategic narrative relates to and codifies ideas and values that exist 'out there' already as the cultural boundaries inside which a strategic actor operates. The narrative can be constructive, in the sense that these boundaries can be incrementally and cautiously shifted. Yet a complex multi-level actor such as the EU, in particular, has limited control over how the narrative plays out when confronted with other actors and real-world events. A strategic decision, Carl von Clausewitz reminds us, will always have both intended and unintended consequences that reflect back on an actor in ways over which it has very limited control. A decision to intervene in one situation at one point may create expectations or precedents for similar situations in the future. Likewise, a repeated focus on the EU's unique potential as a comprehensive security actor will create an expectation that it will also act decidedly comprehensively, and invite criticism if it fails to produce ways, means and results that reflect this.

So far, the European Union has not carried out any fully integrated civil–military operations. The operations in Africa in particular have for the most part been traditional low-intensity military peacekeeping. Most of them have also been pushed forward by France, relied on French military capabilities and been evaluated on their military accomplishments.[83] It seems that the EU is constantly drawn into a discourse where military robustness in itself is treated as the only or most important benchmark for successful intervention, while the EU often fails to 'sell' the point about the 'upsurge in civilian crisis management' as the *real* 'success of the ESDP'.[84] However, the European Union cannot continue to dodge the question whether its own perceived key assets are, in fact, reflected in the operations it carries out. The contributions to this special issue aim to shed light on this.

NOTES

1. Paul Cornish and Geoffrey Edwards, 'Beyond the EU/NATO Dichotomy: The Beginnings of a European Strategic Culture', *International Affairs*, Vol. 77, No. 3 (2001), pp. 587–603; Paul Cornish and Geoffrey Edwards, 'The Strategic Culture of the European Union: A Progress Report', *International Affairs*, Vol. 81, No. 4 (2005), pp. 801–820, Stine Heiselberg, 'Pacifism or Activism: Towards a Common Strategic Culture within the European Security and Defence Policy?', IIS Working Paper 4, Danish Institute for International Studies, 2003; Adrian Hyde Price, 'European Security, Strategic Culture and the Use of Force', *European Security*, Vol. 13, No. 4 (2004), pp. 323–343, Per Martin Martinsen, 'Forging a Strategic Culture - Putting Policy into the ESDP', *Oxford Journal on Good Governance*, Vol. 1, No. 1 (2004), pp. 61–66; Janne Haaland Matlary, 'When Soft Power Turns Hard: Is an EU Strategic Culture Possible?,' *Security Dialogue*, Vol. 37, No. 1 (2006), pp. 105–121; Christoph O. Meyer, *The Quest for a European Strategic Culture: A Comparative Study of Strategic Norms and Ideas in the European Union* (Basingstoke: Palgrave Macmillan, 2006); Per Martin Norheim-Martinsen, 'European Strategic Culture Revisited: The Ends and Means of a Militarised European Union', *Defence and Security Studies*, Vol. 1, No. 3 (2007); Sten Rynning, 'The European Union: Towards a Strategic Culture?', *Security Dialogue*, Vol. 34, No. 4 (2003), pp. 479–496; Kerry Longhurst and Marcin Zaborowski, 'The Future of European Security', *European Security*, Vol. 13, No. 4 (2004), pp. 381–391; Jolyon Howorth, *Security and Defence Policy in the European Union* (Basingstoke: Palgrave, 2007); Asle Toje, *The EU, NATO and Strategic Culture: Renegotiating the Transatlantic Bargain* (London: Routledge, 2008).
2. Colin Gray, *Out of the Wilderness: Prime Time for Strategic Culture* (Fort Belvoir, VA: Defence Threat Reduction Agency, 2006).
3. Hyde Price, 'European Security, Strategic Culture and the Use of Force' (note 1)' Matlary, 'When Soft Power Turns Hard: Is an EU Strategic Culture Possible?' (note 1), Rynning, 'The European Union: Towards a Strategic Culture?' (note 1).
4. Cornish and Edwards, 'Beyond the EU/NATO Dichotomy: The Beginnings of a European Strategic Culture' (note 1); Cornish and Edwards, 'The Strategic Culture of the European Union: A Progress Report' (note 1); Howorth, *Security and Defence Policy in the European Union* (note 1).
5. This view is in line with the broad understanding of (strategic) culture as the context in which all (strategic) acts necessarily take place. See for example Colin Gray, 'Strategic Culture as Context: The First Generation of Theory Strikes Back', *Review of International Studies* 25 (1999), pp. 49–69, David Haglund, 'What Good Is Strategic Culture? A Modest Defence of an Immodest Concept', *International Journal*, Vol. 59, no. 3 (2004), pp. 479–502. I return to this discussion below.
6. European Council, 'A Secure Europe in a Better World: European Security Strategy' (Brussels: endorsed by the European Council, 11–12 December, 2003). Hereafter referred to as ESS.
7. ESS (note 6), p. 11.
8. Sven Biscop, 'The ABC of European Security Strategy: Ambition, Benchmark, Culture', Egmont Royal Institute of International Relations: Egmont Paper 16, 2007; Anne Deighton and Victor Mauer (eds), *Securing Europe? Implementing the European Security Strategy*, Zurich: ETH Centre for Security Studies, 2006, Sven Biscop and Jan Joel Andersson (eds), *The EU and the European Security Strategy: Forging a Global Europe* (London: Routledge, 2008), European Council, 'Report on the Implementation of the European Security Strategy - Providing Security in a Changing World', Brussels: Adopted by the European Council, 11 December 2008.
9. US Government, 'The National Security Strategy of the United States of America', Washington DC: The White House, 2002.
10. Jack L. Snyder, 'The Soviet Strategic Culture: Implications for Limited Nuclear Operations', Santa Monica, CA: RAND Corporation, R-2154-AF, 1977.
11. Ken Booth, *Strategy and Ethnocentrism* (New York: Holmes and Meier, 1979); Colin Gray, 'National Styles in Strategy: The American Example', *International Security*, Vol. 6, No. 2 (1981), pp. 21–47; Carnes Lord, 'American Strategic Culture', *Comparative Strategy*, Vol. 5, No. 3 (1985), pp. 269–293; Richard Pipes, 'Why the Soviet Union Thinks It Could Fight and Win a Nuclear War', *Commentary* 1 (1977), pp. 21–34.
12. Jack L. Snyder, 'The Concept of Strategic Culture: Caveat Emptor', in Carl G. Jacobsen (ed.), *Strategic Power USA/USSR*, (London: Macmillan, 1990), p. 3.
13. For the most notorious account of differing perceptions of security and power on either side of the Atlantic, see Robert Kagan, *Of Paradise and Power: America and Europe in the New World Order* (New York: Knopf, 2003); Robert Kagan, 'Power and Weakness – Why the United States and Europe See the World Differently', *Policy Review*, 113 (June and July 2002). pp. 3–28.

14. David Campbell, *Writing Security: United States Foreign Policy and the Politics of Identity* (Minneapolis: University of Minnesota Press, 1992); Bradley S. Klein, 'Hegemony and Strategic Culture: American Power Projection and Alliance Defence Politics', *Review of International Studies*, Vol. 14, No. 2 (1988); Bradley S. Klein, 'The Textual Strategies of the Military: Or, Have You Read Any Good Defence Manuals Lately?', in James Der Derian and J. Shapiro (eds), *International/Intertextual Relations: Postmodern Readings of World Politics* (Lexington, MA.: Lexington Books, 1989).
15. Rynning, 'The European Union: Towards a Strategic Culture?' (note 1).
16. Simon Duke, 'CESDP and the EU Response to 11 September: Identifying the Weakest Link', *European Foreign Affairs Review*, Vol. 7, No. 2 (2002); Julian Lindley-French, 'Terms of Engagement. The Paradox of American Power and the Transatlantic Dilemma Post-11 September', Paris: EU Institute for Security Studies, Chaillot Paper No. 52, 2002.
17. Gilles Andréani, Christoph Bertram, and Charles Grant, *Europe's Military Revolution* (London: Centre for European Reform, 2001); Charles Cogan, *The Third Option: The Emancipation of European Defense, 1989-2000* (Westport, CT: Praeger, 2001); Jolyon Howorth, 'The CESDP and the Forging of a European Security Culture?', *Politique Européenne*, Vol. 8 (2002), pp. 88–109.
18. Christopher Hill, 'The Capability-Expectations Gap, or Conceptualising Europe's International Role' *Journal of Common Market Studies*, Vol. 31 (1993), pp. 305—328.
19. According to Johnston, behaviour (dependent variable) may causally follow from strategic culture (independent variable), defined as 'a limited ranked set of strategic preference'. In that case, the validity of strategic culture as an explanatory variable is verified, whereas in cases of non-compliance between strategic culture and behaviour, the theory must be discarded. Alastair Iain Johnston, 'Thinking About Strategic Culture', *International Security*, Vol. 19, No. 4 (1995), p. 48. See also Elizabeth Kier, *Imagining War: French and British Military Doctrine between the Wars* (Princeton, NJ: Princeton University Press, 1997); Jeffrey Legro, *Cooperation under Fire: Anglo-German Restraint During World War II* (Ithaca, NY: Cornell University Press, 1995).
20. Gray, 'Strategic Culture as Context: The First Generation of Theory Strikes Back' (note 5). See also Johnston and Gray's subsequent replies and replies to replies. Johnston's definition of culture has been generally discredited, since it represents a sharp departure from definitions in sociological and anthropological literature. For a detailed discussion, see Iver B. Neumann and Henrikki Heikka, 'Grand Strategy, Strategic Culture, Practice. The Social Roots of Nordic Defence', *Cooperation and Conflict*, Vol. 40, No. 1 (2005). pp. 5–23.
21. Gray, *Out of the Wilderness: Prime Time for Strategic Culture* (note 2), p. ii.
22. Alexander Wendt, *Social Theory of International Politics* (Cambridge: Cambridge University Press, 1999), Alexander Wendt, 'On Constitution and Causation in International Relations', *Review of International Relations*, Vol. 24, Special Issue (1998). See also John Gerard Ruggie, 'The False Premise of Realism', *International Security*, Vol. 20, No. 1 (1995).
23. Milja Kurki, *Causation in International Relations: Reclaiming Causal Analysis* (Cambridge: Cambridge University Press, 2008), p. 181. See also Colin Wight, *Agents, Structures and International Relations: Politics as Ontology* (Cambridge: Cambridge University Press, 2006).
24. Kerry Longhurst, 'Strategic Culture', in Gerhard Kümmel and Andreas D. Prüfert (eds), *Military Sociology: The Richness of a Discipline* (Baden Baden: Nomos, 2000).
25. *Ibid.*, p. 305.
26. Ole Waever, 'Insecurity, Security and Asecurity in the West European Non-War Community, in Emanuel Adler and Michael Barnett (eds), *Security Communities* (Cambridge: Cambridge University Press, 1998), pp. 71, 75.
27. Longhurst, 'Strategic Culture' (note 24), p.305, my emphasis.
28. Neumann and Heikka, 'Grand Strategy, Strategic Culture, Practice' (note 20).
29. Cf. Ann Swidler, 'What Anchors Cultural Practices', in Theodore M. Schatzki, Karin Knorr Cetina, and Eike von Savigny (eds), *The Practice Turn in Contemporary Theory* (London: Routledge, 2001). pp. 74–92.
30. John Arquilla and David Ronfeldt, *Networks and Netwars: The Future of Terror, Crime and Militancy* (Santa Monica, CA: RAND Corporation, 2001); Lawrence Freedman, 'The Transformation of Strategic Affairs', Adelphi Paper 379 (London: IISS, 2006); Mary Kaldor, Mary Martin, and Sabine Selchow, 'Human Security: A New Strategic Narrative for Europe', *International Affairs*, Vol. 83, No. 2 (2007), pp. 273–288.
31. Freedman, *The Transformation of Strategic Affairs* (note 30), pp. 22–23.
32. Campbell, *Writing Security: United States Foreign Policy and the Politics of Identity* (note 14).

33. Cf. John L. Austin, *How to do Things with Words: The William James Lectures Delivered at Harvard University in 1955* (Oxford: Clarendon, 1955); Barry Buzan, Jaap de Wilde, and Ole Waever, *Security: A New Framework for Analysis* (Boulder, CO: Lynne Rienner, 1998); Ole Waever, 'Securitization and Desecuritization', in R.D. Lipschutz (ed.), *On Security* (New York: Columbia University Press, 1995), pp. 46–86.
34. Martin Ortega, 'Building the Future: The EU's Contribution to Global Governance', *Chaillot Paper No. 100* (Paris: EU Institute for Security Studies, 2007), p. 93.
35. Mark Gilbert, 'Narrating the Process: Questioning the Progressive Story of European Integration', *Journal of Common Market Studies*, Vol. 46, No. 3 (2008), pp. 641–662.
36. Francois Heisbourg, 'Europe's Strategic Ambitions: The Limits of Ambiguity', *Survival*, Vol. 42, No. 2 (2000).
37. Jolyon Howorth, 'Discourse, Ideas, and Epistemic Communities in European Security and Defence Policy', *West European Politics*, Vol. 27, No. 2 (2004), pp. 211–243. Some would, however, question whether Germany is still pursuing the 'federalism' line.
38. *Ibid.*, p. 228.
39. Alyson J.K. Bailes, 'The European Security Strategy. An Evolutionary History', Policy Paper No.10, SIPRI, Stockholm, 2005, p. 1.
40. 'Sarkozy in Drive to Give EU a Global Goal', *Financial Times*, 27 July 2007.
41. European Council, 'Report on the Implementation of the European Security Strategy – Providing Security in a Changing World' (note 8), p. 3.
42. US Government, 'The National Security Strategy of the United States of America' (note 9); Alyson J.K. Bailes, 'EU and US Strategic Concepts: A Mirror for Partnership and Difference?', *The International Spectator*, Vol. XXXIX, No. 3 (2004), pp. 19–33; Bailes, 'The European Security Strategy. An Evolutionary History' (note 39); Simon Duke, 'The European Security Strategy in a Comparative Framework: Does It Make for Secure Alliances in a Better World?', *European Foreign Affairs Review*, Vol. 9 (2004), pp. 459–481; Felix Berenskoetter, 'Mapping the Mind Gap: A Comparison of US and EU Security Strategies', *Security Dialogue*, Vol. 36, No. 1 (2005); Asle Toje, 'The 2003 European Union Security Strategy: A Critical Appraisal', *European Foreign Affairs Review*, Vol. 10 (2005), pp. 117–133; Sven Biscop, 'The European Security Strategy. Implementing a Distinctive Approach to Security', Brussels: Royal Defence College (IRSD-KHID), Paper No.82 (March), 2004.
43. Quoted in Toje, 'The 2003 European Union Security Strategy: A Critical Appraisal' (note 42), p. 120.
44. Duke, 'The European Security Strategy in a Comparative Framework: Does It Make for Secure Alliances in a Better World?' (note 42); p. 461; Bailes, 'The European Security Strategy. An Evolutionary History' (note 39), p. 32.
45. Haine and Lindström, quoted in Duke, 'The European Security Strategy in a Comparative Framework: Does It Make for Secure Alliances in a Better World?', (note 42), p. 460.
46. Toje, 'The 2003 European Union Security Strategy: A Critical Appraisal', (note 42), p. 121.
47. Frank Schimmelfennig, *The EU, NATO and the Integration of Europe: Rules and Rhetoric* (Cambridge: Polity Press, 2003), pp. 265–278. However, see Gilbert, 'Narrating the Process: Questioning the Progressive Story of European Integration' (note 35).
48. ESS, (note 6) p. 1. The exception was the accession of Greece, Spain and Portugal, which was a testing ground for the EU's ability to promote stability and democracy in the region. The success of this venture later became an important reference point for Eastern enlargement. See Kristi Raik, 'The EU as a Regional Power: Extended Governance and Historical Responsibility', in Hartmut Mayer and Henri Vogt (eds), *A Responsible Europe? Ethical Foundations of EU External Affairs* (London: Palgrave Macmillan, 2006), p. 78.
49. ESS (note 6), p. 1.
50. Hyde Price, 'European Security, Strategic Culture and the Use of Force' (note 1).
51. Peter van Ham, 'Europe's Strategic Culture and the Relevance of War', *Oxford Journal of Good Governance*, Vol. 2, No. 1 (2005), pp. 39–43; Peter van Ham, Europe's Postmodern Identity: A Critical Appraisal', *International Politics*, Vol. 38, No. 1 (2001), pp. 229–252.
52. Van Ham, 'Europe's Strategic Culture and the Relevance of War' (note 51), p. 40.
53. The fact that neither the Cold War nor the war on terror were wars in the conventional meaning of the term makes references to them as such appear all the more conspicuous in the sense that they create a feeling of urgency and lack of safety, as well as commanding a certain way of dealing with the problem.
54. The 'war against terror' was rebaptized 'the long war' in the 2006 NSS, which signified a somewhat reluctant acceptance of the fact that it was going to be protracted *struggle* rather than a war, with all the costs (the Iraq war was and remains the most expensive ever fought by the United States) and suffering it is bound to incur.
55. ESS (note 6), p. 5, emphasis added.

56. Howorth, 'Discourse, Ideas, and Epistemic Communities in European Security and Defence Policy' (note 31).
57. ESS, p. 1.
58. ESS, p. 1, and NSS, p. 3. Commentators differ on what to make of the frequent use of the term 'global' in the ESS. Bayles sees a 'truly global approach' as a feature it shares with the NSS: Bailes, 'The European Security Strategy. An Evolutionary History' (note 39), p. 15. Duke and Berenskoetter, in turn, recognize the ESS' global outlook, but conclude that it is, nonetheless, primarily concerned with regional security. Duke, 'The European Security Strategy in a Comparative Framework: Does It Make for Secure Alliances in a Better World?' (note 42), Berenskoetter, 'Mapping the Mind Gap: A Comparison of US and EU Security Strategies' (note 42).
59. See ESS, p. 7, and Berenskoetter, 'Mapping the Mind Gap: A Comparison of US and EU Security Strategies' (note 42).
60. See for example Toje, 'The 2003 European Union Security Strategy: A Critical Appraisal', (note 42), p. 121.
61. ESS, p. 7.
62. Berenskoetter, 'Mapping the Mind Gap: A Comparison of US and EU Security Strategies' (note 42).
63. ESS, p. 11.
64. See the debate on the EU as a civilian or normative power. Francoise Dûchene, 'Europe in World Peace', in R. Maine (ed.), *Europe Tomorrow* (London: Fontana/Collins, 1972); Karen Smith, 'The End of Civilian Power EU: A Welcome Demise or a Cause for Concern?' *International Spectator*, Vol. XXXV, No. 2 (2000); Stelios Stavridis, 'Militarising the EU: The Concept of Civilian Power Revisited', *International Spectator*, Vol. XXXVI, No. 4 (2001); Mario Telo, *Europe: A Civilian Power? European Union, Global Governance, World Order* (Basingstoke: Palgrave, 2006); Ian Manners, 'Normative Power Europe: A Contradiction in Terms?', *Journal of Common Market Studies*, Vol. 40, No. 2 (2002), pp. 235–258; 'Normative Power Europe Reconsidered: Beyond the Crossroads', *Journal of European Public Policy*, Vol. 13, No. 2 (2006), pp. 182–199.
65. According to Asle Toje, the EU acts in accordance with what Max Weber refers to as *Wertrationalität* (or value rationality) rather than traditional *Zweckrationalität* (ends/means rationality). Toje, 'The 2003 European Union Security Strategy: A Critical Appraisal' (note 42).
66. See for example James March and Johan P. Olsen, *Rediscovering Institutions: The Organizational Basis of Politics* (New York: Free Press, 1989).
67. Cf. Campbell, *Writing Security: United States Foreign Policy and the Politics of Identity* (note 14); van Ham, 'Europe's Strategic Culture and the Relevance of War' (note 51); van Ham, 'Europe's Postmodern Identity: A Critical Appraisal' (note 51).
68. The ESS adds organized crime and regional conflicts to the list. Note also the difference between 'rogue' and 'failed' states. While a failed state is in the ESS seen as a catalyst for other threats to emerge, a rogue state is in the NSS seen as a threat in itself, either by its own direct actions, its sponsorship of terrorists, or failure to prevent these from hurting US interests. Each term anchors fundamentally different opinions about when forceful intervention is considered legitimate.
69. NSS, p. 19.
70. Preventive engagement is described in ESS, pp. 9–11. Solana quoted in Toje, 'The 2003 European Union Security Strategy: A Critical Appraisal' (note 42), p. 128.
71. Barcelona Report, 'A Human Security Doctrine for Europe', Report of the Study Group on Europe's Security Capabilities, Barcelona, 15 September 2004, Biscop, 'The European Security Strategy. Implementing a Distinctive Approach to Security' (note 42); Biscop, 'The ABC of European Security Strategy: Ambition, Benchmark, Culture' (note 8).
72. Sven Biscop, 'The European Security Strategy in Context: A Comprehensive Trend', in Sven Biscop and Jan Joel Andersson (eds), *The EU and the European Security Strategy: Forging a Global Europe* (London: Routledge, 2008), p. 13.
73. *Ibid*; Ulrich Schneckener, 'Theory and Practice of European Crisis Management: Test Case Macedonia', *European Yearbook of Minority Issues*, 1 (2002).
74. European Council, 'The Stability Pact for Central and Eastern Europe', Paris, adopted by the European Council, 20–21 March 1995.
75. ESS, p. 7.
76. *Ibid*.
77. Biscop, 'The European Security Strategy in Context: A Comprehensive Trend' (note 72), p. 16.
78. NATO, 'The Alliance's Strategic Vision: The Military Challenge' ACO/ACT, Mons/Norfolk, 2004.
79. ESS, p. 1.
80. See for example Richard Gowan, 'Good Intentions, Bad Outcomes', *E!Sharp*, 1 (2009).

81. See Kagan, *Of Paradise and Power* (note 13).
82. Cf. Gilbert, 'Narrating the Process: Questioning the Progressive Story of European Integration' (note 35).
83. For an in-depth analysis of these operations, see Per M. Norheim-Martinsen, 'Our Work Here is Done: European Union Peacekeeping in Africa', *African Security Review*, Vol. 20, No. 2 (2011), pp. 17–28.
84. Xymena Kurowska, 'The Role of ESDP Operations', in Michael Merlingen and Rasa Ostrauskaite (eds), *European Security and Defence Policy. An Implementation Perspective*, 25-42 (London: Routledge, 2009), 34.

Strategic Culture and the Common Security and Defence Policy – A Classical Realist Assessment and Critique

STEN RYNNING

The European Union once appeared destined to become the 'dishwasher' of security operations, as the United States seemed strong and capable enough to do the cooking by itself.[1] Dishwashing was not a European ambition but Europe's disorganization, along with what seemed to be a valid distinction between war and stabilization missions, pointed in this direction. Change may now be coming, nourished by the EU's crafting of the Common Security and Defence Policy (CSDP – up until 2010 known as the ESDP) and the widespread realization that war and stabilization, diplomacy and development, and in fact the whole gamut of policy tools must be applied simultaneously in the management of 21st century conflicts. The EU, favoured by its broad toolbox and likewise broad foreign policy approach, might be destined to become head chef, determining in one go who should do the cooking and who should do the dishes.

Alas, this scenario is both unlikely and undesirable, as we shall see. The turn to greater complexity may feed European Union hopes but it does not resolve the underlying political problems of EU ambition in general and the CSDP in particular. The trouble is not so much the bargaining, dispute, and organizational complexity that comes with being a club of 27 countries mixed in with supranational institutions, though these obstacles to policy relevance are important.[2] The trouble lies in the political foundations of the EU project itself.

Nation-states and nationalism continue to dominate European politics even as the European Union – to an extent – seeks to move beyond them. Conditions for political leadership, which is the central concern of classical realism, are therefore difficult. Statesmen are not free agents who dispose of brute power and other instruments of policy; they grow out of and are tied into national histories and cultures. In his study of military leadership and command, John Keegan writes that '[w]hat is interesting about heroic leaders ... is not to show that they possessed unusual qualities, since that may be taken for granted, but to ask how the societies to which they belonged expected such qualities to be presented'.[3] It is this interconnection between political leadership on the one hand and national expectations and legacies on the other that tells us why the CSDP should be considered a fragile tool resting on a delicate balance of political power within Europe. We engage the basic argument of classical realism in the first section of the article.

The second section deals with the EU from a power political perspective. When looked at from the outside – as many contemporary (realist) observers of power politics do, which we shall see shortly – the EU appears to be a grab for power in one form or another because power is what it takes to shape global events. It is hardly the case. While the EU admittedly is an attempt to create a kind of European capacity that can shield the EU heartland from global turbulence and also become a platform for global engagement, it is a very limited actor undertaking minor operations and has trouble doing even that. The contrast between power politics and the EU CSDP record is stark, in other words, and we need a more refined framework of thought than mere power politics to understand why this is so.

An alternative framework could be sociological and elitist, zooming in on Brussels to locate the type of political outlook and strategic culture that European Union governments and institutions can concoct. The argument is that as European policy elites meet again and again, and as they socialize their way of thinking, the end result is a kind of strategic culture unique to the EU that may tell us what the CSDP is really about. We engage this perspective in the third section of the article, where we shall see that the case for it builds on two weaknesses. Culture is not leadership, first of all, and deriving operational capacity from a single outlook will be a challenge because of the EU's complex Brussels set-up. Moreover, and more fundamentally, a Brussels culture does not mobilize European populations who predominantly identify with their nation-states, however challenged these nation-states may be. This disconnect between Brussels and the European populace sets strict limits on how many resources in the shape of manpower, money, machines and popular support can be channeled into CSDP undertakings, even if policymakers find certain missions highly desirable.

Classical realism is thus a criticism of two perspectives on European Union strategic culture – as resulting from power calculations and Brussels socialization, respectively. These perspectives get the CSDP foundations wrong. Strategic power and culture in Europe are predominantly national, and while there is an EU CSDP denominator it is weak. If policymakers believe the CSDP is powerful or can somehow be manipulated according to a Brussels-based world view, they will overreach and wreak havoc. Classical realism therefore favors a prudent CSDP policy or a strategic culture of restraint, which can be achieved by embedding the CSDP in a wider Atlantic framework of security cooperation.

A Critique of Buoyant Progress: Classical Realism

Classical realism, as the name indicates, is old, and some contemporary observers may question the utility of reviving it. Not many contemporaries use it, they might argue, and in the lexicon of realism we have plenty of alternatives to the classical brand – variants such as structural, defensive, offensive, fine-grained and even neoclassical realism. However, the fact of the matter is that classical realism has been sidetracked, not because it does not generate insight, which it does, but because it does not fit into the canon of scientific inquiry that has come to dominate academia for the past forty years.

Classical realism's emphasis on politics and political ambition sets it against theories biased in favour of rationality. One such theory is modern or structural realism. However, it is liberalism to which classical realism historically has been opposed on the grounds that its ideas of rationalized progress empty politics of substance. To classical realists, liberalists committed the sin of grossly simplifying human nature and advancing the false belief that good societies could be engineered by liberal wit.[4] Politics – a source of war and tragedy – was to be controlled from the outside: the main tool to be used was human reasoning, and the main constraints on politics were law, trade, and societal representation (that is, parliaments). Liberal theory lacked a positive view of politics: the political domain was viewed either negatively, as something to be reined in, or instrumentally, as a tool for progress defined not politically but in varying aesthetic, moral, religious and economic terms.[5] Progressive theory, with the faculty of human reasoning as its driver, could overcome princely power politics and ensure human improvement. Today, the CDSP might easily be seen as a case for needing rationalized cooperation where declining national defence budgets demand new collective initiatives for the pooling and sharing of defence resources.[6] The political desirability hereof is taken for granted: if it is rational to pool defence forces, then it is also desirable.

All of this neglects politics as a driver of history and a cause of enduring power confrontations, and from this neglect arose classical realism. It happened as scholars and observers looked to the dark side of the liberal tidal wave that the Enlightenment had stirred and saw human misery and a desire for revolt.[7] Some of the critical observers of liberalism thus had a Marxist leaning, such as Karl Polyani and E.H. Carr; the latter became one of classical realism's founding fathers.[8] Stability and even progress do not emerge from the invisible hand of markets but preponderant power or empire, Carr wrote as the Second World War came to a close, thereby arguing that we must understand politics not just as a handmaiden but as a project in and of itself.[9] The most virulent critic of liberalism's apolitical approach was perhaps Carl Schmitt, who in 1926 sought to define 'the political' and anchor it in the state.[10] Schmitt's view was extreme, reducing the political to friend-enemy distinctions. Classical realism sympathized with liberalism where Schmitt did not, but classical realism did share with Schmitt a concern with the political as an independent and critically important domain.

This led classical realism to a dualist and hermeneutical view of the world. Dualism regarded the essence of reality: there were historical legacies and dreams and visions for particular groups – the stuff of politics – on the one hand, and brute power on the other. Ideas *and* power thus define reality, classical realists would argue. This is their ontology. Today's social scientists prefer simple views of reality (ontology) because they enable theory, but classical realists discarded theory because it was not possible and thus useless.[11] In epistemological terms they were therefore hermeneutics. To do political analysis one does not need the methodological sophistry that comes with big theory exercises, but should instead read history and current affairs and conceptualize their meaning.[12] What did power and purpose mean in Europe in the late 1930s, classical realists asked then – just as today they would ask what CSDP power and CSDP purpose mean.

They would be struck by some similarities. In the CSDP we encounter a desire to build instruments of progress similar to that which grew out of the Enlightenment and which motivated liberals in the early 20th century. There is no need to stereotype the EU as 'idealist' or 'naive' because it generally is not – at least not in the strong sense that these labels have come to indicate. However, the EU's strong attachment to liberal goals and proclamations is indicative of a desire to control or tie down the beast of politics, just as was the case some hundred years ago: free trade, democratic institutions, and international organizations are tools to calm political tempers. This is becoming the EU's strategic culture, but it should be brought into dialogue with classical realist insights into the nature of anarchy, the drivers of policy, and the possibility for international cooperation.

First of all, anarchy happens because units diverge, not the other way around. Put differently, the international system does not drive states to diverge; states diverge first, and the international system reflects this underlying condition of diversity. In 1966 Stanley Hoffmann, who is still a major thinker in the area, wrote a classical realist assessment of why the European political project was bound to be tied down by sovereign nations rather than lifted up by federal and communitarian movements. 'Domestic differences and diverging world-views' will reproduce diversity, Hoffmann stated.[13] This conclusion was also reached by Robert Gilpin, who, in his study *War and Change in World Politics*, took note of the enduring inability of 'the human race' or 'mankind' to solve problems associated with international political change and power transitions in particular. Nuclear weapons, open economies and global society favour problem-solving, Gilpin observed, but humans act within political contexts that diverge and thus inhibit problem-solving and nourish tensions, and this must be the fundamental starting point for international analysis.[14]

Second, conditions for European statesmanship are fragile. Henry Kissinger once noted that statesmanship grows out of 'the study of history and philosophy', and Europe's history is diverse, as we have seen.[15] Diversity was managed through the Cold War by the United States, but today the Atlantic relationship is changing and Europe and the United States are drifting apart. This is change wrought by history, and Atlantic statesmanship must grapple with two conditions: first that the United States remains a nation-state with a vast range of interests which national leaders can invoke to ask for the American people's sacrifice;[16] second that Europe in contrast is moving beyond the nation-state, but only partially so. Its common institutions are too weak for strategic policy, and European nations 'have lost their historic convictions about a national foreign policy'.[17] The transatlantic alliance may not be doomed, Kissinger concludes, but the United States needs to think carefully about what it can and cannot ask of its European allies.[18]

Third, appeals to broad international cooperation are not a solution. Such cooperation is part of the orthodoxy and indeed strategic culture of the EU, and promises to confer legitimacy on the EU and embed it within a wider global network of actors who are equally willing to confront the obstacles of cooperation and progress. However, politics is not about solving generic and abstract problems but particular problems with real and concrete stakes, classical realism cautions, and problem solving will work only when nations and other actors are in quite strong alignment on these stakes. Statesmen have leeway to be ethical in foreign affairs, Reinhold Niebuhr noted, but only, and critically, when they deal with like-minded nations.[19]

In sum, classical realism offers a critical reading of the CSDP's potential. The CSDP is an institutionalization of weakness that grows out of the eroding strength of European nation-states and Europe's pluralist heritage. Strength may be gained from international partners but they, or the goals of partnerships, should be selected with care, because underlying political conceptions must align for cooperation to work. This reading runs counter to the CSDP as a power project or as the social mechanism through which policy elites can control policy, two perspectives to which we now turn.

The CSDP as Limited Power

Contemporary realists agree on one thing – the birth of a European Union security and defence policy is an instance of power politics – but then take three divergent views of it: the CSDP as a balance of American power; the CSDP as a tool to engage the United States in Europe's regional security order; and the CSDP as a balance of German power in which the United States should play a limited role. The positions are clearly defined and eloquently argued but generally off the mark, as we shall see.

Defensive realists' claim that the world is not terribly dangerous is based on an 'offence-defence balance' composed of military technology, geography, and strategic beliefs, and the balance mostly favours defensive strategies.[20] The preponderance of American power may add to the defensive comfort but it may actually also worry Europeans who fear uncontrolled power and what it can do to their neighborhood. They therefore check the American power, the hegemon, which is power politics. They are mostly subtle about it because the CSDP is still weak and they want to avoid Atlantic acrimony, but the trend is clear, according to Barry Posen:[21]

> I argue that the EU is preparing itself to manage autonomously security problems on Europe's periphery and to have a voice in the settlement of more distant security issues, should they prove of interest. It is doing so because Europeans do not trust the United States to always be there to address these problems and because many Europeans do not like the way the United States addresses these problems. They want another option, and they realize that military power is necessary to have such an option.

Some defensive realists sympathize with Posen's argument but prefer to soft pedal the balance-of-power argument because European states are too weak at present to really 'balance'. They instead use institutional and diplomatic means to break US policy – 'soft balancing.'[22] A degree of ambiguity sets in here. Soft balancing can be seen as either a precursor of real balancing, which is the Posen option, or as a means to redress grievances outside a power balancing framework and thus inside the confinements of US unipolarity.

Some defensive realists enlarge the latter point and discard the balancing option. They perceive durable unipolarity and rely on the multifaceted thinking inherent in balance-of-threat thinking where balancing happens not against 'power' but against 'threats' – which are a mix of power, military capabilities, political intentions, and geographic proximity.[23] On the two latter scores – intentions and proximity – European allies have nothing to fear from the United States, they argue.[24] The EU is therefore not motivated by balancing but rather by regional security needs and the desire to influence US policy, which is a different thing entirely.[25] In this light, it makes sense for the United States to encourage as much 'pooling and sharing' of defence resources in Europe as possible because it will make for a more efficient and weighty European partner.

Offensive realists define the third position in the debate. They have a less sanguine view of American power and find a historical 60 per cent success rate for offensive strategies.[26] Defensive states must thus prepare for war in order to avoid it: hence Mearsheimer's advice from 1990 that Europe should begin a 'well-managed' process of 'nuclear weapons proliferation'.[27] Europe's underlying problem is that the United States, for reasons of geopolitics and the 'stopping power of water', is inclined to detach itself from Europe and go offshore: it leaves Europeans to face the underlying question of hegemony in Europe, which really is a question of German power.[28] It would be bad news for everyone if 'pooling and sharing' in Europe recreated Germany's international ambitions, even if by way of rationalized EU cooperation. The CSDP is about containing German power, not building it up, according to offensive realists; and the offshore balancer, the United States, should aim for the middle ground where the EU is strong enough to tie down Germany but weak enough that it will not become a reincarnation of Germany's past.[29]

The empirical record does not fit particularly well with these schools of thought. The problem is that they are all forward looking: the United States will soon disengage; Europe will soon balance; Europe will not balance any time soon. Cases and events from the CSDP experience can then be used to illustrate either position without great difficulty, with the argument that these bits of evidence are a window to the future world. However, the thrust of the CSDP experience runs counter to all three.

The CSDP record shows a burst of operational activity for most of the 2000s, followed by a loss of momentum. It is as if the European Union needed to demonstrate the worth of its new tool but then hit limitations. In the past two years (looking back from mid-2011) nothing major has happened: in April 2010 the EU did launch a Somali police training mission in Uganda, but it terminated in 2011 after two consecutive training periods involving 150 deployed personnel. It has hardly been an impressive grab for international influence. In relation to Somalia the EU continues to run its first-ever naval operation, the anti-piracy Atalanta operation; while important, it is not having a great effect on the pirates (as with other anti-piracy missions in the area).

Africa is generally not a European Union CSDP success story either. The Congo missions (see Peter Schmidt's article in this issue) have been important flag missions but they targeted small segments of a very large refugee problem and did little, if anything, to dent the overall conflict. The Libyan descent into the early stages of civil war in February–March 2011 led in mid-March to the United Nations' authorization of the use of force to protect civilians, as well as a no-fly zone and an arms embargo. After some diplomatic wrangling NATO became the operational lead. It was the

Balkans redux: the same type of action (no-fly zone; arms embargo) and the same division of labour (with the EU trailing). The difference is that the EU has developed a Mediterranean policy since then and has sought to position itself as a leading interlocutor of North African events by developing a EUFOR Libya mission and wider partnership perspectives with post-Qaddafi Libya and other states in the region. Still, the wrangling in the run-up to the NATO no-fly zone, which witnessed great European divisions – including, notably, one between France and Germany – was a bad omen for European unity and it remains to be seen whether the CSDP can come into play in a meaningful way with respect to the North African crises and political transitions.

The European Union has in fact by invitation established a CSDP mission in the heart of the Middle East, on the Rafah border crossing between the Gaza Strip and Egypt. This mission, which began in 2005, has been of some use in managing local relations but it has not been a leveller of influence *vis-à-vis* Hamas, which controls the Gaza Strip, or the Israeli and Egyptian governments, both of whom loathe Hamas (regime change in Egypt could change this situation, of course). The Rafah mission is in fact indicative of a type of powerlessness, because what the local players needed – and found – was an honest broker with few capacities. The same can be said of the CSDP border-monitoring mission established in Georgia in 2008 following the Russia-Georgia war over South Ossetia. Russia would not have agreed to a real power broker entering into Georgia, which could have been NATO led by the United States; and while it has acquiesced to the EU mission, it continues to deny the EU mission access into Soviet-held territory in Georgia. The EUPOL mission in Afghanistan is another case in point. The EU falls notoriously short of the modest 400 police trainers it must deploy to its police academy in Kabul, which is bad as it is.[30] The really bad news is that European countries, led by Germany, the Netherlands, Denmark, and Italy, are in fact deploying far more than 400 police trainers to Afghanistan. One might reasonably ask why they are not committed to the struggling EUPOL mission. The troubling fact is that EU members do not want to pool resources under a complex and tortuous Brussels-led mission, preferring instead to use them flexibly. EUPOL allows only for HQ deployments in Kabul and provincial capitals, not in the field, and the national experience is that EUPOL is being run by an inexperienced and overtly bureaucratic staff back in Brussels.[31] To bypass Brussels red tape and restrictions the preferred option is to run concurrent bilateral police missions, and the unintended outcome is a kind of EUPOL failure.

One final observation can be made in relation to defence planning in Europe. With the CSDP was launched a Headline Goal process that promised more and better military goods for European missions. It set the bar at 60,000 deployable troops with various types of equipment, but this goal has proven elusive. The EU has tried to boost the process with bottom-up initiatives, beginning with so-called battlegroups and proceeding to 'permanent structured cooperation', which is written into the Lisbon Treaty and which was reinforced by a 'Ghent initiative' in late 2010 that asked countries to define the priorities from which momentum – the aforementioned 'pooling and sharing' – could be gained.[32] Not much has happened, though, and the top-down component of the EU's defence planning process, the European Defence Agency (EDA), has received neither the formal powers nor the ongoing political attention that could make it effective. As the financial crisis in Europe deepens and Germany and its partners struggle to rescue the common currency, the Euro – which will entail a new type of political-economic order in Europe – the prospects of radical defence change are nil.

All this is not to say that the EU's CSDP is a failure, but it *is* a troubled policy that is representative of a fragile construction in search of solidity. It does not resemble the power moves that most modern realists depict, though they may be right that the EU at some times worries about unchecked US power and at others hopes to draw the United States further into European affairs.

The CSDP as Prudence

It is possible that the CSDP represents a Brussels-centred attempt to construct a policymakers' community of meaning that can then serve as a launching pad for CSDP missions. This type of crafting of political meaning is difficult for contemporary realism to fit into its framework because it is so heavily rationalist. Neoclassical realism does bring in ideas, but when confronted with the conundrum of building general theory on contextual ideas opts for theory and turns ideas into the kind of "intervening variable" that would shock classical realists. Mainstream neoclassical realism thus deliberately brackets 'variations in the interests of states' for reasons of theory building, which has led one critical reviewer to advocate a change of label from neoclassicism to neostructuralism.[33] Constructivism is differently (but still well-) positioned to analyse constructs of meaning, and the question we shall confront here is whether the constructivist interpretation of the CSDP has greater merit than that of classical realism.

The gist of the constructivist argument is that the CSDP has quite a potential because it builds on a process of 'transgovernmentalism' that takes place among political elites and causes the erosion of deep-rooted differences.[34] In this view, the CSDP is what networks of policymakers make of it, though policymakers from powerful states will be better able to shape new networks than less well-endowed actors.[35] Socialization at elite levels, involving both government and EU officials and representatives, becomes the driver in the making of a cohesive policy community. In turn, as these people launch missions and achieve some measure of success, they can mobilize public opinion behind the CSDP and draw wider circles of practitioners into a CSDP 'community of practice'. There is a distinct flavour of functionalism in this argument – functionalism being the original theory of European integration – but the sociological and ideational elements have been brought out much more clearly.

Classical realism is fundamentally opposed to this line of thinking, which resembles the kind of political engineering that classical realists abhor, though that is putting the point in stark terms. Henry Kissinger wants us to understand the transatlantic relationship via the dire fate of the European nation-state and would oppose the suggestion that policymakers are the engines of change. Policymakers –

statesmen, Kissinger would call them – manage change and choose the lesser of two evils, but they are also fundamentally what their nations have made them into. To Kissinger the CSDP has precious little power potential, and this will not be fundamentally altered by exercises in political alignment in Brussels.

David P. Calleo, another contemporary classical realist, looks at diverging national goals in Europe and Europe's diplomatic system and finds different kinds of Europe – a 'Europe of states', 'Atlantic Europe', and 'Federal Europe'.[36] This may resemble the constructivist idea about meaning underpinning the CSDP but the point is a broader one. Europe's roots are pluralist and this heritage must be managed: it cannot be superseded by a new CSDP project anchored in Brussels. There are several distinct ways to manage it – from Hobbes' centralization of authority, to Rousseau's spiritualized contract, to Montesquieu's intricate balance of power – but they all grow out of Europe's past. Calleo finds that integration is anchored in Western Europe, and warns policymakers that this anchor is adrift. If they do not manage change, the entire Pan-European construction could be brought down.

Kissinger and Calleo reach conclusions in terms of policy advice that differ starkly from those of constructivists: where the latter would give the green light to Brussels-based efforts, the former caution about the need to manage the CSDP context – with this context being the critical community of meaning for the CSDP. Kissinger looked inside Europe and became fearful that the European political community will be made shallow and weakened by the lack of strong and historical ties between its governing elites (the statesmen) and the governed. Atlantic cooperation is one way to offset this weakness, but it is a challenge in itself because the American heritage is different – Hobbesian and unipolar.[37] Still, this opens the door to constructive engagement, because both sides of the Atlantic need the other to create what we might call a balance of pathologies.[38]

We know these pathologies well: American policymakers tend to focus too narrowly on America's power and primacy and ignore conditions for stability and cooperation in Europe,[39] and European policymakers tend to use anti-Americanism as a platform for their individual projects. If locked into opposition to the United States, Europe's unification project cannot succeed. As Calleo observes, the CSDP should therefore not be considered the embryonic European pillar in security, operating on a par with a Russian and an American pillar, but should instead be regarded as an integral part of a transatlantic project of power management.[40]

Classical realism and constructivism do sometimes share a fundamental understanding of politics as being rooted in strongly conservative cultures (or identities). At this point the two schools of thought become more difficult to disentangle.[41] My reading of this debate is akin to that of Jennifer Sterling-Folker, who commends constructivism as a tool that can help realists think through their ideas on threats and threat formation.[42] It is to recognize the creative contribution of constructivism but also to be cognizant of its status as an approach: it is not a theory; it does not tell us what to look for. Classical realism does, and constructivism can help classical realism do a better job. The enterprise remains, therefore, fundamentally classical-realist.

The point of departure for this enterprise could well be classical realism's 2,500-year track record of pondering tragedy and criticizing modernity's blindness to its own capacity for destruction, which is where this article began.[43] How should we in this context assess contemporary statesmanship and the current stewards of the CSDP, the EU's Herman Van Rompuy and Catherine Ashton? The traditional classical realist position is first of all that we cannot judge statesmen according to the standard ethics of interpersonal relations: a special set of ethics applies to intergroup relations and therefore statesmanship.[44] By this standard, EU and other leaders must free themselves of ethical foreign policy expectations back home and charter a prudent foreign policy course that minimizes evil more than it seeks the greater good for the greater number. It is far from clear that the current stewards are strong enough to do this. They instead appear to be captured by the liberal ideology of EU institutions, according to which the EU is a different kind of normative power that can do good.

A dialogue with constructivism, however, could bring about a slightly different perspective. The constructivist emphasis on the role of transnational or supranational ideas dovetails with a different type of prudence that continues to be focused on preventing adventurous statesmanship and turns the classical realist view of ethics on its head. According to it, statesmen should indeed follow standard ethics in their conduct of foreign affairs, not because the purpose is noble (it is, but this would be idealism) but because it leads to proper prudence.[45] If statesmen can nourish the idea among themselves that regular ethics actually make them all safer, as a kind of diplomatic community of ethics, then prudence will prevail. This idea of a common vision shared by political leaders is not foreign to classical realism – Hans Morgenthau wrote about statesmen's society and Henry Kissinger about statesmen's concert – but has been highlighted by constructivism.[46] A wedding of constructivism's transnational ideas and classical realism's prudence could yield the view that the EU institutions are critically important in anchoring European foreign policies – of nation-states as well as the EU itself – in a common and truly collective set of ethics.

At this point constructivism's implicit optimism might take over, had classical realism's stark outlook not drawn us back into the twilight zone defined by Reinhold Niebuhr and touched on in the first section of this article: statesmen may be ethical in foreign affairs, but only when they deal with like-minded nations. There is a dark side to international pluralism, which is captured by the categories of status quo and revisionism, and it could well be that the benevolence that western states tend to observe in international relations is enabled by the superior position that western powers have traditionally enjoyed. As this power wanes, the EU should not worry about benevolent cooperation but the management of differences, and such management entails not only the identification of like-mindedness and potentials for shared standards of ethics – which would be the liberal impulse – but also the identification of deep-seated political and cultural differences that inhibit the facile integration of ethics and policy and demand prudent statesmanship.

Herman Van Rompuy and Catherine Ashton appear as incarnations of Europe's complex and pluralist order, which is laudable, but classical realism would caution that a cocktail of benevolent ideology (EU liberalism) and weak institutions in need of legitimacy could push weak leaders into foreign policy adventures. The CSDP in some ways invites tragedy. A conscious and consistent effort to promote policy prudence is therefore necessary.

Conclusion

There are no fixed answers in classical realism – no place to stand to move the earth. Insights are interpretive and historical, and by definition contextual, and in this case the context is Europe's complex communitarian and pluralist history and political reality. Classical realism tells us that Europe cannot be like a nation, whereby a people creates its state, nor can it be like a state, whereby a political elite creates the people; Europe must build its political institutions, including the CSDP, on an evolving and in some ways threatened model of nation-states. It is the de facto capacities of Europe's nation states, the implications of 'nation-statehood', as Stanley Hoffmann once noted[47] – and the fate of Europe's nation states in a changing world, one might add – that will tell us about the scope and purpose of the CSDP.

Classical realism thus finds no resting place. It sees the CSDP as an evolving institution and the theory itself contains no conception of an end-state – a pole, a power, or an actor of some kind – that it expects to come about. It is an open and dynamic framework for understanding the intersection between power and purpose. If there is a bottom line it is that the CSDP is a fragile policy with two primary purposes: it should maintain prudence inside Europe, and it should help to maintain a transatlantic balance of pathologies that seems necessary to provide a coherent and long-term western footprint on international affairs.

It follows that efforts to augment the European Union's external action capacity must be carefully crafted. If people push too hard, either for reasons of European enthusiasm in the case of Europeans or frustration on the part of Americans who want more from Europe, they will not advance the CSDP but cause it to fail. Michael Loriaux instructively writes that '[t]he commitment to European Union is an affair of realist prudence born of scepticism'.[48] French and German leaders, in particular, support the EU because they likely would be worse off without it; and American leaders have with some hesitation come to support it as well because they too would be worse off without it. It is restrained behaviour on the part of important states that explains institutions, rather than vice versa. If the institutions – such as the CSDP – were to undermine the prudence that fathered them, tragedy could follow.

The purpose of writing articles such as this one is therefore not only to take part in the academic debate but also to make statesmen cognizant of the dangers they face. Classical realists must 'speak truth to power'. Two brief conclusions by way of policy advice follow. First, there is a temptation to provide mechanisms for greater political leadership in Europe because the collective institution tends to be lethargic, and we see the leadership drive in the Franco-British partnering that caused the ESDP in 1998 and drove the intervention in Libya in 2011. It is reminiscent of the type of 'concert' of great powers that Julian Lindley-French once argued should drive the CSDP.[49] It follows from this analysis that such concerts should be treated with caution because they might easily tear apart the fragile CSDP and EU construction, and it may be better instead to organize as a matter of policy flexible operational coalitions.[50] Such flexibility is built into the CSDP, it should be noted, but the point is that operational flexibility should not get tangled up in controversial designs for political directorates or concerts.

Second, the CSDP should at heart be about Europe's contribution to transatlantic dialogue and world order. This is a challenge because the EU tends to become engulfed by constitutional debates – which regard the end-point of European integration and therefore its identity – and because in its self-imaginary it is (destined to become) a fully-fledged foreign policy actor. In this light, the CSDP is about bolstering the EU. However, when apart, Europe and the United States become 'dangerously provincial', as Calleo reminds us.[51] The United States can balance some of Europe's pathologies, just as Europe can balance some of America's. Moreover, transatlantic unity in the sense of a balanced partnership represents the hope that the West can accommodate the new Asia and meet growing challenges of global governance. 'The twenty-first century may then come to reflect Europe's new model for peace rather than its old model for war.'[52]

None of this is easy to do politically. Politics is about dreams and visions and moving people see into the future, and prudence sits uneasily with dreaming. The aspirations of politics are not favourably biased toward the need to 'strike a precarious balance' between tragedy and order. As Hans Morgenthau once wrote, the maintenance of order requires moral courage, moral judgement, and political wisdom.[53] It naturally follows that any system that feeds off dreams and vision will easily imperil these requirements of order.

We thus return to the conclusion of this article that the CSDP should be concerned with the preservation of restraint in Europe. There can be no strong and autonomous CSDP. Strong ambitions will wreck the collective commitment to restraint and open a race for national influence that will be to Europe's detriment. The CSDP should be made to work, though, as Europe's contribution to a functioning Atlantic partnership. The project of European integration has historically been tied into this partnership, which today serves to incur restraint both in Brussels and Washington as Europe and North America seek influence in their environments. Such a partnership is often frustrating and tedious to maintain, which is why moral courage, moral judgement, and political wisdom are indispensable, just as speaking truth to power is.

ACKNOWLEDGEMENTS

The author is grateful to the editors and anonymous reviewers for constructive criticism. The author is likewise grateful to colleagues who, at the Twelfth Biannual EUSA conference, March 2011, generously agreed to discuss some of the issues that I raise here.

NOTES

1. See Robert Kagan, 'Power and Weakness', *Policy Review*, No. 113 (June–July, 2002), pp. 3–28.
2. There were 27 EU countries in 2011, though the number will increase to 28 when Croatia becomes an EU member state in July 2013.
3. John Keegan, *The Mask of Command: A Study of Generalship* (London: Pimlico, 2004), pp. 10–11.

4. Hans Morgenthau famously argued that liberalism overlooked mankind's biological and spiritual dimensions and instead greatly exaggerated its rational dimension. Liberalism thus came to argue that the weapons of true order that had helped liberalism prevail against vested (feudal) interests – positive law, written constitutions, independent courts, and elected parliaments – applied everywhere. Rationality told them so. Liberalism thus became a science akin to engineering, missing out on the stuff of politics. Or, as Morgenthau wrote in *Scientific Man vs. Power Politics* (Chicago: University of Chicago, 1946), 'Politics is an art and not a science, and what is required for its mastery is not the rationality of the engineer but the wisdom and the moral strength of the statesman' (p. 10). This revolt against rational engineering – and the hope that we can muddle our way through to progress if only we persist – fed not only classical realism but also the theology of the English School study of diplomacy as an international institution and source of stability. Such stability can be achieved if we give up on the idea that we are well-meaning and ultimately progressive and instead come to realize that we are 'miserable sinners'. For more on Martin Wight, Hedley Bull and others, see Robert Jackson, *Classical and Modern Thought on International Relations* (New York: Palgrave, 2005), pp. 55–58.
5. It is commonly agreed that classical realists tended to depict their liberal opponents in naïve terms in order to promote their own realist position. E.H. Carr has widely debated the ideas of liberal thinkers such as John Stuart Mill, Immanuel Kant, and Normann Angel. See *The Twenty Years' Crisis, 1919-1939: An Introduction to International Relations* (Basingstoke: Palgrave, 2001), pp. 1–62. However, it is uncontestable that liberals did tend to see the state as essentially a 'structure' which, if properly construed (as a democracy), would promote peace. This disregard for politics led to the revival of Realpolitik in the 1940s, spurred by Friedrich Meinecke and others. For liberal theory, see Kenneth Waltz, *Man, the State, and War: A Theoretical Analysis* (New York: Columbia University Press, 2005), pp. 80–123. For Realpolitik, see Jonathan Haslam, *No Virtue Like Necessity: Realist Thought in International Relations Since Machiavelli* (New Haven, CT: Yale University Press, 2002), pp. 183–186.
6. Pooling and sharing have been on the EU agenda since late 2010, when EU defence ministers defined the terms and urged EU action. By July 2011 the EU's Catherine Ashton (in a classified report to the EU Council) defined the issue as 'a necessity rather than a mere option'. See *Defense News*, 'Pooling, Sharing a "Necessity"' EU Report, 19 July 2011, http://www.defensenews.com/story.php?i=7134177&c=EUR&s=TOP. Necessity has impacted on NATO as well, where pooling and sharing come wrapped in the agenda of 'smart defense' as defined in the fall of 2010 by the Secretary General.
7. Liberal trends 'increase the problems and issues between nations much more rapidly than the intelligence to solve them can be created', wrote Reinhold Niebuhr in 1932, continuing that impartial solutions are impossible because solutions are political, and strong nations have a greater say in them. *Moral Man and Immoral Society* (London: Continuum, 2005), pp. 57 and 72. This insight also formed the basis of E.H. Carr's *The Twenty Years' Crisis*.
8. Karl Polyani, *The Great Transformation* (Boston, MA: Beacon Press, 2001). E.H. Carr wrote fourteen volumes in his series *A History of Soviet Russia*, which is considered his idealist view of the Cold War (he believed or perhaps hoped western capitalism would fail).
9. E.H. Carr, *Nationalism and After* (London: Macmillan, 1945), pp. 13–19. Hans Morgenthau later wrote in a similar vein that '[t]he kind of freedom a particular society is able to realize in a particular period of its history … depends upon the kind of political order under which it lives'. 'The Dilemmas of Freedom', *American Political Science Review*, Vol. 51, No. 3 (September 1957), pp. 714–723.
10. Carl Schmitt, *The Concept of the Political* (Chicago: CUP, 2007).
11. A classical realist would accept that we can generalize about power dynamics. However, motives are by definition contextual.
12. The most eloquent statement in this respect continues to be Hedley Bull, 'International Theory: The Case for a Classical Approach', *World Politics*, Vol. 18, No. 3 (April 1966), pp. 361–377. Ido Oren has more recently criticized modern realists for being confused by their own calls for scientific objectivity while admonishing decision-makers to favour certain policies over others, which is akin to political thought in action. Classical realism is built on this idea of political thought in action, Oren concludes, which modern and scientifically ambitious theory is not. 'The Unrealism of Contemporary Realism: The Tension between Realist Theory and Realists' Practice', *Perspectives on Politics*, Vol. 7, No. 2 (2009), pp. 283–301.
13. Stanley Hoffmann, 'Obstinate or Obsolete? The Fate of the Nation-State and the Case of Western Europe', *Daedalus* Vol. 95, No. 3 (1966), pp. 862–915.
14. Robert Gilpin, *War and Change in World Politics* (Cambridge: Cambridge University Press, 1981). For 'human race' see p. 213; for 'mankind' p. 230. Gilpin's book deals essentially with power dynamics or transitions – the rise and decline of big powers. This is an inherently classical realist

preoccupation because classical realists saw power as contested and therefore dynamic. Structural realists – who we shall encounter in the next section – see power as locked into structure or certain distributions of it, which leads to a preoccupation with balances of power in various guises. This view of power tends to be less dynamic, therefore. The body of thought that today comes under the heading of power transition theory belongs to the former tradition. Its origins are found in A.F.K. Organski, *World Politics* (New York: Knopf, 1968), though today power transition theory tends to get mired in the kind of data computation and statistical sophistry that takes it away from the concerns with political ideas and order that were at the heart of the classical enterprise.

15. Henry Kissinger, *Does America Need a Foreign Policy? Toward a Diplomacy for the 21st Century* (New York: Simon and Schuster, 2001), p. 286.
16. The nation-state is in fact thriving only in North America and Asia. Henry Kissinger, *Does the West Still Exist? America and Europe Moving Towards 2020*, Speech, Washington DC, 23 February 2007.
17. Henry Kissinger, 'A Global Order in Flux', *The Washington Post*, 9 July 2004, http://www.henryakissinger.com/articles/wp070904.html. Colin Gray has written that among his great geopolitical fears is an independent Europe (EU) because it will be weak and dependent on Russia for energy, and it will therefore align with a Sino-Russian alliance. Colin Gray, 'Document No. 1: The Quadrennial Defense Review (QDR), 2006, and the Perils of the Twenty-First Century', *Comparative Strategy*, Vol. 25, No. 2 (2006), pp. 141–148.
18. Henry Kissinger, *The Intellectual Underpinnings of the Trilateral Partnership in the 21st Century*, Remarks to the Trilateral Commission Tokyo Plenary Meeting, April 26, 2009. Julian Lindley-French is less downbeat than Kissinger when it comes to the potential of the transatlantic alliance. Lindley-French perceives a European opportunity to shed its role as a 'junior partner' by taking on vital 'stability and reconstruction'. For Lindley-French Europe can choose to make itself strong; for Kissinger this choice is less real because the limits of the CSDP are rooted in the dissolution of the nation-state. Julian Lindley-French, 'Enhancing Stabilization and Reconstruction Operations: A Report of the Global Dialogue between the European Union and the United States', CSIS Report, January 2009, http://csis.org/files/media/csis/pubs/090122_lindley_enhancingstabil_web.pdf, and 'Stabilisation and Reconstruction: Europe's Chance to Shed its "Junior Partner" Status', *Europe's World*, Autumn 2009, http://www.europesworld.org/NewEnglish/Home_old/Article/tabid/191/ArticleType/articleview/ArticleID/21472/Default.aspx, last accessed 31 October 2011.
19. Reinholdt Niebuhr, *Moral Man and Immoral Society: A Study in Ethics and Politics* (New York: Charles Scribner's Sons, 1960), p. 234.
20. Robert Jervis, 'Cooperation under the Security Dilemma', *World Politics*, Vol. 30, No. 2 (1978), pp. 167–214; Stephen Van Evera, *Causes of War* (Ithaca, NY: Cornell University Press, 2001). Kenneth Waltz is regularly cited as a father of defensive realism but the link is not unambiguous. Waltz developed structural realism (neorealism) and did not make strong claims regarding the motives of states: states 'are unitary actors who, at a minimum, seek their own preservation and, at a maximum, drive for universal domination'. Kenneth N. Waltz, 'Anarchic Orders and Balances of Power', in R. Keohane (ed.), *Neorealism and its Critics* (New York: Columbia University Press, 1986), p. 117. This overview and the following three paragraphs draw on Sten Rynning, 'Realism and the Common Security and Defence Policy,' *Journal of Common Market Studies*, Vol. 49, No. 1 (2011), pp. 23–42.
21. Barry Posen, 'European Union Security and Defense Policy: Response to Unipolarity?' *Security Studies*, Vol. 15, No. 2 (2006), pp. 149–186; Barry Posen, 'ESDP and the Structure of World Power' *The International Spectator*, Vol. 39, No. 1 (2004), pp. 5–17.
22. T.V. Paul, 'Soft Balancing in the Age of U.S. Primacy', *International Security*, Vol. 30, No. 1 (2005), pp. 46–71; Robert J. Art, 'Europe Hedges its Security Bets', in T.V. Paul, J.J. Wirtz and M. Fortmann (eds), *Balance of Power: Theory and Practice in the 21st Century* (Stanford, CA: Stanford University Press, 2004).
23. For balance-of-threat theory, see Stephen Walt, *Origins of Alliances* (Ithaca, NY: Cornell University Press, 1987); for an overview of this debate see Anders Wivel, 'Balancing Against Threats or Bandwagoning with Power? Europe and the Transatlantic Relationship after the Cold War', *Cambridge Review of International Affairs*, Vol. 21, No. 3 (2008), pp. 289–305.
24. William Wohlforth, 'The Stability of a Unipolar World', *International Security*, Vol. 24, No. 1 (1999), pp. 5–41; Stephen Brooks and William Wohlforth, 'American Primacy in Perspective', *Foreign Affairs*, Vol. 81, No. 4 (2002), pp. 20–33; Stephen Brooks and William Wohlforth, *World Out of Balance: International Relations and the Challenge of American Primacy* (Ithaca, NY: Cornell University Press, 2008); Stephen Brooks and William Wohlforth, 'Reshaping the World Order', *Foreign Affairs*, Vol. 88, No. 2 (2009), pp. 49–63; also Joseph M. Grieco, 'Realism and Regionalism:

American Power and German and Japanese Institutional Strategies During and After the Cold War', in E.B. Kapstein and M. Mastanduno (eds), *Unipolar Politics* (New York: Columbia University Press, 1999); Jeffrey W. Taliaferro, 'Security Seeking under Anarchy: Defensive Realism Revisited', *International Security*, Vol. 25, No. 3 (2000/01), pp. 128–161; and Anders Wivel, 'The Power Politics of Peace: Exploring the Link between Globalization and European Integration from a Realist Perspective', *Cooperation and Conflict*, Vol. 39, No. 1 (2004), pp. 5–25.
25. Stephen Brooks and William Wohlforth, 'Hard Times for Soft Balancing', *International Security*, Vol. 30, No. 1 (2005), pp. 72–108; Kier A. Lieber and Gerard Alexander, 'Waiting for Balancing: Why the World is not Pushing Back', *International Security*, Vol. 30, No. 1 (2005), pp. 109–139; G. Press-Barnathan, 'Managing the Hegemon: NATO under Unipolarity', *Security Studies*, Vol. 15, No. 2 (2006), pp. 271–309; Stephen Walt, 'Alliances in a Unipolar World' *World Politics*, Vol. 61, No. 1 (2009), pp. 86–120.
26. John J. Mearsheimer, *The Tragedy of Great Power Politics* (New York: Norton, 2001), p. 38.
27. John J. Mearsheimer, 'Back to the Future: Instability in Europe after the Cold War', *International Security*, Vol. 15, No. 1 (1990), pp. 5–56.
28. Mearsheimer, *Tragedy* (note 26), pp. 393–396.
29. John J. Mearsheimer, 'The Future of the American Pacifier', *Foreign Affairs*, Vol. 80, No. 5 (2001), pp. 46–61; Seth Jones, 'The European Union and the Security Dilemma', *Security Studies*, Vol. 12, No. 3 (2003), pp. 114–156 and 'The Rise of a European Defense', *Political Science Quarterly*, Vol. 121, No. 2 (2006), pp. 241–267.
30. EU, *EU Police Mission in Afghanistan Fact Sheet*, January 2011; Luis Peral, 'EUPOL Afghanistan', in G. Grevi, D. Helly, and D. Keohane, (eds), *European Security and Defence Policy: The First Ten Years, 1999-2009* (Paris: EUIIS, 2010), pp. 325–338. Available at http://www.iss.europa.eu/uploads/media/ESDP_10-web.pdf, last accessed 31 October 2011.
31. House of Lords, *The EU's Afghan Police Mission*, European Union Committee – Eighth Report, 1 February 2011, http://www.publications.parliament.uk/pa/ld201011/ldselect/ldeucom/87/8702.htm, last accessed 31 October 2011.
32. Sven Biscop, 'Permanent Structured Cooperation and the Future of the ESDP: Transformation and Integration', *European Foreign Affairs Review*, Vol. 13, No. 4 (Winter 2008), pp. 431–448; Nicolai von Ondarza, 'Less than the Sum of its Parts: The CSDP Capability Gap and Prospects of EU Military Integration', *Studia Diplomatica*, Vol. 63, Nos. 3/4 (2010), pp. 81–104; Sven Biscop, 'Permanent Structured Cooperation: Building Effective European Armed Forces', Paper for 12th biannual EUSA conference, 3–5 March 2011, http://euce.org/eusa/2011/papers/4i_biscop.pdf, last accessed 31 October 2011.
33. For neo-classical realism see Stephen E. Lobell, N.M. Ripsman, and Jeffrey W. Taliaferro (eds), *Neoclassical Realism, the State, and Foreign Policy* (Cambridge: Cambridge University Press, 2009), pp. 31 and 224; for the critique see S. Rynning, S., 'The High Cost of Theory in Neoclassical Realism,' *H-Net/H-Diplo* (July 2009), http://www.h-net.org/reviews/showrev.php?id=24339. For an attempt to apply neo-classical realism to the EU's CFSP/CSDP, see Z. Selden, 'Power is Always in Fashion: State-Centric Realism and the European Security and Defence Policy', *Journal of Common Market Studies*, Vol. 48, No. 2 (2010), pp. 397–416. For the argument that the study of ideas is incompatible with general theory, see Raymond Aron, *Paix et guerre entre les nations* (Paris: Calman-Lévy, 1984).
34. Jolyon Howorth, 'European Defence and the Changing Politics of the European Union: Hanging Together or Hanging Separately?' *Journal of Common Market Studies*, Vol. 39, No. 4 (2001), pp. 765–89; "Discourse, Ideas, and Epistemic Communities in European Security and Defence Policy," *West European Politics*, Vol. 27, No. 2 (2004), pp. 211–234; 'The Political and Security Committee: A Case Study in "Supranational Intergovernmentalism"', *Les cahiers Européens*, No. 1, March 2010; Jolyon Howorth and Anand Menon, 'Still Not Pushing Back: Why the European Union is not Balancing the United States', *Journal of Conflict Resolution*, Vol. 53, No. 3 (2009), pp. 727–744.
35. See Frédéric Mérand, Stéphanie Hofmann, and Bastian Irondelle, 'Governance and State Power: A Network Analysis of European Security', *Journal of Common Market Studies*, Vol. 49, No. 1 (2011), pp. 121–147.
36. David P. Calleo, *Rethinking Europe's Future* (Princeton, NJ: Princeton University Press, 2001); *Follies of Power: America's Unipolar Fantasy* (Cambridge: Cambridge University Press, 2009).
37. Calleo, *Rethinking Europe's Future* (note 36).
38. For this balance of pathologies, see Rynning, 'Realism and the Common Security and Defence Policy' (note 20).

39. Stanley Hoffmann concurs, arguing that US policy reflects 'dogmatism' where European policy builds on 'empiricism'. Stanley Hoffmann, 'US-European Relations: Past and Future', *International Affairs*, Vol. 79, No. 5, pp. 1029–1036. True, Europe was split on the issue of Iraq and it may be difficult therefore to speak of 'Europe' but, as Hoffmann also writes, the Bush administration deliberately – aided by Tony Blair – sought to divide the European Union by soliciting the support of Atlantic-minded political leaders. Stanley Hoffmann, *America Goes Backward* (New York: New York Review of Books, 2004).
40. Russia has long pushed for just one security pillar from Vancouver to Vladistok, which of course would put it at the main table next to the Western powers. Atlanticists typically prefer a two-pillar scenario whereby Russia is outside and Western Europe and the United States and Canada are united on the inside. Some Europeanists and, as we have seen, American 'offshore' proponents prefer a three-pillar structure with Russia, the EU, and the United States. For Calleo, see *Follies of Power* (note 36).
41. Michael Williams, *The Realist Tradition and the Limits of International Relations* (Cambridge: Cambridge University Press, 2005); Casper Sylvest, 'John H. Herz and the Resurrection of Classical Realism', *International Relations*, Vol. 22, No. 4 (2008), pp. 441–455; J.S. Barkin, *Realist Constructivism: Rethinking International Relations Theory* (Cambridge: Cambridge University Press, 2010).
42. It should be noted that Sterling-Folker is mostly known as a neo-classical realist, but it should be noted that she has a very broad understanding of neo-classical realism. Jennifer Sterling-Folker, 'Realism and the Constructivist Challenge: Rejecting, Reconstructing, or Rereading', *International Studies Review*, Vol. 4, No. 1 (2002), pp. 73–97; 'Realist Theorizing as Tradition: Forward Is As Forward Does', in A. Freyberg-Inan, E. Harrison, and P. James (eds), *Rethinking Realism in International Relations: Between Tradition and Innovation* (Washington, DC: Johns Hopkins University Press, 2009). The observations in this paragraph on classical realism and contructivism draw on Rynning, 'Realism and the Common Security and Defence Policy' (note 20).
43. For the pedigree of classical realism and also this view of modernity, see Richard Ned Lebow, *The Tragic Vision of Politics: Ethics, Interests, and Orders* (Cambridge: Cambridge University Press, 2003), especially chapters 7 and 8.
44. Hans Morgenthau, 'The Evil of Politics and the Ethics of Evil', *Ethics*, Vol. 56, No. 1 (1945), pp. 1–18.
45. S.S. Monoson and M. Loriaux, 'The Illusion of Power and the Disruption of Moral Norms: Thucydides' Critique of Periclean Policy', *American Political Science Review*, Vol. 92, No. 2 (1998), pp. 285–297.
46. Hans Morgenthau, *Politics Among Nations: The Struggle for Power and Peace* (Boston, MA: McGraw Hill, 1993), pp. 235–250; Henry Kissinger, *A World Restored: Metternich, Castlereagh, and the Problems of Peace, 1812–1822* (London: Phoenix, 2000), pp. 1–6 and 144–176.
47. Hoffmann, *Obstinate or Obsolete* (note 13), pp. 914–915.
48. M. Loriaux, 'Realism and Reconciliation: France, Germany, and the European Union', in E.B. Kapstein and Michael Mastanduno (eds), *Unipolar Politics* (New York: Columbia University Press, 1999), p. 378.
49. Julian Lindley-French, 'In the Shade of Locarno: Why European Defence is Failing', *International Affairs*, Vol. 78, No. 4 (2002), pp. 78–812.
50. Sten Rynning, 'Toward a Strategic Culture for the EU', *Security Dialogue*, Vol. 34, No. 4 (2003), pp. 479–496; 'Less May Be Better in EU Foreign and Security Policy', *Oxford Journal of Good Governance*, Vol. 2, No. 1 (2005), pp. 45–50.
51. Calleo, *Follies of Power* (note 36), pp. 165–166.
52. *Ibid.*
53. Morgenthau, 'The Evil of Politics and the Ethics of Evil' (note 43); also and more generally *Politics Among Nations* (note 45).

From Words to Deeds: Strategic Culture and the European Union's Balkan Military Missions

CHARLES C. PENTLAND

Is the European Union (EU) acquiring its own strategic culture? Almost since its inception (as the European Economic Community) it has been an actor in international relations, although in its early years such action was largely confined to negotiating on behalf of its member states in trade and other aspects of international economic policy. Since the end of the Cold War, however, the EU's range of competence in foreign affairs has expanded dramatically. The Maastricht Treaty established the Common Foreign and Security Policy (CFSP) in its own 'pillar' (based in part on the two-decade legacy of collective diplomatic action under European Political Cooperation) and hinted at the prospect of 'a common defence policy which might in time lead to a common defence'.[1] A joint UK–French declaration at Saint-Malo in 1998 triggered a phase of uneven progress toward a European Security and Defence Policy (ESDP) capped, in 2003, by agreement on access to NATO assets (Berlin-Plus), the launching of the first two ESDP missions – one military, the other civilian – and the promulgation of a European Security Strategy (ESS).[2] The Treaty of Lisbon, which came into force on 1 December 2009, updates the language of Maastricht, referring to 'the progressive framing of a common Union defence policy' which, it adds, 'will lead to a common defence, when the European Council, acting unanimously, so decides'. It also opens up the possibility of 'permanent structured cooperation' among smaller groups of EU states, in the framework of what it rebrands as the EU's Common Security and Defence Policy (CSDP).[3] On paper, in the eyes of its member states, in the expectations of others and, increasingly, on the record of events, the EU has at last come to resemble a full-service international actor. Can we therefore take for granted that the answer to our opening question is an unequivocal 'yes'?

Those who write about strategic culture tend to assume that any state – certainly any great power worth its salt – will have one of its own, based primarily on a distinctive blend of geography, ethnicity and history. Whether this assumption can be extended to groupings of states such as the EU, which aspire to or have achieved the capacity to act as a state in at least some areas of international relations, is at least open to debate. The fact that NATO has just completed another of its periodic revisions of its 'strategic concept' suggests that the search for guidelines linking 'ends to means, intentions to capabilities, objectives to resources'[4] can be very much the business of alliances and other multilateral actors. But even if we set aside doubts as to whether the strategic concept truly reflects a collective transatlantic strategic culture, NATO may still be an exception. The EU might seem a harder case. First, the idea of Europe as a fully fledged strategic actor is less than two decades old.[5]

Second, the EU is a diverse assemblage of 27 states which lacks a hegemonic leadership that might be tempted and able to impose its view of the world. Third, the rapid emergence of a plethora of institutions for planning and managing ESDP operations, both military and civilian, does not disguise the resolutely intergovernmental character of the enterprise. That the key decisions about missions require unanimity suggests that it might be difficult for a common strategic culture to take root.

Whether, despite these obstacles, one has nevertheless done so is the central question of this article. As other contributors to this collection have underlined, strategic culture is an elusive and contested concept. Rather than engaging in the debates it has engendered, I propose in this article to work with an understanding of strategic culture distilled from Jack Snyder's early definition which takes it to consist of ideas, emotions and habits that members of a strategic community have learned and shared over time.[6] Strategic culture is not in itself strategy, but the intellectual, normative and behavioural setting which generates and sustains it. It may on occasion seem indistinguishable from 'policy', but it is better seen as inspiring, shaping and constraining the choices from which policy is built. If that is its role, the character of a strategic culture should be discernible in the strategy, the institutions, the decision-making process, the substance and the operations of foreign and security policy.

It made sense for Snyder, writing in the 1970s about US–Soviet relations, to take a narrow view of strategic culture focused on nuclear weapons. That need not preclude our now embracing a more expansive view, extending its scope beyond military applications to broader realms of foreign and security policy and embracing the instruments of soft power. In this light, there is no need to introduce 'security culture' as a competitive or overlapping concept. Strategic culture is about context, process and decisions; security is one of the ends sought through the application of instruments of power, whether hard or soft.

EU Strategic Culture in Words

All this presumes, of course, that we will be able to recognize elements of an EU strategic culture when we see them. In turn, that presumes that we know where, and how, to look for them. First, since strategic culture is above all a set of ideas, we would be well advised to pay attention to the authoritative declarations of policy-makers and the reflections of the broader security and defence community. In addition to the ESS, these sources would include, at the member-state level, major speeches of leaders, periodic defence and foreign policy reviews, and reports from influential think tanks. Whether or not it is always explicitly directed at the formation of a European strategic culture, this material constitutes the primordial intellectual and political soup from which such culture must emerge. What are its main constituents?

The ESS, first drafted by High Representative Javier Solana in early 2003 and approved in slightly modified form later that year, can be taken as capturing the consensus of the EU's member states at that time on the character of their security environment and their priorities with respect to threats, responses, processes, capabilities, institutions and partnerships. If the results of a five-year review of the ESS conducted in 2008 are any indication, that consensus remains pretty much in place, aside from some adjustments to the list of threats (adding energy and cyber insecurity) and some updating elsewhere.[7] In most of the other reflections by scholars and think tanks on the question of Europe's strategic culture over the past five years, a very similar set of themes and priorities emerges.

These include the conviction that the European Union has become a 'global player' and a 'more credible and effective actor' whose international identity is now firmly established. This is a consequence partly of the convergence of member states' interests and partly of the emergence of a more multipolar world. The assertion is that the EU is now fully established as a provider of security,[8] seen in turn as a precondition for development, democratization and other goals to be sought on a global scale. The ESS identifies five principal threats – terrorism, the proliferation of WMD, regional conflicts, state failure, and organized crime – to Europeans' collective interests.[9] And it pointedly makes a distinction between what seems a primary focus of attention – building security in the EU's neighbourhood (the Balkans, eastern Europe, the Caucasus, the Middle East and the Mediterranean littoral) – and the exercise of 'effective multilateralism' in the wider world to promote institutions and 'best practices' of governance, both global and regional. To this reading of the state of the international system and the EU's emergent role status, the ESS adds, finally, a set of prescriptions common to practically all such papers: the EU must become more active, assertive and robust in its approach to security; it must develop its own, autonomous capabilities for the planning and conduct of military missions; its actions must become more genuinely comprehensive with respect to the integration of institutions and instruments both military and civilian; and it must cultivate more effective collaboration with international agencies and strategic partners, especially in action beyond its immediate neighborhood.[10]

In 2005, Paul Cornish and Geoffrey Edwards made a first attempt at defining an EU strategic culture: 'the political and institutional confidence and processes to manage and deploy military force, coupled with external recognition of the EU as a legitimate actor in the military sphere'.[11] The ESS and its five-year assessment represent a set of claims that, at least with respect to those elements that are under its control, the EU has in fact acquired the fundamentals of a unique strategic culture. External recognition as a legitimate actor is, of course, for outsiders to determine, and makes the existence of an EU strategic culture hostage, in part, to their views. But one might argue that this would just be icing on the cake: a group has a culture if it so believes and acts, regardless of what others perceive and believe.

Others are less sure that the European Union has reached even this minimal stage. Posing the apocalyptic question of whether Europe is 'doomed to fail as a power', Charles Grant discerns the lack of a common strategic culture in the fact that some member states take defence seriously, while others (most?) do not.[12] He faults an aversion to hard power, attributed particularly but not exclusively to Germany. Others, however, turn this into almost a virtue, celebrating soft power and human security as integral to the EU's strategic vision. Alvaro de Vasconcelos underlines the uniqueness of EU soft power and claims that its security culture is based on 'delegitimizing power politics'. He writes that the EU 'remains essentially a civilian power that confines the use of force to the most exceptional circumstances and broad international legitimacy'.[13] While he does argue elsewhere for a more robust ESDP with greater autonomy and (hard-power) capabilities, his characterization of the prevailing culture may well ring true both with those who approve and those who despair of it.

These necessarily brief references to the declaratory dimension of European strategic culture reveal both a broad agreement on its main ingredients and a continuing disagreement over the priority to be accorded to some of them – and, more fundamentally, whether it makes sense yet to proclaim the existence of a distinctive strategic culture at the European Union level. Those debates are, rightly, far from exhausted.

Strategic Culture in Words and Deeds

Words, however, are not enough. What we encounter on the declaratory level is largely aspirational and inspirational. In itself that may herald an emergent strategic culture – of which aspiration and inspiration are important ingredients – but the skeptic might reasonably press for harder evidence. With a passing nod to the Johnston–Gray debate,[14] therefore, we should also direct our attention to the operational level, seeking evidence of a European strategic culture as it is manifested in how the European Union conducts itself in the field. It is, after all, conceivable that whatever emerges on the declaratory level has precious little to do with how the EU actually responds to demands for action. The history of NATO's past strategic concepts, or of any number of national defence white papers, reminds us that events have a way of compromising the best laid of plans. It would thus be a good test for the existence and vigour of an EU strategic culture to look for its traces in the aims, instruments and conduct of ESDP missions. Is there a compelling pattern to the types of mission that the EU has taken on, how it determines their objectives and instruments, how it sets up and manages them, and how it puts into play such key governing themes as the comprehensive approach and effective multilateralism?

The argument for going beyond the declaratory version (or versions) of the EU's strategic culture is that strategy is, in the end, about choice in specific and often difficult circumstances. To be sure, a document such as the ESS is not, any more than NATO's strategic concept, just an abstract, frivolous wish-list; it is the product of intense deliberation and negotiation at the highest levels of the organization. What it says – and does not say – tells us much about the organization's collective view of the world: how it is, how it should be, and what is to be done about it. What it cannot tell us is which of the intellectual constructs, normative preferences and ways of doing things will come to the fore or fade to the rear, which will be strengthened and which found wanting, as they engage the real world in a military or civilian mission. Truths about the EU's strategic culture will no doubt be revealed by both words and actions, but of the two, actions may ultimately prove more reliable.

Some of this insight is likely to come from an overview of the 24 missions so far mounted under the auspices of the ESDP.[15] First, there have been more than twice as many civilian as military missions. This reflects need, opportunity, the comparative state of military and civilian capabilities, and the persistent appeal of the EU's self-definition as above all a civilian power.[16] Second, most missions have been modest in numbers and cost, and of relatively brief duration. Exceptions here are, with respect to scale, Althea (see below) and Artemis (2003, in eastern Congo) on the military side and the EU Police Mission (EUPM, in Bosnia), Afghanistan and Kosovo on the civilian side; with respect to duration, Althea, EUPM and in all likelihood Kosovo. This prevalent pattern reflects collective caution, which was no doubt appropriate in the early stages of the ESDP's development but was also a sign that the bigger member states were not fully invested, except with respect to south-east Europe. Third, the EU's European neighbourhood – the Balkans and the Caucasus – accounts for almost a third of all missions, including some of the biggest and longest-lived. This emphasis is in line with the stated priorities of the ESS. On the other hand, the Middle East, often identified as an EU priority, accounts for only three small civilian missions, while Africa – usually ranked as less important – accounts for ten missions overall.[17] This seems a good illustration of the disruptive power of events over planning. Fourth, roughly half of the missions have been either downscaled follow-ons to UN, NATO or other relatively robust missions, or have been conducted jointly with other regional bodies – evidence, perhaps, that the language of comprehensiveness and effective multilateralism that marks the EU's declaratory security culture carries real weight in the field.

These 24 cases are not the empirical universe of the EU's strategic culture. The actions they have entailed may put some meat on its doctrinal bones, but so, too, may cases of inaction, or of action by EU member states under auspices other than ESDP. Libya is a case in point. EUFOR Libya, a military/humanitarian mission proposed in March-April 2011, never materialized because of disagreements between national capitals. Individual member states nevertheless mounted a major military campaign under a UN mandate and NATO command. As in the case of Lebanon in 2006, although for different reasons, they chose not to deploy under an ESDP flag. Such decisions help sketch the shifting behavioural boundaries of the EU's emergent strategic culture.[18]

The assigned task of this article, however, is to focus more narrowly, exploring in greater depth the European Union's two military missions in south-east Europe: Operations Concordia, in the Former Yugoslav Republic of Macedonia (FYROM), and Althea, in Bosnia-Herzegovina. The aim is less to tell their stories in great detail or to assess their impact – those jobs have been well done by others[19] – than to seek the outlines of a European strategic culture at work in shaping the conception and execution of the two missions. The rationale for this choice of cases is that as military missions in the Balkans, they are undeniably 'strategic' for the EU in a way that many of the other missions may not be. First, each – especially Althea – involved a significant deployment of armed forces to a theatre where danger had been reduced but not eliminated. In this respect, only Artemis and possibly the more recent mission to Chad are comparable. Second, they were set in a region to which the EU had an exceptional long-term commitment, represented by the institutional framework of the Stability Pact for South Eastern Europe and the long civilian arm of Brussels working to prepare the western Balkan states for eventual membership.

To borrow language from another strategic context, these two Balkan operations could be described as missions of necessity, and most of the rest as missions of choice. Of course, how that distinction is drawn is itself a reflection of strategic culture. More importantly, we might expect the elements and the profile of a European strategic culture to emerge most starkly where the identity and interests and indeed the very 'idea of Europe' are so clearly seen to be at stake. Missions of choice may well provide other windows into Europe's strategic soul, but if we are to find strong evidence of an extant or emergent strategic culture, the Balkan military missions are a promising point of departure. If we had only these two missions as evidence, then, what would we be able to infer about strategic culture in the EU?

The Former Yugoslav Republic of Macedonia: Operation Concordia

From the outbreak of the Yugoslav wars in 1991, observers predicted that it was only a matter of time before Macedonia went up in flames as had three of its sister republics. In fact, from the time it declared its independence in 1992, the FYROM has been a showcase for judicious international intervention. While Croatia and Bosnia burned, the UN's protective force in those theatres, UNPROFOR, kept a wary eye on Macedonia. After Dayton, while NATO forces secured Bosnia, a new UN preventive deployment (UNPREDEP) helped to deter potential ethnic violence between Macedonia's Slavic majority and Albanian minority. It was assisted in this by the fact that – again, contrary to many expectations – neighbouring Kosovo, with its ethnic Albanian majority, and Albania proper had stayed relatively quiet through the worst of the Bosnian war.

Two developments in the wake of the Dayton Accords changed the FYROM's immediate environment, with direct impact on its domestic stability: first, the breakdown in domestic order in Albania in 1997 and second, NATO's war with Serbia over Kosovo in the spring of 1999. The contiguity of the FYROM's Albanian regions with both Albania and Kosovo, and the porosity of those borders, led to an influx of weapons and fighters and the radicalization of Macedonia's Albanians, with their many grievances over language rights, education and economic opportunity Rapid escalation in the number, scope and intensity of violent incidents along the ethnic fault lines and in disputed towns in western Macedonia led the government in Skopje and many in the international community to believe that the long-avoided civil war might at last be imminent.[20] At the same time, a Chinese veto in the Security Council in February 1999 had prevented the renewal of UNPREDEP's mandate.

Diplomatic intervention by the United Nations and the European Union led to a negotiated Framework Agreement between the government and the Albanian leadership, signed at Ohrid, Macedonia in August 2001. The agreement called for a NATO force to provide a secure environment for the implementation of its provisions. A one-month NATO operation to collect and destroy the insurgents' weapons was succeeded by Operation Amber Fox, which commenced in September under German command, with a complement of about 1000 troops. It was succeeded in December 2002 by Operation Allied Harmony, with a reduced force complement and a mandate to support the peace monitors and advise the government on security sector issues.

The Ohrid Agreement held, the government undertook a number of political and economic reforms, and the NATO force found itself with relatively little to do. Even as Allied Harmony was being deployed, while some narrow, specific security issues persisted, it seemed that the international military presence could safely be drawn down, if not yet ended.

For the European Union the timing was opportune. The institutional structure of the ESDP was newly in place, and the member states had tasked themselves with meeting the Helsinki 'headline goals' by the end of 2003. They had agreed to undertake a civilian police-training operation in Bosnia, starting on 1 January 2003. Macedonia now provided a promising venue for the first ESDP military mission. The EU's capabilities – and its initial ambitions – might still be modest, but it was important to demonstrate that the ESDP was more than just another set of institutions, that it could marshal resources and put boots on the ground.

In early 2003 the government in Skopje agreed to a transfer of responsibility from NATO to the European Union for keeping the civil peace. Like its predecessor, the EU mission – Operation Concordia – drew its authority from a UN Security Council resolution (1371).[21] It was the first invocation of the recently agreed Berlin-Plus arrangement whereby the EU could avail itself of NATO assets both institutional and material.[22] The EU's planning and operational headquarters was set up at Supreme Headquarters Allies Powers Europe (SHAPE), in Mons, Belgium and, as Berlin-Plus envisaged, the Deputy Supreme Allied Commander Europe (SACEUR), a German admiral at the time, was appointed operation commander. France agreed to serve as the 'framework' (that is, lead) nation, with a French general taking initial command of the forces on the ground.

With a complement of just over 350 troops – about 300 of them from 13 EU members, with France providing the largest single contingent – Concordia was modest in scale. Expectations, too, were fairly modest, since the worst of the ethnic tension seemed to have dissipated. The forces were lightly armed, with restrictive rules of engagement, and organized into over twenty field liaison teams whose tasks were patrolling, observation and reporting, largely in the border areas and the Albanian communes of western Macedonia.[23] The mandate was initially set for six months from 31 March, although it was subsequently extended to December 2003.

On balance, as a first test of Berlin-Plus, Concordia was deemed a success by both the EU and NATO. Coordination and intelligence sharing between the two organizations were less than perfect; nor, in practice, were all aspects of the division of labour between them as clear as they might have been. On the whole, however, the command arrangements worked well, to some extent because the operation inherited much of what NATO had already set up, both at SHAPE and in Macedonia.[24] The mission also benefited from the presence of various EU civilian agencies, building on their earlier success in crisis management and engaging the FYROM in the early stages of the Stabilization and Association process. Here too, however, coordination fell somewhat short of what was required by a truly comprehensive approach. Finally, this first EU military mission was too small, too brief and too much in NATO's shadow to establish the ESDP as a visible, credible provider of security in the FYROM or the region at large. Nevertheless, as Eva Gross notes, it was 'high on symbolism for ESDP but also for the development of the EU as a comprehensive crisis manager'.[25]

Since, in the eyes of both the European Union and the government, Concordia had fulfilled its core mandate to maintain a secure environment, there was really no argument over terminating the ESDP's military involvement in the FYROM at the end of 2003. Concordia was, however, followed by two successive civilian police-training missions, EUPOL Proxima and the short-lived EUPAT, which was concluded in June 2006.[26]

Bosnia-Herzegovina: EUFOR Althea

When the Bosnian war concluded in late 1995, it was clear that to provide the secure environment required for reconstruction, a robust international military presence would be needed. To that end, the Dayton Accords called for an initial insertion of 60,000 troops under NATO command. While some were European and Canadian – many of them re-hatted veterans of the much-maligned UNPROFOR – the Implementation Force (IFOR) had a notably strong American contingent, as well as contributions from non-NATO and even non-European countries. Its successor, the Stabilization Force (SFOR), which took over at the end of 1996, continued that pattern, although with a reduced complement of 32,000 troops. Over its eight-year history, SFOR was able gradually to reduce that number to 12,000.

Based on a Security Council resolution (1031), NATO's operations in Bosnia had as their primary mission implementation of the military aspects of the Dayton Accords as set out in Annex 1A. At the outset, IFOR was faced with a daunting list of tasks: to secure and maintain the cessation of hostilities; to separate the armed forces of the Bosniak-Croat Federation and the Republika Srpska; to oversee the transfer of land between the two newly formed 'entities'; and to move the armies' personnel and heavy weapons into approved and controlled sites. In fact IFOR managed to accomplish most of these tasks by mid-year. From then on, its main job was to patrol the demilitarized inter-entity boundary and inspect the cantonment sites containing heavy weapons and other equipment. In carrying out these tasks it also re-opened roads and railways, restored bridges, and brought Sarajevo airport back to full operation.

IFOR's mandate was for one year. While it had accomplished a great deal, it was clear in late 1996 that a follow-on operation would be necessary to maintain the secure environment established by IFOR, by deterring or preventing a resumption of hostilities or new threats to the peace, promoting a climate in which the peace process could continue, and providing support to civilian organizations. The last of these included working with the international police-training mission IPTF and its successor, the European mission EUPM, and providing a secure environment for the UN High Commission for Refugees (UNHCR) in assisting refugee returns and for the Organization for Security and Cooperation in Europe (OSCE) in overseeing a series of elections. Authorized by a new UN Security Council resolution (1088), SFOR had the same command structure as its predecessor, with the force commander under Allied Forces Southern Europe reporting to SACEUR and ultimately responsible to NATO's North Atlantic Council. SFOR inherited the geographic areas of command into which IFOR had divided Bosnia and, like IFOR, included contingents from non-NATO countries such as Russia.

Over its eight-year span, SFOR went through a number of modifications to its structures and activities, as well as a series of reductions in its force complement. By 2004, a number of considerations converged to compel a bigger change. First, with Bosnia having achieved a degree of political stability and taken the first steps on the long road to EU accession, and with reform well along in the security sector, the consensus in the international community was that the security problem was much diminished.[27] Second, with the wars in Afghanistan and Iraq, the US was anxious to reduce its military presence in the Balkans and to take NATO global.[28] Third, the EU was ready and willing to charge the ESDP with a task which, while more demanding than others it had taken on, had its foundations already laid and was in a region with a declared 'European perspective'.

At the June 2004 NATO summit in Istanbul, the alliance therefore agreed to terminate SFOR at the end of the year. In November the UN Security Council passed a resolution (1575) authorizing the EU to launch a follow-up mission. On 25 November the EU Council agreed on a Joint Action to establish EUFOR under the rubric of Operation Althea, which took effect in December.[29] EUFOR's objectives are the same as SFOR's – essentially to ensure the implementation of the security provisions in Annexes 1A and 2 of the Dayton Accords. Being an EU mission, however, it is necessarily also closely associated with the broader, long-term objective of bringing Bosnia and its Balkan neighbours into the EU.

As was the case with Concordia, the European Union Force Commander reports to Deputy SACEUR in Mons. Overall decision-making authority lies with the EU Council, while under it the Political and Security Committee exercises day-to-day political control and strategic direction and the EU Military Committee, in turn, oversees the military side of operations. Like Concordia, Althea is a Berlin-Plus mission, making use of NATO institutions and assets. It consults and shares intelligence with the alliance at all levels, both in Brussels and in the field, where NATO retains a small but visible presence in security-sector reform, counter-terrorism and the pursuit of accused war criminals. Like its two NATO predecessors, finally, EUFOR has included contingents from non-NATO and non-EU countries, although most of the initial complement of 7,000 troops was contributed by the UK, Germany and the other larger EU member-states. At the outset, the majority of these were simply re-hatted contingents carried over from SFOR.

Six years after its initial deployment, EUFOR Althea remains in place. To date it has faced no serious challenges to its authority or its capacities. While the Bosnian political system continues to verge on the dysfunctional, the security environment is largely stable, such that a reconfiguration of EUFOR (in 2007) and subsequent cuts to personnel had reduced its force complement to about 2,200 by early 2010. By November 2010, when the UN Security Council renewed the mission's mandate for a further twelve months, that number had dropped to about 1,500, in the form of a multinational manoeuvre battalion based in Sarajevo and a number of small liaison and observation teams in other parts of the country. EUFOR can also call for support from abroad, including NATO forces still in Kosovo.

Throughout its existence, EUFOR's role in Bosnia-Herzegovina has frequently been adjusted and refined. It continues the work it inherited from NATO's SFOR: deterrence of threats to security and reassurance of the population remain, officially, its priority tasks. In practice, it has devoted as much time to assisting with refugee returns (although that process is winding down), electoral supervision, security sector reform, police training and the hunt for accused war criminals.[30] The fight against organized crime, with its links to political corruption and its transnational reach, was for some time one of EUFOR's principal tasks, deploying the Integrated Police Unit (IPU) it inherited from SFOR. In 2006, however, more of this work was devolved to the EUPM in order to disentangle the roles of the two EDSP missions in Bosnia. A distinction is now more clearly drawn between EUFOR's 'executive' functions, where it may take direct action to deter or suppress threats to the domestic order, and its 'non-executive' functions which, as of January 2010, are to include support for capacity-building and training of the Bosnian armed forces.[31]

In most of these areas EUFOR works in partnership with other international agencies, including the UNHCR, NATO, the UN, and the Hague Tribunal, as well as with the Bosnian defence ministry. The Balkans in general, and Bosnia in particular, remain thickly populated with such actors, whose roles and ambitions occasionally overlap. The EU is, however, the acknowledged lead international agency in the region. Over the past decade it has driven and overseen the Stability Pact for South Eastern Europe – succeeded in early 2008 by the Regional Cooperation Council – and encouraged the western Balkan states in their 'European vocation' through Stabilization and Association Agreements and the promise of eventual membership negotiations. In Bosnia, however, the EU's presence is especially intense. In addition to the two ESDP missions and a panoply of other EU agencies, its Special Representative, who is also the international community's High Representative, retains some residual governing powers in the name of the international protectorate established under Dayton. It is not surprising that problems of coordination have arisen from time to time between EUFOR and some of the other players on this crowded field.

Over the past three years, there has been a muted debate among the EU's member states as to whether and when EUFOR Althea might be terminated. The argument for ending the mission stresses that the sort of security threat against which EUFOR was needed to provide deterrence, insurance, and defence is no longer likely to arise. The real security threats now come from trafficking of money, drugs, weapons, and people, and the nexus between organized crime and war criminals. As destabilizing and draining as these problems might be to the Bosnian state, it is argued, they are dealt with better by policing and intelligence than by military forces. Others caution that it is premature, given the ethnic tensions that continue to poison much of Bosnian politics, to declare the central mission accomplished. This debate continues amid general agreement that EUFOR Althea has been a very successful peace operation.[32]

Tracing Strategic Culture in the Balkan Missions

The two European Union military missions to the western Balkans have much in common, however much they may differ in ambition, scale and duration. Each was mounted early in the life of the ESDP, as a follow-on to an NATO mission that had dramatically, if not completely, dampened down significant threats to the domestic security of a Yugoslav successor state. In pursuing their carefully delimited objectives each had to operate in a complex of multilateral security and development agencies, and in the framework of the EU's programme of stabilization, association and ultimate accession for the states of the region. It would be too much to expect either of these missions to serve as the definitive showcase of an emergent EU strategic culture. It should, nevertheless, be possible to detect intimations of its central ideas, even in those early days. It is not a matter of using these cases to 'prove' the existence – let alone the causal force – of a European strategic culture, but of tracing in their conduct the dominant themes evoked by those seeking to articulate such a culture.

First, the discourse of European strategic culture is consistent in identifying the prime threats to Europe's and the world's security. Of the five listed in the ESS, the two Balkan missions were squarely aimed at three: regional conflict (in these cases the resurgence of inter-ethnic violence); state failure (as a consequence of chronic domestic disorder); and transnational organized crime. Terrorism, first on the ESS list, was less prominent, although there was concern about some Albanian groups, as well as residual 'jihadists' in Bosnia. Only the proliferation of WMD did not really figure among the threats engaging these two missions.

Second, the objectives set out for both Concordia and Althea were clear, limited and consistent with the interests and values of the EU's member states. In the formation and execution of these two missions there was strong evidence of the 'convergence' in these matters proclaimed at the declaratory level in the ESS and elsewhere. Of course, the modest ambitions of each mission helped in this respect, as did two other factors. The first was the strong awareness among proponents of the ESDP that these were tests that it must not fail. The second was that, as successors to NATO missions in which many EU members had participated, both were unlikely to embody objectives at odds with those they had already been pursuing.

Third, the geographic setting was in that most uncomfortably intimate quarter of the EU's designated neighbourhood, the Balkans. Eastern Europe, the Caucasus, the Middle East and the Mediterranean mattered, of course, but by 2003 among these officially proclaimed 'neighbours', only states in the Balkans had been granted the prospect of membership. There was also a sense that for Brussels the Balkans represented unfinished business – an exercise in redemption for the failures of 1992–1995 and a way back from its marginalization at Dayton. The two police assistance missions that followed Concordia, and the EUPM, which has been in Bosnia even longer than Althea, add to the evidence that the EU's strategic culture continues to give geopolitical priority to the nearest of its 'near abroad'.

Fourth, both Balkan military missions resonated to the theme of 'effective multilateralism', so prominent in the discourse of Europe's strategic culture.[33] For both, the foundation for this was authorization by the UN Security Council. It is worth recalling that in 2003 we were still in the early days of an emerging practice – seen first in Africa – in which the Security Council would delegate (occasionally after the fact) the maintenance of peace to a regional organization, as envisaged by the rarely invoked Chapter Eight of the UN Charter. Beyond this, as already noted, these missions both followed more robust and largely successful NATO operations. After the handovers, vestiges of NATO remained in both Macedonia and Bosnia. While this presence was an aid to intelligence gathering and signalled the availability of backup, it also gave rise to some coordination problems and perhaps undermined the EU's efforts to be accepted as the 'new sheriff'.

Problems of coordination, of course, went well beyond the EU–NATO relationship. With so many international agencies on the ground, involved in security-sector reform, human rights, refugee issues, and development, multilateralism is the name of the game. 'Effectiveness' is an aspiration not yet fully realized.

Fifth, another prominent theme of the European strategic-culture literature is 'coherence', which is, in a sense, the intra-EU equivalent of effective multilateralism. Its primary reference is to the need for a comprehensive approach to security and state-building, in which the military arm of the EU (the ESDP mission) works in seamless coordination with its civilian side – itself a multifaceted presence, including representatives of the Commission charged with overseeing each country's progress through the successive processes of stabilization, association and application for membership, as well as, in Bosnia, the EUPM and the powerful office of the EU Special Representative. Moreover, given the likelihood that certain member states will continue to pursue their own agendas in the region, it is not surprising to see increasing calls for greater coherence and comprehensiveness in EU operations,[34] although it is not evident that the 'coherence deficit' is worse in the Balkans, or in the European Union, than elsewhere.

Sixth, most elaborations of Europe's strategic culture have something to say about the EU as a 'civilian power' which, notwithstanding its acquisition of an institutionalized military arm, continues to use 'soft power' as its primary mode of influence and to seek 'human security' as its primary goal.[35] Some may see this as making a virtue of necessity, since that military arm remains underdeveloped. Others will defend it as a realistic assessment of the present global security environment, which demands a large measure of non-military capacity. Still others will note that both Concordia and Althea have ended up devoting the majority of their resources to what are, in effect, soft-power tasks in aid of enhanced human security. There is, however, a certain tension in the discourse on Europe's strategic culture, where an insistence on the uniqueness and importance of the soft-power, human-security agenda coexists uneasily with calls for a robust EU military army making full use of its member states' considerable capabilities.

This leads to the seventh, and last, point. The supreme aspiration of the strategic-culture discourse is that Europe establish itself as a recognized global player, willing and able to share responsibility for regional and global security. Whatever the stated aims of the two Balkan military missions, then, they have borne the additional burden of establishing the EU's credibility as a provider of military security. It could hardly be overlooked that each was descended from a NATO mission and would have to call for the alliance's assistance in the event of a dire emergency. That said, the two missions were an attempt to, as soon as possible, demonstrate that the new ESDP meant a Europe that was increasingly able to deploy quickly and decisively, that had access to a large pool of sophisticated military assets, and that was capable of serious commitment to a long, expensive and arduous mission when and where necessary. Concordia's part in this demonstration was to get out of the gate quickly, as soon as the Berlin-Plus agreement was finalized and even before Solana's draft of the ESS was circulated. EUFOR Althea's contribution has of course been more substantial: a major commitment of troops over eight years (and counting) and a suite of security-related tasks beyond the fundamental one of providing a secure environment for the transformation of the Bosnian state.

Conclusion

This article has proceeded from the expectation that if we know how and where to look for it, we are likely to discover that the European Union has acquired at least the rudiments of a distinctive strategic culture. It has argued that since the core of a culture consists of ideas about the world – perceptions, normative preferences, visions for the future, prescriptions for action – it is appropriate to seek the EU's strategic culture first in the world of words. Official documents and the commentary that surrounds them, attempting to define, develop, and direct common foreign and security policy, are the starting point – the wellsprings of declaratory strategic culture. They are the manifestations of an intellectual, psychological, and political process through which, over time, a compromise may be reached among the interests and values of 27 member states. To be of any use as a guide to security and defence policy – whether to direction or to interpretation – that compromise must have produced something reasonably clear, distinctive, and coherent – not an easy task. It should provide a strategic reading of the international system, complete with threats, policy priorities and a vision for the future.

But a culture is also a way of living and doing. In the absence of any plausible theory linking culture as cause with policy as effect, actions themselves can at least provide further evidence – beyond words – of the existence and the constituent elements of a strategic culture. There must be a presumption of consistency here: we ought to be surprised and look for explanations if there is a striking lack of fit between what is said and what is done. The 24 missions so far conducted under the auspices of the European Union's Security and Defence Policy are the obvious – if not necessarily the only – actions to examine for traces of a nascent strategic culture. Taken in aggregate, they reveal a pattern that is indeed broadly congruent with the ideas expressed in the ESS. Only the geographical distribution of missions and the ratio of military to civilian actions seem somewhat at odds with the rhetoric. A closer analysis of the two ESDP military missions to the Balkans strengthens the general impression of consistency between words and deeds, although EUFOR Althea, as a long-running mission with major capabilities and multiple tasks, is the more revealing of the two with respect to signs of a EU strategic culture in action.

As Cornish and Edwards suggested in their seminal article, there are other forms of action that can provide markers for the existence and elements of a European strategic culture. In particular, they single out the development of capabilities and policy processes.[36] How and to what extent they are developed is an indicator of what matters; even more so are the disputes to which they give rise, both among the European Union member states and between them and, for example, their non-EU NATO allies. The theological arguments over the meaning of 'autonomy' and the more tangible disputes over command structures, the location of planning cells and the sharing of assets are also rich in evidence of a European strategic culture in formation.

A final word of caution is perhaps in order. It is one thing to assert, as this article does, that gaining as full and clear a picture as possible of the European Union's strategic culture would be of great value in understanding its security and defence policy, whether that understanding be interpretive or causal. There is a parallel here with using personality or 'character' to understand the actions of individuals. But states and other international actors may be as capable as human beings of acting 'out of character'. Any account of the EU's policy that does not make allowance for the realist calculus of power, for the path-dependent momentum of institutions, or for the random, unpredictable quality of events, is bound to remain incomplete.

NOTES

1. European Communities, 'Treaty on European Union', Brussels-Luxembourg, 1992, Article B.
2. European Union, 'A Secure Europe in a Better World: European Security Strategy', Brussels, 12 December 2003.
3. For the new language agreed at Lisbon, see European Union, 'Consolidated Version of the Treaty on European Union', Brussels, March 2010, Article 42, paragraphs 2 and 6. This article uses the earlier designation, ESDP, since both military missions to be discussed were initiated before Lisbon.
4. John Lewis Gaddis, *Strategies of Containment: A Critical Appraisal of Postwar American National Security Policy* (Oxford: Oxford University Press, 1982), p.viii.
5. From the collapse of the initiative for a European Defence Community in 1954 until the end of the Cold War, a common defence was virtually a taboo topic for the architects of European integration. On its re-emergence, see Anand Menon, Anthony Forster and William Wallace, 'A Common European Defence?', *Survival*, Vol. 34, No. 3 (1992), pp. 98–118.
6. Jack L. Snyder, *The Soviet Strategic Culture: Implications for Limited Nuclear Operations* (Santa Monica, CA: RAND, 1977), p. 8.
7. European Union, 'Report on the Implementation of the European Security Strategy: Providing Security in a Changing World', Brussels, 11 December 2008.
8. Sven Biscop and Joel Coelmont, 'A Strategy for CSDP: Europe's Ambitions as a Global Security Provider', *Egmont Paper* 37, Academia Press for the Royal Institute for International Relations, Gent, October 2010.
9. EU, 'European Security Strategy' (note 2), pp. 3–5.
10. *Ibid.*, pp. 11–14.
11. Paul Cornish and Geoffrey Edwards, 'The Strategic Culture of the European Union: A Progress Report', *International Affairs*, Vol. 81, No. 4 (July 2005), p. 802.
12. Charles Grant, 'Is Europe Doomed to Fail as a Power?', *CER Essays* (Brussels: Centre for European Reform, July 2008), p. 18. On the military diffidence of some EU members, see also Biscop and Coelmont (note 8), pp. 22–23.

13. Alvaro de Vasconcelos (ed), 'A Strategy for EU Foreign Policy', Report No. 7, European Union Institute for Security Studies, Paris, June 2010, pp. 3, 9–10.
14. Alastair Iain Johnston, in *Cultural Realism, Strategic Culture and Grand Strategy in Chinese History* (Princeton, NJ: Princeton University Press, 1995), views strategic culture as distinct from, and potentially accounting for, foreign policy behaviour, while Colin Gray takes behaviour to be part of culture. For comment on this debate, see Colin Gray, 'Out of the Wilderness: Prime Time for Strategic Culture', *Comparative Strategy*, Vol. 26, No. 1 (January–February 2007), pp. 2–3, and David G. Haglund, 'What Good is Strategic Culture?', in Jeannie L. Johnson, Kerry M. Kartchner, and Jeffrey A. Larsen (eds), *Strategic Culture and Weapons of Mass Destruction: Culturally Based Insights into Comparative National Security Policymaking* (New York: Palgrave Macmillan, 2009), pp. 15–31.
15. For concise accounts of these missions, see Giovanni Grevi, Damien Helly and Daniel Keohane (eds), *European Security and Defence Policy: The First Ten Years (1999-2009)* (Paris: European Union Institute for Strategic Studies, 2009).
16. On 'civilian power', see Christopher Hill, 'European Foreign Policy: Power Bloc, Civilian Bloc, or Flop?', in Reinhardt Rummel (ed), *The Evolution of an International Actor: Western Europe's New Assertiveness* (Boulder, CO: Westview Press, 1990), pp. 31–55, and Alex Lofthouse and David Long, 'The EU and the Civilian Model of Foreign Policy', *Journal of European Integration*, Vol. 19, Nos. 2–3 (1996), pp. 181–96.
17. Including the anti-piracy mission EUNAVFOR off the Somali coast and counting the Support To AMIS mission in Darfur as half-military gives a total of $5\frac{1}{2}$ military and $4\frac{1}{2}$ civilian missions in Africa.
18. For a critical view of the EU's response to Libya, see Ana Gomes, 'Was EUFOR Libya an April Fool's Joke?', *EUObserver*, 13 July 2011; a more optimistic view can be found in Thomas Valasek, 'What Libya says about the Future of the Atlantic Alliance', *CER Essays* (London: Centre for European Reform, July 2011). Valasek's essay is partially a response to the criticism of NATO Europe voiced in June by the outgoing American Secretary of Defence. See 'Transcript of Defense Secretary Gates's Speech on NATO's Future', *The Wall Street Journal*, 20 June 2011.
19. For an earlier assessment of Operation Concordia, see Annalisa Monaco, 'Operation Concordia and Berlin Plus: NATO and the EU Take Stock', *NATO Notes*, Vol. 5, No. 8, International Security Service Europe, Brussels, December 2003. On Operation Althea, see Frank Kupferschmidt, 'EU and NATO as "Strategic Partners": the Balkans Experience', in Peter Schmidt (ed.), *A Hybrid Relationship: Transatlantic Security Cooperation Beyond NATO* (Frankfurt am Main: Peter Lang, 2008), pp. 127–46.
20. See International Crisis Group, 'Macedonia: No Room for Complacency', *European Report*, No. 149, 23 October 2003; for the broader context see Misha Glenny, 'The Kosovo Question and Regional Stability', in Judy Batt (ed), 'The Western Balkans: Moving On', *Chaillot Papers*, No. 70, EUISS, Paris, October 2004, especially pp. 92–94.
21. EU authorization was by Council Joint Action 2003/92/CFSP, 27 January 2003.
22. A concise account of the Berlin-Plus agreements can be found in the *NATO Handbook* (Brussels: NATO Public Diplomacy Division, 2006), pp. 248–9.
23. Eva Gross, 'EU Military Operation in the Former Yugoslav Republic of Macedonia (Concordia)', in Grevi, Helly and Keohane, *European Security and Defence Policy* (note 15), pp. 175–7.
24. *Ibid.*, pp. 177–80.
25. *Ibid.*, p. 174.
26. See Arnold Kammel's article, 'Putting Ideas into Action: EU Civilian Crisis Management in the Western Balkans', *Contemporary Security Policy*, Vol. 32, No. 3 (2011) for details.
27. On the establishment of Althea, see Thomas Bertin, 'The EU Military Operation in Bosnia', in Michael Merlingen and Rasa Ostrauskaite (eds), *European Security and Defence Policy: An Implementation Perspective*, (Abingdon: Routledge, 2008), pp. 61–77.
28. On the debate over NATO's future, see Ivo Daalder and James Goldgeier, 'Global NATO', *Foreign Affairs*, Vol. 85, No. 5 (September–October 2006), pp. 105–14.
29. Council Joint Action 2004/803/CFSP, 25 November 2004.
30. Daniel Keohane, 'The European Union Military Operation in Bosnia and Herzegovina (Althea)' in Grevi, Helly, and Keohane, *European Security and Defence Policy* (note 15), pp. 216–7.
31. *Ibid.*, pp. 217–8.
32. On the success and prospects of EUFOR, see Kupferschmidt, 'EU and NATO as "Strategic Partners"' (note 19), pp. 130–3, and Keohane, 'The European Military Operation in Bosnia and Herzegovina' (note 30), pp. 218–20.
33. See EU, 'Report on the Implementation of the ESS' (note 7), pp. 9–12, and de Vasconcelos, 'A Strategy for EU Foreign Policy' (note 13), pp. 4–5 and 16–17.

34. See, for example, de Vasconcelos, 'A Strategy for EU Foreign Policy' (note 13), passim.
35. *Ibid*, pp. 15–19. On interests and values in EU foreign policy see also Albert Bressand, 'Between Kant and Machiavelli: EU Foreign Policy Priorities in the 2010s', *International Affairs*, Vol. 87, No. 1 (January 2011), pp. 59–85.
36. Cornish and Edwards, 'The Strategic Culture of the European Union' (note 11), pp. 802–6 and 810–14.

The EU's Military Involvement in the Democratic Republic of Congo: Security Culture, Interests and Games

PETER SCHMIDT

Strategic culture (SC) is a vague concept.[1] Used in the 1970s to explain differences between the United States and the Soviet Union with regard to nuclear strategy,[2] it was then extended to the function of the military in international relations by states in general and – especially with regard to the European Union – also to the influence of 'soft power instruments' in security policy.[3] The methodological status of the concept is also contested: strategic culture is seen variously as a 'cause', as sheer 'context' or, as David Haglund proposes in this volume, as 'cognition'. In addition, as Charles Pentland points out, there is a question of whether a concept that originated in the analysis of the behaviour of states may be applied to the EU, with 27 member states and a still curious mix of inter-governmental and communitarian decision-making. Some commentators have therefore looked at the European Union's SC as a two-level system.[4] As we will see, the situation is even more complex: when it comes to the deployment of troops, the UN must be included as a third level in order to get a meaningful understanding of the EU's behaviour with regard to the use of the military. This study has, however, a specific focus which allows one to avoid some of the intricacies of the SC concept. It covers two cases of EU military operations in the Democratic Republic of Congo. By this it is therefore indicated that I refer to use of the military only and place 'soft instruments' apart.

A conference at the American-based Center for Contemporary Conflict in 2006 reached a consensus on a definition on strategic culture, which is taken as a starting point. Strategic culture is understood as 'a set of shared beliefs, assumptions, and modes of behavior, derived from common experiences and accepted narratives (both oral and written), that shape collective identity and relationships to other groups, and which determine appropriate ends and means for achieving security objectives.'[5]

From a methodological point of view, this approach understands strategic culture as a 'system of preferences' and not as a concept for the explanation or understanding of specific decisions: it only represents a – sometimes – contradictory context for the employment of military forces abroad. In order to make it a useful tool for the understanding of the EU's behaviour, specific interests, which might even overrule SC premises, must be taken into account alongside the way in which the decision-making 'game' is played across the various levels.

Against this background, the following analysis aims at answering the following questions: 1) Is there something that can be called strategic culture – not just a concept on paper, but something that plays a role 'in action', regardless of the fact that member states have the major say in defence affairs? 2) What are the constituent 'preferences' of this culture? 3) How does the interaction between general preferences, particular interests and the way the 'game' is played influence operations?

We will see that, regardless of the fact that member states have the major say in defence affairs, one can indeed recognize some sort of European SC, including a strong emphasis on supporting peace in Africa. The extent and form of European military engagement alongside the UN in Africa seems, however, to remain a disputed matter, though, especially between France and Germany.[6]

The analysis is an explorative one, with its well-known limitations: generalizations are very tentative and, in the case of the European Union, later changes with regard to the institutional and legal framework, such as those brought into being by the Lisbon Treaty, may well have an influence on member states' behaviour in later operations. From today's perspective, however, major changes are not discernible.

Artemis

EUFOR Artemis (12 June–1 September 2003) was the second military operation after EUFOR Concordia. Whereas Concordia was based on the Berlin-Plus agreement, meaning it relied on NATO assets and support,[7] Artemis was the first fully independent military operation undertaken by the Union and the first one outside of Europe. It came as a response to Under-Secretary General for Peacekeeping Operations Jean-Marie Guéhenno's raising of the first call for international intervention on 9 May 2003.[8] UN Secretary-General Kofi Annan endorsed this afterwards through an appeal to the international community to provide support to the large UN operation (MONUC). The UN forces were not able to provide sufficient security for Congo. The situation was especially severe in the Ituri region, where the UN estimated 500,000 displaced and 60,000 casualties. The 712 Uruguayan UN troops were much too few to address the problem of security sufficiently.[9] Kofi Annan's request came on 30 May 2003 and the EU agreed on a 'joint action' on 5 June 2003. The short space of time between Guéhenno's and Annan's requests, the Council's decision and the deployment of 500 French troops in Bunia only one day later indicates that the mission on the French side was not only militarily but also politically well-prepared by substantial informal communication on all involved political levels.[10]

Artemis is a clear indication not only of the fact that military involvement in Africa is part of France's strategic culture, but also its strong interest in restoring its influence in the Great Lake Region, where French interests had been waning in the years before the operation.[11] After French colonies gained independence in the 1960s, France signed bilateral treaties with many of them, containing various degrees of military cooperation. In the 1970s this system of treaties was expanded to more countries, including the Democratic Republic of Congo. France was – and still is – militarily engaged in the neighbouring Central African Republic.[12] It was no surprise that France restarted its military cooperation with the DR Congo just after Operation Artemis.[13] These agreements and its ongoing military presence indicate that engagement in many parts of Africa was indeed one of France's major foreign policy preferences.

France not only contributed the bulk of forces on the ground (about 2000 troops, roughly 85 per cent) but was also appointed Framework Nation, while the Operational Headquarters was located in Paris (*Centre de Planification et de Conduite des Operations*) and a French general, Bruno Neveux, was appointed Operation Commander. In addition, France had already prepared detailed contingency plans for a national operation, on which the European Union operation later relied strongly.[14] Other countries' contributions were minimal: 70 Swedish troops and 100 British engineers are 'outstanding' figures in this context. The composition of the Operation HQ personnel in Paris, however, was far more multinational, with almost 50 per cent of the staff coming from other European Union member states.[15] Despite this, Artemis was basically a French operation in a European Union framework. Beyond France's specific interest of restoring its influence in the region, there were at least two French strategic preferences related to this operation: to engage the EU alongside French interests in Africa, which – in general – was the foremost reason for France to push forward the EU's defence dimension; and to run European Union operations without NATO's support, which was for the French defence community an objective that goes without saying.[16]

It is revealing to contrast the French approach with that of Germany. The latter country took a cautious approach to participation in Artemis – partly because of its traditional anxiety about contributing to combat operations, and partly because Artemis looked very much like a French operation in European Union disguise.[17] Its reluctance was heightened by the specific German strategic culture and the fear that France would use the European Security and Defence Policy (ESDP) to promote primarily its own interests. Indeed, while Germany's strategic culture developed throughout the 1990s – moving from a 'culture of reticence' to become increasingly robust through, for example, the deployment of forces to the Balkans in the 1990s and to Afghanistan in the new century – Africa has never represented a strategic preference for German military operations.[18]

However, this German lack of strategic interest in Africa was overruled by three general political preferences. All three referred to long-standing elements of German foreign policy: European integration, support of the UN, humanitarian values: a) The German government felt a certain need to demonstrate European togetherness after the major split among European countries with regard to US policy towards Iraq.[19] b) The operation was properly legitimized by the UN Security Council, which was from Germany's vantage point not only a prerequisite for an operation but also a certain obligation to support it. c) The objective of the operation was to stop a humanitarian crisis.

Germany's approval of Operation Artemis was therefore based on partly contradictory preferences which were part of Germany's strategic culture. Beyond the political acceptance of the operation, there was very limited physical support for the operation: two staff officers were engaged in the Operational Headquarters, some Transall C-160 provided air transport capability (30 sorties) and Germany also offered capacities for strategic transport and transport capacity for bringing injured soldiers home (neither of which were required in the end).

What does this tell us from the strategic culture point of view? We will discuss this question by referring to Simon Duke's analysis. He argues that the European Union has an SC and, in the case of Artemis, identifies an 'abundant normative "framing" of the decision-making environment'[20] as a major cause of the EU's military involvement. For a proper understanding of the matter, we also have to discuss the methodological status of Duke's notion of 'framing',[21] which is another contextual expression widely used in SC studies to explain the methodological status of the analysis.

According to the SC approach, Simon Duke argues that the 'extent of the normative commitments, ranging from the TEU[22] and its invocation of the United Nations Charter, to the more specific commitments made at St Malo and Le Touquet, all created the expectation of support, if not actual physical involvement'[23] and concludes that 'it would therefore have been difficult for any EU member to adopt a "no action" position...'[24].

The situation is, however, more complex than is assumed by Duke, mainly because of the multi-level character of the decision-making in this case. What looks obvious is that this general approach is not unique to the European Union. In its vagueness, this approach is formally accepted by all European Union state signatories of the UN Charter and, indeed, by the UN itself. Against this background, Artemis looked more like a 'coalition of willing' using the EU as a platform than an operation based on a specific SC of the European Union as a whole. In addition, France was in the driving seat and only six member states accepted the operation by actively taking part.[25] The majority of EU states appeared to give reluctant backing, although they did not oppose the general idea of an operation. There were clearly different understandings of situations in which use of the national military is appropriate. Through this the existence of different national SCs in the European Union became evident.[26]

In addition, the summits in St Malo (1998) and Touquet (2003), which were taken by Simon Duke as reference points for the African focus of the ESDP, were not European Union summits but meetings of the French and British governments only.[27] The outcome of both conferences was an emphasis on ESDP operations in Africa, an emphasis which was not shared to the same extent by other member states. For example, Germany saw ESDP primarily as a further step in the European integration process, not something that was meant to deal primarily with African contingencies. In addition, the use of the military in crisis management was greatly restricted by Germany's SC and by the very fact that the employment of military assets has to be accepted by the German parliament.

One should also not overlook that the first initiative at the United Nations level was taken by the French Deputy-Secretary General, Jean-Marie Guéhenno. He may not have acted on behalf of the French government; however, it is plausible that as part of French diplomatic culture he may be very open to the French approach to matters, which includes a 'culture of intervention' in Africa: between 1960 and 2006, France launched 37 major military operations in Francophone sub-Saharan Africa.[28] In addition, as a permanent member of the UN's Security Council,

France had plenty of opportunities to promote its views. Taking this into consideration, Operation Artemis should be regarded as an operation based on French interests and SC implemented in the framework of the European Union, rather than one primarily based on a European strategic culture.[29] Indeed, there was a normative context which supported the idea of an EU operation – the accepted process of building up a military capacity to be used in international crisis management was especially important in this regard. In addition to differences regarding specific interests, however, it was clear that member states had dissimilar understandings of the conditions under which force should be used, and – especially – where.

There is also a need to reply to Duke's argument that it was 'difficult for any European Union member to adopt a "no action position"', by which he supports his positive view of the existence of a European Union SC. Acceptance of an operation with no substantial contribution is hardly the same as being covered by a common SC – free riders do not really share the same preferences. The policy of the reluctant states appeared to be based much more on defensive interests – seeking to ensure that the buildup of the EU's defence dimension was not disturbed or interrupted – than on the security problem at hand. Above all, the focus of most member states was avoiding any disturbance of European capacity building in a political sense, not the security problems in DR Congo. Most states' policies were dominated by an inward-looking approach, not an outward-looking one.[30]

As Martinsen argues in this volume, the notion of 'comprehensiveness' is the major feature of the EU's strategic culture.[31] It is, however, difficult to observe whether this principle was implemented by Artemis. Indeed, one has to take into account that the ESS was only affected in November 2003, after the end of the operation. However, the principle was already in discussion and, indeed, was in the interest of EU bodies aiming at the 'Brusselisation' of foreign and security policy by the application of a 'comprehensive approach' that integrated national policies and assets and the Commission's civilian resources in a EU framework. The EU Commission was lobbying for a military operation at this time to protect the programmes run by the Commission in the DR Congo and to safeguard its investments.[32] However, member states' limited contributions make it difficult to understand Artemis as an application of the principle of comprehensiveness, regardless of the cooperation between the EU troops and ECHO on the ground.[33] At this time, the principle could not be applied fully due to differences in member states' interests and SC.

In analysing the European Union's strategic culture, one should not overlook the role and policy of the UN's Secretary General. He does not merely represent an apolitical personality without specific interests and positions. He released the earlier discussed request to the international community with the obvious understanding that France – and possibly the entire European Union – were prepared to act. In addition, it was a good chance to put the United States at the fringes of the process,[34] as it was overstretched by the Iraq operation. Kofi Annan seemed to be interested in setting the United States aside for a time and including Europeans as partners in order to create a more positive perception of the UN after the Americans side-stepped the UN by launching their operation against Saddam Hussein without Security Council authorisation, which was regarded by the UN's Secretary General just as 'illegal'.[35] The

Secretary General's preference is to establish a special relationship with actors who support the UN as strongly as possible.

Against this background there is sufficient evidence to argue that Artemis was not 'the' product of a specific European Union strategic culture, but was primarily based on an interactive system of SCs across various levels: member states of the European Union, the European Union itself, and the United Nations. The major actor, however, was one single member state: France, which had its own specific SC and interests in the region. France acted on all levels in order to make the operation work. In addition, the UN's Secretary General had a situational interest in establishing a special relationship between the UN and the EU. That the European Union represented the framework for Artemis was due more to situational concerns than to its being a product of the European Union's SC. The European Union served as a platform of national and UN preferences. It didn't – in this case – represent a strategic actor for its own sake; the way this operation was run was much more an indication of national interests and preferences than of the preferences of the European Union.

EUFOR RD Congo

Under Secretary General of the UN Jean-Marie Guéhenno also submitted a request in the case of EUFOR RD Congo (July–November 2006[36]), this time in a formal letter sent directly to the Presidency of the EU Council, asking for a 'deterrent force' which 'could take the form of a suitably earmarked force reserve that could enhance the quick reaction capabilities of MONUC during or immediately after the electoral process'.[37] Given Germany's policy in the Artemis case, it came as a surprise that it took the lead in EUFOR RD Congo. In addition, a much more balanced structure of military contributions by member states was observable.[38] Altogether, 21 member states, plus Turkey, contributed troops. The operation incorporated approximately 2,450 soldiers, among them about 1,000 French, 780 German, and 130 each from Spain and Poland; Belgium, the former colonial power of the Congo, sent 100 soldiers.[39] This structure meant EUFOR RD Congo looked much more like a self-contained, fully-fledged EU operation than Artemis.

Germany's lead role and member states' broader and more equal participation in comparison to Artemis, however, complicated the planning and force generation process enormously. The German journal of the Bundestag, *Das Parlament*, illustrated this process in the title 'Desperate search for troops' (*Truppen verzweifelt gesucht*).[40] It took almost half a year to finalise the political decision-making process, starting with the EU's agreement of general preparedness to support the Congolese people during the transition to a democratic government on 12 December 2005 and moving to the formal request by the UN's Under-Secretary General on 27 December 2005, to the Franco-German Council meeting dealing with the issue on 14 March 2006, to the 28 March letter from the Austrian Foreign Minister on behalf of the European Council stating that the European Union was ready to deploy troops, to the UN Security Council resolution approving the European Union's readiness to deploy troops on 25 April 2006, to the 'common action' of the EU on 27 April, and culminating in the approval by the Bundestag on 6 June 2006.

One of the major reasons was that the German government – and other European Union members – were still hesitant to contribute to the operation or represent the lead nation. This time, however, Germany lost the fight against French pressure and accepted the lead role. It seems quite plausible that this was not due to Germany's interests in the region, nor to established general preferences like the commitment to 'effective multilateralism'[41] or establishing ESDP as a foreign policy tool of the European Union, but to changes in EU-UN relations.

Two relevant changes which put pressure on Germany occurred on the European Union-United Nations level. First, shortly after Operation Artemis, on 19 September 2003, the European Union and United Nations decided 'to establish a joint consultative mechanism at the working level to examine ways and means to enhance mutual co-ordination and compatibility'.[42] Second, in summer 2004 the United Nations and the European Union agreed on approaches by which the EU could operate militarily in support of the UN. Special emphasis has been placed on the 'launching and conduct of an EU operation in support of the UN' and support of the UN namely by deploying forces in order to fill an operational gap until UN forces arrive or to hold in readiness forces for the UN,[43] by which the European Union created the expectation that operations like Artemis could become relatively common.

The EU-level changes supporting the decision were the following: 1) In December 2003 member states agreed on the European Security Strategy (ESS), stipulating that the EU needed 'to develop a SC that fosters early, rapid and when necessary, robust intervention'.[44] 2) The EU's decision to generate so-called battle groups – national and (mostly) multinational units of about 1,500 soldiers on a rotational basis capable of quick reaction – also created some expectation that they would be deployed, especially should the UN be unable to act in time. 3) In December 2005 the EU approved a concept linking security and development in Africa, stipulating that 'without peace there can be no lasting development'.[45] These decisions created a set of preferences in favour of EU operations in support of the UN, especially in Africa, where most UN operations take place.

All of these changes can be understood as being part of the European Union's evolving SC. They all made it arduous for national governments – at least in the larger countries – to escape participation in a military operation on African soil, presuming that two preconditions have been met: there has to be as well a major push by an influential EU member as a formal request and authorisation by authoritative UN bodies. It may be too deterministic to brand these cases 'normative entrapment', as Simon Duke does, but the pressure on individual nations which hold significant capacities and are able to deliver indeed became substantial.

The notion of a 'push by an influential EU member' leads us, however, beyond the EU level. In the case of EUFOR RD Congo, France was once more the driving force on all levels: at the UN, the EU and in the Franco-German Security Council. France applied a strategy which could be called 'multiple bi- and multilateralism' or a 'play on many pianos'[46] and reflects the shrinking of the country's resources for foreign policy engagements. Several factors prepared the ground for the French success in overcoming other countries' reluctance – especially Germany's – including convergence of the European Union and United Nations' strategic cultures, as analysed by

Ingo Peters in this volume and expressed on the EU level by the notion of 'effective multilateralism'; the French preference to engage European partners alongside its interests in Africa; and the German view of the operation as part of European capacity building.[47]

However, this success was limited, which complicates the analysis. Germany confronted France and the European Union with concrete preconditions, indicating differences with regard not only to the national strategic cultures but also to interests. Germany's political moves counteracted the established political top-down approach of the EU's planning process, which starts with the formulation of a 'common action' by which decisions about, for example, operational headquarters and operational commanders are taken. The latter should be engaged in the establishment of the operational concept. Germany's preconditions were far-reaching:[48] 1) approval by RD Congo; 2) a robust mandate from the UN's Security Council; 3) substantial contributions by other member states, not only France and Germany, 4) limitation of the operation to the Congolese capital Kinshasa; and 5) a time frame of only four months. The mandate accepted by the Bundestag later on included even more restrictions:[49] most German forces should be stationed in nearby Gabun as so-called 'on call forces' only, and German forces could undertake evacuation operations, but only to free individuals from hazardous situations.

Through this Germany showed on the one hand its readiness in the end to represent the lead nation, and on the other its reluctance and misgivings about the operation, which surfaced during the process of formulating the concrete mandate of EUFOR RD Congo and its implementation, which occurred during a crucial phase of the election-related turmoil.[50] This can also be interpreted as a tactic by the German government aiming at avoiding, as far as possible, any conflict with the Bundestag; it can also be seen as a conflict between the nascent European SC and German interests and strategic culture.

The specifics of the situation are due to the European Union's two-level character in defence affairs. You cannot analyse the European Union's security culture without taking the national security cultures and interests – in these cases especially the French and German –into account and, just as importantly, understanding them as the driving force behind decisions on the deployment of troops. And, due to the entangling relationship between the EU and the UN, you have to incorporate the UN too. The deployment of troops in the framework of ESDP is a three-level, not a two-level, affair.

The involvement of several political levels in the decision creates a highly complicated bargaining process. The specific interests of the actors involved and the 'games' they play on various levels have an important influence on the overall outcome of the decision-making process. In the case of EUFOR RD Congo, this even suggests that Germany's lead role may have been less related to German preferences than it was to a certain level of reluctance during the negotiation process. In general terms, one has to take this situation into account in order to understand the EU's SC and specific decisions on the deployment of troops.

In the following I focus on two examples: one concerns force generation process between the European Union and the member states, while the other pertains to all three levels, but with a view from below – that is, from the concerned member states of the EU. [51]

The Barrack Yard Syndrome

As stated earlier, strategic culture, as said in the introduction, is not regarded as a deterministic concept, nor even as a simple soft independent variable. The complex nature of the European Union, an institution with 27 member states, suggests this view. In such a structure there is always some freedom of manoeuvre for individual member states when it comes to the question of deploying troops. In the case of EUFOR RD Congo and the German readiness to take the lead regardless of its lack of enthusiasm or even aversion, the way in which European Union member-state negotiations are conducted and how the players play the game had an important impact on the outcome of decision-making, and these should be regarded as part of the European Union's strategic culture.

This feature comes into the foreground when looking at the political economy of the decision-making process regarding the operation, and especially the political and financial risks of the operation for the member states. The objective of achieving political stability in RD Congo was, for many member states, a typical 'collective good': if it is achieved, every member states can enjoy its benefit whether it paid for it or not. In these kind of decision-making processes, free riders are a regular phenomenon. In order to enjoy the benefits of a 'free rider' in such a dense system of institutional cooperation like the EU, a phenomenon that can be called 'barrack yard syndrome' must be taken into account. This behaviour reflects the hypothetical reaction of a soldier to the commander's appeal: 'Volunteers to the front!' Soldiers' experience tells us that those who don't step back will be the losers. In the European Union's case, the positive cost-benefit ratio for such behaviour goes back to the regulation that about 90 per cent of the costs of the operation have to be carried by the operating countries. This explains the lengthy force generation process. On the one hand, the European Union's SC, as developed after Operation Artemis, advised all member states to actively support the UN in Africa; on the other hand the question is must be raised: who carries costs and risks? Does this include the deployment of troops? And if yes, what should the size, structure and mandate of the contingent look like?

The problem is that although European Union member states share the preferences set up in the European Union framework, they may not share the concrete interests suggesting such an operation. Germany was exposed to a contradictory set of preferences and interests: it did not share France's special interest in the region, but supported the building up of ESDP capacities and a strong European Union-United Nations relationship. The question for the German government was: why should it support French special interests in a region which was not on their list of regional preferences? This particularly explains Germany's reluctance at the beginning, its preparedness to represent the lead nation in the middle, and its desire to restrict the mandate as far as possible at the end of the decision-making process. Germany's only chance to avoid taking the lead in the operation came at the very beginning of the EUFOR discussions.

The contradictory character of Germany's strategic preferences made it not impossible, but certainly difficult for Berlin to take this step. It is interesting to note that Germany did not take part in the subsequent, also French-promoted, operation in Chad. Germany's early refusal to take part may well be understood as being based on a learning process rooted in its experience with EUFOR RD Congo.[52] Berlin started to understand how to play the game.

As we can see, EU's SC does not lead to a foreseeable outcome. You can follow wise soldiers' advice, take a step back early on and signal to partner countries that you are not ready to take on this task. Or you can wait and see, and become a captive of your non-decision.

One general lesson can, however, be drawn: If European Union bodies or member states try to compel a reluctant country to engage in a military operation, the result is quite likely to be sub-optimal.

Multilateral Caesarism

Analysing the multi-level process from the perspective of the national parliamentary institutions brings another feature of the multi-level decision-making process to the surface,[53] which also has an impact on the outcome of national and European Union decisions in the field of military deployment.

The complexity of the lengthy negotiations on and between various levels, as shown above, means there is almost no freedom of manoeuvre for national parliaments to influence the process directly – negotiations are all led by the government and members of parliament may not be easily able to follow these complex consultations, with their lack of transparency and likely need for compromise. This is especially the case in Germany, where the Bundestag has to approve every military operation. Criticism of the operation by a German member of parliament would have meant substantial opposition to the UN, the EU and the special Franco-German relationship, all – in general terms – major preferences of the German foreign policy. It is highly likely that this 'multilateral Caesarism'[54] paradoxically added to the caveats that Germany applied to EUFOR RD Congo and, through this, led to a sub-optimal outcome: the government wanted to preempt possible criticism by members of parliament displeased by a mandate which was not suited to the situation but substantially reduced the risks for the German contingent.[55]

Conclusions

While member states have the major say in defense affairs, one can indeed disclose some sort of European Union strategic culture, based on the following preferences: strengthening and supporting of the UN in certain operations and the tackling of humanitarian crises; more coherence between European Union and member states' policies; an outward-looking approach also in the military sphere; capacity building; and a stronger emphasis on supporting peace in Africa. Visible changes in this direction took place between 2003 and 2006, including the following. 1) As part of an emphasis on 'effective multilateralism', a stronger link between the European

Union and the United Nations has been established, including the possibility for the EU to support UN missions by separate military operations. 2) As part of a so-called 'comprehensive approach', an attempt was made to embed member states more closely in common European policies, the military included (battle groups). 3) EU member states agreed on the ESS emphasising the need for outward-looking actions of the EU, including, if necessary, support of robust intervention by the development of national and multinational military units which are capable of quick reaction. 4) A stronger emphasis on Africa's security dimension.

The above mentioned evolution has created a strategic culture which is focused not only on the European Union, but also on interaction between member states, the EU and the UN; the European Union's SC may be understood as a system of outreaches to member states and the UN. The system can be dubbed a 'cultural space'. This assessment is close to Andrew Moravcik's view that 'the relationship of states to the domestic and transnational social context in which they are embedded [...] ha[s] a fundamental impact on state behavior in world politics'.[56] However, as shown by the two cases above, when the deployment of military forces is at stake, member states' policy and their respective SCs play the predominant role. The preferences established on the EU level may not be understood as a deterministic concept. We have to realise that it is impossible in this field to detach the EU's strategic culture from national versions and concrete national interests. The two cases suggest that member states' SCs share some of the EU's preferences in the military field, but only some. During Artemis and EUFOR RD Congo, it became clear that the overarching SC does not replace the national ones. From a national viewpoint, and in the cases above especially from a French perspective, the European Union system enlarges the outreach and potential of member states, but at the same time constrains EU members' freedom of manoeuvre.

This applies particularly to France and Germany. Military activity in Africa is part of France's SC and interests, but not Germany's, as demonstrated in the recent Libyan case, too. This did not prevent the two operations, but did have a substantial impact on the quantity and quality of Germany's and France's contributions and the overall mandate of the troops. This became evident during EUFOR RD Congo, when Germany was the lead nation: the mandate disclosed Germany as a reluctant ally in Africa.

It became also obvious that a lot of 'games' go on, on various levels: bottom-up, from member states to the United Nations, and top-down, from the UN to the European Union and member states. In the two cases analysed, it was certainly France that was in the driving seat and attempting to steer the development of the EU's strategic culture in its preferred direction. Antoine Sadoux accordingly designated the three functions of Common Foreign and Security Policy from a French point of view: 1) To involve European partners in military operations in Africa, in order to fill French military gaps; 2) To eliminate through European operations prejudice against French engagement; 3) To consolidate French efforts at military cooperation through multilateral programs.[57] France wishes to establish a close relationship between the European Union's SC and French interests and preferences. From the top down, UN requests for military EU engagements in Africa were based not only on 'need', but also on political considerations about establishment of a UN-European relationship apart from the United States.

There is no space to analyse the 'games' played across all levels in great detail. Taking the view from states upwards, two features of these 'games' can be understood as part of the type of strategic culture which could be identified during the two European Union missions. The first one, the 'barrack yard syndrome', is an indication of the volatile force-generation process of ESDP at that time. This is a consequence of the fact that the European Union does not represent a single actor and of the heavy hand played by the member states in this area. One could argue that this type of 'syndrome' cannot be regarded as part of a 'system of preferences', as it is too much a hidden feature of the EU's political decision-making processes. This argument cannot be easily refuted. There is, however, one overarching principle of the EU's force generation process which is decisive for the EU's military engagements, which better suits the definition of SC: flexibility. Indeed, with regard to the question of whether and how member states take part in an operation, flexibility can be considered to be part of the 'preferences' of the European Union's military engagements.

It is more difficult to situate the second feature, 'multilateral Caesarism', under the umbrella of SC. Indeed, it is apparent that 'multilateral Caesarism' is not a formulated concept but much more an unintended consequence[58] of the political structure established by European Union member states in the area of security and defence. However, it has had a significant impact on the formulation of the EU, and especially the mandate for the German forces. In addition, it may well be regarded as a permanent feature for the system. This author feels that changing the definition and including this as an unintended but permanent feature of decision-making in this field would create a more meaningful understanding of strategic culture.

NOTES

1. Melanie Graham rightly writes in reference to a conference which was held at the American-based Center for Contemporary Conflict in 2006 to address the ongoing debate over a definition of strategic culture: 'While it is gratifying that consensus was reached at the conference, the agreed upon definition still leaves much to be desired as a tool or analytic process for identifying and comparing specific strategic cultures in any reliable or verifiable manner. What are the common experiences that are relevant? What identifies narratives as valid in terms of shaping a collective identity?' Melanie Graham, 'Defining Strategic Culture: A Thesis Prospectus', University of Northern British Columbia and Royal Roads University, 1 October 2007, p. 6.
2. Jack Snyder, *The Soviet Strategic Culture: Implications for Nuclear Options* (Santa Monica, CA: RAND Corporation, 1977).
3. See, for example, Sven Biscop, 'The ABC of European Union Strategy: Ambition, Benchmark, Culture', Royal Institute for International Relations, Brussels, October 2007, pp. 17–21.
4. See, for example, Michael Smith, 'Toward a Theory of EU Foreign Policy-making: Multi-level Governance, Domestic Politics, and National Adaptation to Europe's Common Foreign and Security Policy', *Journal of European Public Policy*, Vol. 11, No. 4 (2004), pp. 740–758.
5. Darryl Howlett, 'The Future of Strategic Culture', Defence Reduction Agency Advanced Systems and Concepts Office, Comparative Strategic Culture Curriculm Contract No. DTRA01-03-D-0017, Technical Instruction, 18 June 2002.
6. This study focuses on Germany and France. The reasons: a) France is the major European player in Congo and was the foremost 'demandeur' of European operations in RD Congo; b) Germany is the major member state with a skeptical view on military engagements in Africa, despite having taken

the lead in EUFOR RD Congo. In this way it is possible to show the major features of the EU's SC without being forced to analyse the approaches of most or all member states.

7. See Eva Gross, 'Operation Concordia', in Giovanni Grevi, Damien Helly and Daniel Keohane (eds), *European Security and Defence Policy. The First 10 Years (1999-2009)* (Paris: Institute for Security Studies, 2009), pp. 173–180.
8. See Paraswchos Lianos, 'European Strategic Culture: Assessing the ESDP Years (1998-2005)', PhD thesis, University of Leicester, 2008.
9. See Simon Duke, 'Consensus Building in ESDP: Lessons of Operation Artemis', European Institute Working Paper 09-07, Dublin, July 2008, p. 11.
10. See *ibid.*, pp. 12ff. and Peter Petrov, 'Early Institutionalization of the ESDP Governance Arrangements: Insights From Operation Concordia and Artemis', in Vanhoonacker, Sophie Hylke Dijstra and Heide Maurer (eds), 'Understanding the Role of Bureaucracy in the European Security and Defence Policy', *European Integration online Papers (EIoP)*, Special Issue, Vol. 14, No. 1, p. 10, http://eiop.or.at/eiop/texte/2010-008a.htm (accessed 20 April 2011).
11. See Duke, 'Consensus Building' (note 9), p. 17.
12. Today France maintains about 230 troops in the CAR capital Bangui. See 'France Seeks New Military Deal with Africa, *Defence Web*, 21 June 2010, http://www.defenceweb.co.za/index.php?option=com_content&view=article&id=8560:france-seeks-new-military-deal-with-africa-&catid=56:Multi-National & Inter-Agency&Itemid = 111 (accessed 20 April 2011).
13. See http://www.diplomatie.gouv.fr/fr/pays-zones-geo_833/republique-democratique-du-congo_376/france-republique-democratique-du-congo_1219/presentation_3672/index.html (accessed 20 April 2011).
14. See Petrov, 'Early Institutionalization' (note 10), p. 8.
15. See Lianos, 'European Strategic Culture' (note 8), p. 212.
16. See Peter Schmidt, 'Frankreichs Schwierigkeiten mit den Vereinigten Staaten und der NATO - Entwicklungstrends einer mühsamen Partnerschaft', in Jens van Scherpenberg and Peter Schmidt (eds), *Stabilität und Kooperation: Aufgaben internationaler Ordnungspolitik* (Baden-Baden: Nomos, 2000), pp. 245–246.
17. See Duke, *Consensus Building* (note 9), p. 21.
18. Peter Schmidt, 'Stability Operation and Alliance Management – The German View', Paper for the Senior Course on Security Policy in a New Europe, Swedish National Defence College, April 2009; Sebastian Harnisch and Raimund Wolf, 'Germany – The Continuity of Change', in Emil Kirchner and James Sperling (eds), *Global Security Governance. Competing Perceptions of Security in the 21st Century* (London: Taylor & Francis, 2010), pp. 43–65; K. Longhurst, *Germany and the Use of Force: The Evolution of German Security Policy 1990–2003* (Manchester: Manchester University Press, 2005). During the formulation of the ESS, '...Germany wanted the EU to focus on particular areas instead of boldly pretending at a global role. Particularly Foreign Minister Fischer insisted on the Middle East, where he had personally been involved, and the European neighbourhood, mainly the Balkans, as key areas for European responsibility' (Claudia Major, 'Europe is what Member States Make of it. An Assessment of the Influence of Nation States on the European Security and Defence Policy', PhD thesis, Uinversity of Birmingham. In the 'Leitlinien für die Afrika-Politik', Germany's Foreign Office (2009) emphasizes above all the fostering of African capabilities, the German readiness to support the building-up of African capabilities for crisis management, and humanitarian aid, not military deployment –see http://www.auswaertiges-amt.de/cae/servlet/contentblob/357282/publicationFile/3715/2009-LeitlinienAfrikapolitik.pdf;jsessionid=D93061A8DEBAC75601D078614D82087B (accessed 28 April 2011).
19. Duke, 'Consensus Building' (note 9), p. 8.
20. *Ibid.* p. 4.
21. Duke's notion of 'framing' is here understood as another expression for SC.
22. Treaty of the European Union (Maastricht Treaty).
23. Duke, 'Consensus Building' (note 9), p. 22.
24. *Ibid.*
25. Only six member states contributed forces or force elements to the operation (see 'Personnel Contributions Source Fact Sheet on the Artemis, July 2003, Council of the European Union' (European Council 2003).
26. Certain problems arise with this argument. It may be that a certain 'strategic culture' was not the cause for this behaviour but rather, for example, a free-rider attitude. In the German case, however, it is very plausible to place the responsibility on Germany's strategic culture.
27. See Tony Chafer, 'The AU: A New Arena for Anglo–French Cooperation in Africa', *The Journal of Modern African Studies*, Vol. 39, No. 1 (2011), pp. 55–82. See also 'Franco–British Summit

Declaration on Franco-British cooperation in Africa, Le Touquet 4.02.2003', http://www.ambafrance-uk.org/Franco-British-summit-Declaration,4972 (accessed 8 August 2011).
28. David Chuter, *Humanity's Soldier: France and International Security* (London: Berghahn Books, 1997). Chuter argues convincingly that France enjoys a solid consensus on defence issues. To this day, the French national strategy explicitly declares 'intervention' as one of its basic principles (see Fabio Liberti and Camille Blain, *France's National Security Strategy*, WP 3/2011 - 17/1/2011). See also Christopher Griffin, 'French Military Interventions in Africa: French Grand Strategy and Defense Policy since Decolonization', Paper prepared for the International Studies Association 2007 Annual Convention, Chicago, 28 February–3 March 2007.
29. See Bagayoko, Niaglé, 'L'Opération Artémis, un Tournant pour la Politique Européenne de Sécurité et de Défense?', *Afrique Contemporaine*, Vol. 209, pp. 101–116.
30. For a similar argument with regard to the EU's civilian operation in Africa see Reinhardt Rummel's contribution in this collection.
31. From the EU's viewpoint, this principle is a major tool for integrating the EU's policies with national ones (see Damien Helly, 'L'UE et l'Afrique: Les Défis de la coherence', Paris: Institut d'Etudes de Sécurité, Cahiers de Chaillot, Novembre 2010).
32. See Petrov, 'Early Institutionalization of the ESDP' (note 9), p. 13.
33. See Kees Homan, 'Operation Artemis in the Democratic Republic of Congo', in Andrea Ricci and Eero Kytömaa (eds) *Faster and more United? The Debate on Europe's Crisis Response Capacity* (Office for Official Publications of the European Communities, 2007), p. 4, http://www.clingendael.nl/publications/2007/20070531_cscp_chapter_homan.pdf (accessed 30 April 2011).
34. Simon Duke, *Consensus Building* (note 9), p. 212.
35. See *BBC News*, 'Iraq War Illegal, Says Annan', http://news.bbc.co.uk/2/hi/3661134.stm; (accessed 30 April 2011).
36. The overall presence lasted 5–6 months, including pre-deployment and the pulling out of forces.
37. Letter dated 27 December 2005 from the Under-Secretary-General for Peacekeeping Operations to the Secretary of State for Foreign and Commonwealth Affairs of the United Kingdom of Great Britain and Northern Ireland.
38. The operation made use of 2276 soldiers: Germany and France each contributed about one-third of the troops, with the rest provided by 13 additional member states plus Turkey (see Denis M. Tull, 'EUFOR DR Congo: ein Erfolg, aber kein Erfolgsmodell', in Muriel Asseeburg, Ronja Kempin (eds), *Die EU als strategischer Akteur in der Sicherheits- und Verteidigungspolitik* (Berlin: SWP-Studie, S32, 2009), p. 54).
39. Claudia Major, 'EU-UN Cooperation in Military Crisis Management: The Experience of EUFOR RD Congo in 2006', Occasional Paper No. 72, Institute for Security Studies, Paris, September 2008, p. 18.
40. Das Parlament, 13 March 2006.
41. See Harnisch and Wolf, 'Germany – The Continuity of Change' (note 18), p. 45.
42. Joint Declaration on UN-EU Co-operation in Crisis Management (New York), 24/9/2003.
43. See EU-UN co-operation in Military Crisis Management Operations. Elements of Implementation of the EU-UN Joint Declaration, adopted by the European Council /17–18 June 2004. For a more detailed analysis of the development see Peter Schmidt, 'La PESD et l'ONU: un couple parfait?', *Politique étrangère*, Vol. 70, No. 3, (2005), pp. 613–624.
44. 'A Secure Europe in a Better World. European Security Strategy', Brussels, 12 December 2003. http://www.consilium.europa.eu/uedocs/cmsUpload/78367.pdf (accessed 20 April 2011), p. 11.
45. Council of the European Union, 'The EU and Africa: Towards a Strategic Partnership', 15961/05 (Presse 367), Brussels, 19 December 2005, available at http://consilium.europa.eu/uedocs/cms_data/docs/pressdata/en/er/87673.pdf
46. See Schmidt, 'Frankreichs Schwierigkeiten' (note 16), pp. 234–255.
47. For evidence of this German view see Ludwig Jacob, 'Im Interesse der EU oder der DR Kongo?', in Heinz-Gerhard Justenhoven and Hans-Georg Erhart (eds), *Intervention im Kongo. Eine kritische Analyse der Befriedungspolitik von UN und EU* (Stuttgart: Kohlhammer, 2008), p. 117.
48. See Tull, 'EUFOR DR Congo' (note 38), p. 53.
49. See Peter Schmidt, '"Freiwillige vor!" Bundeswehreinsatz im Kongo – zur Dialektik einer Führungsrolle wider Willen', *Internationale Politik* (November 2006), p. 75.
50. See Thomas Jäger, 'EUFOR DR Congo: Defizite eines glücklich verlaufenen Einsatzes', in Hans J. Gießmann and Armin Wagner (eds), *Armee im Einsatz* (Baden-Baden: Nomos, 2010), p. 20.
51. For the following see Schmidt, "Freiwillige vor", (note 49) pp. 70-75.
52. Jean Y. Haine's analysis of the Chad operation is an excellent expression of the contradicting strategic cultures in Europe.

53. Anne-Marie Slaughter regards government networks as a major, positive feature of the new world order in *A New World Order* (Princeton, NJ: Princeton University Press, 2004). The bargaining on certain formal levels but also, more informally, between the levels, can be regarded such a network.
54. I choose this notion in consideration of Laurence Whitehead, who used 'democratic Caesarism' to describe the political circumstances in Latin America. The gist of this notion was to describe tendencies to constrain liberal democracies (see Laurence Whitehead. The Alterantives to "Liberal Democracy": a Latin American Perspective, *Political Studies*, Vol. 40, No. 1 (1992), pp. 146–159.
55. From a national point of view, multilateral Caesarism is under the current circumstances the downside of EU's pursuit of 'effective multilateralism'.
56. Andrew Moravcsik, 'Taking Preferences Seriously: A Liberal Theory of International Politics', *International Organization*, Vol. 51, No. 4 (Autumn 1997), p. 513.
57. See Antoine Sadoux, 'La PESD: un moyen d'assurer la position de la France en Afrique?', *Revue Défense Nationale*, No. 10 (2005), pp. 70–71. For this 'multilateral turn' of French African policy see also Sylvain Touati, 'French Foreign Policy in Africa: Between Pré Carré and Multilatilateralism. An Africa Programme Briefing Note' (London: Chatham House, February 2007).
58. However, there is the widespread argument, that governments like international cooperation not only because it is needed, but also because it provides them more freedom of manoeuver with regard to their national parliaments.

The Failure of a European Strategic Culture – EUFOR CHAD: The Last of its Kind?

JEAN YVES HAINE

Since the European Security Strategy first invited European Union member states to develop and implement a strategic culture that 'fosters early, rapid, and when necessary, robust intervention', questions have arisen about the actual prospects and specific nature of such a strategic culture at the European level.[1] Indeed, the literature on a nascent European strategic culture seems to have flourished. Of course, an official aspiration, even one from Brussels, does not mean that such a culture could be created *ex nihilo*. It is worth noting that the Solana document expressed such an ambition in December 2003 when the Artemis Operation (June–September 2003) was already underway. At least implicitly, the document was not only an endorsement of that kind of operation but also an encouragement to build on its perceived success. After all, looking at the development of institutions and practices so far for the Common Security and Defence Policy (CSDP), European deployments were focused on low-intensity, classic peacekeeping operations mostly in the Balkans. It was not obvious at the time that the first autonomous European operation would have taken place in a remote part of Congo where European strategic stakes were debatable, to say the least. In a sense, that operation served as the template to be followed; and indeed, subsequent developments in European capabilities, notably the Battle Groups initiative, referred specifically to the Artemis operations.

This double feature of encouragement and endorsement – or, to put it differently, of beliefs and practices – symbolizes the traditional ambiguities about the concept of strategic culture in general, and its European dimension in particular. Beyond the familiar controversies around the very concept of culture, the two qualifiers, 'European' and 'strategic', also raise a number of difficulties that need to be carefully addressed. After reviewing the implications of this complex trilogy, this paper will focus on the Chad operation and will argue that the European Chad mission was not strategic in the classic sense, but rather embodied a specific set of European *political* and *security* beliefs that should not be confused with a *strategic* culture.[2] Finally, it will offer some tentative conclusions about the crisis of the Common Security and Defence Policy as a strategic endeavour and as a European policy. It is not a coincidence that the European Chad mission has been the last of this kind in CSDP developments and that, as a whole, CSDP is suffering from a general fatigue. Compared to the enthusiasm of 2001, it must be recognized that support for CSDP has clearly faded, although for different reasons in different countries.

The socialization and the learning by doing processes, the building of collective capabilities and the strategy itself at the core of the CSDP endeavour have shown their limits. Specifically among the main European powers, France, which has carried the torch of this endeavour nearly alone, seemed to prefer a much more intergovernmental process based on a narrower definition of national interests. The United Kingdom, always sceptical about the 'Brusselization' of defence and security issues, seems to have embraced this new approach, while Germany has witnessed to its dismay an increasing 'Africanization' of military operations which Berlin does not support or share.[3] In its current format, CSDP is nearly dead; its life support rests either on institutions' inertia or on small and medium powers in Europe that are just nursing it, while the capable doctors – the big European powers – have left the room. Concert of great powers in and outside Europe, shaping *ad hoc* coalitions of willing partners and associates, will increasingly become the favoured format of collective actions, rather than the institutionalized minimal consensus of the European Union. As the operation in Libya illustrated, Europe has ceased to be the point of reference and the centre of initiatives. Instead, the impetus came from national capitals, mostly Paris and London, in coordination with Washington and other permanent members of the United Nations Security Council and supported by other crucial forums, like the Arab League. Europe was divided and Brussels irrelevant. Protection of a civilian population against a dictator's brutality in a country neighbouring Europe should have brought Europeans together into an autonomous military operation under a CSDP umbrella. This combination of strategic interests, humanitarian emergency and American ambivalence was a textbook case to support Europe's security and defence ambitions. And yet NATO became the main institutional player instead.

Born out of the tragedy of Bosnia, the Common Security and Defence Policy seems to have been buried in the sands of Libya. After more than a decade of the Saint-Malo process, the frustration in London and Paris regarding the lack of progress is not only linked to the continuing gaps in crucial capabilities and decreasing military budgets throughout Europe, but also, and more crucially, is about the overall narrative and substance of the European security strategy that informs CSDP missions and military deployments. The very legitimacy of the Union as a security actor has been damaged in the process, from outside and from within Europe.[4] In this story of disillusionment, missions like EUFOR Chad played an important role.

A Delicate Trilogy: Culture, Strategy and Europe

Since its introduction at the end of the 1970s, the concept of strategic culture has both enriched debate and divided security and defence scholars.[5] As such, the controversies around this concept were part of a larger debate about realism versus constructivism, which was itself an illustration of the ongoing, long-standing dispute about the nature of causality in International Relations. Belonging to an Aronian tradition in international relations, which emphasizes a 'historical and sociological' *understanding* of international politics rather than abstract generalizations deduced from *explaining* the international system,[6] I largely share Colin S. Gray's puzzlement about the overzealous but ultimately fake rigour and artificial demarcation between causes and effects. At the same time, I also empathize with Ian Johnston's attempt to make the role played by ideas and beliefs more rigorous and clearer.[7] The tendency of academia to forge and entertain dichotomies or clashes and to impose labels or schools is not conducive for synthesis, and the concept of strategic culture has suffered from it. Yet, as Theo Farrel states:

> [E]ach approach has its uses. Gray's all-encompassing concept of strategic culture is useful for considering the cultural context of state action. However, if one wishes to explore culture as a cause of state action, then Johnston is quite right in arguing for a narrower conceptualization, which allows for consideration of rival, non-cultural causal variables, and which avoids being deterministic by excluding behaviour.[8]

As long as we remember that what is ultimately voluntary cannot be made necessary – or, to put it another way, that ideas belong to human *virtu*, not to mechanistic *necessita* – a middle ground can and should be found. The common foe is about reification and structure – material *and* ideational – that deny human freedom, responsibility and thus tragedy. The common aversion is about causal determinisms that exclude the contingent, the unexpected and thus also the tragic. It is ultimately a matter of using common sense with regard to what realism and constructivism can achieve, and the pragmatic compromise offered by David Haglund in this volume offers an excellent illustration of this.[9] In this spirit, reviewing a specific operation does not imply subscribing to the vocabulary of dependent and independent variables, but it does mean assessing a strategic culture in practice. So, with a premium on understanding rather than explaining, the concept of strategic culture offers a context – the historical contingency – and a framework of shared beliefs – the sociological milieu – that informs and is informed by practices. As we shall see, the context helps us to better understand the European insistence on autonomous actions and its focus on Africa, while shared beliefs help us to better define the specific nature of European 'security' objectives and the risks it is acceptable to take in order to achieve them.

The two other qualifiers are equally contentious and, in the present case, both are intimately intertwined. I will start with the strategic dimension. Several aspects must be introduced to assess the genuine 'strategic' character of the European security culture. At the most general level, a grand strategy, traditionally defined, is '... the capacity of a nation's leaders to bring together all of the elements, both military and non-military, for the preservation and enhancement of the nation's long-term, that is, in wartime and peacetime, best interests'.[10] Essentially, a grand strategy is the adaptation of domestic and international resources to achieve the foreign and security objectives of a state. Despite the usual imprecision attached to such documents, a grand strategy represents an important element in foreign and security policy formations and as such an essential element in a strategic culture.[11] The European Security Strategy, which failed to be meaningfully revised in 2008, had the ambition, at least on paper, to offer such a framework. Its remarkable characteristic was the identification of threats and vulnerabilities for Europe as a whole. The document was relatively precise about the nature of these threats – international terrorism, WMD proliferation, regional conflicts, failed states and organized crime – even though they were presented in a very generic fashion and without any hierarchy attached to them.[12] Much more problematic was the common design by which to address them, and it has been widely noted that two essential concepts at the core of the document – 'preventive engagement' and 'effective multilateralism' – were vague means rather than specific ends.[13] As a strategic document and as a framework for foreign policy choices, the ESS stood out for what was lacking. First, and most crucially, a strategy is about dealing with significant others, friends and foes. Making a difference *vis-à-vis* the second determines the kind of relationships possible with the first. With the nascent CSDP and the overall ESS framework, it was more the other way around. Its relative position to the United States largely determined the shape and the content of the European security framework. For instance, as far as international terrorism was concerned, the common European dimension was limited to stress differences with Washington's global war on terror, while actual counterterrorism policies remained a matter for individual member states. The same can be said about Iran, a common approach developed outside CSFP structures and before the European Security Strategy aimed at engaging a dialogue which was, at the time, taboo in Washington. This tendency to mark a difference with a friend, rather than setting the conditions and objectives 'to influence an adversary's will', became even more pronounced with the CSDP's first missions.[14] As we shall see, the Chad mission was in that regard a particularly non-strategic operation.

This leads to the second gap, the relationship between objectives and resources – the essence of what a strategy is all about. The discrepancy between the European security framework and the actual development of resources and capabilities to fulfil it is indeed striking. If an essential part of *strategic* culture is the 'art of distributing and applying military means to fulfill the ends of policy',[15] then the CSDP process has been both a quantitative and a qualitative failure, even though military capabilities were at the core of the Saint-Malo grand bargain. Moreover, one may argue that these capabilities were developed in a strategic void and the ESS did nothing to clarify their organic and command structure, their necessary transformation and their doctrinal framework. The CSDP process was much more capacity-driven than strategy-led, and a 'capability-strategy mismatch' occurred. The saga of the much discussed but never used Battle Groups illustrates this discrepancy.[16] Beyond military capabilities, other crucial resources –diplomatic assets, intelligence services, civilian officials, assistance budgets – need to be streamlined and adjusted to the overall strategy, but developments in all these areas have lagged behind what is necessary to fulfil the proclaimed ambition of a strategic role. The Lisbon Treaty was supposed to address some of these shortcomings,[17] but the process is painstakingly slow and, most importantly, the strategic vacuum remains. It will increasingly be filled by European great powers outside European structures, in *ad hoc* configurations; for this very reason, the External Action Service is unlikely to deliver on its promises.

The last gap is more familiar and is, of course, a consequence of the above discrepancy. The link between an overall strategy and actual operations is tenuous at best. The Petersberg Tasks, now extended and formally codified in the Lisbon Treaty, offered a framework for European Union military missions, but by themselves they do not constitute a strategic umbrella; they only translate vague security preferences.[18] As R. Betts has noted, strategy is a distinct plan between policy and operations, 'an idea for connecting the two rather than either of the two themselves'.[19] This 'idea', which – as we shall see – can be summed up in the concept of human security, as it was understood by Brussels, was too vague and too nebulous to represent a guiding principle for the use of force. Each individual mission has been justified on an *ad hoc* and political basis, without a clear overall strategy defining the stakes and guiding their prioritization. Their rationale had more to do with Europe's image and legitimacy than with Africa or the Balkans' strategic relevance for Europe. They were more symbolic than strategic operations.

This leads to the difficulties around the second qualifier: the *European* character of the strategy, which, not surprisingly, has been the focus of intense scholarly debates. For some, the very idea of a European strategic culture is something like an oxymoron. Precisely because Europe is not a state and never will be, it cannot have a proper strategy, since the unity of command and the legitimacy of the decision to use force will always escape it.[20] A key component of the Saint-Malo process was to recognize that the European Union would increasingly become the main legitimate framework of external actions. Indeed, institutions were rapidly set up after Saint-Malo, offering the necessary – but not a sufficient – framework for socialization, for sharing beliefs and for learning best practices. By serving as 'repositories' of shared ideas and as 'placeholders' for expected practices, and by binding friends to a specific agenda, institutions are a key component of a socialization process which over time would lead to a normative convergence on strategy among European members.[21] Yet this socialization process has severe limitations. First, the legitimacy of the European framework itself may be contested. Institutions may be disregarded if they do not offer meaningful and relevant added value, if they do not respond to expectations and interests, or if they are instrumentalized towards strictly national purposes.[22] They become obsolete if cheating and free-riding repeatedly occur with impunity, if their voice remains unheard and their loyalty unrewarded. Then the exit option becomes the preferred choice – sometimes officially, as in the case of Denmark, which opted out of CSDP at its creation, but more often implicitly, as in the cases of the Netherlands, the United Kingdom and, to some extent, Germany, which has contributed only minimally to CSDP operations. At the same time, 'loyalty' is often hypocritically exercised by contributing only symbolically to the institution.[23] It is fair to say that the legitimacy of the European Union as a meaningful strategic actor, weak from the start, has now reached a crisis point. France was the most loyal player but came to consider the burden-sharing too disproportionate – or, to put it another way, came to feel that its own loyalty was not matched by others'. The Chad operation played a significant role in this French disillusionment and estrangement. If the *European* strategic culture rested on 'the institutional confidence and processes to manage and deploy military force as part of the accepted range of legitimate and effective policy instruments, together with the general recognition of the *EU's legitimacy* as an international actor with military capabilities', then the socialization process is weaker now than it was at its creation.[24] Or, in other words, Europe has failed to mobilize and generate enough traction to have a role at the strategic level.[25] Moreover, the involvement of the European

Union in security affairs has been contested from the start through its rivalry with NATO. As we shall see, this institutional competition heavily influenced the scope of its actions and the nature of its security beliefs.

Second, in security matters, institutions remain fragile, commitments provisional and solidarity weak. As all realists know, because national interests and stakes are the crucial determinants of state's actions, security institutions are rarely more than a temporary marriage of convenience, based on a common threat and a favourable aggregation of forces.[26] The European case, because it is not an Alliance – despite assertions to the contrary in the Lisbon Treaty – suffers from a different centrifugal tendency. As it is not in the business of collective defence –NATO has the monopoly on that – the EU has focused on a liberal internationalist agenda based on peacekeeping and humanitarian interventions. In this framework, participation in operations is a matter of national choice, not of collective necessity. This leads to the domestication of foreign policy issues and the predominance of national sensitivities, preferences, constraints and caveats. The collective dimension is lost through the prism of national experiences.[27]

Moreover, some European countries have committed troops in other theatres, such as Afghanistan, Lebanon or Iraq, either nationally or through NATO. For them the Common Security and Defence Policy is a futile luxury that they cannot afford. All security institutions suffer from this unavoidable predicament and the European Union is no different. Situations, not institutions, shape foreign policy choices. Neither the position of a European 'Foreign Minister' nor the External Action Service will change this fundamental dynamic. The Europeanization of national interests can only happen if it follows a strategic, not a political, logic. If discussions in the European Council address the threat posed by a resurgent Russia, then Finland's high stakes in this regard cannot be reduced to Austrian's complacency or Portugal's indifference. The qualified majority voting cannot be politically defined *semper idem*, it has to be strategically measured *hic et nunc*. That was and remains the crucial advantage of core and flexible groups.[28] In practice, CSDP is thus reduced to *à la carte* groupings whose actions are triggered by the thrust of the big powers' agendas or the congruence of some members' foreign policy objectives, but not by a sense of collective obligations. Every crisis thus demands an intense and difficult debate about the rationale and the stakes of a potential mission. If CSDP military operations have been collectively endorsed, in practice they have been implemented by few, with symbolic contributions being the rule rather than the exception. The political conditions that make a European mission possible are far away from the strategic requirements that would make it successful.

The third obstacle to a European socialization process concerns a different level of analysis, that is, the military themselves. First, it should be noted that, at the highest level, European defence ministers still rarely meet. At a lower level, the European Union military staff could in theory represent a nexus for exchanging best practices, yet turnover of military personnel is high and, for officers of the most powerful nations, it is not clear whether a 'tour' in Brussels represents an actual promotion. More importantly, operational headquarters remain largely national. In the same vein, the battle groups have been useful exercises in interoperability, in standards harmonization, in shared practices – but they remain just that, exercises, and in some instances even temporary ones.[29] Most importantly, however, the real test for emergence of a strategic culture occurs in actual engagement, where the enemy has a vote. Precisely because strategy is about an adversary's will and behaviour, relevant learning occurs in battlefields, not in Brussels seminars.[30] Transformation, adaptation and innovation are as much a product of engagement with enemies as of socialization between, emulation of or imitation of friends. Was the conscription system in Germany reconsidered because of European peer pressures or because of the experience of the Bundeswehr in Afghanistan?[31] Wasn't Srebrenica a decisive learning moment for the Dutch troops? The Battle Groups concept itself was a key lesson from the CSDP engagement in Ituri, Eastern Congo.

Given the above mentioned caveats about a European strategic culture, one may be tempted to conclude that such a culture does not exist in Europe. Others may contend that CSDP developments and European security were never about fighting a war or winning against an enemy and that the use of armed forces was responsive to other goals, namely a liberal agenda based on human security and peacekeeping. But in that case, the sources of this peculiar security culture and its lack of strategic content must be addressed.

Culture, Context and Cognition

Taking the middle ground suggested by David Haglund, historical context and shared beliefs help us to better understand why this security agenda emerged among European elites and how it was implemented. The historical context brings us back to the core of the ambiguity of the Saint-Malo agreement, the UN's complex relationship with NATO and the relative position of Europe *vis-à-vis* the United States. This background is well known and thus does not demand elaborate discussion here. Less well known, however, is the flipside of the Anglo-French cooperation, that is, the status of the African theatre as the pre-eminent zone of potential actions. As for security beliefs developed within the Union from Saint-Malo onwards, it is not an exaggeration to sum them up through the concept of human security and an implicit zero-casualties doctrine attached to it. Human security is a people-centred approach which differs from classic, state-centric conceptualizations of security. It emphasizes freedom from want and freedom from fear. It is about 'protecting people from critical or pervasive threats and situations. It means using processes that build on people's strengths and aspirations. It means creating political, social, environmental, economic, military and cultural systems that together give people the building blocks of survival, livelihood and dignity'.[32] As we shall see, this concept informed CSDP missions.

Essentially, Saint-Malo was the last section of a decade-long question about the role of the United States in Europe with regard to European crises. The 'Europeanization' of NATO, through a separate identity and separable (but not separate) forces within a Combined Joint Task Force, could not hide the fundamental discrepancies between on the one hand, American selective and non-negotiable engagement and on the other, Europe's increasingly inadequate military capabilities after a decade of peace dividends. Against the background of the Bosnian tragedies and bittersweet success in Kosovo, the pragmatic British approach focused on the second disparity, while the more political French approach focused on the first imbalance and led to a fragile but genuine compromise that became the founding act of CSDP.[33] Overall, for Washington the reorganization of European military capabilities within NATO but under an EU umbrella was tolerable, but it was unacceptable for any political body to reflect this military impetus. The conundrum was partially solved, within these strict American limits, by the Berlin-Plus agreement, and the implementation of the nascent CSDP naturally took place in the Balkans, as a belated redemption for Europe's 'hour' failure.[34] In practice, Washington was not really interested in protracted state-building missions in a zone that was Europe's responsibility and CSDP was a benign addendum of 'a foreign legion of peace-keepers' to the Pentagon's and NATO's fighting forces.[35]

This initial *modus vivendi*, uneasy but practical, did not hold up against the shock of the 11 September attacks and the American reaction to them. With the Global War on Terror mantra and the war in Iraq, the fundamental equation of the transatlantic partnership changed dramatically: it was no longer about the US' role in Europe supporting European security, but about Europe's place in the American strategy for global security. The unilateral and revolutionary character of US foreign and security policy as embodied in the National Security Strategy (NSS) of the United States in 2002 changed the nature of the debate on decoupling: the American fear of Europe decoupling from NATO was replaced by the reality of Washington's estrangement from NATO.[36] This fundamental shift gave new momentum to the French ambition of building Europe's military autonomy and a new credibility to the traditional French objective of an independent political Europe. Yet while Europeans – albeit with significant internal dissonances – could agree that they opposed the American way forward for global security, a consensus about what Europe should do in world affairs was more difficult to reach. It was one thing to emphasize the divergence with the US, quite another to demonstrate this difference in practice. Given that gap, the 'African' chapter of the Franco-British rapprochement of 1999 became suddenly very convenient, at least for France. Before and at Saint-Malo, London and Paris bilaterally strengthened their defence cooperation through several instruments aimed at joint crisis management operations in Africa.[37] A significant agreement in defence cooperation was signed at the Cahors Franco-British summit in February 2001, and subsequently in Le Touquet in February 2003, where Paris and London set up the framework for a European role in African crises.[38]

After the debacle of the 'Praline' summit of April 2003 – when Belgium, France, Germany and Luxembourg proposed the creation of an European Headquarters for Common Security and Defence Policy missions – and in a deleterious atmosphere among Europeans and *vis-à-vis* Washington after the start of the Iraqi war, President Chirac seized the opportunity offered by UN Secretary General Kofi Annan to put this Franco-British agreement in practice by accepting the offer for a UN bridging mission in the Ituri region in Congo. France was determined to demonstrate that the European Union could act autonomously and in a distinct and contrasting manner from the Americans and their focus on unilateral regime change.[39] It was an ideal case to contrast with the Iraq war: legitimacy was ensured by a UN Security Council Resolution; the ownership of the process belonged to the African Union; the use of force was only a temporary expedient to restore order and to prevent further atrocities; and a devolution to African peacekeepers would deny any imperial design. What actually happened militarily in Bunia was far less important than the political objective of branding an autonomous Europe as a legitimate and legal force for good. To achieve this, France was the main, if not the sole, leader of the mission. The command was entirely French, with the OHQ (Operational Headquarters) located in the Defence Ministry in Paris and with a Force Headquarters in Entebbe, where London provided logistical and engineering support for the setting up of a joint support base. Operations in the town of Bunia were conducted mostly by French soldiers.[40]

Although the European force secured Bunia, the rest of Ituri remained a theatre of massacre, and the strict exit date clearly signalled the intervention's transitory nature to the armed belligerents. Bunia itself saw renewed violence a year after the Artemis operation.[41] The strategy of quick-in, quick-out by its nature thus had a limited impact. Humanitarian operations are extremely demanding and always precarious: they need to be forceful in order to create buffers and no-fly zones where assistance can be provided; they need to involve a large number of troops to defend these safe areas and to punish the spoilers; they need to be long-lasting to allow for reconstruction and reconciliation. To put it briefly, they may be nasty, brutish and long. They require commitments, sustainability and risks that Europe is reluctant to endorse. So, when the then French Defence Minister Alliot-Marie declared – in an unfortunate choice of words – 'mission accomplished' at the end of August 2003, she was obviously referring to the accomplishment of political rather than military objectives. Indeed, in European rhetoric, the mission was deemed successful precisely because it was an autonomous operation. Instead of a means to an end, it became an end in itself, setting the pattern for future operations in Africa. Building on that 'success', France and the United Kingdom fleshed out the role of the EU military in Africa in November 2003.[42] Using the Battle Groups, which would become operational in 2005, the EU should be able to respond quickly to a crisis, giving the AU or United Nations time to prepare for a longer-term intervention. Short-term military missions – 'quick in and quick out' – to support the United Nations or African Union became the strategic framework. This was echoed by the Solana paper's call for a European strategic culture aimed at 'early, rapid and robust interventions' and in the agreement on the Battle Groups concept. Yet the Europeanization of this agenda turned out to become far more difficult than Paris and London had expected.

The emergence of the Common Security and Defence Policy in Africa was not unanimously supported among Europeans. The obvious instrumentalization by France of CSDP structures and goals was met by reticence from European members with no tradition and no willingness to play an active military role in Africa, most notably Germany, which started to call the CSDP 'the French Africa Korps'. A majority of European actors favoured other ways of achieving progress in Africa through a more consensual agenda based on human security rather than militarization through CSDP. Moreover, if Africa was to become the main theatre of EU's military operations, other Brussels institutions were keen to reassert their specific role and add value in that region.

First, with the enlarged membership in the Union, it was not obvious that Africa should represent a priority for CSDP. As long as other missions in the Balkans continued, few were ready to object but fewer still were ready to participate – all the more so because in 2003–2004 Afghanistan started to emerge as a theatre of deployment of European troops under ISAF and national mandates. Since Europeans have only one set of forces, the strategic reserve to conduct operations in Africa was severely reduced.

Second, Brussels institutions, mostly the Commission, reasserted their authority on Africa by issuing a series of 'strategic' documents to contain the militarization of Europe's policies in Africa and to dilute it into broader objectives linked to poverty and development.[43] These documents called for 'a more comprehensive approach' than the narrow military quick fixes, promoting a natural linkage with the United Nations and a reinforced partnership with the African Union. The First Action Plan for the Implementation of the Africa-EU Strategic partnership led to more streamlined support of the AU, based on 'commitments to equality, partnership and ownership'.

More crucially, it focused on the development of African capabilities through the Europeanization of the French Recamp Programme, initiated by Paris in 1997 to reinforce and train African peacekeeping capacities. The EU was willing to help build African capabilities with military, logistics and financial aid but believed the process should be 'demand-driven'.[44] It was thus a firm reminder to France and others that the EU was not in the business of 'colonial' interventions and that, if forces needed to be sent, they should remain a small part of a larger political framework aimed at assistance, development, state-building and democracy. The Congo operation in 2006 illustrated the significant reduction of CSDP through the overall European instruments used towards Kinshasa. The mission, controversial from the start, caught the Germans in a classic entrapment dilemma and was framed in such a way that 'nobody could test the European forces and nothing dangerous could happen during the mission', with the bulk of German forces outside the country in neighbouring Gabon. After the French 'non' and Dutch 'nee' to the Constitution, it served the purpose of reaffirming that the EU was still a player in foreign affairs.[45]

Third, this dilution was helped by the emergence among European security circles of an agenda inspired by the concept of human security. Without addressing the history and the ambiguity of the concept itself, it can be said that human security offered, at least in theory, a convenient compromise between the traditional European civilian power and its military role. If the 'postmodern' identity of Europe has to include a place and a role for the armed forces, then the areas of human rights, peacekeeping and state-building became the obvious arenas for their actions, however limited. The Barcelona Report commissioned by Javier Solana and presented at the end of 2004 was a clear attempt to reconcile armed forces and Europe's 'ethical' or 'humanitarian' beliefs and values.[46] The report laid out seven principles of actions for the use of armed forces – the primacy of human rights, clear political authority, multilateralism, a bottom-up approach, regional focus, the use of legal instruments, and the appropriate use of force.

These principles were supposed to inform and guide CSDP operations. To that end, the Report called for the creation of a human security response force which emphasized its police and civilian elements. This civilian component was very popular throughout Europe, for at least three reasons. First, it underlined again the difference between the Venusian Europe and the Martial US at the moment at which the attempt at regime change in Iraq started to turn into a disaster, despite President Bush's continual denials. Second, it enhanced small and medium European powers' positions and influence in security and defence policies, where the modesty of their actual military capabilities would have reduced their role to a marginal one.[47] It was an opportunity to Europeanize CSDP, and was indeed duly seized. Lastly and most importantly, it led to the framing of CSDP operations in a 'postmodern' manner – one that did not entail any risk of actual combat against an identified enemy; that reduced significantly the scope of the Petersberg tasks; that could not lead to casualties among European forces; that domestic public opinion would support. It fit the risk-averse preferences of most decision-makers and political parties in Europe, an aversion that goes well beyond the use of force.[48] Embraced by the Commission, supported by Solana, shared by a majority of European actors, human security as a concept and as a guiding principle for actual operations was thus an extremely useful tool to avoid a deemed excessive militarization of security policies in Africa. It became the consensual buzzword of the time. Following the same trajectory of its sister concept, normative power, it flooded official documents and was referred to as the main, if not the unique, 'strategic' narrative for European external actions.[49] As elaborated by Brussels, this narrative however became the opposite of genuine strategic thinking. The human security concept, as conceived at the EU level, denies the possibility and disregards the probability of influencing a state or a sub-state actor by deterrence, compelling or coercion. It presupposes a posture of neutrality and impartiality while neglecting the geopolitical environment. It ignores the very essence of what a soldier does, and dismisses how his mere presence is perceived. It considers the EU as a NGO and conflates the rank of its armed forces to the status of Red Cross personnel. As an alternative to 'early, rapid, and when necessary, robust' interventions, human security is a dangerous illusion.[50] As we shall see, EUFOR Chad in that respect was a close call. Needless to say, European members of NATO, especially the ones actually fighting in Afghanistan – the Dutch, the Danes and the British – had an entirely different *strategic* conception of that issue.

The historical context and the security beliefs based on human security help us to understand how the Saint-Malo focus on autonomy was translated into an exercise of assertive difference with Washington, why it was implemented in Africa, and how in that context it triggered a European reluctance to the actual use of force and led to the emergence of humanitarian security beliefs that informed Europe CSDP practices.

EUFOR Chad: The Last of its Kind?

The actual European Union operation in Chad was a Plan B. It was intimately linked to a failed European attempt to address the humanitarian crisis in Darfur. Despite repeated calls and pressure on President Al-Bashir from the EU to ensure the protection of the civilian population, the Union made clear that it would not act without the consent of and collaboration with the Sudanese government and that the main actor should be the African Union, although the refusal of the first and the weakness of the second were well known. The European Union repeatedly expressed 'concerns' but essentially did nothing to address the crisis,[51] despite having the capability and the forward bases to at least police the refugee camps in Darfur. However, after a short fact-finding mission Peter Feith, a close adviser of J. Solana, declared in summer 2004 that the crisis in Darfur did not amount to genocide and so did not justify an intervention, while France made clear that the Union was not 'in the business of invading an Islamic country'.[52] Moreover, at the Council level it was assessed that the EU could not afford to antagonize the regime in Khartoum for the sake of the peace agreement between North and South Sudan.[53] At the same time, Britain was contemplating an intervention but realized that without French forward bases and troop contributions, its military, already overstretched in Iraq, would not have sufficient weight to make a difference on the ground. So Europe, despite its very public humanitarian and ethical agenda, went 'back to sponsoring peace talks and bankrolling other actors, back to applying measures [it] knew were ineffective'.[54] The inaction in Darfur was more than a embarrassing display of political cowardice and hypocrisy; it demonstrated the limits of the 'human security' concept that presupposed a world without power and interests, a world made of consent and neutrality, a world that did not exist.

That failure in Darfur largely explained the European willingness to act when the worsening conflict in Sudan spilled over into Chad. From a strategic culture point of view, however, this operation illustrated how lessons from that failure were not learned, how the 'human security' umbrella remained prevalent in Brussels and how this led to serious strategic miscalculations and mistakes. The mission's objective was to create humanitarian corridors and safe havens where European peacekeepers and humanitarian relief workers could operate to protect and assist the estimated 460,000 internally displaced persons and refugees from Darfur. This goal was first presented in May 2007 by French Foreign Minister Bernard Kouchner, a leading figure in the humanitarian NGO community. In October, four months later – with the time lag already a good indication of the sense of urgency and a clear sign of hesitation among Europeans – the Council approved the operation, based on UN Security Council Resolution 1778.

The UN resolution framed the mission in its usual manner, whereby the EUFOR Chad/CAR mission would represent a bridging deployment to be replaced by a UN follow-on force in March 2009 and would complement the work of UNAMID, the UN–African Union peacekeeping force being deployed to Darfur in neighbouring Sudan, as well as that of MINURCAT, the UN mission in Chad aimed at improving police and judicial infrastructures.[55] All EU instruments – diplomatic, political and financial – were mobilized, including substantial European Commission assistance for the establishment of a UN police force, a €10 million programme to train and equip a special Chadian police/gendarmerie (the DIS Détachement Intégré de Sécurité, a force specially set up to provide security for refugee camps in the East) and €28 million for justice reforms. All in all, the European Union allocated nearly €300 million for Chad and €137 million to CAR over a five-year period. The European Union also sponsored a peace process between Chad and Sudan in March and established a contact group with Libya, Senegal, the Republic of Congo, Eritrea, Gabon, Chad and Sudan to monitor the situation and to facilitate an AU border protection mission between N'Djamena and Khartoum. However, President Déby, despite French pressure, only agreed to the European force on the condition that it would not deploy on the border between Chad and Sudan.[56] The deployment of forces was thus only one element in a broader approach which reflected the EU Commission's agenda in Africa.

Europeans by and large were hesitant to be involved in such a demanding, potentially long-lasting and complex operation in which few had any stake or interests, while France retained a significant military force and an influential political presence. Several reasons explain this reluctance.

First, the concept of the operation, adopted in November 2007 by the Council, took great care to avoid any confusion with the French heritage in Chad. Emphasis was repeatedly put on the 'neutral, impartial and independent manner' in which EUFOR would operate. General Nash, from Ireland – a country deeply attached to the value of neutrality, speaking at a moment when Dublin was voting on the Lisbon Treaty – insisted that neutrality and independence were crucial elements.[57] The reluctance of Europeans, despite this reassurance that the force would not take sides and that it would stick to a human security agenda, translated into a very painful force generation process. After the Council's endorsement, five force generation conferences were required; thus the mission suffered many delays as Europeans struggled to meet planned targets. Originally set at 5,000 troops, despite the UN's estimation that an adequate force level would be twice that level, the European Union had to settle for 3,700, with a strategic reserve of 600 remaining in Europe. Again France carried the bulk of the deployment, sending 2,000 troops – some of which were part of the permanent French presence in Chad – while Ireland and Poland each sent one battalion.[58] The Commission made clear, however, that the costs would have to be supported mostly by contributing countries, and that the common costs package would have to be reduced.[59]

Second, the logistical aspect of the mission was a nightmare. The area of operations, which covered approximately 200,000 km^2, was one of the furthest African points from the sea. Air deployment was constrained by the very limited facilities in N'Djamena and in Abéché, both being able to handle only a very small number of aircrafts like Hercules C-130s at any one time. While France, Poland and Ireland flew their forces on their own, the European Union had to rely on Russian Transport helicopters and on the seaport of Douala in Cameroon as a transit hub. Few countries in Europe could afford to cover these costs in personnel and in budgets without them affecting simultaneous NATO requests to strengthen contributions in Afghanistan. Given these logistical difficulties and the existing gaps in European strategic lift capabilities, the operation became fully operational only on 17 September 2008, 10 months after the EU's endorsement.

Third, the environment was particularly challenging. The Déby regime in Chad lacked the ability to establish effective control of its entire territory, and diverse ethnic groups and tribal clans contested the regime's power. Moreover, Sudan had blamed Chad for cooperating with the Darfurian rebels, some of whom were from Déby's own clan, the Zaghawa. The result was a proxy war between Chad and Sudan.[60] In the Central African Republic, the situation was roughly the same – a failed state facing regular rebellions, often funded by Sudan. Overall, the deployment was not unlikely to face a mix of Janjaweed militias from Khartoum, various rebel groups in Chad and several bandit gangs, some of which were known to be well organized and heavily armed.[61] Meanwhile, the Chadian and CAR armies of 25,000 and 3,150 forces respectively were deemed poorly trained and had very limited capabilities.[62] This balance of forces on the ground was thus potentially very risky. And yet this was not the main preoccupation among European countries and in Brussels.

This leads to the fourth and most important reason why Europeans were reluctant to participate in this mission. France had maintained a heavy presence in Chad and played a crucial part in supporting the autocratic Déby regime. With 1,500 troops – part of Opération Epervier – permanently stationed in Chad since the mid-1980s, France was a kingmaker, a role that the European Union was keen not to be associated with. ESDP was not designed to take over the traditional colonial role of saving or deposing troubled regimes in Africa, so the insistence on neutrality was an obvious political way to avoid any such confusion. Yet the EU operation was mainly French, and this ambiguity plagued the mission's initial phases.[63] Brussels was thus more preoccupied with distancing itself from France than with assessing the strategic situation on the ground. In France itself, the objective of protecting civilians did not seem to be in contradiction with strengthening the Déby regime against Sudan. The French press emphasized the second as well as the first.

The painful birth of the Chad mission worsened at the moment it started. As early as September 2007, one important rebel group, the RFC (Rassemblement des Forces pour le Changement), had warned EUFOR not to obstruct their struggle to topple President Déby, threatening that otherwise they may fight against EUFOR. On the very day that the first elements of the mission were to be deployed, rebels mounted a flash attack, leaving the Sudanese border on 28 January and reaching the capital in N'Djamena four days later after a 700km dash in the desert. Paris spotted the manoeuvre with its satellites but did not stop the column, as it had in similar circumstances in November 2006 by flying over French Mirages. However, Paris did warn Déby and help to defend the regime, and the attack was repelled. If France had intervened sooner, however, hundreds of people may not have been killed in N'Djamena and thousands would not have been forced to flee to Cameroon. In Brussels, there were frantic discussions about possible cancellation of the European Union mission and further deployments were postponed. On March 2008, a reconnaissance patrol operating near Tissi in the tri-border region between Chad, Sudan and CAR inadvertently strayed 3km across the border into Sudan, where it met hostile fire, leading to the death of a French peacekeeper, Gilles Polin. Speaking at Polin's funeral, French President Nicolas Sarkozy angrily denounced the Sudanese, accusing them of 'premeditated murder'.[64] Meanwhile, the cooperation between the DIS and the UN was obstructed by Déby's attempts to use this force – sponsored by the EU – to launch an incursion against Sudan. In June, a rebel offensive took place in Goz Beida. Irish and Dutch troops did not intervene but had to evacuate hundreds of UN and NGOs workers. The pretence of neutrality made the mission far more difficult than it already was.

In sum, collective action is about aggregating power, not taming it. French leverage in the region was a crucial enabler of the mission, not an obstacle to it. To cling to a neutral posture when your potential adversaries have denied it amounts to strategic shortsightedness. The long-standing relationships between Paris and N'Djamena and the French support to President Déby were a strategic asset, not a political liability. That France eschewed crucial leverages of influence to please Brussels reveals the mission's ambiguity.[65] Sending troops into Chad was doomed to raise tensions with Sudan and change the security landscape in Chad itself. The hope in Brussels was that the Sudanese government and the Chadian rebel groups would not confront European forces, but that wishful thinking was denied by the reality on the ground, and it could have turned into a nightmare for EUFOR.[66] Even the United Nations DPKO (Department of Peacekeeping Operations) considered that the conditions identified by the Brahimi Report – peace to keep, a firm commitment of troops and clarity of mandate – were not met.

The mission's impact is debatable. Over 2,500 short-range patrols and 260 long-range patrols were conducted during the operation, but according to European Union military officials, EUFOR spent too much time 'aimlessly patrolling the vast deserted lands along the Chad-Sudan border'.[67] Because of the limited number of troops, the operations could not intervene in troublespots, and in October 2008 NGOs had to evacuate their operations in some cities – notably Dogdore and Ade, which were flooded with refugees. The mission helped to build six camps, which were handed over to Minurcat when the EUFOR handed the baton to the UN in March 2009. This transition turned out to be difficult. Polish, Irish and French troops simply changed their hat from European blue to the blue of the UN. Overall, humanitarian agencies and NGOs acknowledged EUFOR's positive contribution, yet they all underlined that the humanitarian situation remained precarious and relations between Chad and Sudan had deteriorated. For Oxfam, although the European troops made some civilians feel safer, 'the underlying security situation has not significantly improved'.[68] Criminality and banditry continued unabated, refugee and IDP flows increased, and failed governance in Chad has been left unaddressed. For the International Crisis Group, while EUFOR has contributed to an improvement in the infrastructure of territorial security, the operation 'has failed to achieve its main goal, the creation of an environment that would favour the return of displaced people and protect the civil population and humanitarian workers against attack'.[69] The EU Defence Ministers praised the mission as a success, yet also recognized that 'obviously the operation was not a game changer at the national or regional level nor a transformer of the root causes of the crisis in the area of operation'.[70]

CSDP in Crisis

The Chad operation may prove to be the last of its kind. At an estimated cost of more than €1 billion, it is not clear that European countries will be willing to get involved again in an African environment where their impact is likely to remain limited and temporary. The economic crisis, and the absence of any common funding process, will severely constrain those kind of African adventures. Granted, the EU suffers the same difficulty as the UN in these Sisyphean tasks of humanitarian relief. Yet Europe has its own specific flaws.

First, the EU's understanding of the human security concept and the zero-casualty mantra led to contradiction with the few lessons learned on peacekeeping. The current premises of neutrality, casualty avoidance and early exit are the opposite of a humanitarian intervention strategy that would have been meaningful in Bosnia – one that takes sides, uses force and is sustained in order to rebuild a state after conflict. As an alternative to 'early, rapid, and when necessary, robust' interventions, human security is a negation of what Europe had learned painfully in the Balkans. Saint-Malo was about building capabilities that could be employed in a battle, preferably alongside the United States under a NATO framework, to make a difference on the ground. The Europeanization process has seriously downgraded this initial objective, both quantitatively – from the initial 60,000 troops of the Helsinki Headline Goal of 1999, the number is now two Battle Groups on standby – and qualitatively – there is no battle to fight and only peace to keep. The amalgamation of armed forces into this postmodern European framework was not what London and Paris signed up to.

Second, beyond Chad, Common Security and Defence Policy operations in Africa had been driven more by political agendas regarding Europe's own image than by the defence of European strategic interests. For Great Britain, this confirmed that the 'Brusselization' process in security and defence was a dangerous illusion. If there is a future for CSDP, it will be based on common national interests between Europeans who have the power and the responsibility to act militarily. The intrusion of the Commission, which possessed neither, is seen as a strategic oxymoron. The Atalanta mission, off the rather large coast of Somalia, is precisely about defending vital strategic interests. Here lies CSDP duty. France was the main supporter of a European role in security and defence, mainly because of its traditional political ambition to build a Europe independent from Washington. Paris has always endorsed the role of a would-be soft-balancer.[71] But France may not want to repeat the experience of taming its own interests and leverage in Africa for the sake of a minimal European consensus while Paris has to carry the bulk of such operations. The CSDP exercise in difference may not be worthwhile if it means the deference of French interests and power to a Europe which seems so reluctant to be engaged in power politics. In others words, the current European *security* culture framework that emphasizes human security, by contrast with a *strategic* culture that would focus on an adversary, has become a burden to the classic French ambition of a *Europe puissance* and, most importantly, an obstacle to French strategic interests and roles. For Paris, Europe has ceased to be useful. The translation of this Brussels security culture into deployments in Africa has also triggered an estrangement process for Berlin, not based on the culture itself, but on the stakes at hand. Germany having been dragged into one such operation in Congo, it is extremely unlikely that it will be caught twice. Moreover, the 'early, rapid and robust' deployments envisaged in the ESS were always at odds with Germany's core pacifist culture. The Solana paper's call has thus been left unanswered.

Third, when the three most powerful countries in Europe are dissatisfied with a process, it can only lead to a crisis of legitimacy of the institution itself. The sense of solidarity, of obligations, of 'European-ness' of the CSDP has waned.[72] The combination of vastly different strategic cultures at the national level could only lead to minimal consensus and to figurative operations aimed at fostering the European institution itself. Claiming ownership, difference and success very loudly, as European officials have done for years about CSDP missions, is what one would expect from a weak and young institution trying to build its legitimacy inside and outside. But these public relations exercises involved soldiers, the use of force and ultimately questions of life and death, the core of national sovereignty. To dispatch soldiers to remote places where no strategic interests are at stake may have been an acceptable, although onerous, option to strengthen the process itself. But it was acceptable precisely because there were no risks involved, no stakes to defend, no strategy to implement. In this sense, there was never a European strategic culture, only chimerical security beliefs.

Lastly, the role of posturing differences with America has ceased to be relevant, since the Obama administration has significantly altered the course chosen by his predecessor. Now that America is 'appropriate' again, as the constructivists would say, the opposing mirror image of Venus does not particularly stand out. But because the United States has seriously shifted the exercise of its power, and because the emerging multipolarity may compel Washington to look elsewhere, Europeans may realize that America is not a European power anymore. Then they may be willing to reconsider a CSDP that would defend and protect their interests – a realist Common Security and Defence Policy based on strategic calculations, not on political chimera.

NOTES

1. See The European Security Strategy. Translated into military preparedness and doctrine terms, the Headline Goal 2010 envisioned that the EU Military Staff would 'be able by 2010 to respond with rapid and decisive action applying a fully coherent approach to the whole spectrum of crisis management operations covered by the Treaty on European Union'.
2. I distinguish between 'security' and 'strategic' culture for reasons explained below.
3. The inter-governmental approach favoured by Paris and London seems to occur more and more outside Brussels. The Lancaster House Defence Treaty of November 2010 is significant in this regard. It is striking how this Franco-British cooperation is about Paris and London's respective power perceptions as declining world powers rather than as leaders of Europe. Indeed, Europe and CSDP are barely mentioned in the Treaty. See Ben Jones, 'Franco–British Military Cooperation: A New Engine for European Defence?' Occasional Paper No. 8, EU-ISS, Paris, February 2011. As one scholar has argued, 'The real threat [to CSDP], then, is not the Franco-British agreement, but the fact that the strengthening of Franco-British defence cooperation is taking place against a background of significant frustration in both London and Paris over EU defence efforts'. See Clara Marina O'Donnell, 'Britain's Coalition

Government and EU Defence Cooperation: Undermining British Interests', *International Affairs*, Vol. 87, No. 2 (March 2011), p. 428.
4. As one Australian general quipped, 'CSDP? This European device whereby Europeans send their best troops where they are not needed?' (Author's conversation, London, June 2005).
5. Alastair Iain Johnston, 'Thinking about Strategic Culture', *International Security*, Vol. 19, No. 4 (Spring 1995), pp. 32–64; Colin S. Gray, 'Strategic Culture as Context: The First Generation of Theory Strikes Back', *Review of International Studies*, Vol. 25, No. 1 (January 1999), pp. 49–69; and Alastair Iain Johnston, 'Strategic Cultures Revisited: Reply to Colin Gray', *Review of International Studies*, Vol. 25, No. 3 (July 1999), pp. 525–530.
6. Raymond Aron, *Peace and War: A Theory of International Relations* (New York: F.A. Praeger, 1967); Anne Ahonen, 'The Contemporary Debate in International Relations Theory and Raymond Aron's Epistemology and Ontology', *Cooperation and Conflict*, Vol. 29, No. 1 (March 1994), pp. 77–94; Hollis Martin and Steve Smith, *Explaining and Understanding International Relations* (Oxford: Clarendon Press, 1991).
7. See Michael C. Desh, 'Culture Clash: Assessing the Importance of Ideas in Security Studies', *International Security*, Vol. 23, No. 1 (Summer 1998), pp. 141–170; Stephen M. Walt, 'Rigor or Rigor Mortis, Rational Choice and Security Studies', *International Security*, Vol. 23, No. 4 (Spring 1999), pp. 5–48, and the courageous but flawed attempt by Robert O. Keohane and Judith Goldstein (eds), *Ideas and Foreign Policy: Beliefs, Institutions and Political Change*, (Ithaca, NY: Cornell University Press, 1993).
8. Theo Farrel, 'Culture and Military Power', *Review of International Studies*, Vol. 24, No. 3 (July 1998), p. 408. Or as Gray puts it: 'Should I lose sleep worrying about whether I am a neoclassical realist or a constructivist? Could I possibly be both? Well, I think I am indeed both' (Colin S. Gray, 'Out of the Wilderness: Prime Time for Strategic Culture', *Comparative Strategy*, Vol. 26, No. 1 [January–March 2007], p. 3).
9. Classical realism was much more sophisticated and cautious than its neo version. As Hans Morgenthau argued, '[New theories] do not so much try to reflect reality as it actually is as to superimpose upon recalcitrant reality a theoretical scheme that satisfies the desire for throughout rationalization. Their practicality is specious since its substitutes what is desirable for what is possible' (Hans Morgenthau, 'Common Sense and the Theories of International Relations', *Journal of International Affairs*, Vol. 2, No. 2 [1967], p. 209). It is a pity that we have to live with an awful and absurd neologism, 'neoclassical realism'.
10. Paul Kennedy, 'Grand Strategy in War and Peace: Toward a Broader Definition', in Paul Kennedy (ed.), *Grand Strategies in War and Peace* (New Haven, CT: Yale University Press, 1991), p. 5.
11. For a good overview of the usual deficiencies of a grand strategy, see Richard K. Betts, 'Is Strategy an Illusion?', *International Security*, Vol. 25, No. 2 (Fall 2000), pp. 5–50, and Robert Jervis, 'U.S. Grand Strategy: Mission Impossible', *Naval War College Review*, Vol. LI, No. 3 (Summer 1998), pp. 22–36.
12. See Jean Yves Haine, 'The European Security Strategy and Threats: Is Europe Secure?', in Sven Biscop and Jan Joel Andersson (eds), *Forging a Global Europe – The EU and the European Security Strategy* (Abingdon: Routledge, 2007), pp. 21–40.
13. See, among many, Jolyon Howorth, 'The EU as a Global Actor: Grand Strategy for a Global Grand Bargain?', *JCMS: Journal of Common Market Studies*, Vol. 48, No. 3 (June 2010), pp. 455–474; Pascal Vennesson, 'Competing Visions for the European Union Grand Strategy', *European Foreign Affairs Review*, Vol. 15, No. 1 (February 2010), pp. 57–75; Alyson Bailes, 'The European Security Strategy', SIPRI Policy Paper No. 10, Stockholm, February 2005.
14. As Colin Gray reminds us, 'Strategy is about influencing the will of an adversary' (Colin S. Gray, 'Strategic Thoughts for Defence Planners', *Survival*, Vol. 52, No. 3 [June–July 2010], p. 161).
15. Basil H. Liddell Hart, *Strategy* (New York: Meridian, 1954/1991), p. 319. On the consequences of the budget crisis see, among others, Bastian Giegerich, 'Budget Crunch: Implications for European Defence', *Survival*, Vol. 52, No. 4 (August–September 2010), pp. 87–98.
16. Ursula C. Schroeder, 'Strategy by Stealth? The Development of EU Internal and External Security', *Perspectives on European Politics and Society*, Vol. 10, No. 4 (December 2009), pp. 486–505. On the Battle Groups, see Jean-Yves Haine, 'Battle Groups: Out of Necessity, Still a Virtue?', *European Security Review*, No. 39 (July 2008), pp. 1–5.
17. Antonio Missiroli, 'The New EU "Foreign Policy" System after Lisbon: A Work in Progress', *European Foreign Affairs Review*, Vol. 15, No. 4 (November 2010), pp. 427–452.
18. In the Lisbon Treaty (Art. 43.1 TEU) member states agreed on an extended definition of the Petersberg Tasks, stating that they: '[...] shall include joint disarmament operations, humanitarian and rescue tasks, military advice and assistance tasks, conflict prevention and peacekeeping tasks, tasks of

19. combat forces in crisis management, including peace-making and post-conflict stabilization. All these tasks may contribute to the fight against terrorism, including by supporting third countries in combating terrorism in their territories'.
19. He added: 'Among practitioners, politicians often conflate strategy with policy objectives, focusing on what the desired outcomes should be, simply assuming that force will move the adversary toward it while soldiers often conflate strategy with operations focusing on how to destroy targets or defeat enemies tactically assuming that positive military effects mean positive policy effects' (Betts, 'Is Strategy an Illusion?' [note 11], p. 7). This was underlined as soon as the ink of Saint-Malo was dry, yet more than 10 years after, it is still missing. See for example Alfred Van Staden et al., *Towards a European Strategic Concept* (The Hague: Netherlands Institute of International Relations 'Clingdael', November 2000), available at http://www.nbiz.nl/publications/2000/20001100_cli_ess_staden.pdf, and Sven Biscop and Jo Coelmont, 'A Strategy for CSDP: Europe's Ambitions as a Global Security Provider', Egmont Paper No. 37, October 2010, available at http://www.egmontinstitute.be/paperegm/ep37.pdf
20. As noted by F. Heisbourg, 'The EU cannot have a proper security strategy as long as decisions on the use of force rest in the hands of its member governments'. François Heisbourg, 'The "European Security Strategy" is Not a Security Strategy", in Steven Everts et al., *A European Way of War* (London: Centre for European Reform, 2004), p. 28. See also Sten Rynning, 'The European Union: Towards a Strategic Culture?', *Security Dialogue*, Vol. 34, No. 4 (December 2003), pp. 479–496.
21. Felix Berenskoetter and Bastian Giegerich, 'From NATO to ESDP: A Social Constructivist Analysis of German Strategic Adjustment after the End of the Cold War', *Security Studies*, Vol. 19, No. 3 (2010) p. 422. See also Jolyon Howorth, 'Discourse, Ideas, and Epistemic Communities in European Security and Defence Policy', *West European Politics*, Vol. 27, No. 2 (2004), pp. 211–234; Christoph O. Meyer, 'Convergence towards a European Strategic Culture? A Constructivist Framework for Explaining Changing Norms', *European Journal of International Relations*, Vol. 11, No. 4 (December 2005), pp. 523–549; Alessia Biava, 'The Emergence of a Strategic Culture within the Common Security and Defence Policy', *European Foreign Affairs Review*, Vol. 16, No. 1 (February 2011), pp. 41–58.
22. On the first point, see Helga Haftendorn, Robert O. Keohane and Celeste A. Wallander (eds), *Imperfect Unions; Security Institutions over Time and Space* (Oxford: Oxford University Press, 1999), especially pp. 1–18. The other two are classically known as the chain-gang and the entrapment dilemma. See Thomas J. Christensen and Jack Snyder, 'Chain Gangs and Passed Bucks: Predicting Alliance Patterns in Multipolarity', *International Organization*, Vol. 44, No. 2 (Spring 1990), pp. 137–168.
23. As Albert Hirschman has noted, 'Loyalty, far from being irrational, can serve the socially useful purpose of preventing deterioration from becoming cumulative, as it so often does when there is no barrier to exit... While loyalty postpones exit, its very existence is predicated on the possibility of exit. That even the most loyal member can exit is often an important part of his bargaining power vis-à-vis the organization' (Albert O. Hirschman, *Exit, Voice and Loyalty: Responses to Declines in Firms, Organizations and States* [Cambridge, MA: Harvard University Press, 1970], p. 78 and pp. 80–81).
24. That definition is from Paul Cornish and Geoffrey Edwards, 'Beyond the EU/NATO Dichotomy: The Beginnings of a European Strategic Culture', *International Affairs*, Vol. 77, No. 3 (July 2001), pp. 587.
25. For a nice summary of the importance of social mobilization in strategy, see Michael Howard, 'The Forgotten Dimensions of Strategy', *Foreign Affairs*, Vol. 57, No. 5 (Summer 1979), pp. 975–986, and Stephen Peter Rosen, 'Military Effectiveness: Why Society Matters', *International Security*, Vol. 19, No. 4 (Spring 1995), pp. 5–31.
26. The reference work is Stephen M.Walt, *The Origins of Alliances* (Ithaca, NY: Cornell University Press, 1987).
27. As a scholar of alliances noted long time ago, 'The fact of entering into alliances does not transform national actors into coalition actors. The discrete members of the alliance retain all of their individuality, all of their separateness despite assumptions to the contrary' (Edwin H. Fedder, 'The Concept of Alliance', *International Studies Quarterly*, Vol. 12, No. 1 [March 1968], p. 81).
28. 'A policy cannot be branded "EU" unless backed by all 27. But 27 cooks in the kitchen is too many. On particular issues, the EU should encourage smaller groups of the most interested countries to draw up policy. It has done this already for Iran, where Britain, France and Germany take the lead' (Charles Grant, *Is Europe Doomed to Fail as a Power?* [London: CER, 2009], p. 25).
29. For example, the Nordic Battle Group, led by Sweden, has now been dismantled.
30. See Robert T. Foley, Stuart Griffin and Helen McCartney, '"Transformation in Contact": Learning the Lessons of Modern War', *International Affairs*, Vol. 87, No. 2 (March 2011), pp. 253–270; Theo

G. Farrell and Terry Terriff, *The Sources of Military Change: Culture, Politics, Technology* (Boulder, CO: Lynne Rienner, 2002).
31. There are of course many reasons why the conscription system was reconsidered in Germany, budgetary constraints being one of them. But the question of efficiency in engagement seems the most important. Former Army Chief Klaus Naumann argued that 'I would like to hold on to [conscription]. If it still made sense, if you could still use it to form units in which the young man can say at the end of his service: "OK, I've learned how it works, I have the confidence to go into battle with this company, with this battery and survive", but you can't do that in six months'. (*Der Spiegel*, 24 August 2010). According to a Nato official, 'what's really lacking in zu Guttenberg's vision is the European dimension' (quoted in Quentin Peel and James Blitz, 'Security: A German Military Overhaul', *Financial Times*, 31 January 2011).
32. See Final Report of the Commission on Human Security, (May 2003), http://www.humansecurity-chs.org/finalreport/English/FinalReport.pdf
33. As early as October 1998, Prime Minister Tony Blair argued that 'a common foreign and security policy for the European Union is necessary, it is overdue, it is needed and it is high time we got on with trying to engage with formulating it'. See 'European Defence: From Pörtschach to Helsinki', House of Commons, Research Paper 00/20, (21 February 2000), available at http://www.parliament.uk/documents/commons/lib/research/rp2000/rp00-020.pdf. See also Jolyon Howorth, 'Britain, France and the European Defence Initiative', *Survival*, Vol. 42, No. 2 (Summer 2000), pp. 33–55, and Robert E. Hunter, *The European Security and Defense Policy: NATO's Companion- or Competitor?* (Santa Monica, CA: RAND Corporation, 2002).
34. Beyond Albright's three Ds – no decoupling, no discriminating, no duplicating – the American reaction to Saint-Malo was rather negative. As US Ambassador to NATO Alexander Vershbow had argued in May 2000, 'the danger here is that, if autonomy becomes an end in itself, ESDP will be an ineffective tool for managing crises and transatlantic tensions will increase'. Quoted by Barry R. Posen in 'ESDP and the Structure of World Power', *The International Spectator*, Vol. 39, No. 1 (2004), pp. 10–11.
35. William Pfaff, 'A Foreign Legion for the Pentagon', *International Herald Tribune*, 7 November 2002, quoted in Ulriksena Ståle, 'Requirements for Future European Military Strategies and Force Structures', *International Peacekeeping*, Vol. 11, No. 3 (2004), p. 461.
36. Jean-Yves Haine, 'ESDP and NATO', in Nicole Gnesotto (ed.), *EU Security and Defence Policy: The First Five Years (1999–2004)* (Paris: EU ISS, 2004), p. 143. For detailed accounts, see Elizabeth Pond, *Friendly Fire: The Near-Death of the Transatlantic Alliance* (Washington DC: Brookings Institution Press, 2004); Phillip H. Gordon and Jeremy Shapiro, *Allies at War: America, Europe, and the Crisis over Iraq* (New York: McGraw-Hill, 2004).
37. This less well known aspect of the Franco-British rapprochement to cooperate on African policy is sometimes called 'Saint-Malo II'. On this, see Tony Chafer and Gordon Cumming, 'Beyond Fashoda: Anglo–French Security Cooperation in Africa since Saint-Malo', *International Affairs*, Vol. 86, No. 5 (September 2010), pp. 1129–1147.
38. In Le Touquet on 4 February 2003, Paris and London declared that 'preventing conflict and keeping or re-establishing peace in Africa are our constant concern. Both countries would like to emphasize that primary responsibility falls on Africa in this matter. We will take joint initiatives to that end at the United Nations and within the European Union and G8, ensuring in particular that they support the efforts of the African Union and of the sub-regional organizations, and that they strengthen Africa's peacekeeping capability' ('Franco-British Summit, Declaration on Franco–British Cooperation in Africa, Le Touquet 4.02.2003', available at http://www.ambafrance-uk.org/Franco-British-summit-Declaration, 4972.html).
39. As one scholar noted, 'France badly wanted a mission to show the EU was capable of acting alone, where NATO would not be involved'. See Catherine Gegout, 'Causes and Consequences of the EU's Military Intervention in the Democratic Republic of Congo: A Realist Explanation', *European Foreign Affairs Review*, Vol. 10, No. 3 (September 2005), pp. 437–438.
40. The French forces in Bunia interpreted the EU mandate extensively and some operations were carried outside it, that is, under strict French orders. Interview with Artemis Commander General Neveux, Paris, October 2003.
41. See UNDPKO, *Operation Artemis: The Lessons of the Interim Emergency Multinational Force* (New York: United Nations Department of Peacekeeping Operations, Peacekeeping Best Practices Unit, 2004); S. Ulriksen, C. Gourlay and C. Mace, 'Operation Artemis: The Shape of Things to Come?', *International Peacekeeping*, Vol. 11, No. 3 (2004), pp. 508–525, and Fernanda Faria, 'Crisis Management in Sub-Saharan Africa: The Role of the European Union', Occasional Paper, EU ISS, April 2004.
42. 'We now propose that the EU should build on this [operation Artemis] precedent so that it is able to respond through ESDP to future similar requests from the UN, whether in Africa or elsewhere'

(Franco–British Declaration, 'Strengthening European Cooperation in Security and Defence', 24 November 2003, http://www.fco.gov.uk/Files/kfile/UKFrance_DefenceDeclaration,0.pdf).
43. In December 2005, the European Council endorsed a document entitled 'The EU and Africa: Towards a Strategic Partnership', largely inspired by the Millennium Goals. This document was written by the Commission, hardly discussed by the COREPER, barely overseen by the PSC. This institutional imbalance triggered a brief statement by J. Solana, the High Representative for CFSP, to remind the Commission that the Council and the ESDP-CFSP framework could not be bypassed. See also Niagale Bagayoko and Marie V. Gibert, 'The Linkage between Security, Governance and Development: The European Union in Africa', *Journal of Development Studies*, Vol. 45, No. 5 (May 2009), pp. 789–814.
44. EU, Council of the European Union, General Affairs and External Relations, 2760th Meeting, Brussels, 13 November 2006. See also Thierry Tardy, 'EU–UN Cooperation in Peacekeeping: A Promising Relationship in a Constrained Environment', in Martin Ortega (ed.), 'The European Union and the United Nations. Partners in Effective Multilateralism', Chaillot Paper no 78, EU ISS, Paris, 2005.
45. Gorm Rye Olsen, 'The EU and Military Conflict Management in Africa: For the Good of Africa or Europe?', *International Peacekeeping*, Vol. 16, No. 2 (2009), p. 254. Jean-Yves Haine and Bastian Giegerich, 'In Congo, a Cosmetic EU Operation', *International Herald Tribune*, 12 June 2006.
46. See *Barcelona Report of the Study Group on Europe's Security Capabilities: A Human Security Doctrine for Europe*, (September 2004), available at www.lse.ac.uk/collections/pressAndInformation Office/newsAndEvents/archives/2004/HumanSec_Doctrine.htm. See also Janne Haaland Matlary, 'When Soft Power Turns Hard: Is an EU Strategic Culture Possible?', *Security Dialogue*, Vol. 37, No. 1 (March 2006), pp. 105–121. One scholar uses the term 'humanitarian power Europe'. See Christoph O. Meyer, *The Quest for a European Strategic Culture: Changing Norms on Security and Defence in the European Union*, (Basingstoke: Palgrave, 2006), p. 141, and also Ian Manners, 'The Normative Ethics of the European Union', *International Affairs*, Vol. 84, No. 1 (January 2008), pp. 45–60.
47. The civilian side of CSDP has not been a great success either. See Daniel Korski and Richard Gowan, 'Can the EU Rebuild Failing States? A Review of Europe's Civilian Capacities', ECFR, October 2009.
48. Zaki Laïdi, 'Is Europe a Risk Averse Actor?', *European Foreign Affairs Review*, Vol. 15, No. 4 (November 2010), pp. 411–426. According to transatlantic polls in 2007, only 20 per cent of Europeans supported committing more troops for combat actions in general (see *Transatlantic Trends*, available at www.transatlantictrends.org).
49. Mary Kaldor *et al.*, 'Human Security: A New Strategic Narrative for Europe," *International Affairs*, Vol. 83, No. 2 (March 2007), pp. 273–288.
50. For a trenchant critique, see Roland Paris, 'Human Security. Paradigm Shift or Hot Air?', *International Security*, Vol. 26, No. 2 (Fall 2001), pp. 87–102, and Jean-Yves Haine, 'The European Crisis of Liberal Internationalism", *International Journal*, Vol. LXIV, No. 2 (Spring 2009), pp. 453–479. As one scholar put it, the military ethos that it induces is: 'pretend to be warlike but don't fight' (Tommi Koivula, 'Towards An EU Military Ethos', *European Foreign Affairs Review*, Vol. 14, No. 2 [May 2009], p. 171). Some, at last, have recognized that the operational meaning of the concept is a failure. See Janne Haaland Matlary, 'Much Ado about Nothing: The EU and Human Security', *International Affairs*, Vol. 84, No. 1 (January 2008), pp. 131–143; Mary Martin and Taylor Owen, 'The Second Generation of Human Security: Lessons from the UN and EU Experience', *International Affairs*, Vol. 86, No. 1 (January 2010), pp. 211–224.
51. As former Commissioner Chris Patten recorded, 'EU foreign ministers have since early 2004 issued 19 Darfur statements using phrases such as "serious concern" or "profound concern" a total of 53 times in a period that has seen some 200,000 slaughtered and 2.5 million displaced by government forces or government-backed militia, the Janjaweed. When something more than words is needed, the EU does not have much to boast about...' (quoted in Andrew Rettman, 'Ex-Commissioner Attacks EU Verbalism on Darfur', *EU Observer*, 20 March 2007).
52. Private conversation with French officials, Paris and Brussels, September 2004.
53. See Paul Williams and Alex Bellamy, 'The Responsibility to Protect and the Crisis in Darfur, *Security Dialogue*, Vol. 36, No. 1 (March 2005), pp. 27–47.
54. EU diplomat, quoted by Asle Toje, *The European Union as a Small Power after the Post-Cold War* (New York: Palgrave Macmillan, 2010), p. 106.
55. As always, the UN mandate was extensive. The EU 'multidimensional' force was 'to help create the security conditions conducive to a voluntary, secure and sustainable return of refugees and displaced persons, *inter alia* by contributing to the protection of refugees, displaced persons and civilians in danger, by facilitating the provision of humanitarian assistance in eastern Chad and the north-eastern Central African Republic and by creating favorable conditions for the reconstruction and economic and social development of those areas' (UN Security Council, 'Security Council Resolution 1778

Authorizing the "Establishment Of 'Multidimensional Presence" in Chad, Central African Republic', 25 September 2007, available at http://www.un.org/News/Press/docs/2007/sc9127.doc.htm).
56. 'Not having the European force deployed directly on the border enables President Déby to continue to freely intervene in Darfur' (Bjoern H. Seibert, 'EUFOR Tchad/RCA: A Cautionary Note', *European Security Review*, No. 37 [March 2008], p. 3).
57. He later recalled: 'It was important for EUFOR to remain neutral and it had to learn how to refuse offers that would threaten its own neutrality without humiliating the parties involved'. See 'Ensuring Peace and Security in Africa: Implementing the New Africa–EU Partnership', Summary of Conference held on 27–28 October 2010, (London: Chatham House), p. 18. Available at www.chathamhouse.org.uk/files/17861_1010confsummary.pdf
58. The contributions were as follows: France (2,000); Ireland (450); Poland (400); Austria (210); Sweden (200); Romania (120); Belgium (120); Spain (80); Netherlands (60); Finland (40); and Slovenia (15).
59. On this see Alexander Mattelaer, 'The Strategic Planning of EU Military Operations: The Case of EU for Chad/RCA', IES Working Papers, No. 5, 2008, p. 18.
60. Roland Marchal, 'Chad/Darfur: How Two Crises Merge', *Review of African Political Economy*, Vol. 33, No. 109 (September 2006), pp. 467–482.
61. These groups put together represented well above 10,000 men. Of course, none were coordinated. For a detailed account of these potential 'enemy' forces, see Bjoern H. Seibert, 'African Adventure? Assessing the European Union's Military Intervention in Chad and the Central African Republic', MIT Security Studies Program Working Paper, November 2007, pp. 11–15.
62. See International Institute for Strategic Studies, *The Military Balance* (London: Taylor and Francis, 2007), pp. 267–268.
63. 'France's intentions were unclear for many Europeans who feared Paris would use the European flag to mask a policy aimed at supporting an authoritarian regime. Many who had a genuine interest in acting on the margin in Darfur and in promoting CSDP feared being dragged into a mere regime protection measure.' Damien Helly, 'EUFOR CHAD/CAR', in Giovanni Grevi, Damien Helly and Daniel Keohane (eds), *ESDP: The First 10 Years (1999-2009)*, (Paris: EU ISS, 2009), p. 346.
64. Quoted in 'EUFOR in Chad and CAR: The EU's Most Taxing Mission Yet', *IISS Strategic Comments*, Vol. 14, No. 4 (May 2008), p. 2.
65. Rebels were one element, banditry another. The lessons learned report noted that 'de-linking the security crisis in the East from internal Chadian politics was a deliberate decision made during the planning phase, and there was a "debate" on whether or not this was appropriate'. It also noted that 'NGOs regretted EUFOR's inadequate understanding of the context, particularly the security situation and the conditions needed to be created for long-term IDP returns'. See Helly, 'Lessons from EUFOR Chad/CAR' (note 63), p. 10.
66. As Colin Gray argued, 'adversity cannot cancel culture'. In the European case, the 'security' culture was far away from strategic realities. (Gray, 'Strategic Culture as Context' [note 5], p. 62).
67. Quoted in Toje, *The European Union as a Small Power* (note 54), p. 111.
68. Oxfam International, 'Insecurity still Rampant in Chad as UN Takes over from EU', 13 March 2009.
69. See International Crisis Group, 'Chad: Powder Keg in the East', Africa Report, 15 April 2009, No. 149, p. 19.
70. Helly, 'Lessons from EUFOR Chad/CAR' (note 63), p. 11.
71. CSDP had been associated with a 'soft-balancing' exercise against US power. But CSDP had been about Europe's own image and about differentiating, not balancing, the US. See T.V. Paul, 'Soft Balancing in the Age of U.S. Primacy', *International Security*, Vol. 30, No. 1 (Summer 2005), pp. 46–71 and Jolyon Howorth and Anand Menon, 'Still Not Pushing Back: Why the European Union is Not Balancing the United States', *Journal of Conflict Resolution*, Vol. 53, No. 5 (October 2009), pp. 727–744.
72. And as realists know, 'alliances have no meaning unless the human actors feel bound by their obligations' (Lauren Paul Gordon, 'Diplomacy: History, Theory and Policy', in Gordon, *Diplomacy: New Approaches in History, Theory and Policy* [New York: Free Press, 1979], p. 5).

In Search of a Trademark: EU Civilian Operations in Africa

REINHARDT RUMMEL

How Strategic is a Civilian Intervention?

Is it conceivable that strategic culture, which is traditionally related to the military sphere, could be based on civilian assets only? Or – in the case of the European Union, in particular – do we have to define strategic culture as consisting of a mixture of civilian and military elements? Further, is it conceivable that a collection of states like the EU could acquire the ability to develop a common strategic culture, and, if so, would this culture see the EU become a unified actor in security and defence matters? Or does the EU first have to become a security actor before it is capable of 'strategic culture'?

Based on Paul Cornish and Geoffrey Edwards' definition of strategic culture, which notes that not only 'operations' but also 'capabilities and policy processes' are part and parcel of a strategic culture, the answer to all of these questions starts from the fact that the present European Union does not have a strategic culture. Instead, to assess the civilian missions of the Common Security and Defence Policy (CSDP) in Africa one needs to admit from the outset that EU security policy is a relatively new factor in international relations and has little textbook knowledge to draw on, especially regarding the nexus of 'civilian' and 'security', 'civilian' and 'defence', or even 'civilian' and 'strategic culture'. As a newcomer to the constellation of relevant powers in international governance, the EU has only seen the inclusion of political practitioners and academic analysts as it has built up over the past couple of years.[1] Its security focus on Africa via the European Security and Defence Policy (ESDP) is even younger.[2] Since 2003, five military operations have been launched – three of them completed, two ongoing. Five civilian missions have been dispatched since 2005 to the African continent, again with three completed and two still running.

A few characteristic elements of European Union foreign and security policy can be distilled from these pioneer missions, but the empirical basis is too small to allow serious conclusions about the potential future for the strategic culture of the EU, let alone about any potential interplay with the strategic cultures (to the extent that there are any) of the 27 member states. Things improve slightly once we widen the scope of analysis to include two further empirical fields: EU external action beyond ESDP and the internal build-up of the Union's security sector. This double extension is more than a methodological trick to widen the narrow database. It is an analytical necessity, because European civilian missions in Africa are part of a broader bureaucratic and political context, even though they are often portrayed – and even conducted – as 'surgical strikes'.

Unlike CSDP, the wider platform of European external action has been in operation for many decades and has substantially contributed the Union's civilian external outlook, based on an internal consensus. The main responsibility for the EU's description as a 'civilian power'[3] lies after all with its traditional approach to external relations, comprising diplomacy, trade, development aid, humanitarian support, and multilateral cooperation regarding cross-cutting worldwide challenges such as international terrorism, organized crime, energy security, and the proliferation of weapons of mass destruction. All of these components allow a unified European international engagement thanks to a civilian approach and the exclusion of the use of military force.

The truth is that CSDP missions are not isolated from these foreign policy traditions of the EU, just as they are today intertwined with the gradual construction of a whole new sector of the Union: a collective foreign, security and defence policy, a plan that has only begun to be implemented. Neither the provisions in the Lisbon Treaty, nor the ESDP/CSDP missions – intergovernmental as they are – can avoid the strategic traditions of the EU's member states and their security policies either as individual nations within a collective defence organization, or within the ideological framework of non-aligned/neutral countries. Groups of member states have contributed according to their history, standards, and interests to the EU's stand as an actor in international security.

Will their imprint continue to dominate the perception of the Union from outside? Will, for example, France's record of dealing with African cases of conflict override the influence of the EU's collective policies there or will the Union take over, flanked by the member states? Indeed, Brussels' Africa policy today has been born out of a mixture of activities at both national and EU levels, within which ESDP missions are only a very recent addition, focusing on conflict prevention, crisis management, and post-conflict stabilization. This innovation is of potential importance for the Union as a security actor, but what is the dynamic size of this work in progress? Is Brussels on its way from civilian power to military superpower?[4] Is it specializing in soft security according to the view that the Europeans have neither the political will nor the military substance to forcefully defend their vital interests?[5] What is particular in the European assessment of present security challenges and in the responses that flow from such?

The view taken in this article is that the European Union – far short of strategic culture – is testing its potential for greater powers of intervention. It runs an internal build-up process and a series of individual external operations. To raise its impact, Brussels primarily combines civilian and military tools on both the European and the national levels. Cases of EU African intervention are certainly show projects for its increasingly comprehensive approach. Thus, Brussels may assume it is on its way to establishing a trademark European intervention policy. However, all of its efforts toward methodological and material sophistication in this regard cannot hide the fact that the EU remains a group of very different states that lack political unity when it comes to serious questions of security. The Union has neither a common defence policy nor a common defence that would allow and require a strategic culture.

The research approach taken in this article is duly restricted to the development of civilian ESDP both in geographical and in institutional terms. The (geographical) first part illustrates the political situation in African countries that called for civilian intervention and describes the five European civilian missions undertaken in response. Do these interventions reveal a strategic content? The (institutional) second part looks into the build-up of the civilian component of CSDP and asks a similar question: how much strategic content can be found in the new institutional structures as amended by the Lisbon Treaty? The empirical record of these two arenas, however embryonic they are, should serve to offer some tentative conclusions regarding the texture and strength of the EU's mode of intervention.

Civilian ESDP Engagement in Africa: Innovative Intervention?

Not long ago, European relations to African countries were rather compartmentalized. One major sector consisted of humanitarian aid, another of development cooperation, with a third devoted to trade, and other sector-policies related to security, technology, finance, and culture. Today these sectors interact to the degree that they are no longer easily separable. This is particularly striking in cases of state fragility where the causes for failure are manifold and where the best strategy to re-stabilize a rundown country is not always obvious. Should law and order be re-established first? Can this be done without a minimum degree of security? Should one start with fixing the economy to feed the people? Or should the priority lie with building up the institutions to allow good governance and progress in all sectors mentioned above? To the extent that the EU is asked to intervene and help in those cases, Brussels has to find innovative answers which include political choices regarding where to assist and how.

African Security Challenges: A Call for European Answers?

In the 1990s, when the European Union's foreign policy was largely preoccupied with the end of the Cold War and the start of the hot wars in former Yugoslavia, and when the shaky transitions in Eastern Europe, including the dissolution of the Soviet Union, determined the security agenda in Brussels, the European continent seemed to form the EU's strategic horizon. The massacres of Srebrenica and the Kosovan war were trigger events and test cases for more substantial action of CFSP and for the creation of ESDP. Some professionals, however, anticipated that the African continent would soon appear on the EU's radar screen simply because it was in a similar state – multiple conflicts with the potential to escalate all the way up to genocide (as indeed happened in Rwanda in 1994). After the Western Balkans, Africa would be the next theatre for ESDP operations. Paris and London, at least, were sure about that and helped to inspire the size and function of the EU's intervention forces accordingly.[6]

At academic conferences and in political circles, comparisons were made between the task of transition inside Europe and the challenge of change inside Africa. Strange as it seemed, with regards to changes of regime, Africa faced a set of problems somewhat similar to those experienced by central and eastern European transformation countries. However, African cases of failed states were clearly of a distinct and more alarming nature. At the turn of the millennium most of the African countries were struggling with factors of instability such as corrupt governments, bands of warlords, violence among ethnic groups, rotten legal systems, massive violations of human rights, an institutional breakdown, and poor economic prospects. The G8 and others recognized that Africa needed particular support in order to achieve the Millennium Development Goals adopted at the UN General Assembly in September 2000.[7]

In addition to those more long-term goals, Africa suffered from immediate shortages and medium-term needs. The enlargement process (both of the European Union and of NATO) and the European neighbourhood policy helped to deal with system change and restructuring in Europe, but Africa did not qualify for those programmes. The Cotonou Agreement with the ACP countries was not designed to cope with short-term reactions to turmoil and intra-state conflict.[8] New approaches combining security and development were in demand.[9] The EU claimed to have those answers. Brussels was identifying and building up capabilities to intervene outside Europe if called upon. In fact, the need for a more proactive approach was discussed in the policy circuits of EU capitals, inspired by concepts of conflict prevention, the responsibility to protect, and human security.

These reflections entered into the spirit and the wording of the European Security Strategy (ESS), in which the EU member states stated that in the recent past no region of the world had been untouched by armed conflict and that the Union 'should be ready to share in the responsibility for global security and in building a better world'.[10] Several interest- and value-related reasons are given in the ESS as to why the EU should bring stability to crumbling regions. The ESS starts with the self-assessment that 'the increasing convergence of European interests and the strengthening of mutual solidarity of the EU makes it a more credible and effective actor'[11] to deal with global challenges and key threats. While such a statement raises hope that the prophecy will be self-fulfilling, in reality the EU could only be rated as a global player if it was capable of using its strategic potential.

Among the global challenges, the connection between economic failure and violent conflict is regarded as crucial, particularly in crisis-torn Africa. According to the assessment of the ESS, 'Sub-Saharan Africa is poorer now than it was 10 years ago' and 'security is a precondition of development'. The EU member states were concerned because 'conflict not only destroys infrastructure, including social infrastructure; it also encourages criminality, deters investment and makes normal economic activity impossible'. Regional conflicts, like those in the Great Lakes Region, could 'threaten minorities, fundamental freedoms and human rights. Conflict can lead to extremism, terrorism and state failure; it provides opportunities for organised crime. Regional insecurity can fuel the demand for WMD'.[12] No doubt, the EU and its member states felt indirectly and directly threatened by these mutually reinforcing cycles of violence and by the privatization of force. A key concern of EU member states is failing states and their impact on the international order. The functioning of the international system and the commitments to international regimes and treaties depends on the quality of the governments that are its foundation.

Obviously, European leaders have a common reading of risks and challenges to their countries, and also seem to agree on how to respond. In the ESS the Heads of State and Government therefore note: 'The best protection for our security is a world of well-governed democratic states. Spreading good governance, supporting social and political reform, dealing with corruption and abuse of power, establishing the rule of law and protecting human rights are the best means of strengthening the international order.'[13] It is a European priority to support the United Nations and regional organizations in order to strengthen global governance: '... regional organisations such as ASEAN, MERCOSUR and the African Union make an important contribution to a more orderly world.'[14] This approach is a central part of the Union's concept of effective multilateralism and of its missionary reflex to bring democracy and human rights to others. The assumption is that all players in international relations are partners in the dissemination of the European way. Rivals, competitors, or even adversaries are not mentioned.

Equally strong seems the Union's desire for the export of its regional integration model. Member states compare regional constellations in other parts of the world to the pre- and post-war situations on the European continent and conclude that their own experience of the past 60 years, of dealing peacefully with disputes and cooperating through common institutions, was a powerful method that might help others as well. Obviously, the extension of the rule of law and the spread of democratic behaviour has led to authoritarian regimes in Europe transitioning to secure, stable and dynamic democracies.[15] Many regions of crisis badly need reconciliation between former belligerents, a ban on discrimination against minorities, and to embark on joint projects. In this respect, the EU feels that it has rare knowledge to offer, a concept that works if the conditions are favourable: the integration process of the European Community.

Despite the self-assertive cases made in the ESS for assisting regions in conflict, the views of EU members were differentiated (and still are). While some felt that the EU had a responsibility to provide help to poor regions of the world, given the EU's stability and wealth, others asked why the Union should intervene in remote places of little economic or strategic importance like those in Africa. It is true that some EU citizens and politicians had asked the same question in relation to the nearby Western Balkans when local ethnic cleansing and religious wars were ravaging the area. To most of the new EU member states from Eastern Europe it was disappointing to see large proportions of the Union's programmes devoted to uncharted African territories when funds were badly needed in the heart of Europe.[16] Germany, Austria and the Scandinavian countries shared this opinion to some extent.[17] By contrast, former colonial powers like France, the United Kingdom, Belgium, Italy and Portugal stressed their continued cultural, economic and political ties.[18] They felt that the eastern enlargement made the EU tilt toward the 'East'.

The former colonial powers saw African conflicts and their implications as a pressing issue. They had carried the burden of stabilizing their former colonies via bilateral agreements and manifold support while their economic and political profit from these engagements was decreasing and local conflict increasing. Sustaining peace and good governance in their partner countries was too much to handle for once glorious imperial powers like Belgium and Portugal. Even France and the United Kingdom felt their capabilities were overstretched and were searching for an arrangement that allowed them to share the responsibility and cost for crisis management and post-conflict reconstruction in some of the African states with their European partner countries.[19] A number of demanding practical factors like the long distance from home, the fragile infrastructure, and the particular geographical and cultural environment would make interventions difficult. In some cases an EU intervention would help to win back credibility which was lost in (partisan) bilateral relations with local governments.

To sum up, one can find a number of good reasons why there was and remains demand for the EU and its member states to assist and intervene in Africa. Some of these reasons are present in other regions as well; some are specific to African countries. Likewise, it turns out that EU member states have divergent interests regarding the size and the mode of intervention. Individual member states expect their fellow EU members to support their individual approach. These differentiations point to the challenge of establishing coherence within the EU's definition of security risks, policy agenda, and priority of action. It is a tall order for the EU and its member states to sort out a balanced approach to intervention in a specific state or region. A common document like the ESS is a helpful means to guide the consensus building process in the EU but remains far too general to help with the operational side of intervention. It neither connects objectives and capabilities, nor specifies the enemy.

Civilian Interventions in Africa: Rational Choices?

As civilian interventions may contribute decisively to deescalation of a dispute or to restoring law and order in a failed state, the European Union seems to regard this approach as being as powerful as military peacekeeping or strategic defence. How did the EU select the cases for its civilian interventions? Generically, the answer to such a difficult question is easy. Drawing on the analysis above one can identify several obvious sets of motivations within groups of EU member states: historical affiliation, economic interest, personal relationships between heads of state, altruistic impulses, normative drives, security implications, global player competition, and many more. In the abstract, one can find enough actors at EU level and within member states who would be likely to advocate for or against a particular CSDP mission. In a concrete case, however, it remains difficult, if not impossible, to determine the exact mix of motivating or demotivating factors. Let us see if a description of the civilian missions to Africa can offer some clarification and allow for some conclusions on the dominant factors in the decisions for and the implementation of civilian missions. Did the European Union make rational choices, and would these lead to powerful interventions?[20]

Geographically speaking, Africa is today CSDP's second centre of gravity, next to the Western Balkans. In terms of numbers, four of a total 17 civilian missions (and five of a total of seven military operations) have been sent to the African continent. The Democratic Republic of Congo (DRC) received three of the EU's four civilian missions, Guinea-Bissau one. Two of the four are police missions (EUPOL Kinshasa, EUPOL RD Congo) and two are Security Sector Reform (SSR) operations (EUSEC

RD Congo, EU SSR Guinea-Bissau). Africa is also the region in which CSDP launched what has so far been its only combined civil–military action, which was aimed at supporting an operation of the African Union in favour of Sudan (AMIS). The AU also profited from EU support (Africa Peace Facility) regarding the buildup of conflict prevention and peace-building capabilities at the headquarters in Addis Ababa, a cooperation that is to be placed in the much wider EU–Africa strategic partnership inaugurated in 2007 and includes economic and development aspects as well as political and security cooperation. CSDP is a player both in conducting individual operations and in shaping the EU–AU group-to-group relationship.

Civilian Missions in DR Congo and Guinea-Bissau

ESDP started its civilian actions in Africa with two missions to the Democratic Republic of Congo: EUPOL Kinshasa in April 2005 and EUSEC RD Congo in May 2005.[21] The police mission was confined to the Congolese capital and lasted until June 2007, when it was replaced by EUPOL RD Congo – another police mission, but with a wider reach.[22] After several renewals EUPOL RD Congo is still ongoing at the time of writing, having been extended to September 2012; EUSEC RD Congo has been extended to September 2012. The EU's missions to the DRC certainly represent a longer-term commitment which was, at first glance, not the case with EU SSR Guinea-Bissau, which started in March 2008 and was ended in September 2010.[23] Currently the EU seems to put all its civilian eggs in one basket, the DRC. What is the reason for this focus – or did it come about by accident?

EUPOL Kinshasa was a rather small mission which began with 23 international staff and a budget of €4.3 million.[24] A peace agreement had been reached among the fighting factions in the DRC in 2003 and elections were scheduled for 2006. The Congolese authorities had asked the EU to help with stabilization in the transitional period. Orderly preparation of the elections was the priority and the Europeans were mandated to monitor, mentor, and advise the Integrated Police Unit (IPU) located in the Congolese capital. The IPU at the time was a potentially important stabilizing instrument, created by the Congolese transitional government and designed to replace the multitude of militias owned by influential local politicians and businessmen. With support from the European Commission and from member states, IPU officers had been trained in dealing with political unrest and in protecting state institutions.[25] Aldo Ajello, the EU Special Representative (EUSR) to the region, provided political guidance for the EU's activities in DRC which, for a short period during the national elections, also included an ESDP military mission (EUFOR RD Congo).

Due to the fragile internal situation after the elections, EUPOL Kinshasa was concluded and replaced by EUPOL RD Congo, which had a much wider and more structural goal. In agreement with the new Congolese government, Brussels dispatched a mission of 53 international and nine local staff and an annual budget of some €7 million.[26] As witnessed by EUPOL Kinshasa during the election campaign, the DRC police forces were run down and fragmented and needed reform and reorganization. ESDP's new mission aimed to support Congolese efforts to restructure the police sector and to insert it into the political system. More specifically, the mission was mandated:

- to provide advice and assistance through the Police Reform Committee set up by Congolese authorities;
- to improve the interaction between the police and the justice criminal system;
- to ensure coherence between the three pillars of Security Sector Reform (defence, justice, police).

This programme was later extended geographically and functionally. Originally not deploying to the DRC provinces, EUPOL RD Congo was authorized by the EU Council to send personnel to the Eastern province of Kivu in order to support the implementation of the Goma peace process of January 2008. Likewise, the Council extended EUPOL RD Congo's mandate to allow support of the Congolese border police force and the police inspectorate. The EU had started with a quite limited mandate to assist in the law and order realm of the DRC, but it seemed that need for external assistance was constantly growing.

This changed focus and size through the course of a mission is also true of EUSEC RD Congo. It began in May 2005 with a planned 60 personnel and an annual budget of some €2.5 million.[27] In 2010 the amount had reached some €11 million per year (and rising). The mission was dubbed civilian but was asked to provide military advice. Hence, almost all the mission personnel were active or retired military officers. Originally, EUSEC RD Congo's mandate was:

- to support the integration of the Congolese army;
- to improve good governance in the field of security;
- to assist with the identification and conduct of a series of projects which the EU or its member states would want to support.[28]

Soon, additional tasks were assigned to the mission. When two projects (one on a census of the army, the other on the new chain of payment scheme for military salaries) turned out to be successful achievements, they demanded follow-ups and maintenance. After the formal completion of army integration a DRC Rapid Reaction Force had to be developed. The next extension focused on gender and on the protection of children affected by armed conflict.

The extension dynamic might well be a characteristic of SSR missions and thus could also be expected in the case of EU SSR Guinea-Bissau – even more so given the Council's explicit order to the mission to assess the perspective of continued ESDP engagement.[29] Surprisingly, however, the mission was ended after 28 months, before it could substantially evolve. It had started in June 2008 with a staff of 14 seconded and 13 local experts.[30] The budget was limited to €5.6 million. The mission's mandate was:

- to advise and assist local authorities in the implementation of the national SSR strategy, comprising plans to downsize and restructure the army and the police;

- to support the adoption of SSR legal frameworks and to help with the preparation for further engagement by donors in capacity building and DDR;
- to assess the relevance of a continued ESDP engagement.

The mission was abruptly ended in 2010 because of negative circumstances in the host country. Among those circumstances were an attempted military coup in Guinea-Bissau on 1 April 2010, the growing importance of the country as a trading centre for drugs moving from Latin America into Africa, and the inability of the country's government to undertake serious efforts to fully put into place a legal framework for SSR. Moreover, with ECOWAS and the UN poised to start their own SSR missions in the country, the European Union would have to coordinate its activities with both organizations in order to avoid overlap. Finally, the participating member states held differing views of what SSR actually is and how it benefits the local population. In this regard it seemed clear that far more human and financial resources would be needed in order for the mission to possibly have a measurable impact on comprehensive SSR.

Regarding all civilian missions in specific African countries, the European Union finds itself clearly in a situation of learning by doing. The choice of targeted country is largely determined by the initiative of the one EU member state which has an important national interest. Other member states join in for reasons of integration; in other words, they want to demonstrate solidarity and take pride in the fact that the EU runs an international intervention. These choices do not convey the impression of a programme, let alone a concept for a strategic European presence in Africa.

A Civil–Military Mission in Support of the African Union

In addition to missions aimed at individual countries in Africa, the European Union used the ESDP format alongside CFSP diplomacy and European development policy to support ownership and regional cooperation on the African continent and to raise relations between the European and African Unions to the level of strategic partnership. The EU's approach to security assistance met with the African Union's ambition to elaborate on its own security architecture and to conduct its own stabilization operations. Since its inception in 2002, the AU has been building mechanisms of conflict prevention and crisis intervention at its Addis Ababa headquarters and has undertaken peace missions in half a dozen conflict countries, including in Sudan, the case in which the EU has made a major contribution.[31]

The African Union Mission in Sudan (AMIS) has been one of the AU's most important missions to date, trying to manage and end the conflict in the eastern province of Darfur.

Given that the Sudanese government had refused a United Nations peace operation on its territory, the African Union was called in to monitor and verify the ceasefire agreement concluded by the parties to the Darfur conflict in N'Djamena in April 2004. AMIS I, staffed by several hundred troops from Nigeria and Rwanda, turned out a failure because of inadequate size and experience. The AU's Peace and Security Council increased the number of personnel to 3,320 in October 2004 (AMIS II) and later to 7,730 in April 2005 (AMIS II–Enhanced). To help make AMIS a success the

EU provided operational support, financial aid, and diplomatic assistance throughout the AMIS phase from January 2004 to December 2007, after which the African Union-led mission was replaced by a much wider hybrid AU–UN operation (UNAMID).[32]

The ESDP mission, called 'EU civilian–military supporting action to the African Union mission in the Darfur region of Sudan (AMIS)', was asked to deliver a 'consolidated package of civilian and military measures' to AMIS.[33] This included 30 police officers from the European Union Police Advisory Team (EUPAT), 15 military experts and two military observers, who were dispatched from 15 EU member states and were assigned partly to the AU's Darfur Integrated Task Force (DITF) in Addis Ababa and partly to the AMIS force headquarters in Khartoum and AMIS headquarters in Darfur.[34] ESDP support to AMIS also comprised delivery of equipment (vehicles, generators, water-tankers) and technical assistance (media support, aerial observation, air transport) for 2,000 African troops, over a period of 30 months. Moreover, the EUSR to Sudan would draw on the military and civilian experts of the ESDP mission in order to coordinate with the African Union.

The appointment of a EUSR for Sudan in July 2005 was part of various CFSP support activities to end the civil war and to lubricate the peace-building process in Sudan.[35] Brussels had started by sending a Special Envoy early in 2004 in order to help to overcome hurdles in the way of negotiation and reconciliation.[36] Experts were identified to assist the AU with the N'Djamena ceasefire negotiations. Measures were taken to bring about political initiatives like the Darfur-Darfur Dialogue and the Darfur Assessment and Evaluation Commission. The EU Instrument for Stability (run by the European Commission) funded the AU Ceasefire Commission, which included a certain number of military personnel. The EUSR was responsible for ensuring the coherence of these and other European Union measures and for coordinating with international partners such as NATO, the United States and the United Nations.

The European Union's efforts did not end there. Brussels seemed determined to demonstrate that it was serious about security assistance to the African Union in terms of both capacity building and operational support. By creating a special funding instrument for capacity building and operational support, the African Peace Facility (APF), the EU was able to assist the AU in a tailor-made fashion. More than €300 million from this source was dispensed directly to AMIS. The money was taken from the European Development Fund, which allowed spending only for civilian purposes. Thus, the amounts were used to cover non-military costs such as salaries, allowances, insurance, travel, food rations, and medical care. An additional €200 million was provided by EU member states such as France, the United Kingdom, and Germany on a bilateral basis, raising the sum total to half a billion. Taken together with the almost €700 million in humanitarian aid channelled through ECHO, the European Commission's Humanitarian Aid Office, the EU appeared the most generous supporter of African assertiveness.[37]

The civil–military investment in the Africanization of conflict management and the cases of direct engagement in specific peace support operations in individual African countries are seen as practical steps in the direction of a more advanced

AU–EU strategic partnership which has been celebrated in three Africa–EU summits (2007, 2008, 2010) and two Action plans (2008–2010, 2011–2013). The 2007 Joint Africa–EU Strategy (JAES)[38] defines the long-term policy orientations of the two continents, based on a shared vision and common principles. Regarding the area of security, two goals are prominent: assisting to build the African Peace and Security Architecture (APSA) and strengthening the dialogue between the EU and the AU on peace and security issues.

Without explicitly advertising it, the EU is seeking to seize the chance of winning a partner and of dealing more effectively with competitors for power on the African continent, such as the US and the BRICS countries. The EU's civil–military operations are a distinct feature of European intervention policy. The integration of civilian and military components in one package seems important. It is the symbolic content that is significant, not the achievement of change and stabilization on the ground. Again, the aspect of developing the Union further plays a major role. EU member states are keen to demonstrate that they are capable of implementing a broad approach and that they care about African ownership. Following the definition of strategic culture above, this in itself can be counted as a component of an EU strategic culture.

Assessing the EU's Civilian Engagement in Africa

Taken together, the European Union's support for all-African responsibility and for the stabilization of individual countries looks like a plan. In fact, at the turn of the century, the political assistance from Brussels and particularly by the European members of the G8 contributed to the start of the Millennium Development Goals and to the creation of the AU. ESDP activities started a few years later and could be seen as a sign of intercontinental solidarity and substantial support, small as the contributions may have been. This attempt at EU credibility allowed it to venture into a more comprehensive partnership by the end of the decade and tied in with the ESS' provision to win like-minded partners for global security.[39]

Looking back on these ten years, the European Union's civilian engagement in Africa reveals a mixed record. It embarked in the right direction but has come only halfway, and there is little chance of it going much further. The situation in each of the countries in which ESDP has been involved has not moved on to sustainable stability, let alone to good governance, rule of law, or democratic infrastructure. In Guinea-Bissau, the EU had to leave before finishing its SSR mission. Others, like Angola or the UN, have taken over. In the DRC the two ESDP missions continue but no reasonable exit strategy is in place. In Sudan, some of the country's problems such as the north-south divide have been reduced; the Darfur problem, however, remains basically unsolved, with no more than 'a semblance of stability'[40] in the area. Other dormant conflicts, like those in Nigeria and Côte d'Ivoire, have reignited but seen little substantial effort by the AU or EU to reduce civil war. The inefficiency of both organizations in the 2011 North African liberation movements, particularly regarding Gaddafi's Libya, shed additional light on the limits of collective and transcontinental conflict prevention and crisis management.

While it is certainly major progress for the European Union to go beyond humanitarian aid and economic cooperation and to operate in Africa with specialized intervention teams, the task seems more demanding and complicated than was expected and prepared for. Engaging in security sector reform and in training police forces may be an efficient choice in order to rebuild a failed state and utilize European skills and capabilities, but these sectors happen to be among the most sensitive when it comes to redistribution of internal powers and privileges in authoritarian states. If successful, the EU's civilian operations will lead to a change in the political system (with or without a change in government). European personnel risk getting caught in local political struggles. The European Union deliberately takes sides. Civilian interventions are far from being politically neutral or purely humanitarian; they are partisan, they can be coercive, and they can lead to violence and to casualties.

When the first ESDP civilian mission in Africa started in 2005 the EU could already build on the experience gained in its missions in Europe – EUPOL Proxima in FYROM and EUJUST Themis in Georgia. Each mission, however, had its own features in terms of mandate, mission team, and local environment. It turned out to be particularly difficult to recruit the suitable experts and practitioners for the African missions. Take EUSEC Guinea-Bissau, where one of the criteria for participation in the operation was to be able to speak French and Portuguese. The EU member states lacked lots of these specific, but indispensable, criteria and most of them would take time to overcome. The same applies to providing practical equipment in time, such as sufficient force enablers (vehicles, helicopters, communication equipment). The logistic challenge was as demanding as political coordination with the activities of other actors, like NATO or the UN.[41] These deficiencies highlight that the EU is by no means a professional actor when it comes to establishing security in Africa.

Despite the remarkable level of European Union support for capacity building of the AU and for individual African-led missions like AMIS, no breakthrough was achieved and no self-sustaining process followed, as had been the aim. Some observers claim that the funding level was simply much too low, while others feel that the AU was not experienced enough to handle all the external support it received.[42] The EU constantly underestimated the extent to which the AU was stretching its capabilities. Too much wishful thinking may have misguided the EU. The African claim for ownership lacked substance.

What remains, on the positive side, is the civil–military approach that the European Union managed to project into the African Union's peace-building concepts and structures. The African Standby Force (ASF) has been built on a concept similar to that of the CSDP. It consists of various types of military forces, police forces, and civilian personnel. These forces are located in their respective countries and can be assembled within 30 days, according to an operation plan worked out at the AU headquarters in Addis Ababa and agreed upon by the AU Peace and Security Council. All of these institutional arrangements are new and still weak. There is a so far insurmountable lack of instruments and means by which to plan and implement missions on the continent with some degree of calculability and reliability. The EU can bridge only a small part of this African deficiency. But unlike other strategic regions and major players in the world, the AU seems to know what the appropriate answers are and seems able to work on them.[43]

If the European Union security assistance to the AU via the Africa Peace Facility and the Stability Instrument was largely a choice by design, its selection of the individual ESDP missions was rather driven by a small group of activists among the member states. We find Belgium, Portugal, France, Italy, and Sweden contributing to all civilian and civil–military ESDP missions in Africa, while Germany, the Netherlands, Finland, and the United Kingdom participated only in one or two of them. Two thirds of the EU membership did not join in at all; in particular the east European countries were not active (with the exception of Romania). As expected, the former colonial powers are the most active. The United Kingdom is less involved, probably because of its heavy bilateral engagement in Liberia and other war-ridden places. Sweden is part of the activist group most likely as a consequence of its early and continued championship of civilian interventions by the EU. Germany, the Netherlands, and Finland may have been lured into the process once they saw that the civilian missions made sense and seemed to earn some results. Moreover, it took off some of the pressure from peers to contribute to military operations.

It seems natural that countries like Belgium and France, in the case of the DRC, and Portugal, in the case of Guinea-Bissau, would push for European engagement, given their long-standing political and security involvement with these countries, their cultural affinity, and their important economic interests regarding industrial investment, exploitation of raw materials, and financial cooperation. In the end, these factors determined the choices of the EU as a whole. As bilateral donors, individual member states had been active in 'their' country long before and now decided to engage in a dual-track tactic, contributing both to bilateral projects and to EU missions.

Objectively speaking, in the group of 27 member states, countries with a strong interest and conviction are needed for taking initiatives, reaching a consensus, and carrying it through. The former colonial powers clearly did play this role in the civilian ESDP operations in Africa. The Europeanization of their bilateral interests alleviates part of their burden, at the price of losing part of their bilateral status.[44] African former colonies may find it attractive to deal with the EU – a more powerful, more innovative, and more objective partner than the colonial patron of the past. Overall, the EU adapts its choices of intervention and its method of action to the needs of some of its members while building on their special relationship with individually targeted countries, as well as with the AU as a whole. This pattern of operation may lead to a recognizable international profile for the Union. Some observers may call it a trademark of European intervention policy.

Installing Civilian CSDP in Brussels: Structural Limitations?

Paul Cornish and Geoffrey Edwards rightly claim that not only 'operations' but also 'capabilities and policy processes' are a constituent part of the establishment of strategic culture.[45] This remains true even if the Union seeks a lower-level target first – the development of a distinctive power of intervention. Not long ago, the EU lacked rapidly available civilian police and experts for immediate intervention in crisis situations. Before ESDP was established, CFSP would engage in mediation and organize dialogue between parties in dispute, but had no funds and no instruments to follow on, help to implement peace agreements, and assist with building up state infrastructure.

The Commissioners for external relations and for development would use their funds to intervene in critical cases in the Third World, including African countries, to help with peaceful conflict resolution, post-war reconstruction and training of security forces. However, these activities were mostly separate from the diplomatic circuit of CFSP. In such a system, the legal and the administrative structures of the EU would hamper holistic thinking as well as a comprehensive approach, both of which are indispensable nowadays for efficient crisis management. How did the EU manage to integrate a civilian intervention component in its foreign and security policy, and how does it characterize the EU as a security actor?

Building Up the Civilian Component of CSDP: Responsive Concept or Political Pressure?

The civilian component of ESDP came later than its military counterpart. The idea of an ESDP goes back to the experience of the war over Kosovo, where countries of the European Union felt that their influence on the conflict with Milosevic's Serbia had been insufficient. The EU lacked a collective intervention force. This was the conclusion drawn at an informal meeting in Pörtschach, Austria, in October 1998, which led to the Franco-British Saint-Malo paper of December 1998 that prepared the blueprint for ESDP, adopted at the European Council meeting in Cologne in June 1999. Up to then, ESDP had been a military project. The Finnish EU Presidency (supported by Sweden) added the civilian aspect to the project, but it was not until the European Council of Santa Maria Da Feira, Portugal, in June 2000 that the civilian component of ESDP was specified and a civilian headline goal declared.[46]

The Swedish and Finnish governments had intervened in the early discussion process over ESDP by suggesting an addition to the originally military ESDP concept.[47] Their reasoning was both conceptual and political. In their analysis, the EU was confronted with intervention cases of a kind that mostly demanded civilian expertise and support, a conclusion which was inspired by the August 2000 Brahimi Report of the UN.[48] Military means would be needed in specific cases of peace building and peace enforcement only, said the Report. The two Scandinavian governments also made it plain that their parliaments would refuse the plans for a military European intervention force unless they were assured that, as a rule, the projection of civilian EU power would come first, leaving the use of military means as a last resort. Many of the EU member states followed this line of reasoning as they saw themselves confronted with the same kind of problem of political acceptance at home. In the end, the first series of ESDP operations started with a civilian mission and so far more than two thirds of all the ESDP operations have been civilian in nature. Their scope and strength, on average, has been more moderate than the scope and strength of military operations, and they have also been much less costly.

When the missions began in January 2003, the EU did not create an overall conceptual guideline or a security-related white paper. The European Union Institute for

Security Studies (EUISS), an agency of the Union, was asked to do some strategic reflection but was not allowed to design a white paper.[49] The EUISS study was strong on the military side, the civilian component of crisis management was hardly mentioned. The ESS of December 2003, designed as a counter-document to the US National Security Strategy of September 2002 and adopted before the eastern enlargement of the EU in May 2004, drew attention to the fact that the EU's approach to security was particular. The ESS was pleading not only for a link-up of civilian and military means but also for the centrality of the UN regarding security and for the promotion of international law, as well as for the expansion of effective multilateralism. All of these core features of the EU's security culture are connected to the civilian side of ESDP, with the exception of the ESS's demand for robust intervention when necessary.

Overall, the ESS sounded civilian, while the institutional innovation and the instrumental build-up were military. It is fair to say that in terms of the European integration process, the Union had to catch up most in the military sphere. The establishment of the Political and Security Committee (PSC), the EU Military Committee and the EU Military Staff were all dominated by military requirements, including the operative preparation, implementation, and control capacities created in the Council Secretariat. Most of the European intervention forces had been trained within the NATO context and the ESDP link to NATO (Berlin-Plus) for planning purposes; transport, surveillance and command was all military-related. The civilian side, which did not have NATO as backup and support, was left with the task of identifying and assembling experts scattered all over the EU member states and their provinces. Inside the Council Secretariat, civilian missions lacked a professional infrastructure that would have lived up to the challenges of crisis intervention. The organization of civilian operations was understaffed, the status of the civilian officers was low, and the Committee of the Civilian Aspects of Crisis Management (CIVCOM) had little influence on the political process of the PSC. While ESDP was scheduled to create a military rapid reaction force of 50–60,000 soldiers, the civilian component of ESDP aimed to comprise not more than one tenth of that size.[50]

Since those beginning years the civilian/military asymmetry has changed significantly. Given the growing quantity and size of civilian missions, it was important to raise their professional level as well as their institutional handling. The creation of the Civilian Planning and Conduct Capability (CPCC) in June 2007 introduced a command structure in the civilian realm (Civilian Operations Commander) comparable to the one in the military sector – an innovation as indispensable as it was unusual for non-military personnel from the private and state sectors. Moreover, the quality and specialization of civilian experts has been improving, national and European training centres have been established, and several generations of specialists have been collecting best practices by moving from one ESDP mission to the next. All these ameliorations have not excluded serious constraints of available financial resources, personnel and equipment in particular situations, such as in the African missions described above. But overall, it seems that the civilian strand is on its way to being recognized as an important element within CSDP.

The promotion of the civilian strand of ESDP was a precondition for grasping the EU's full potential by way of Civil–Military Cooperation (CMCO). An attempt had been made already in 2003 with the creation of the Civil–Military Cell, which was meant to provide capacities for early warning and situation assessment and to support strategic planning in case of an ESDP mission. In fact, the Cell has contributed to a number of missions, including the ones to Darfur and to Guinea-Bissau. Within the institutional structure of ESDP, the Cell was of limited reach given that it was located within the EUMS, and suffered from diverging views among the member states, with France's claim for a military planning capacity and London's concern about duplication with NATO facilities.

A more promising move toward an integrated civil–military structure began with the Crisis Management and Planning Directorate (CMPD), as agreed by the Council in December 2008. The CMPD was modelled on the Crisis Response Coordinating Teams (CRCTs), which used to be composed on a case-by-case basis and include personnel from all relevant Council Secretariat geographical task forces, from SitCen, SatCen, from the EUMS, and from the Civil–Military Cell, as well as from relevant Commission services.[51] At that stage, the initial advocacy for a strong civilian ESDP component had moved on from a few pioneer member states' political pressure to an EU-wide conceptual logic. The experience on the ground in crisis management countries had brought the message home to all the EU governments that only the broadest approach would be appropriate to the nature of the security challenges encountered in Africa and other critical regions of the world.

Institutionalizing the Civilian Component: A New Type of Security Actor?

Since the adoption of the Lisbon Treaty in December 2009, the European Union's comprehensive approach to conflict prevention and crisis management has been institutionalized. 'Comprehensive approach' refers to the ability to integrate civilian and military instruments into one policy package and to coordinate civilian and defence agencies closely, and the new High Representative of the Union for Foreign Affairs and Security Policy (HR) is what could be described as the master of comprehensiveness within the new institutional set. As the Chair of the External Affairs Council, the HR is responsible for the intergovernmental CFSP, including CSDP; as Commission Vice-President the HR is responsible for the communitarian external relations of the Commission, including the coordination of the external aspects of other Commission policies. The HR has not only the right and duty of political initiative in both functions, but is asked to interconnect them in a coherent manner and to represent them as the European voice and position toward the outside of the EU. The period since the integration of policy procedures began is too short to extract any reliable outcomes but it will certainly lend itself as test field concerning the horizontal interaction of the communitarian and the intergovernmental components of EU external action. Is the one dominating the other? Will the two merge and lead to an overarching third quality of European policy making in the field of security?

Unlike the first decade of ESDP, when its interconnection with the Commission's external relations happened mostly at random, the EU now has a structural ability to base its initiatives on integrated assessment and planning that allows and demands use of the whole range of the Union's foreign policy instruments in a coherent and focused manner, as well as coordination of the European and national levels of foreign policy-making. Since January 2011 the HR has been supported by the European External Action Service (EEAS), which is composed of foreign-affairs and security-policy experts from the European Commission, the Council Secretariat, and the member states, seconded temporarily from their governments on a rotating basis. The EEAS has one department for global issues and five geographical ones, including one that deals with African affairs. Thus, the HR can rely on the EU's collective European and national expertise, and the member states can profit from the European experience of their rotating staff. The two-level governance of EU foreign and security policy is developing into a two-way street. What is the long-term outcome of this vertical interaction process regarding the EU's mode of intervention?

Some of these interactive horizontal and vertical processes have been studied in the past using concepts of constructivism, socialization, Europeanization or others. This was at the time of the institutional and methodological schism in European Union external relations. Today, a fresh approach will be needed to grasp the new degree of complexity which has come with the practical policy processes seen in the past years and the legal and institutional changes of the Lisbon Treaty. What is the status and the role of civilian missions today? In 2008, when France held the EU Presidency and tried to update and redesign the ESS with a military emphasis, it could not find enough support for the initiative among the member governments.[52] The failure of this attempt led to a relative strengthening of the civilian component of ESDP. The strengthening of the civilian strand seems to be more attractive because it is believed to be less costly and politically more acceptable.[53]

Conclusion: Perhaps a Trademark, but no Strategic Culture

This article started by assessing a few civilian ESDP missions in Africa. Its empirical discussion showed that the missions arrived in places in which the EU had been engaged long before via its diplomatic relations and economic cooperation programmes. EU humanitarian aid as well as development policy had responded to needs of underdevelopment and state failure. In particular, some of the EU's member states had been active on a bilateral basis concerning more long-term business and cultural relations. The civilian ESDP missions arrived late, but seemed timely when they were called in to assist at critical moments and for specific tasks. Their achievements, however, turned out to be marginal rather than decisive.

The missions did not perform tremendously well partly because of objective reasons, partly due to lack of capacity among the receivers, and partly because of deficiencies in the European Union related to the asymmetrical evolution of the various components of the Union's security policy. The EU's approach to intervention is basically interactive and multilateral, and therefore depends on others as much as on its own (lack of) assertiveness. In the African cases described above and within the institutional construction site in Brussels, the EU is driven more by practical goals and integrationist desire than by strategic thinking. National and European actors are preoccupied with individual, largely technical and bureaucratic challenges. How to run an intervention and how to run it without major flaws is the dominant question. The focus is more inward, oriented toward the internal fabric of the EU, than it is led by external assertiveness and geopolitical competition. Under these circumstances the EU may run a remarkable intervention mainly using civilian components or even civil–military coordination. This in itself allows us to infer that there is indeed a component of what can be called strategic culture. However, a more comprehensive strategic culture could not be detected at this point in time.

The article did not analyse or compare ESDP civilian missions in other regions of the world, nor did it include any military ESDP operations, although doing this could lead to a greater understanding of the EU's broader approach to crisis management. Such a widening of the empirical base may lead to a stage of analysis that could detect a strategic threshold. The pure civilian cases are too modest in size and reach to allow a debate of strategic culture, although they did facilitate discussion of the quality of EU modes of intervention. However, among the civilian cases in Africa were hybrid ones – those that included civilian and military strands – as well as those with a goal of security assistance and support of a build-up of partner organizations', such as the African Union's, crisis management capabilities. In these cases Brussels demonstrated that it can enjoy moments of broader response even though the scope and sustainability of assistance remain sub-strategic. The notions 'comprehensive approach' and 'civil–military' should not be misread: there is a vast preponderance of the civilian component in European foreign and security policy.

The cases of civilian intervention in Africa, initiated and pushed by former colonial powers, opened an option for influence to individual member states by Europeanizing (part of) their bilateral relationship with the country in question. This part of the mode of intervention is a unique feature of the European Union. Non-colonial actors like the US or China, cannot profit from such alternative avenues. The advantage of this singularity is reduced by the EU's own heterogeneous membership comprising non-colonial and former colonial states. Homogeneous, or at least like-minded, behaviour is a precondition for the attempt to project power out of Brussels. In this vein the EU as a whole seized the opportunity to export its model of regional integration and to offer a pretty sophisticated concept of conflict prevention and post-crisis rehabilitation to its AU partner. Selling the EU crisis management approach and exploiting the possibility of Europeanization of bilateral relations are so far understudied, maybe also underestimated. If further developed, the typical European comprehensive approach to conflict prevention and crisis management and the EU's specific two-level (Member States and Union) external action could become the trademark of EU security policy.

The European engagement in the DRC, in Guinea-Bissau, and via the AU also in Sudan was aimed at developing the Union and its foreign and security policy. In this perspective, Africa constituted to a considerable extent a test field for the new crisis management machinery in Brussels. It was visible from the civilian ESDP missions to Africa, including the nomination of an EU Special Representative to the Great Lakes, that the EU had tentatively attained a new level of international reach simply by taking responsibility beyond Europe. While praising effective multilateralism with the UN at its core as its prime approach to international security, the Union learned that potential international partners either pursue their own rival programmes (as in the case of the UN), lack absorption power (as in the case of the AU), try in vain to substantiate coordination with a congenial ally (such as the US) or compete conceptually (as Angola did with its own SSR activities in Guinea-Bissau).

With its broad-based civilian instruments and its civil–military approach, Brussels may have a comparative advantage over other international actors, but European actions lack geopolitical leadership, united political will, and reliable resources. The European Council, since the Lisbon Treaty an institution among many in the political system of the EU, has so far not delivered such indispensable ingredients of strategic culture. As long as this situation remains basically unchanged (and the Lisbon Treaty reconfirms the intergovernmental nature of CSDP) we witness a 'mode of intervention' rather than a 'strategic culture'. One should not be deceived by EU rhetoric. Brussels is not defending Europe with a European army – NATO is, and the United States. The CSDP project is neither about building up an EU missile defence system nor about a common nuclear defence.

The ESS optimistically stated: 'Our history, geography and cultural ties link the European Union with every part of the world: our neighbours in the Middle East, our partners in Africa ... These relationships are an important asset to build on. In particular we should look to develop strategic partnerships, with Japan, China, Canada and India as well as all those who share our goals and values, and are prepared to act in their support.'[54] Working in partnership with key actors is as much art as labour, given that all of these partners follow agendas of their own and cultivate their own mode of intervention. Some of them are more competitors than partners. China is a prominent example in this regard, especially in Africa, and especially concerning the comprehensive approach.

NOTES

1. The build-up of an EU intervention capability for crisis management started with the creation of the European Security and Defence Policy (ESDP) at the European Council meeting in Helsinki in December 1999. See http://www.consilium.europa.eu/uedocs/cmsUpload/Helsinki%20European%20Council%20-%20Annex%20IV%20of%20the%20Presidency%20Conclusions.pdf (accessed 7 May 2011).
2. ESDP interventions started with operation CONCORDIA in the Former Yugoslav Republic of Macedonia in January 2003. Three months later the first operation was sent to Africa: ARTEMIS DR Congo. Petar Petrov, 'Early Institutionalisation of the ESDP Governance Arrangements: Insights from the Operations Concordia and Artemis', in Sophie Vanhoonacker, Hylke Dijkstra and Heidi Maurer (eds), *Understanding the Role of Bureaucracy in the European Security and Defence Policy* (European Integration Online Papers 2010, Special Issue 1, Vol. 14, http://eiop.or.at/eiop/texte/2010-008a_htm), pp. 1–22.
3. The term 'civilian power' (Zivilmacht) was first used to describe the European Community, including its European Political Cooperation, by François Duchêne in 1973. François Duchêne, 'Die Rolle Europas im Weltsystem. Von der regionalen zur planetarischen Interdependenz', in Max Kohnstamm and Wolfgang Hager (eds), *Zivilmacht Europa – Supermacht oder Partner?* (Frankfurt: Suhrkamp, 1973), pp. 11–35.
4. Karen E. Smith, 'The End of Civilian Power EU: A Welcome Demise or Cause for Concern?', *International Spectator*, Vol. 35, No. 2 (2000), pp. 11–28.
5. Robert Kagan, Power and Weakness: 'Why the United States and Europe See the World Differently', *Policy Review*, No. 113 (2002). Kagan's argument is built around the notion that Europe's relative military weakness compels it to use fundamentally different foreign policy tools than America.

6. Gisela Müller-Brandeck-Bocquet, 'The Big Member States' Influence on the Shaping of European Union's Foreign, Security and Defence Policy', in Gisela Müller-Brandeck-Bocquet (ed.), *The Future of the European Foreign, Security and Defence Policy after Enlargement* (Baden-Baden: Nomos-Verlag, 2006), pp. 25-53.
7. William Easterly, 'How the Millennium Development Goals are Unfair to Africa', Brookings Global Economy and Development Working Paper 14, Washington, DC, November 2007.
8. http://vlex.com/source/partnership-agreement-acp-ec-signed-cotonou-23-june-2000-revised-luxembourg-25-june-2005-2009
9. Federica Marzo, 'More Trees have Fallen ... but the Forest is Still Growing: Recent trends in African politics', OECD Development Centre Policy Insights No. 63, Paris, 2008.
10. 'A Secure Europe in a Better World', European Security Strategy, Brussels, 12 December 2003, http://www.consilium.europa.eu/uedocs/cmsUpload/78367.pdf
11. *Ibid.*, p. 1.
12. *Ibid.*, pp. 2-4.
13. *Ibid.*, p.10.
14. *Ibid.*, p. 9.
15. Grzegorz Ekiert and Stephen E. Hanson (eds), *Capitalism and Democracy in Central and Eastern Europe* (Cambridge: Cambridge University Press, 2003).
16. Barbara Lippert, 'The Big Easy? Growth, Differentiation and Dynamics of EU-enlargement Policy', in Udo Diedrichs, Anne Faber, Funda Tekin and Gaby Umbach (eds), *Europe Reloaded: Differentiation or Fusion?* (Baden-Baden: Nomos 2011), pp. 238–268.
17. Gunilla Herolf, 'National and Supranational Actors in European Foreign Policy', in K.Y. Nikolov (ed.), *Adapting to Integration in an Enlarged European Union* (Sofia: Bulgarian European Community Studies Association [BECSA], 2008), pp. 312–333.
18. Tony Chafer and Gordon Cumming (eds), *From Rivalry to Partnership? New Approaches to the Challenges of Africa* (Aldershot: Ashgate, 2011).
19. *Ibid.*
20. The following description of the civilian ESDP missions to Africa is based on the information given by Thierry Vircoulon, Caty Clément, Benedict Franke and Damien Helly in Giovanni Grevi *et al.* (eds), *European Security and Defence Policy. The First 10 Years (1999-2009)*, (Paris: EU ISS, 2009).
21. The legal basis was the Council Joint Action 2004/847/CFSP of 9 December 2004, and Council Joint Action 2005/355/CFSP of 2 May 2005.
22. The legal basis is the Council Joint Action 2007/405/CFSP of 12 June 2007.
23. The legal basis is the Council Joint Action 2008/112/CFSP of 12 February 2008.
24. Contributing states at the start of the mission were Belgium, France, Italy, Netherlands, Portugal, and Sweden. Later the UK, Denmark and Romania reinforced the team and non-EU states – including Canada, Turkey, Mali, and Angola – were also added to the list.
25. Support had come from the European Commission, which gave €7 million for technical assistance, training facilities and communication systems; and from member states, which gave €2.4 million for training and equipment. See Thierry Vircoulon, 'EUPOL Kinshasa and EUPOL RD Congo', in Grevi *et al.*, *European Security and Defence Policy*, (note 20) p. 223.
26. Contributing states at the start of the mission were Belgium, Finland, France, Germany, Italy, Portugal, Romania, Spain, and Sweden. The following non-EU states were added to the mission: Angola, Canada, Turkey, and Switzerland.
27. Contributing states at the start of the mission were Belgium, France, Germany, Italy, Portugal, and the UK.
28. The projects included the separation of the chain of payment from the chain of command; a census of the Congolese Army; advisory support to the 2009 Revised Strategic Plan for Army Reform; and a multilateral approach to SSR.
29. The legal basis is the Council Joint Action 2008/112/CFSP of 12 February 2008.
30. Contributing states were France, Germany, Italy, Portugal, Spain, and Sweden.
31. Other AU operations were undertaken in Burundi, the Comores, the Central African Republic and Somalia. Regarding Somalia, the EU Council followed a request by the AU and amended its Joint Action on AMIS on 23 April 2007 to include a military support component for the setting up of the African Union Mission in Somalia (AMISOM). In May 2010 EUTM Somalia was launched as a military training mission taking place in Uganda, where Somali security forces are already being trained, which also facilitates the coordination of the EU action with AMISOM. The mission is conducted in close coordination with EU partners, including the TFG of Somalia, Uganda, the African Union, the United Nations, and the United States of America.

32. The legal basis is UN Security Council Resolution 1769 of 31 July 2007.
33. The main legal basis is Council Joint Action 2005/557/CFSP of 18 July 2005.
34. Member states contributing to the EU Support for AMIS were Austria, Belgium, Cyprus, Denmark, Germany, Finland, France, Hungary, Ireland, Italy, Netherlands, Portugal, Spain, Sweden, and the UK.
35. The legal basis is Council Joint Action 2005/556/CFSP. Pekka Haavisto from Finland was appointed as the EU's first Special Representative (EUSR) for Sudan. He was followed by Torben Brylle in April 2007.
36. Sten Rylander from Sweden acted as Special Envoy for Darfur between early 2004 and December 2005.
37. For the exact figures see Nicoletta Pirozzi, 'EU Support to African Security Architecture: Funding and Training Components,' Occasional Paper No. 76, EU Institute for Security Studies, Paris, February 2009.
38. 'The Africa-EU Strategic Partnership: A Joint Africa-EU Strategy', http://www.africa-eu-partnership.org/partnerships/africa-eu-strategic-partnership
39. Reinhardt Rummel, 'Die EU in Afrika – Regionale Stabilisierungsinterventionen im lokalen und internationalen Kontext', in Walter Feichtinger and Gerald Hainzl (eds), *Krisenmanagement in Afrika* (Vienna: Böhlau, 2009), pp. 51–72.
40. Seth Appiah-Mensah, 'The African Mission in Sudan: Darfur Dilemmas', *African Security Review*, Vol. 15, No. 1 (2006), p.19.
41. Markus Derblom, Eva Hagström Frisell and Jennifer Schmidt, 'UN-EU-AU Coordination in Peace Operations in Africa', Swedish Defence Research Agency Report No. 2602, Stockholm, November 2008.
42. 'Despite multilateral initiatives for information exchange on security assistance and cooperation programmes like the Africa Clearing House and the AU Partners Technical Support Group in Addis Ababa, possible synergies were not always utilised and donor efforts often overlapped leading to unnecessary duplications, which increased the transaction costs for the AU and further strained its absorption capacity.' See Benedikt Franke, 'The European Union supporting actions to the African Unions missions in Sudan (AMIS) and Somalia (AMISON)', in Grevi *et al.* (eds), *European Security and Defence Policy* (note 20), p.259. The author adds the following telling case: 'A good example is the fact that even though both NATO's Strategic Airlift Coordination Centre and the EU's European Airlift Centre are co-located in Eindhoven each dispatched its own liaison team to the DITF in Addis Ababa, thereby unnecessarily multiplying demands on AU staff and facilities.'
43. Jackie Cilliers, 'The African Standby Force. An Update on Progress', ISS Paper 160, Pretoria 2008.
44. Sébastien Bergeon, 'Stratégies africaines - Vers une européanisation de la politique de sécurité et de défense de la France en Afrique?' *Défense Nationale et Sécurité Collective*, Vol. 63, No. 1 (2007), pp. 55–62.
45. See Paul Cornish and Geoffrey Edwards, 'The Strategic Culture of the European Union: A Progress Report', *International Affairs*, Vol. 81, No. 4 (July 2005), p.802
46. http://www.consilium.europa.eu/uedocs/cms_data/docs/pressdata/en/ec/00200-r1.en0.htm (accessed 9 November 2011).
47. Gunilla Herlof, 'Overcoming National Impediments to ESDP', in K Brummer (ed.), The North and the ESDP. *The Baltic States, Denmark, Finland and Sweden*, (Tallinn: EVI Publications, 2007), available at http://www.isn.ethz.ch/isn/Digital-Library/Publications/Detail/?ots591=0C54E3B3-1E9C-BE1E-2C24-A6A8C7060233&lng=en&id=94522, pp. 17–29.
48. http://www.un.org/peace/reports/peace_operations/ (accessed 9 November 2011)
49. The EUISS later produced a volume which picks up the task of strategic thinking ahead. See Álvaro de Vasconcelos (ed.), *What Ambitions for European Defence in 2020?* (Paris: European Union Institute for Security Studies, 2009), available at http://www.iss.europa.eu/uploads/media/What_ambitions_for_European_defence_in_2020.pdf. Other experts have asked for an official strategic document. See Christos Katsioulis *et al.*, 'The European Union needs a Defence White Paper. A Proposal', Berlin, 2010.
50. For a comprehensive record see Agnieszka Nowak (ed.), 'Civilian Crisis Management: the EU Way', Chaillot Paper No. 90, Paris, June 2006.
51. Carmen Gebhard, 'The Crisis Management and Planning Directorate: Recalibrating ESDP Planning and Conduct Capacities', *CFSP Forum*, Vol. 7, No. 4 (2009) pp. 8–14.
52. 'Report on the Implementation of the European Security Strategy – Providing Security in a Changing World', S407/08, Brussels, 11 December 2008, available at http://www.consilium.europa.eu/uedocs/cms_data/docs/pressdata/en/reports/104630.pdf (accessed 9 November 2011).
53. Peter Viggo Jakobsen, 'The ESDP and Civilian Rapid Reaction: Adding Value is Harder than Expected', *European Security*, Vol. 15, No. 3 (September 2006), pp. 299–321.
54. ESS (note 10), p.14.

Putting Ideas into Action: EU Civilian Crisis Management in the Western Balkans

ARNOLD H. KAMMEL

Introduction

Since its first appearance in the late 1970s, the term 'strategic culture' has formed the basis for examining the key priorities of a nation state's security policy. The main goal is to identify the continuity and changes in the behaviour of nation states regarding their security policy.[1] Generated at the crossroads of history, capabilities, geopolitics, and values, the exact meaning of the term varies considerably. Without going into too much detail on the scholarly debate between first and third-generation theorists regarding the definition of the term, there is obviously a rationale behind the action of global players which are not necessarily nation states, but are supranational entities.[2] There is, in the words of Gray, something 'out there'; something perceivable within a security community that influences its behaviour and which needs to be more closely examined.[3] As Toje has pointed out, strategic culture 'indicates but does not determine what is expected of an actor, what the alternatives are or what courses of action are deemed possible.'[4] It is thus necessary to look not only at the declaratory level, but also at the operational actions. Ideas and actions form the key variables for the assessment of a strategic culture.

However, in speaking about the development of a European strategic culture, one has to consider that due to its very nature the European Union is a different actor. Three shortfalls have to be admitted. First of all, the European Union is not a nation state. A widening of the project of enhancing a supranational organization has been on the agenda instead of a deepening of European integration, thus hindering debates on what the real European security interests and objectives are due to member states' increasing lack of cohesion.[5] Secondly, the field of foreign, security and defence policy still remains intergovernmental, leaving decisions on the nation-state level. Thirdly, this policy field is less than two decades old, meaning that work is still in progress and this process will not be finished in the near future. Therefore, an attempt to define what a European strategic culture would consist of will be considerably different from the concept used for nation states. In this context it is also not surprising that the responses to security issues among member states differ.

Is there then a need for the European Union to acquire its own strategic culture? Considering the European Union as a global actor, the answer must be a clear yes.[6] On the declaratory level, the adoption of the European Security Strategy (ESS) in December 2003 clearly demonstrated a consensus among the member states regarding Europe's security environment, threat perception, capability development and interaction with other actors. With the adoption of the ESS, the idea of a common

European Union strategic culture '[fostering] early, rapid and when necessary, robust intervention' became a foreign policy objective and the ESS the reference document by which to measure European action.[7] The ESS clearly focuses on bringing and maintaining stability in the immediate neighbourhood. Thus, the EU takes into account that '[T]he integration of acceding states increases our security but also brings the EU closer to troubled areas. Our task is to promote a ring of well governed countries to the East of the European Union and on the borders of the Mediterranean with whom we can enjoy close and cooperative relations'.[8] Keeping this idea of stability in the neighbourhood, proposed actions should be carried out through an integrated civil-military approach, whereby the civilian dimension based on European values such as democracy, human rights and the rule of law is clearly dominant.

Against this background, the question of what strategic culture really means for a global actor such as the European Union needs to be answered. As stated above, it is not all about words and ideas, but also concrete actions. Therefore a definition of a European strategic culture must consist of elements, words and deeds. Snyder defined strategic culture in 1977 as 'the sum total of ideals, conditional emotional responses, and patterns of habitual behaviour that members of the national strategic community have acquired through instruction or imitation and share with each other with regard to [nuclear] strategy', but my approach to the term strategic culture will be slightly different and shall be tested in relation to the EU's attitude towards civilian crisis management in the Western Balkans.[9] The underlying assumption is based on the first generation of strategic culture theory, namely that when the EU engages itself in post-conflict scenario, this engagement is based within a certain context, that is a strategic culture. In this article, I define EU strategic culture as the sum of ideas, behaviours and mindsets that the EU and its member states have acquired as a result of forming a strategic community, among whose constituent parts instruction and imitation are shared. This does not automatically constitute a strategy in itself but lays the normative and behavioural foundations for the generation and sustainability of a foreign policy strategy for the EU, and encompasses also the capabilities and actions of this strategy.

The objective of this paper is to analyse and chronologically describe the four civilian missions carried out under the framework of the European Security and Defence Policy (ESDP)/Common Security and Defence Policy (CSDP) in the Western Balkans.[10] As the deployment of missions and operations can be considered an important way to infer insights about its strategic culture, and based on the assumption that the European Union clearly possesses the prerequisites to form a strategic culture in terms of having extensive interests, obligations, and capabilities, the paper will take a closer look at the civilian missions that have taken place in the Western Balkans and that were carried out within the framework of ESDP.[11] This makes it necessary to briefly describe the development of EU civilian crisis management to illustrate how possible prerequisites for a genuine strategic culture were built up. After an analysis of the four missions, their possible contribution to the development of a European strategic culture will be assessed by examining whether the two poles, namely ideas and action, match. The decisive question hereby will be to what extent the four missions have influenced the ideas and behaviour of European foreign and security policy and to what extent the different mindsets of EU member states have guided the EU's interests with regard to its action in the field.

Putting its Civilian Powers in Action: the Development of Civilian Crisis Management in the Framework of ESDP

The development of a European Security and Defence Policy (ESDP), at least in its initial phase, has moved with 'almost breathtaking rapidity'.[12] While European crisis management in general has never been a top priority with regard to European integration, due to the fact that that economic integration was considered its main tool for integration, the rapid development of a Common Foreign and Security Policy (CFSP) and ESDP as a component of the EU's external action was unexpected. These developments, however, were the consequence of the European inability to deal with the Balkan crisis and the break-up of the former Yugoslavia, cumulating in the war in Kosovo in 1999. This experience made European leaders aware of the necessity to further advance the project of CFSP, including an autonomous ESDP. It was considered an unavoidable step to overcome the marginalization of the EU as an actor in its immediate neighbourhood. In addition, economic assistance needed to be backed up by a credible external action by the EU.

After the constitutive moments for ESDP in Pörtschach and St. Malo in 1998, the European Union decided at the Nice European Council meeting of December 2000 to bring ESDP on track and to become operational in December 2001.[13] This was underlined by the European Council's Gothenburg summit in June 2001 where the incoming presidency was 'invited to take forward work... and to report on progress towards achieving the objective of making the EU quickly operational. Progress must continue so that a decision to that end can be taken as soon as possible and no later than at the European Council in Laeken.'[14]

However, it took another external event to move ESDP forward. Following the events of 11 September 2001, an extraordinary European Council meeting took place in Stockholm on 21 September 2001 where European leaders underlined the necessity to make CFSP and ESDP operational as fast as possible: 'It is by developing the Common Foreign and Security Policy (CFSP) and by making the European Security and Defence Policy (ESDP) operational at the earliest opportunity that the Union will be most effective.'[15]

The European Council of Laeken adopted the 'Declaration on the Operational Capability of the Common European Security and Defence Policy' on 14/15 December 2001, signalling that 'the EU is now able to conduct some crisis-management operations'.[16] The declaration made it very clear that the operationality was linked almost completely to the military dimension of ESDP. Nonetheless, at that time the general perception of the European Union was that of a normative and mainly civilian power applying soft power rather than military means.[17] In short, the European Union had established a perceived reputation as a reliable civilian crisis manager, using military force under the most exceptional circumstances and based on a broad legitimating international consensus.[18]

In the meantime, the Feira European Council in June 2000 defined four action areas of priority with a view to improving the Union's civilian capabilities, namely the police sector, the rule of law, civil administration and civil protection.[19] These capabilities should be available either for autonomous EU-led missions or for operations conducted under the lead of other international organizations such as the United Nations (UN) or the Organization for Security and Cooperation in Europe (OSCE). Effectively, however, operationality in civilian capacities was achieved in 2002.[20]

By 2004 the EU was involved in both military operations and civilian missions. It had also developed its own formal security strategy, the European Security Strategy, as a guidance document for the further development and implementation of ESDP.[21]

After the first five years of ESDP, however, the dynamics slowed down and the various headline goals adopted in order to develop the necessary capabilities turned out to be aspirational targets. Christopher Hill's 'capability-expectations gap' could also be detected in the area of civilian crisis management capabilities.[22]

As a consequence, developments within the first ten years of operationality in the area of EU civilian crisis management can be described as two steps forward, one step back, due to the fact that ESDP had to start from scratch. Since the initiation of a foreign, security and defence policy on the European level, which was developed largely as a consequence of the EU's failures to react to and manage the events in the Western Balkans, priority was given to ensuring and improving stability in the immediate European neighbourhood. Essentially the ethnic conflict in Kosovo and NATO's military interventions indicated to the EU that it was time for it to show a stronger commitment to the region by offering clear membership prospects as the only way to promote stability and democracy in the countries of the Western Balkans.[23] Against this backdrop, it was not surprising at all that the first civilian mission under the framework of ESDP would take place in the Balkans.

EU Police Mission (EUPM) (Table 1)

In the absence of the Serbian members, the parliament of Bosnia and Herzegovina (BiH) declared its independence in March 1992, placing the country on the brink of civil war. The Serbs themselves had already announced their own 'Republika

TABLE 1
EU POLICE MISSION (EUPM)

Duration	2003–present
Territory	Bosnia and Herzegovina
Type	Police Mission
Legal framework	Council Joint Action 2002/210/CFSP
Aim	Support to local police in fight against organized crime
	Accountability of local police
	Support to Police Restructuring Implementation
Mission strength	Approximately 300 personnel
Head of Mission	Stefan Feller (Germany) since 1 November 2008
Costs	€ 76,950,000 (2003-2008)
Countries engaged	33 countries (27 EU and 6 non-EU)
Status	Ongoing

Srpska' two months previously, on 9 January 1992. In April 1992, the United States and the European Commission officially recognized the independence of BiH. However, the recognition of Bosnia's sovereignty neither calmed nor stabilized the situation on the ground, but rather sparked an attack on Muslim cities and villages in Eastern Bosnia by Serb irregulars and army reservists.[24] A few days later the Yugoslav People's Army itself joined the fighting. Despite numerous diplomatic efforts by the United Nations (UN) and the European Communities (EC) to bring the fighting to an end, the conflict lasted for more than three years.[25] With the signing of the Dayton Peace Agreement in 1995, the war in BiH officially ended. The main purpose of this agreement was to promote peace and stability in BiH, and to support and endorse regional balance in and around the former Republic of Yugoslavia. However, the Agreement did not succeed in all parts of the former Republic. Between 1998 and 1999 violent clashes between Albanians and Serbs occurred regularly. Nonetheless, as the situation in BiH slowly began to improve, the EU's efforts concentrated on helping the newly built country to develop its own structures of government. In that sense, the EU's first mission was to deploy a mission to BiH and to show that the European Union had learned its lessons from the failures a decade earlier. Brussels also wanted to demonstrate that the EU could ensure security and stability in its immediate neighbourhood.

The European Union Police Mission to Bosnia and Herzegovina was the first mission to be carried out in the framework of ESDP. More specifically, it was an integral part of a comprehensive programme of measures that were aimed at establishing the rule of law in BiH. Beginning in January 2003, EUPM/BiH followed the UN's International Police Task Force. It also marked the beginning of ESDP's work on civilian crisis management, especially in the area of promoting security sector reform (SSR). From an international law perspective, EUPM derived its legitimacy in part from Security Council Resolution 1396 of 5 March 2002. Through a decision of the Steering Board of the Peace Implementation Council of 28 February 2002, the EU accepted the offer to deploy the police mission. It thus followed the UN's Mission in Bosnia and Herzegovina (UNMIBH).

The mission itself can be divided into three phases: EUPM I, which was deployed from the beginning of the mission in 2003 until the end of 2005, EUPM II, from 2006–2008, and EUPM III, which is ongoing. The original mandate of the mission for the initial three-year period sought to preserve the existing level of institutional and personal proficiency through continuity with the achievements of the IPTF mission.[26] It furthermore called for an enhancement of police managerial and operational capacities through monitoring, mentoring and inspecting. The importance of greater professionalism at a high level within the ministries, as well as at the senior officers' level through advisory and inspection functions, was particularly highlighted. Lastly, the mission called for a politically monitored control over the police. At the beginning of the mission it was made clear that it would not include executive powers and no armed personnel would be deployed. This subsequently became the guiding principle for other police missions in the framework of ESDP. Moreover, the mission's mandate included monitoring political control over the police as well as policing functions, such as fighting trafficking and organized crime. It also led to the establishment of institutional structures on security and borders, which were supported by Commission funding.

After the deployment of the mission, critics emphasized its weak mandate and encountering of political difficulties with local authorities. In response, the EU admitted that the mission's goal was far from being achieved and that the original mandate would need some amendments. Ensuring coherence with the other actors in the field, mainly with the EU Special Representative (EUSR), and increased consultation by the EUSR with the ALTHEA EU Force Commander and Head of EUPM, was set as one of the priorities for the continuation of the mission. The first amendments of the mandate were introduced with the replacement of EUPM I with EUPM II, which entered into force at the beginning of 2006.[27] The EU's evaluations showed that the local law enforcement agencies had clearly not yet become self-sustaining.[28] Acting on behalf of the High Representative/Secretary General Javier Solana,[29] the mission statement clearly defined that the EUPM would carry out its tasks under the guidance and coordination of the EUSR. The EUPM was determined to become an integral part of the EU's broader rule of law approach in BiH, which aims at establishing a sustainable, professional, and multiethnic police service, while operating in accordance with the best European and international standards of mentoring, monitoring and inspecting.[30]

The next rotation, from EUPM II to EUPM III, took place at the end of 2007.[31] The responsibilities of the new police contingent included the necessity of maintaining the lead in coordinating the policing aspects of the ESDP in their efforts to fight organized crime. Generally, the EUPM was tasked to assist local authorities with planning and conducting investigations into major and organized crime, contributing to improved functioning of the whole criminal justice system in general, and enhancing police–prosecutor relations in particular. In conjunction with the European Commission, the EUPM was tasked with helping BiH authorities to identify remaining police development needs that could be addressed through Community assistance.

The final adjustment of EUPM's mandate took place in December 2009, when the mission was extended for another two years, until 31 December 2011.[32] This means that the prolongation of the deployment with EUPM III was decided upon under the new provisions of the Lisbon Treaty. Thus for the first time the mission statement, including the key tasks of the mission, was based on a new legal instrument, namely a Council decision. The Council not only focus on the work that has been carried out, but also extend their reach into new areas such as strengthening the operational capacity and joint capability of Law Enforcement Agencies engaged in the fight against organized crime and corruption, providing systematic assistance and support in the planning and conduct of investigations in the fight against organized crime and corruption and promoting the development of BiH's criminal investigative capacities. The new mandate also aimed at improving and enhancing the cooperation between police and prosecution authorities, strengthening cooperation between the police and the penitentiary system in BiH and ensuring that BiH authorities' accountability to the population was at a suitable level.

In sum, it can clearly be shown that the mandate of the mission was continuously adapted due to the changing operational environment in BiH. However, the established lessons, learned mechanisms and constant review process need to be highlighted in this respect, because they are crucial elements for the success of the operation after eight years of deployment.

With a view to some of the most salient improvements, the mission has succeeded in the following areas: making the local police more accountable (for example by setting up, training and mentoring internal control units that investigate police misconduct); professionalizing police training; implementing modern human resource management in the Bosnian police apparatus; and changing how the police deal with crime scene management.[33] To be more precise, the mission's successes to date include the transformation of the State Investigation and Protection Agency (SIPA) into an operational police agency with enhanced executive powers to fight organized crime and corruption. Furthermore, other actors in the security sector, such as the Ministry of Security and the Border Policy, have developed steadily. However, in the case of EUPM, there was a long lead-time for preparation of the mission and, especially at the beginning, the mission was rather sluggish.

All in all, the EUPM has proved the EU's ability to carry out a mission over a longer period of time without losing sight of the main objectives. At the same time, it has also shown that there is a need for a long-term strategy and a comprehensive approach to crisis management for which the EU needs to be prepared. Above all, stability and security in BiH cannot be achieved by a single police mission, as all the actors involved in CFSP need to address issues in a coherent and coordinated manner. The shortfalls at the beginning of EUPM have been addressed and this lessons-learnt mechanism has helped to make the mission a successful one. The whole-of-government approach laid down in the different mandates of the mission has clearly demonstrated that the EU places the mission in a wider spectrum, beyond a purely police mission. Finally, the deployment of its first mission to BiH, and keeping it in place, also demonstrates the importance that the immediate vicinity of the EU has for its foreign, security and defence policy. This can be seen as an indicator of a gradually developing European strategic culture.

EUPOL Proxima (Table 2)

The Yugoslav Republic of Macedonia declared its independence in the fall of 1991. Yet, unlike the cases in Slovenia and Croatia and, later, Bosnia, the move triggered

TABLE 2
EUPOL PROXIMA

Duration	15 December 2003–14 December 2005
Territory	Former Yugoslav Republic of Macedonia
Type	Police Mission
Legal framework	Council Joint Action 2003/681/CFSP
Aim	Monitoring, mentoring and advising the country's police and thus helping to fight organized crime as well as promoting European policing standards.
Mission strength	Approximately 200 personnel
Head of Mission	Jürgen Scholz (Germany) 15 December 2004-14 December 2005 Bart D'Hooge (Belgium) 29 September 2003-14 December 2004
Costs	€38,015,000 all from CFSP budget
Countries engaged	24 Member States plus four non-EU countries
Status	Concluded

neither a civil war nor an intervention by the Yugoslav national army. Nonetheless, internal conflicts between the Macedonian majority and the Albanian minority of the population emerged. These internal disputes were solved by the so-called Ohrid Framework Agreement – a peace deal signed by the Government of the Republic of Macedonia and ethnic Albanian representatives on 13 August 2001 which ended the armed conflict between the National Liberation Army and the Macedonian security forces. The agreement also laid the groundwork for improving the rights of ethnic Albanians. More specifically, the compromise between these two largest communities in Macedonia encompasses two important goals. On the one hand, the Framework Agreement called upon the signatories to introduce a number of constitutional amendments, legislative modifications and structural reforms designed to end inter-ethnic tensions and restore a stable political environment. On the other, it explicitly paved the way for 'the development of closer and more integrated relations [with] the Euro-Atlantic community'.[34] The Framework Agreement addressed most of the identity-related grievances of the Albanian minority. However, from a Macedonian perspective, little compensation was offered to the Macedonian majority beyond a (promised) peace which they feared would not last very long.[35]

In the case of Macedonia, the EU's expression of continuing commitment to support the peace process within the country and to bring the country closer to the Union translated into both European Commission instruments and Council tools playing a role in the reform of Macedonian institutions, starting in 2001. The actions undertaken by the European Union in this country are often perceived as a success story for ESDP.[36] Essential for the successful role of the Union was the fact that after the outbreak of the violence in Macedonia, the European Union responded very quickly and, most importantly, on the basis of a unified position of the EU member states. In short, the EU member states were acting jointly, and there were no divisions among the countries regarding the position the EU should take in the Macedonia case.[37]

Against this backdrop, the European Union established an EU Police Mission in the former Yugoslav Republic of Macedonia (FYROM). It was designed in line with the objectives of the Ohrid Framework Agreement of 2001 and in close partnership with the country's authorities. Despite the European Commission's contribution to the reconstruction of the country through development aid in the framework of the Rapid Reaction Mechanism (RRM) and the Community's assistance for reconstruction, development and stabilisation (CARDS) programme, as well as the presence of the NATO operation Allied Harmony, followed by the EU military mission Concordia, the political and security situation in FYROM remained fragile in 2002, as weak public institutions, failed exercise of state power in the Albanian-controlled areas, and uncontrolled possession of arms in the population led to an unstable situation in the country.[38] This was the background of a police mission named EUPOL Proxima which was launched on 15 December 2003.[39] EU police experts were deployed to monitor, mentor, and advise the country's police force and to help them fight organized crime, as well as to promote European policing standards. In particular, the main activities of EUPOL Proxima alongside their host country counterparts were general improvement of the performance of FYROM's police force, supporting them in crime investigations – in particular the fight against organized crime – and assisting the border police as part of the wider EU effort to promote integrated border management throughout the region. Moreover, it sought to help to build the different ethnic communities' confidence in the police, promote European standards of policing in all areas of operation and assist with the comprehensive reforms within the Ministry of Interior.

The mandate was translated into 28 activities and covered all the functions of the subsequent five programmes: uniformed police, criminal police, department for state security and counter-intelligence, internal control, and border police.[40] Originally, the mission was intended to last for one year. However, in December 2004 it was extended for another year, and the operation was finally completed on 14 December 2005. The mission continued to pay particular attention to the upper and middle management of police authorities, but reduced the number of staff and focused functionally on specific challenges in the police reform process. The five programmes of Proxima were restructured and reduced to three programmes in Proxima II, concentrating on organized crime, public peace and order, and border police aspects. At the same time, Proxima expanded its geographical coverage to a countrywide deployment, though it retained a greater presence in the former crisis area.[41]

To sum up, EUPOL Proxima marked the second consecutive police mission deployed to the Western Balkans. However, the situation on the ground was slightly different than that of EUPM due to the fact that the European membership perspective seemed to be a stronger catalyst for changing internal policies in FYROM than in BiH. During the first year of its existence, Proxima had become unable to tackle the more demanding facets of its mandate, especially in the area of organized crime.[42] Therefore adjustments had to be made concerning the mandate of the mission. As in BiH, inter-institutional arrangements were needed to ensure the necessary coherence of EU action in FYROM. Furthermore, the Macedonian government did not always perceive Proxima as having added value for the country. The mission's weak exit strategy further aggravated the situation. Hence the decision to terminate the mission in December 2005 was largely predetermined for political reasons, namely the Macedonian government's perception that the presence of a crisis management mission in the country could jeopardize its chances of getting a positive avis from the European Commission regarding its prospects for EU membership.[43] Nonetheless, these fears did not become reality, and EUPOL Proxima is very often referred to as a success story – an EU mission that completed its tasks, in which a country was set on the right track with the support of the EU.[44] Characteristically, the end of the mission also coincided with the granting of EU accession candidate country status on 17 December 2005, and can therefore be seen in the light of the process of FYROM moving closer towards the European Union. After the termination of the mandate, the mission was taken over by an EU policy advisory team (EUPAT) and thus the focus was shifted slightly. However, it still continued the whole-of-government approach in the field of security sector reform in FYROM and more generally throughout the region of the Western Balkans.

EU Police Advisory Team (EUPAT) (Table 3)

TABLE 3
EU POLICE ADVISORY TEAM (EUPAT)

Duration	15/ December 2005–14 June 2006
Territory	Former Yugoslav Republic of Macedonia
Type	Police Mission
Legal framework	Council Joint Action 2005/826/CFSP
Aim	— Monitoring, mentoring and advising on priority issues in the field of border police; public peace, order and accountability. — The fight against corruption and organised crime. — Overall implementation of police reform in the field. — Police-judiciary cooperation; and professional standards/ internal control.
Mission strength	Approximately 30 personnel
Head of Mission	Jürgen Scholz (Germany)
Costs	€1,500,000
Status	Concluded

The launch of EUPAT on 14 December 2005 followed the termination of the mandate of the EU Police Mission Proxima on 15 December 2003. The mandate of EUPAT was mainly aimed at continuing the work of Proxima and further supporting the development of an efficient and professional police service based on European standards of policing. Under the guidance of the EUSR and in partnership with the host government authorities, EU police experts monitored and mentored the country's police with regard to priority issues in the field of border police, public peace and order, and accountability, as well as in the fight against corruption and organized crime. EUPAT activities focused on the middle and senior levels of management.

To this end, the key tasks to which EUPAT paid special attention were the overall implementation of police reform in the field, cooperation among the police and judiciary authorities and the implementation of professional standards, accompanied by mechanisms of internal control.[45]

EUPAT included some 30 police advisors who supported the development of an efficient and professional police service based on European standards of policing. Under the guidance of the European Union Special Representative and in partnership with the host government authorities, EU police experts monitored and mentored the country's police on the above mentioned priority issues. The operational phase of EUPAT began on 15 December 2005 and lasted for half a year, to mid-June 2006.

When evaluating EUPAT, the mission has to be seen in the broader context of the European approach to bringing stability and European policing standards to FYROM. However, it cannot be evaluated without taking into account its predecessors, namely the military mission Concordia and EUPOL Proxima, and thereby following the logic of a combined civil–military approach as stressed in the ESS. The duration of half a year, however, raises the question of whether a new mission was really needed or whether Proxima could have achieved the same results with a changed mandate only. Nevertheless, European action in FYROM has produced concrete results and has further paved FYROM's way towards EU membership, in the sense that both missions fulfilled to a large extent the objectives laid down in the mandates of the two missions.[46] Despite the lack of coherence among the various actors and of a clear and sustainable strategy for the country, the EU's comprehensive approach to FYROM has certainly achieved its goals. Moreover, a sense of a European strategic culture with regard to crisis management in FYROM can be found as the ideas of stabilizing the country based on the Ohrid Framework Agreement was followed by concrete and coherent action – the two civilian missions, plus the military mission Concordia.

EULEX Kosovo (Table 4)

TABLE 4
EULEX KOSOVO

Duration	16 February 2008–ongoing
Territory	Kosovo
Type	Rule of Law Mission
Legal framework	Council Joint Action 2008/124/CFSP
Aims	Monitor, mentor and advise competent Kosovo institutions in all areas related to the wider Rule of Law
	Ensure the maintenance and promotion of the rule of law, public order and security
	Help ensure that all Kosovo Rule of Law services are free from political interference
	Ensure that cases of war crimes, terrorism, organized crime, corruption, inter-ethnic crimes, financial/economic crimes and other serious crimes, as well as property related issues are properly investigated, prosecuted, adjudicated and enforced according to the applicable law
	Contribute to strengthening the co-operation and coordination throughout the whole judicial process, particularly in the area of organized crime
	Contribute to the fight against corruption, fraud and financial crime
	Contribute to the implementation of the Kosovo Anti-Corruption Strategy and Anti-Corruption Action Plan
	Ensure that all its activities respect international standards concerning human rights and gender mainstreaming
Mission strength	Approx 2,800 personnel
Head of Mission	Xavier Bout de Marnhac (France)
Costs	€165,000,000 for the period 15 October 2010–14 October 2011
Status	Ongoing

At the beginning of this paper, I stated that the war in Kosovo in 1999 and the failure of the European Union and its member states to react to the crisis led to the development of CFSP and ESDP.[47] Therefore, it was not surprising that the EU supported the developments in Kosovo in spite of internal discussions about whether an independent Kosovo would be able to survive and what European support for independence would mean for EU countries facing separatist movements, such as those in Spain. EULEX was designed to take over the work of the UN mission in Kosovo (UNMIK) and was prepared by a two-year EU planning team mission (EUPT Kosovo).[48] It was also in line with the so-called Arthisaari Plan of 2007, which anticipated the independence of Kosovo.[49] However, on 16 February 2008, one day before

Kosovo declared its independence from Serbia, the EU decided to launch its largest civilian crisis management mission (EULEX Kosovo) with the aim of assisting Kosovan authorities with the consolidation of the rule of law, and in contributing to the creation of a safe and secure environment for all inhabitants, regardless of their ethnic origins.[50] The EU hereby used a comprehensive approach, meaning that the mission mandate comprised all issues linked to the wider areas of rule of law, from strengthening cooperation and coordination within the judiciary to fighting corruption and investigating war crimes. Nonetheless, the mission had to face several obstacles, especially with regard to the definition of its mandate and its actual deployment. Serbian opposition to dealing with the EU mission and allowing EULEX to operate in the Serb enclaves in Kosovo was only recently overcome, and so the mission only reached its full operational capability on 6 April 2009. Nevertheless, the takeover of capacities from UNMIK could not be fully completed, as the UN mission has maintained its presence in the field and still exercises its authority over the autonomous police force established in Serb-majority areas. In addition, the EU has arranged with Serbian authorities to keep its mission neutral with regards to questions of Kosovo's independent status. It just aspires to prevent a negative image of EULEX developing among the population of Kosovo. In order to allow the implementation of its mandate, the EU mission has now been called to engage in a series of outreach actions to gain the trust of both the civil society and the Kosovar government.

According to the mission statement in Article 2 of the Council Joint Action, EULEX Kosovo 'shall assist the Kosovo institutions, judicial authorities and law enforcement agencies in their progress towards sustainability and accountability and in further developing and strengthening an independent multi-ethnic justice system and multi-ethnic police and customs service, ensuring that these institutions are free from political interference and adhere to internationally recognized standards and European best practices'.

In Article 3, the Joint Action further subdivides the mission mandate into a number of operational 'tasks' horizontally for the three different components of EULEX, these being the justice, police, and customs components. As described above, the mandate comprises a nine tasks, including monitoring, mentoring and advising the competent rule-of-law institutions. In order to ensure the maintenance and promotion of the rule of law, public order and security, the mandate grants the EULEX staff executive powers, enabling them to reverse or annul operational decisions taken by the competent Kosovan authorities after consulting their Kosovan counterparts. Additionally, the mission should help to ensure that the Kosovan rule-of-law services are free from political interference. Moreover, cases of war crimes, terrorism, organized crime and other serious crimes should be properly investigated and cooperation and coordination throughout the whole judicial process should be ensured. Other key tasks include the contribution to the fight against corruption and the implementation of the Kosovo Anti-Corruption Strategy and Plan, as well as ensuring that all its activities respect international standards of human rights and gender mainstreaming.

Besides the more general and expected tasks foreseen in Article 3, it is notable that the mandate grants the executive the right to overrule and annul Kosovan authorities' operational decisions in order to ensure the maintenance and promotion of the rule of law, public order and security (subparagraph b). Such an annulment could take place after consultation with relevant international civilian authorities; these are, however, not clearly defined in the mandate.[51]

The EULEX Programme Strategy affirms a three-pronged approach of 'monitoring, mentoring and advising' and seeks to define these individual elements.[52] Advising is referred to as 'providing professional counselling to the Kosovo authorities to assist them in the development of those elements which lead to the establishment of required structures, including the appropriate legislation, as well as the improvement of the authorities' performance'. This means that EULEX should provide expert information for their Kosovan counterparts with respect to European best practice, internationally recognized standards, multiethnicity, sustainability, and accountability. As for monitoring, it is advised to apply a system in order to measure performance, namely an agreed method of accurate recording and reporting, in order to identify changes and improvements.[53] This will be carried out by observing and assessing how the Kosovan rule-of-law institutions and their personnel perform in relation to the aims of the EULEX mission.

This is linked to a programming method which foresees six-month cycles of activity. Thereby, analyses of the data, output and performance indicators after each six-month period of operations are intended to result in modifying, adapting and reorienting performance indicators. In that sense, a permanent evaluation mechanism has been integrated. Lastly, the term mentoring describes the ways and means by which EULEX advises and monitors the Kosovo law enforcement authorities. It is based on mutual trust and professional respect between EULEX officials and the Kosovan rule-of-law institutions' staff. Through these principles, the overall thrust and rationale of the mission clearly relies on an existing level of professionalism in the local law enforcement sector to such an extent that it can eventually reach a level of efficiency and sustainability sufficient for the administration and governance of the sector.[54]

In conclusion, EULEX Kosovo has to be considered a different case than the other missions. It was launched with the objective of proving the European Union's ability to support stability in the Balkans, but strong disagreements between the EU member states regarding Kosovo's independence have severely hindered comprehensive action in the region, as decisive actions can rarely be taken without strong political backing by both the EU and the member states.[55] The dividing lines between the EU member states were clearly visible even in the planning and preparation phases of the mission. Whereas the majority of EU member states, including *inter alia* Germany, France, the United Kingdom, and Austria, recognized the independence of Kosovo, five member states, namely Spain, Cyprus, Greece, Bulgaria, and Romania, expressed their anxiety about the signals that recognition might give to separatist movements in their countries.[56] Furthermore, the mandate of the mission contained a problem in itself. The creation of government institutions without the necessary executive authority to strengthen independent statehood has not only been difficult, but has also led to the development of two different legal realities in theatre due to the fact that both UNSCR 1244 (1999) and the new constitution were considered to be applicable and thus sources of law. Despite the mission's noticeable impact in terms of the technicalities of policing, political disagreement within the EU remains the fundamental barrier to structural reforms.[57] As long as not all EU member states recognize Kosovo, the signing of the Stabilisation and Association Agreement is not feasible. This impedes the development of a really coherent European Union external policy regarding Kosovo.

Nevertheless, deploying the largest civilian mission to Kosovo continued the traditional whole-of-government approach towards reforming the security sector in the countries of the Western Balkans. However, much still remains at stake. Thus, the EU has to continue its efforts to establish a well-governed country based on the rule of law and separation of powers on the one hand; on the other, it has to convince those member states who are concerned about independence that this direction is the right one. So far, there is uncertainty about how the European Union may be able to bridge this gap. A lot will depend on the concrete results EULEX Kosovo can achieve. In spite of the status conundrum and the division of member states on the question, EULEX operational deployment was relatively successful and the mission has provided assets in civilian crisis management and rule of law promotion, although results are unlikely to be immediately visible.[58] That said, these achievements, as well as further progress in strengthening the overall rule-of-law sector in Kosovo, will only prove sustainable if more fundamental challenges are successfully addressed. Three top the agenda, namely: improving inter-ethnic relations, which are still very tense; fighting pervasive organized crime; and dealing with widespread corruption, including in political circles and public administration.[59] However, the political interest in EULEX Kosovo and in civilian crisis management seems to be waning in Brussels and in many EU member states.[60]

Since Kosovan membership of the European Union does not seem to feature realistically on its agenda in the foreseeable future, the EU has to broaden its approach in order to keep Kosovo on the right track regarding Europe, without promising it EU membership. Only the future will show whether or not this two-pronged approach will turn out to be as successful as the EU's actions in FYROM. The EU's unclear position is most certainly disadvantageous to Kosovo. Furthermore, as the EU is attempting to be the central major actor in the region, the success or failure of Kosovo as an independent state will, in both cases, lie within the responsibility of the EU and as a consequence will fall back on the Union.[61] As Pirozzi and Sandawi point out: 'Especially Kosovo could become an acid test, because the EU mission, which aims especially to fight organized crime, is not only the largest but also the most ambitious civilian ESDP mission so far. It is fair to say that the risk of mission failure in the long run can be assumed substantial, yet the consequences of such a failure would be immeasurable'.[62]

Civilian Crisis Management Missions in the Western Balkans – Four Parameters to Detect Strategic Culture

So far, the European Union has carried out four civilian missions in the Western Balkans: one in BiH, two in FYROM and one in Kosovo. These four missions differ in their ambition, scale and duration. Whereas the missions in BiH and Kosovo are large-scale missions planned for longer-term deployment, the missions in FYROM fulfilled their mandate in a shorter period of time and could therefore be terminated earlier. EUPM, EUPOL Proxima and EUPAT were more general, focusing on police issues while EULEX Kosovo rather concentrated on rule-of-law aspects. Nonetheless, they do have much in common. All four missions are based on the concept of security sector reform with the objective of strengthening state authorities. Recalling the definition of strategic culture as the sum of ideas, behaviours and mindsets acquired and shared among the EU and its member states, the time has come to examine whether both ideas and actions match. Obviously, such an examination has to take into account that these four missions, of a total of 24 missions and operations, can only provide parameters for detecting strategic culture by identifying common approaches and behaviours with regard to civilian crisis management in the Western Balkans.

First, geography matters. The fact that all four missions were deployed to the immediate neighbourhood was coherent with the approach of the ESS, declaring that a foreign policy aim would be to bring stability to the neighbourhood and to create a ring of well-governed states at the EU's border. Historically speaking, ESDP has returned to the places in which the failure of the early 1990s gave rise to its development. Furthermore, it must be stressed that the Western Balkans can clearly be seen as the area in which the EU's action was the most coordinated. Obviously, it is also the area in which the EU had the most interest in producing stability and of which it had strong knowledge.

Second, there is a visible tendency to react rapidly to crises, especially in post-conflict stabilization. Nevertheless, in all four missions the EU was never the first actor in place. In BiH, FYROM and Kosovo, the EU engaged either after the termination of a UN mission (BiH, Kosovo) or following a NATO operation which was taken over by a military operation and then followed by civilian missions (FYROM). In the case of FYROM, EUPOL Proxima had to start from scratch and was the first civilian mission following military engagement in the country. However, this approach is completely in line with the targets laid down in the various civilian headline goals – for instance that the EU should deploy its capabilities on short notice and be able to respond upon a request from other international organizations, mainly the UN.

Third, the four missions clearly demonstrate a whole-of-government approach which in the end is based on a wider understanding of a security sector reform in the Western Balkans by not just focusing on either police or judiciary, but also considering European values of democracy, rule of law, and human rights, which in turn have formed the basis of all four operations. They were also aimed at responding to three of the five threats highlighted in the ESS, namely regional conflict, state failure, and organized crime. The EU provides comprehensive assistance to build well-functioning authorities, ranging from purely reforming police structures, to better cooperation between policy authorities and the judiciary, to a more integrated security system.

Fourth, it is necessary to take a closer look at the coherence of EU actions when talking about a possible EU strategic culture. As demonstrated in all four missions, there are a variety of actors in the field, and the Western Balkans has become something of a meeting point for many EU officials in order to properly conduct and evaluate operations and missions. For instance, ESDP missions in Bosnia-Herzegovina have been bringing together officials from different EU institutions for a period of more than eight years now and have also visibly improved the interplay between civilian and military actors in the region. During this time, EU officials have had the chance to get to know each other, discuss various issues concerning the future of the area and take common decisions. This has taken place not only among civilian actors, such as the EUSR, the Commission and the mission in place, but has also seen interplay with EU military action (as perfectly illustrated in the case of FYROM).

EU Strategic Culture in Formation

As this paper has demonstrated, there is a high declaratory level in official documents and headline goals that aim to define the foreign and security policy of the European Union. At this declaratory level, European Union Member States have managed to form a strategic community by bridging diverging national interests and behaviour and defining a common mindset.

However, as is shown in the empirical section, strategic culture requires more than just a declaratory level. It needs to be put into action. The missions and operations so far deployed under the framework of ESDP give evidence that there is a European strategic culture. They match to a large degree the ideas laid down at the declaratory level. More specifically, the four missions described have clearly shown that there is consistency between the idea of bringing stability to the immediate neighbourhood and action by applying a comprehensive whole of government approach to the countries of the Western Balkans. Therefore, they have influenced the rationale of European foreign and security policy with regard to civilian crisis management in this region. EULEX Kosovo, on the contrary, demonstrates that internal divergences among member states limit the actions of the EU. Thus, strong national strategic cultures defer the development of a common, genuine, and comprehensive strategic culture at European level. Nonetheless, these contradictions among member states are also crucial elements in the formation of European strategic culture.

In general, ESDP is still to be considered a work in progress, and so is European strategic culture. As a strategic community formed by its member states, the EU certainly has a strategic culture based on the nexus of ideas and actions. Hence, the progressive development of civilian crisis management capabilities also provides a marker for the existence of a European strategic culture – an emerging culture in the process of formation.

NOTES

1. Bezen Balamir Coşkun, 'Does "Strategic Culture" Matter? Old Europe, New Europe and the Transatlantic Security', *Perceptions*, Vol. XII (Summer-Autumn 2007), pp. 71–90.
2. See Colin S. Gray, 'Strategic Culture as Context: The First Generation of Theory Strikes Back', *The Review of International Studies*, Vol. 25, No. 1 (1999), pp. 49–69; Alastair Ian Johnston, 'Thinking

about Strategic Culture', *International Security*, Vol. 19 (1995), pp. 36–43, *Cultural Realism: Strategic Culture and Grand Strategy in Chinese History*, (Princeton, NJ: Princeton University Press, 1995), pp. 4–22.
3. See Gray, 'Strategic Culture as Context', (note 2), p.50.
4. Asle Toje, 'Strategic Culture as an Analytical Tool. History, Capabilities, Geopolitics and Values: The EU Example', *Western Balkans Security Observer*, No. 14 (July–September 2009), pp. 3–23.
5. On the debate about widening vs. deepening see, for example, Fraser Cameron, 'Widening and Deepening', in Fraser Cameron (ed.), *The Future of European Integration* (New York: Routledge, 2004), pp. 1–17. For the mismatch between widening and deepening see Ludger Kühnhardt, 'Introduction: European Integration: Success through Crises', in Ludger Kühnhardt. (ed.), *Crises in European Integration. Challenges and Responses 1945–2005, New German Historical Perspectives Vol. II* (Oxford/New York: Berghahn Books, 2011), pp. 1–17.
6. The term 'global actor' is preferred by the EU when describing its role in foreign, security and defence policy on an international level. In this context the question has to be raised: what kind of power is the EU actually perceived as in international affairs? Due to the very specific nature it is difficult to describe the EU as a 'great power' in the classical sense as defined by Barry Buzan, for example, in *The United States and the Great Powers* (Cambridge: Polity Press, 2004), p. 69. The author however favours the definition of Andrew Moravcsik: the EU has to be considered as a quiet superpower having civilian, military and normative abilities at its disposal. Andrew Moravcsik, 'The Quiet Superpower', *Newsweek*, 17 June 2002, p. 23.
7. Kühnhardt, 'Introduction: European Integration: Success through Crises' (note 5), p. 11; Sven Biscop, 'The ABC of European Security Strategy: Ambition, Benchmark, Culture', Egmont Paper, No. 16 (2007).
8. European Union, 'A Secure Europe in a Better World: European Security Strategy', Brussels, 12 December 2003, pp. 7–8, available at http://www.consilium.europa.eu/uedocs/cmsUpload/78367.pdf
9. Jack Snyder, *The Soviet Strategic Culture: Implications for Nuclear Options* (Santa Monica, CA: Rand Corporation, 1977), p. 8.
10. For an easier reading of the text, the abbreviation of ESDP will also be used for the post-Lisbon period, when after the entering into force of the Lisbon Treaty on 1 December 2009 ESDP was renamed Common Security and Defence Policy (CSDP).
11. Toje, 'Strategic Culture as an Analytical Tool' (note 4), p. 9.
12. As commented on by Paul Cornish and Geoffrey Edwards in 'Beyond the EU/NATO Dichotomy: The Beginning of a European Strategic Culture', *International Affairs*, Vol. 77, No. 3 (2001), p. 587. For an in-depth analysis of civilian capabilities development see Giovanni Grevi and Daniel Keohane, 'ESDP resources', in *European Security and Defence Policy. The First Ten Years* (Paris: EU Institute for Security Studies, 2009), pp. 98–111.
13. European Council: Presidency Conclusions, Nice, 7–9 December 2000, [400/1/00].
14. European Council: Presidency Conclusions, Gothenburg, 15–16 June 2001, [SN 200/1/01 REV 1], p. 11.
15. European Council: Conclusions and Plan of Action of the Extraordinary European Council Meeting on 21 September 2001, [SN 140/01], p. 3.
16. Draft Presidency Report on European Security and Defence Policy further to the General Affairs Council on 10 December 2001, including Annex I and II: Doc. 15193/01.
17. See, for instance, Karen Smith, 'The Instruments of European Foreign Policy', in Jan Zielonka (ed.), *Paradoxes of European Foreign Policy* (London: Kluwer International Law, 1998), p. 67, or Catriona Gourlay and Eric Remade, 'The 1996 IGC: The Actors and Their Interaction', in Kjell Eliassen (ed.), *Foreign and Security Policy in the European Union* (London: Sage, 1998), pp. 58–93.
18. Alvaro de Vasconcelos, 'A Strategy for EU Foreign Policy', EUISS Report, No. 7, European Union Institute for Security Studies, Paris, June 2010, p.3.
19. The EU does not have a legal text defining this type of assistance. In practice, however, civil protection assistance is delivered during the immediate phase of a disaster and in the case of third countries usually works parallel with or hands over to humanitarian aid. See the website of the European Commission DG Humanitarian Aid and Civil Protection, http://ec.europa.eu/echo/civil_protection/civil/prote/cp01_en.htm (accessed 11 April 2011).
20. See 'Speaking points of Javier Solana, EU High Representative for CFSP, at the Civilian Crisis Management Capability Conference at Ministerial Level', General Affairs and External Relations Council, Brussels, 19 November 2002 [S0217/02], p.1.
21. Jolyon Howorth, 'From Security to Defence: the Evolution of the CFSP', in Christopher Hill and Michael Smith (eds), *International Relations and the European Union* (Oxford: Oxford University Press, 2005), pp. 179–204.

22. Christopher Hill, 'The Capability-Expectations Gap, or Conceptualizing Europe's International Role', *Journal of Common Market Studies*, Vol. 31, No. 3 (September 1993), pp. 305–328.
23. Ana E. Juncos, 'Police Mission in Bosnia and Herzegovina', in Michael Emerson and Eva Gross (eds), *Evaluating the EU's Crisis Missions in the Balkans* (Brussels: Centre for European Policy Studies 2007), pp. 46–80.
24. For a detailed description of the events in BiH see Wolfgang Petrisch, *Bosnien und Herzegowina. 5 Jahre nach Dayton* (Klagenfurt: Wieser, 2001).
25. With the entry into force of the Maastricht Treaty on European Union in November 1993 the EC became the EU. Michael Merlingen and Rita Ostrauskaite, *European Union Peacebuilding and Policing. Governance and the European Security and Defence Policy* (London: Routledge, 2006), p.53.
26. See Council Joint Action 2002/210/CFSP 11 March 2002, Official Journal of the European Communities Nr. L70/5 from 13 March 2002.
27. Council Joint Action 2005/824/CFSP of 24 November 2005 on the European Union Police Mission (EUPM) in Bosnia and Herzegovina (BiH), Official Journal of the European Union, L 307/55 of 25 November 2005.
28. Stefano Recchia, 'Beyond International Trusteeship: EU Peacebuilding in Bosnia and Herzegovina', EUISS Occasional Paper, No. 66 (2006), p.16; Agnieszka Nowak (ed.), 'Civilian Crisis Management: the EU Way', EUISS Chaillot Paper, No. 90 (2006), p.26.
29. Javier Solana was appointed High Representative of the Common Foreign and Security Policy on 18 October 1999 and became *ex officio* the Secretary General of the Council of the EU. See Art. 18, Treaty on the European Union in the consolidated version of the Treaty of Amsterdam, Official Journal of the European Communities, C 340 of 10 November 1997.
30. The meaning of the term 'inspecting' remained unclear, especially due to the fact that the mission had not been granted executive policing powers (such as arrest and prosecution powers). See Michael Merlingen, 'EUPM (Bosnia and Herzegovina)', in *European Security and Defence Policy*. (note 12), pp. 161–171.
31. Council Joint Action 2007/749/CFSP of 19 November 2007 on the European Union Police Mission (EUPM) in Bosnia and Herzegovina (BiH), Official Journal of the European Union, L 303/40 of 21 November 2007.
32. Council Decision 2009/906/CFSP of 8 December 2009 on the European Union Police Mission (EUPM) in Bosnia and Herzegovina (BiH), Official Journal of the European Union L 322/22 of 9 December 2009.
33. Michael Merlingen, 'EUPM (Bosnia and Herzegovina)' (note 30), p. 169.
34. The English version of the Ohrid Framework Agreement is available at http://www.president.gov.mk/eng/info/dogovor.htm (accessed 27 March 2011).
35. Stojan Slaveski, 'Macedonian Strategic Culture and Institutional Choice: Integration or Isolation?', *Western Balkans Security Observer*, No. 14 (2009), pp. 39–56.
36. Isabelle Ioannides, 'Police Mission in Macedonia', in Emerson and Gross (eds), *Evaluating the EU's Crisis Missions in the Balkans* (note 23), pp. 81–125.
37. Marija Risteska, 'The Macedonian Accession to the European Union', in David Kral (ed.), *Bulgaria, Romania... and Who Next? Perspectives of Further EU Enlargement as Seen from the Newmember statesmember states and EU Hopefuls* (Prague: Europeum, 2007), pp. 89–113.
38. Isabelle Ioannides, 'EUPOL PROXIMA/EUPAT (fYROM)', in *European Security and Defence Policy* (note 30), pp. 187–199.
39. Council Joint Action 2003/681/CFSP of 29 September 2003 on the European Union Police Mission in the Former Yugoslav Republic of Macedonia (EUPOL Proxima), Official Journal of the European Union, L 249/66 of 1 October 2003.
40. Ioannides, 'EUPOL PROXIMA/EUPAT(fYROM)', (note 38), p. 190.
41. *Ibid*, p. 191.
42. Ioannides, 'Police Mission in Macedonia' (note 36), pp. 81–125.
43. Ioannides, 'EUPOL PROXIMA/EUPAT (fYROM)' (note 38), p. 195.
44. See, for example, Franz Halas and Cornelia Frank,'Friedenskonsolidierung mit polizeilichen Mitteln? Die Polizeimission EUPOL-PROXIMA auf dem Prüfstand', *DIAS-Kommentar*, No. 72 (2006), p.8, or Xira Ruiz 'La evolución de las misiones civiles de la Política Europea de Seguridad y Defensa', UNISCI Discussion Papers, No. 16 (2008), pp. 61–84.
45. Council Joint Action 2005/826/CFSP of 24 November 2005 on the establishment of an EU Police Advisory Team (EUPAT) in the Former Yugoslav Republic of Macedonia (fYROM), Official Journal of the European Union L 307/61 of 25 November 2005.

46. Ruiz, 'La evolución de las misiones civiles de la Política Europea de Seguridad y Defensa' (note 44), pp. 61–84.
47. For an excellent in-depth analysis on the mandate of EULEX Kosovo see M. Spernbauer, 'EULEX Kosovo – Mandate, Structure and Implementation: Essential Clarifications for an Unprecedented EU Mission', CLEER Working Papers 2010/5, The Hague, 2010. The author agrees with the views contained concerning the mandate and has therefore based the argumentation in this section on this study.
48. For a detailed analysis of the role of UNMIK see Calin Trenkov-Wermuth, *United Nations Justice. Legal and Judicial Reform in Governance Operations* (Shibuya-ku, Tokyo: United Nations University Press, 2010), pp. 50–94. The mission was based on UNSCR 1244(1999).
49. It is worth mentioning that the role former Finnish President Maarti Arthisaari played in elaborating his Plan was heavily discussed with respect to his impartiality on Kosovo. See M.J. Barceló, 'EULEX-Kosovo: ¿la misión imposible?', Documento de Trabajo N° 42/2008, Real Instituto Elcano, Madrid, 2008, p. 8.
50. Cyprus has formally abstained from adopting the joint action on EULEX Kosovo. This has been reportedly the first and only case of recourse to constructive abstention as provided for in the Treaty in the context of ESDP.
51. Spernbauer describes in more detail the different actors to which this definition could apply. See Spernbauer, 'EULEX Kosovo' (note 47), p. 17.
52. Access via http://www.csfederalismo.it/images/stories/PESD/eulex-kosovo/eulex_programme-strategy.pdf (accessed 27 March 2011).
53. Spernbauer, 'EULEX Kosovo' (note 47), p. 17.
54. *Ibid*, pp. 17–18.
55. Tanja Tamminen, 'High Expectations – Limited Resources. The Bottlenecks of EU Civilian Crisis Management in Kosovo', UPI Briefing Paper, No 70 (2010), p. 7.
56. See for example 'EU splits on Kosovo recognition', *BBC News*, 18 February 2008, http://news.bbc.co.uk/2/hi/europe/7249909.stm (accessed 11 April 2011).
57. An Jacobs, 'EU Civilian Crisis Management: A Crisis in the Making?', *CSS Analysis in Security Policy*, No. 87 (February 2011), p. 3.
58. David Cadier, 'EU Mission in Kosovo (EULEX): Constructing Ambiguity or Constructive Disunity?', Transatlantic Security Paper, No. 3 (2011), p. 7.
59. Giovanni Grevi, 'EULEX Kosovo', in *European Security and Defence Policy* (note 12), pp. 353–368.
60. Tamminen, 'High Expectations – Limited Resources' (note 55), p. 5.
61. Vibeke Brask Thomsen, 'One Year On: What is Next for Kosovo?', *European Security Review (ISIS Europe)*, No. 43 (2009), p. 8.
62. Nicoletta Pirozzi and Sammi Sandawi, 'Military and Civilian ESDP Missions: Ever Growing and Effective?', Documenti IAI No. 09/29 (November 2009), p. 13.

Strategic Culture and Multilateralism: The Interplay of the EU and the UN in Conflict and Crisis Management

INGO PETERS

How does the European Union's strategic culture relate to other international organizations, here specifically the United Nations? Do both organizations' strategic cultures (SC) differ, and do these differences impact on inter-organizational cooperation? What is the significance of SC for inter-organizational cooperation problems compared to material or institutional factors? Since the 1950s, multilateralism and international cooperation have been integral parts of the European integration process; both have also been guiding principles for the Union's international engagement, whether with states and governments or with international organizations. Hence it comes as no surprise that the European Security Strategy (ESS) of 2003 refers to 'effective multilateralism' and 'working with others' as the best strategy to tackle challenges 'in a world with global threats, global markets and global media'. More precisely, it is a strategy that envisions 'a stronger international society, well-functioning international institutions and a rule-based international order.'[1] In view of the EU's ambition to become a global actor, its relations and cooperation with the United Nations, as the prime global international organization, become paramount. However, the qualification of multilateralism as 'effective' indicates that multilateral cooperation may in fact not always live up to expectations. This is also indicated by the organizations' individual or joint statements, with the United Nations praising achievements while simultaneously emphasizing the need for further improvements of their cooperative relationships.[2]

The European Union and United Nations cooperate across a range of policy issues. Those overlap horizontally, first and foremost in the realms of humanitarian aid and development policy and of promoting democracy, rule of law, human rights, conflict resolution and post-conflict rehabilitation and peace-building. Moreover, both organizations cooperate vertically across all levels of the institutions' structures, ranging from general and specific consultation of the organizations' political leadership, to coordinating their efforts by desk-to-desk consultations, to operational cooperation in the field. Cooperation in the realm of conflict and crisis management, which will be the focus of this analysis, has become increasingly institutionalized according to respective joint declarations since 2003.[3]

This process is driven by three main factors: the two organizations' complementary political interests, shared norms and values, and operational interdependence. Firstly, in terms of complementary interests, the United Nations is lacking specific capabilities which the European Union started to develop with the emergence of

ESDP since 1999 and which can also be used for UN operations. In turn, the UN can provide legitimacy for the EU's conflict and crisis management activities as much as for its drive to become a significant global security actor. Secondly, the UN and the EU are supposedly natural partners, since they share a wide range of norms and values, culminating in the ideal of a democratic peace and world order. Thirdly, as the UN reports, cooperation with the EU covers a wide spectrum of activities, ranging from concerns of peace and security to development and humanitarian assistance in more than 100 countries worldwide. Overall, the UN (as of March 2010) had deployed 89,000 troops and 13,000 police officers overall, as well as 22,000 civilians on the ground. The EU's contribution amounted to 8 per cent of troops and police officers and 40 per cent of the funding. And from the European Union point of view, 15 of the 23 missions and operations launched between 2003 and 2009 were deployed in countries that were also hosting UN peacekeeping and peace-building missions.

Hence, consultation and cooperation are imperative for the effectiveness and efficacy of conflict and crisis management activities, which could possibly lead to a win-win outcome for both organizations.[4] However, as will become obvious in the empirical sections below, a relatively high degree of institutionalization or numerous practical instances of policy coordination and cooperation do not *per se* rule out inter-organizational cooperation problems. In fact, many cooperative endeavours are impeded by the divergent interests and preferences of member states, by collective action problems or lack of military or civilian capabilities, by intra-organizational (intra to the European Union or United Nation) hurdles to policy coordination or conflicting procedures of both organizations, and maybe also by strategic culture.

The objective of this study is to identify cooperation problems originating from any mis-fit between the European Union's and the United Nations' strategic cultures. In the IR community, the concept of 'strategic culture' is defined and used in various ways. Here Iain Johnston's conceptualization is adopted, since it is conceived as a (soft) independent variable and can appropriately be operationalized. As a 'soft independent variable', strategic culture may not determine the specific political choices of actors, but it confines the range of choices in the sense of an enabling or inhibiting condition. According to Johnston, 'strategic culture' refers to actors' normative presumptions about 1. the origins and role of war in human affairs, 2. the nature of the adversary and the risks and threats challenging security, 3. the efficacy of force, and the conditions under which force is useful, and – against the backdrop of the first three points – 4. the efficacy of different available strategic options. The characteristics of the respective policies along the lines of these criteria are significant for the formation of political preferences and actors' operational choices in a given situation.[5]

Strategic culture as a social structure is an intangible factor influencing policy-making, and as a constructivist concept is based on the assumption of mutual constitution of structure and agent. It is important to note that strategic culture as social structure and its influence on policies here is 'bracketed' (Figure 1).[6] Hence, the opposite constitutive dimension – that is, the actors' policy practices' impact on strategic culture – will be left aside. In that sense, strategic culture is kept apart from policy practices and the former is assumed to influence the latter. Most importantly this conceptualization, in contrast to some contributions to this field of study in which the concept encompasses norms *and* practices as an integral part of SC, avoids invalidating strategic culture as an 'independent variable' and generating tautological results. Moreover, as with international cooperation, cooperation between the EU and the UN may be hampered by cooperation problems due to factors other than strategic culture, including material factors such as budgetary interests, institutional factors and operational practices; for example decision-making rules, or standard operational procedures for conducting missions and operations.[7]

In this essay, I will argue that Johnston's concept of SC allows us to identify a similar but distinct strategic culture of the European Union and the United Nations in the area of conflict management. Hence, the preliminary hypothesis inferred will be that SC cannot be expected to be a significant cause of cooperation problems between both organizations. The following analysis of actual cooperation problems confirms this hypothesis while at the same time revealing some issues which might be identified as cultural factors, though not necessarily in terms of *strategic* culture.

This investigation proceeds as follows: In section 2, the respective strategic cultures of the European Union and the United Nations are compared based on the self-attribution of these organizations in pertinent documents. This comparison will allow us to formulate expectations and conditions (hypotheses) of cooperation problems before proceeding to the investigation of political practices. Section 3 will focus on the practice of inter-institutional cooperation so as to identify factors hampering this cooperation, by using illustrative examples of cooperation problems drawn from three EU operations conducted in collaboration with the UN (EU Artemis in Congo 2003, EU EUFOR Congo 2006, and EUFOR Chad 2008). In section 4 conclusions will be drawn from the empirical findings in terms of the significance of

FIGURE 1
STRATEGIC CULTURE AS AN EXPLANATORY FACTOR

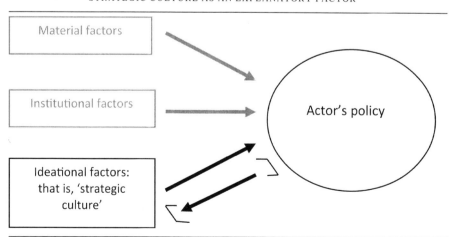

SC in comparison to material or institutional factors influencing, hampering or furthering inter-organizational cooperation among constituent actors.

The Strategic Culture of the European Union and the United Nations in Comparative Perspective

What are the communalities and differences of the strategic cultures of the EU and the UN respectively according to the self-attribution of both organizations? What are the implications in terms of expectations and conditions (hypotheses) for cooperation problems?

A brief review of the pertinent literature quickly reveals that the kind of SC that can be ascribed to the European Union as well as to the UN is remarkably contested. Some experts suggest that the EU/UN does not have a strategic culture yet; or that, if there is one, it is very weak.[8] Others point to an evolutionary path, claiming that the EU/UN is about to develop a common strategic culture, or is already departing from one culture to another.[9] Still other experts confirm without doubt the existence of a distinct EU/UN strategic culture.[10] This broad range of positions can obviously be ascribed to the use of different concepts of SC, as well as varying evaluations of the EU's acute quality as a security actor.

What do pertinent EU and UN documents tell us about both organizations' basic collective assumptions regarding Johnston's criteria?[11] Concerning the role of war and the recipe for taming it (criterion 1), the opening statement of the ESS 2003 directly pinpoints what the EU perceives as its fundamental premises: 'Europe has never been so prosperous, so secure nor so free. The violence of the first half of the 20th Century has given way to a period of peace and stability unprecedented in European history. The creation of the European Union has been central to this development. (...).'[12] In this picture, the bellicose past of the European states and the successful history of European integration convey member states' normative beliefs that power politics and traditional wars have become delegitimized and that state power needs to be domesticated by mutual limitation of sovereignty.[13] This interpretation also rests on the observation that the term 'war' is not used in EU core documents but is circumscribed by references to challenges posed by 'regional conflicts'. In contrast, the UN explicitly uses the term 'war', which apparently starts from the premise that war and 'armed conflicts today, as they have throughout history, continue to bring fear and horror to humanity, requiring our urgent involvement to try to prevent, contain and bring them to an end.' Moreover, the role of power, encompassing 'special responsibilities and temptations' for the powerful, and the great value and importance of the following four principles are stressed: sovereignty, territorial integrity, independence of states, and the principle of self-determination of peoples.[14]

Furthermore, both institutions subscribe to an evolving 'international society' as a manifestation of and recipe for global social integration, with the EU striving for 'a stronger international society, functioning international institutions and rule-based international order'. The UN, on the other hand, discerns 'an increasingly common moral perception that spans the world's nations and peoples, and which is finding expression in international laws, many owing their genesis to the work of this

Organization.' Another common feature is both institutions' appreciation for the democratic-peace paradigm. The UN emphasizes that 'respect for democratic principles at all levels of social existence is crucial' and the EU perceives 'a world of well-governed democratic states' as the best recipe for peace.[15]

Regarding the nature of the adversary and the threats posed to security (criterion 2), the EU and the UN's assumptions show a striking congruence: in view of the end of the Cold War, Europeans no longer perceive any immediate threat to survival and no direct adversary. And the UN stresses 'new opportunities for tackling new threats to common security'. At the same time, both organizations also perceive new security challenges emerging 'ranging from regional conflicts to failed states, from proliferation and terrorism to organised crime', and from ecological damage, unchecked population growth and war between states to poverty and infectious diseases.[16]

Both also agree on the vast impact of globalization. The EU considers these challenges more complex and interconnected, rendering internal and external aspects of challenges and responses 'indissolubly linked' and the increased dependence on 'interconnected infrastructure' a critical challenge. The UN stresses that globalization generates a contradictory process of integration and fragmentation, and renders 'a threat to one a threat to all' eroding state capacity: 'Every state requires international cooperation to make it secure.'[17] Moreover, both organizations apparently ascribe to the view – though they describe it in different terms – that there are a number of 'root causes of conflict' (EU) or 'deepest causes of conflict' (UN) which might easily evolve into acute crisis: poverty, lack of good governance, respect for human rights, and competition for scarce resources (EU), as well as economic despair, social injustice and political oppression (UN).[18]

In view of the wide spectrum of new challenges, the efficacy and usefulness of force (criterion 3) is devalued. In this regard, the EU concludes that 'none of the new threats is purely military, nor can any be tackled by purely military means'. Though this might be interpreted as rendering the use of military force a last resort,[19] the EU includes the need for more flexible and mobile forces and military capabilities in its forecast for the Union's future security.[20] In contrast – as is also shown in the way they address the challenge of war – the UN is more explicit when it comes to the use of force. If prevention fails, 'threats will have to be met by military means'. UN operations cannot only be sent in post-conflict situations but also assigned to assist with peace enforcement, and rules of engagement for these operations should be 'sufficiently robust and not force United Nations contingents to cede the initiative to their attackers'.[21] However, at this point the differences between the EU and the UN appear to be marginal.

The European Union's preferences concerning strategic options (criterion 4) and policy instruments are guided by three basic principles: comprehensiveness, cooperation, prevention. According to the 'comprehensive approach', security problems should be addressed by the full spectrum of instruments for crisis management and conflict prevention at the EU's disposal: political and diplomatic, military and civilian, and trade and development activities. Trade and aid in particular are perceived as powerful tools for promoting reform, and better governance may be induced through assistance programmes, conditionality, and targeted trade measures.[22]

The principle of comprehensiveness is also applicable to the UN, which addresses this in terms of multi-dimensional challenges that require 'multi-dimension responses' or an 'integrated approach' on the various levels of policy-making and across policy areas: 'The efforts to build peace, stability and security post-conflict peace-building must encompass matters beyond military threats in order to break the fetters of strife and warfare that have characterized the past'. And, relating to the sources of conflict and war, it is seen as imperative 'to enhance respect for human rights and fundamental freedoms, to promote sustainable economic and social development for wider prosperity, to alleviate distress and to curtail the existence and use of massively destructive weapons.'[23] Likewise, the terms 'preventive diplomacy', 'peace-making', 'peace-keeping', and 'post-conflict peace-building' are considered as 'integrally related'. With the transformation of the international system, 'a new generation of "multi-dimensional" United Nations peacekeeping operations' is marked by 'a mix of military, police and civilian capabilities'. Moreover, the concept of 'integrated missions' plays 'a critical role in ensuring that the UN system and actors are guided by a common strategic vision'.[24]

Both institutions share also what could be dubbed a 'cooperative approach' to international security, although the EU takes a bottom-up and the UN a top-down perspective. Hence, the EU subscribes to an international order based on effective multilateralism and working with partners from across the Atlantic to form regional as well as global organizations.[25] It also continually stresses its commitment to coordination and cooperation with the UN: 'The fundamental framework for international relations is the United Nations Charter. The United Nations Security Council has the primary responsibility for the maintenance of international peace and security. Strengthening the United Nations, equipping it to fulfil its responsibilities and to act effectively, is a European priority.'[26] Likewise, the UN stresses the need for 'concerted attention and effort of individual States, of regional and non-governmental organizations and of all of the United Nations system'. And based on Chapter VIII of the UN Charter, the UN considers regional organizations 'a vital part of the multilateral system provided they work within the framework of the Charter and the purposes of the United Nations in an "integrated fashion".'[27]

Another common element of the EU's and the UN's principles regarding the efficacy of different strategic options can be subsumed under the concept of a preventive approach. The EU emphasizes the necessity to act *before* crises occur: 'Conflict prevention and threat prevention cannot start too early.' Accordingly, the EU ascribes explicitly to the necessity of developing a SC that fosters early, rapid and when necessary, robust intervention.[28] Likewise, the UN assumes that the 'most desirable and efficient employment of diplomacy is to ease tensions before they result in conflict – or, if conflict breaks out, to act swiftly to contain it and resolve its underlying causes.'[29]

Consequentially, the EU and the UN are formulating operational necessities and best practices inferred from lessons learned of their missions and operations by using different terms for what apparently resemble substantially similar if not identical concepts. The EU stresses the requirement of 'coherence' between different policy areas of the Union, and 'mainstream[ing]' of conflict prevention by all Union institutions.[30]

Moreover, civil-military cooperation (CMCO) for coherence of policies on the operational level is said to require a 'culture of co-ordination' rather than detailed structures and procedures. Nevertheless, permanent institutional structures are created for the handling of conflict and crisis management policies: as part of CFSP/ESDP structures, the Political and Security Committee (PSC) is charged with formulating 'crisis management concepts' and the Council's Secretary General and the Commission, on a case by case basis, establishes a 'Crisis Response Co-ordination Team' (CRCT). Moreover, all EU actors in the field are advised to form a 'Co-ordination group' for co-ordinating the implementation of the EU's response to a crisis, chaired by an EU Special Representative (if one has been appointed!) who reports to the PSC and Secretary General, who is simultaneously the EU's High Representative for Foreign and Security Policy.[31]

On the UN side, the equivalent of those EU operational guidelines were formulated in the Secretary-General's Decision on Integration of June 2008, which relates back to the plea contained in the Brahimi Report of 2000 that 'no amount of money or resources can substitute for the significant changes that are urgently needed in the culture of the Organization'. Accordingly, multi-dimensional peacekeeping operations or political missions and a UN Country Team (UNCT) require an integrated strategic framework (ISF) that reflects 'a shared vision of the United Nation's strategic objectives' and 'a set of agreed results, timelines, and responsibilities for the delivery of tasks critical to consolidating peace.'[32] Like the EU, the UN adds structures for operational guidance by an Integration Steering Group (ISG), headquarters-based Integrated (Mission) Task Forces (IMTF/ITFs). Their purpose is to ensure coherent and consistent policy support and guidance.[33] Moreover, the UN also tries to balance seemingly rigid structural provisions through principles facilitating operational flexibility. This is done by arguing in favour of adapting the configuration and composition of integrated field coordination mechanisms on a case-by-case, country-to-country basis and in line with the principle of 'form follows function' for strategic and programmatic coordination.[34]

In sum, while employing Johnston's analytical framework of strategic cultures, it is hard to identify any differences in the norms and procedures of the pertinent EU and UN documents consulted. What seems to be rather a marginal difference of wording registered under criterion 1, that is, the UN using the more pronounced term 'war', while the EU avoids this term and prefers to talk about 'regional conflicts' instead, appears to be the most obvious difference noted. This difference may be explained by the EU being a *regional* organization, and an institution *sui generis* characterized by its specific history and experience of integration, including some significant *supra*-national elements, while the UN remains an *inter*-national organization with the ultimate mandate to work towards peace and security on a global scale.

The attitudinal congruence could be explained by the fact that both organizations and their member states (MS) are closely interrelated. Above all, it should be noted that the documents studied in this analysis are not evolving independently; rather, EU states and governments work towards the formulation of basic principles for conflict and crisis management on both the regional EU *and* the global UN level. Hence, the documents would probably only differ if one assumes that the EU could possibly agree on a more stringent set of basic principles in this realm on the regional level – which is, in view of the previous analysis, empirically not the case. Moreover, the EU subordinates itself to the UN. It explicitly recognizes the primary responsibility of the UN Security Council for the maintenance of peace and security in accordance with the UN Charter. Therefore the overwhelming normative congruence of EU and UN documents may come as no surprise.[35]

However, one caveat has to be noted: when analysing EU and UN documents in a static manner, the previously depicted self-image of both organizations' strategic culture largely neglects the evolutionary character and thus possible changes of a SC over time. Hence, those expert opinions mentioned above dealing with the evolution of cultures are to be taken into account: the EU's SC changing from a purely civilian power to a 'modest superpower' or 'global power' more inclined to use military intervention as a foreign policy tool, in the view of both van Ham and Rogers. For the UN, Barnett and Finnemore contend a return to a less robust concept of peacekeeping, and to a more traditional concept void of ambitious considerations of human security and democratization. Gowan, in contrast, asserts a continuity of UN premises of the early 1990s and criticizes this as being overoptimistic in view of the repoliticization of the Security Council and peacekeeping activities.[36]

Concerning the basic research question addressed in this study, these intermediate findings suggest that we cannot expect that strategic culture will be accountable for any cooperation problem between the EU and the UN in the area of crisis management. More precisely, if no variance between the two institutions' strategic cultures exists, the concept of a strategic culture cannot help to explain the apparent problems of cooperation between the two institutions. However, if we take into consideration van Ham and Rogers on the one hand, and Barnett and Finnemore on the other hand, we face a remarkably contradictory evolution of both institutions' normative paradigms regarding the efficacy of different strategic options: while the EU is said to be becoming more assertive and ambitious, the UN allegedly appears to be more cautious and constrained regarding its SC in the realm of conflict and crisis management. This could nurture expectations of a possible role for SC in influencing inter-organizational cooperation and contributing to cooperation problems.

The next step of the analysis will be to investigate EU–UN cooperation practices in order to discuss the significance of a SC or other explanatory factors that could explain problems of inter-organizational cooperation between the European Union and United Nations.

Cooperation Problems between the EU and the UN in Conflict and Crisis Management

This section focuses on EU–UN cooperation in the following operations:

- An EU military operation in DR Congo (Artemis, June–August 2003);
- The military operation EUFOR RD Congo (July–November 2006), which, like Artemis, complemented the UN mission (MONUC);
- EU military operations in the Republic of Chad; and

- A mission in the Central African Republic (Operation EUFOR Chad/RCA, March 2008 to March 2009) that complemented the UN Mission to Central Africa and Chad (MÍNURCAT).

In addition, we will examine:

- EUPOL Kinshasa (2004),
- EUPOL DR Congo and UNPOL, as well as the EU assistance mission to security sector reform in the DR of Congo (EUSEC DR Congo, since May 2005).[37]

The choice of these missions holds two advantages: 1) some contextual factors can be kept constant, since all these cases relate to conflicts in Africa and similar conflict environments; 2) these operations cover the time span of 2003 to 2009 and thus allow for a temporary comparison and assessment of progress in terms of institutionalized cooperation among the organizations in question.

All three operations under scrutiny here were – in terms of impact success, that is, concerning their contribution to problem-solving on the ground – more successful in the short term. However, their effectiveness was called into question soon after the European Union operations were terminated.[38] Regarding the output and the European Union-related outcome dimension, the operations enhanced the EU's stance and credibility as a capable actor in spite of some internal shortcomings which questioned its ability to act decisively. These shortcomings also infringed on EU–UN cooperation, internal decision-making structures, the framework-nation concept, and the ability to act without NATO and outside the Berlin-Plus agreement. Operational capacities were tested and – in spite of some shortcomings which will be addressed below – were allegedly an overall success.[39]

Concerning the outcome dimension, most experts have stressed that Artemis reinforced EU links with the UN in crisis management. The UN and the EU took on distinct roles aiming at an operational division of labour. Cooperation in this case was marked by the UN's lead in terms of providing the most troops for the longest time. It also acted increasingly 'as a facilitator and coordinator of the efforts of other international actors'. The EU's contributions were substantial, compared to both previous EU operations and to other international actors in the DRC. For example, the United States provided one quarter of the MONUC budget. Operational coordination was facilitated by a division of labour between the EU's political and military commands, which liaised with the respective partners in the UN.[40]

The EUFOR RD Congo mission in 2006 was also reportedly successful in terms of EU–UN cooperation. It reconfirmed the EU's commitment to 'effective multilateralism' and was its first successful application of the 'standby model', which was identified by both organizations as one of the possible modes of inter-organizational cooperation.[41] In short, in view of EUFOR Chad/RCA's diversity of troop contributors, the complexity of the challenge and the degree of cooperation with the UN is said 'to remain a milestone in the development of ESDP'. This positive assessment was also shared by the High Representative for CFSP, Javier Solana, as well as by UN reports and those of some NGOs.[42]

Helly points to achievements in terms of new modes of coordination at all levels between the EU and the UN – an overall unprecedented level of coordination – as well as new procedures that will be available for future joint operations. Contradictions between the EU and the UN emerged frequently during the coordination process, but allegedly they did not hamper joint work on the ground. Nevertheless, the 'bridging operation' combining EU and UN activities proved difficult to implement efficiently in terms of the impact dimension of an ESDP military umbrella for civilians and the humanitarian community and UN staff and police. Moreover, timely deployments were problematic since, contrary to original plans, they did not occur simultaneously. Overall, the bridging function would not have worked in this case without the significant (although temporary) re-hatting of EU contingents until the arrival of UN follow-on troops.[43]

Overall, experts' assertions can be contradictory: pertinent analyses repeatedly stress that 'there was very good cooperation with the UN on the ground as well as at the highest political level'[44] and the operation has also been dubbed a remarkably positive exercise and a precedent for future cases of crisis-management cooperation between both organizations.[45] According to Martinelli, cooperation achievements were facilitated by the Joint Declaration on Cooperation in Crisis Management agreed upon in 2003.[46] In contrast, Giegerich interprets the recurring insistence on improving cooperation contained in successive EU–UN agreements by saying that this may have 'led to greater institutionalization but not necessarily to better results.'[47] Experts' assessment of EU–UN cooperation was still positive despite the admitted political and operational problems.[48] This inherent tension in expert assessments may be ascribed to diverging points of reference for gauging success which are not always spelled out in a clear and equal manner.

Which causal factors can be identified in view of the actual problems discernible in inter-organizational cooperation in the realm of conflict and crisis management operations selected in this study?[49]

Material Factors: Member States' Interests and Preferences, Collective Action Problems, Military Capabilities

Cooperation with the United Nations' conflict and crisis management activities depends on the member states' positions regarding 1. their respective readiness to go for an ESDP mission, 2. the specifics of the mandate, and 3. the specifics of national contributions in terms of troops, equipment, and finances. Factors defining governments' positions in this regard are 'national interests and preferences', as well as the availability of a respective capability. That is, the members have to be 'willing and able'. These factors are framed here in terms of 'material factors' that are bound by national cost-benefit calculations.[50]

Manifest interests of governments will define their position and role in the process of establishing an ESDP operation in connection with the UN. All three operations considered here (Artemis, EUFOR RD Congo 2006 and EUFOR Chad/CRA 2008) were marked by strong French leadership. Paris not only took the initiative for these missions and for the EU support of existing or planned UN activities, it also contributed most of the troops, capabilities and budget. This, of course, becomes logical against the backdrop of Africa's existing political, social, and economic boundaries and France's history as a colonial power in Africa. However, to some experts France's dominant role questioned the ability of the EU as such to get these operations going in the first place, in the sense of reaching consensus in the EU Council as well as the operation in the field.[51]

The EUFOR Operation in Congo, formally requested by Ban Ki-Moon, failed in December 2005 because member states' divergent positions on the scope and extent of this operation prevented agreement in the EU Council.[52] First, in close contact with the UN's DPKO, France attempted to initiate an operation, while Finland, Ireland, the Netherlands, and Sweden reportedly lobbied for an ESDP operation. In contrast, Britain was strongly against an ESDP engagement because it was reluctant to deploy its 'battle group' while British troops were preoccupied with Afghanistan. Thus London favoured an expansion of the MONUC mission instead of deployment of a separate ESDP operation. Germany at first was also reluctant because of domestic reservations about such an operation as well as a general lack of interest in playing a big role in Africa. Likewise, the EU's internal debate on contributions to the reform of the security sector in Congo was, according to Martinelli, also complicated by diverging national positions.[53]

France could not again become the framework nation and take on the formal leadership role in this operation for fear of suspicion about Paris using ESDP to further the French national interest. Other than France, however, only Britain and Germany have the capacity to provide operational headquarters for such an endeavour. Since Britain was strictly against the mission, Germany became 'the only country without an argument as to why it should not provide the OHQ (in Potsdam)'.[54]

This change of position was apparently due to Germany's determination not to harm the constantly advocated strengthening of ESDP, as well as to show consideration for its relations with Paris. Against this backdrop, Germany's reluctance provided Berlin with some leverage for negotiating a mandate that included some caveats: 'the consent of the government of DR Congo; a robust mandate from the UN Security Council; substantial military participation by other EU member states apart from France and Germany; geographical concentration on the Congolese capital Kinshasa; and duration restricted to four months'. Moreover, Germany refused any discussion of the French and Belgian demands to extend the duration of the mandate.[55] Overall, Brussels responded to the UN request with caution. Initial deliberations by the EU Military Committee and Civcom were followed by a demand for more information on what kind of military force New York was requesting. Also, a mixed EU military-civilian fact-finding team was sent to the DRC, which could be considered a sort of holding operation, and all these factors contributed to the significant delay of the actual start of the operation in March 2006.[56]

EUFOR Chad's mandate was, once again, a compromise resulting from member states' diverging agendas. Paris reportedly pushed reluctant member states for contributions by way of political ambiguity about the forces remaining 'neutral and impartial'. Despite an overall consensus to deploy ESDP forces, debates in the EU sprang from ambiguities and suspicion of French intentions, fearing that they were possibly using 'the European flag to mask a policy aimed at supporting an authoritarian regime.' Britain and Germany only agreed because the mission was limited to a bridging function; Austria, Finland, and Sweden insisted on neutrality and impartiality. In the end, France shouldered the main burdens in terms of troops and costs (80 per cent).[57] Aside from some national caveats posed at the last minute, troop contingents provided by all EU states reportedly supported each other on behalf of the collective European objectives, and caveats were not made public. Despite originally divergent positions there was apparently a convergence of efforts to optimise the operation's conduction.[58]

Another sub-cluster of material factors are national prerogatives and the political control of the military by member states. For example, reportedly Germany was frustrated by its experience of EUFOR RD Congo in 2006, where Berlin was the framework nation and provided the second-largest contingent for the operation: 'Officials in Berlin felt that the UN had pushed them into an unnecessary operation and that the structures put in place in 2003-4 gave EU Member States too little oversight of relations with the UN.'[59] Another example relating to Artemis was that the EU renounced the benefit from the legal agreement of MONUC with the Congolese, because this would have required putting ESDP troops under UN command.[60] This reservation does not relate to the UN alone: sometimes EU governments are even 'reluctant to have their military aid supervised by Brussels'; for example, when it comes to bilateral security sector reform efforts run by EU MS – France, Belgium, Netherlands, and Britain – which are by no means always complementary to or compatible with EU efforts.[61]

Moreover, both costs and existing deployments of member states' troops restrain the EU and national armies from supporting UN peacekeeping missions. A case in point is the British resistance to contributing troops for EUFOR RD Congo 2006 due to London's anxiety not to deploy its 'battle group', which at that time was on duty in ESDP rapid reaction operations, as well as the heavy British involvement in Afghanistan.[62] The strongest expression of national prerogatives might have been to avoid following a UN call for an ESDP operation. This in fact did happen in the wake of Artemis, which had raised great UN expectations concerning EU support: when the UN requested an ESDP force for an intervention in the Kivu region (RD Congo) in late 2008, the EU Council, and thus the member states, refused to follow this call.[63]

Another 'material' factor is the EU's shortage of operational capabilities. To this end, *Artemis* highlighted well-known weaknesses in Europe's military capabilities, including its shortage of strategic transport and the need to improve the interoperability of European armed forces. Moreover, shortcomings in strategic, political or operational intelligence gathering and sharing, and information and communication technology, as well as the obsolescence of certain equipment, became discernible. These weaknesses, however, according to General Neveux, the French commander of *Artemis*, did not put the success of the operation at risk.[64] In the case of the EUFOR Chad operation, even after the UN-SC mandate, some EU members were worried about getting involved, primarily because much of the required equipment was lacking – especially the provision of helicopters and airlifts. The net result was that EUFOR only deployed in March 2008, over a year after the UN Secretary

General had proposed a UN force. Even if the EU was slow to deploy, MINURCAT also struggled to get its personnel in place.[65]

Last but not least, as Gowan has observed, at times the EU neglected a more strategic approach and instead favoured a 'political approach', while 'stressing identity over impact'. EU engagement was to a significant degree driven by internal considerations regarding the European constitution, the search for reassurance about ESDP's credibility, and French-German cohesion.[66] Another expression of this self-centred and inward-looking EU, questioning its cooperation commitment to the UN, could be seen, for example, in the *Artemis* case: according to Giegerich, 'the UN was not directly involved in the planning for the EU operation and was not even informed in advance of the arrival of the EU troops. There were no liaison arrangements in place'.[67]

In sum, material factors are at the heart of EU member states' engagement in an ESDP operation. Collective action problems resulted from divergent national interests and preferences and not only hampered the internal EU decision-making processes but also infringed on the EU's ability to deploy rapidly. Moreover, political leadership in those operations was significant for overcoming these collective action problems and decision-making rules of 'constructive abstention' in the EU's ESDP. Active leadership, as France showed in EUFOR Congo, is also important to facilitate policy coordination with UN counterparts on all levels. Like NATO, the EU has no troops of its own. They remain the sole prerogatives of the member states, which in turn, enhance political opportunity costs for them. Also, assignment of capabilities and availability of equipment remains awkwardly organized and contributes to significant delays in the operations.

Institutional Factors: Internal EU (and UN) Hurdles for Policy Coordination

As Kuehne states, '(t)he complexity of the planning, consultation and decision making process in Brussels is breathtaking'. The trouble starts with the combination of intergovernmental (European Council) and supranational (EU Commission) approaches and activities within the political system of the EU. These structures not only complicate cooperation among the member states, they also confuse UN interlocutors about what the EU is, how it works and who is responsible for what.[68] For example, even after the EU had reached a political consensus on sending an ESDP operation to Congo in 2006, the decision-making process was still cumbersome, as the member states could not agree on specific assignment of who would participate and who would take on a leadership role. This led to irritations in the EU between individual MS and HR Solana, as well as between the EU and the UN. At the same time, the EU Commission – first and foremost Commissioner for Development and Humanitarian Aid (and former Belgian Foreign Minister) Louis Michel, reportedly – strongly argued in favour of an ESDP operation.[69]

In the case of Artemis, intra-EU efforts were obstructed partly because the Commission's development work in Bunia (a conflict-ridden town in eastern Congo) was not coordinated with the operation.[70] In Chad, ESDP–EU Commission cooperation was allegedly suboptimal because the latter had concerns for the humanitarian community on the ground and viewed the military operation with mistrust. This was mirrored in a strained relationship between the Force Commander and the EC Head of Delegation. And 'synergies and coherence between the ESDP operation, French diplomatic representation and the EU Special Representatives could have been optimized, through a more permanent and appropriate EU political presence in Chad'.[71] Likewise, in the realm of security sector reform in the DRC, inter-institutional differences and rivalries occurred which were only partly remedied by an agreement between the Commission and the Council on a comprehensive EU approach.[72]

As another institutional factor hampering inter-organizational cooperation, Martinelli identified differences in the 'institutional cultures' of the EU Council and the EU Commission, which troubled the EU peace-building efforts. This was especially evident in the case of EUPOL Kinshasa. However, this point can be applied more generally. These differences were visible in different conceptions of purpose and modalities concerning security sector reform efforts: '[t]he Council views these efforts in the context of its ESS while the Commission views SSR in terms of state and human security as part of good governance'.[73] Thus, culture – here, institutional culture – is at least shining out once as an explanatory factor for inter-organizational cooperation.

In sum, internal policy coordination between EU institutions and its agencies is often awkward in terms of 'coherence across pillars'. As a comfort for the EU, on at least one occasion, the UN was to be blamed of a lack of clarity and cohesion. With reference to the EUFOR Congo operation, 'EU officials complained that they received mixed signals from their UN counterparts on the necessity and desirability of an ESDP deployment'.[74]

Institutional Factors: Conflicting Procedures of Organizations

'(T)he quality of EU–UN relations cannot only be measured in terms of institutionalisation. It is defined first and foremost by the quality of operational interactions.'[75] Gowan's assertion draws our attention to the cooperative efforts of the EU and the UN prior to and during actual operations, including interactions between Brussels and New York, as well as between ESDP and UN operations and missions in the field. Cooperation problems may arise from misunderstandings due to a lack of knowledge of each side's current political debates, institutional constraints, procedures and capabilities, or problems resulting from the differences of practices and procedures governing the EU or the UN's conflict and crisis management activities.[76]

Differences in organizational structures, decision-making procedures and chain of command issues are encumbering inter-organizational cooperation. Kuehne holds that structural differences in terms of headquarters are apparent, as they are regarding the locations and responsibilities of the different layers of command: 'UN operations are normally placed under the political direction of a Special Representative of the Secretary-General (SRSG), EU Special Representatives or Special Envoys, do not have – when they exist – the same level of prerogatives as UN SRSGs regarding, for instance, the Force Commander or the Police Commissioner as the head of the police.'[77]

In the same vein, some delays in decision-making on the ground occurred due to a cumbersome operational chain of command according to which EUFOR could only act at the request of MONUC, which received its guidance from New York. A case in point was the delayed EUFOR reaction, in August 2006, to the unrest in Kinshasa following the announcement of the election results. Moreover, decision-making on the ground was cumbersome since Brussels was not allowed to communicate directly with Kinshasa, but had to involve the German command in Gabon and finally Berlin.[78]

The planning and implementation of complementary EU and UN operations were according to Kuehne marked by 'very different cultures, institutions and procedures'. Given the problems regarding logistics and financing, planning an ESDP mission under the authority of the European Council is also a cumbersome and lengthy process.[79] Multilevel governance in the EU and forging inter-governmental compromises are demanding in terms of time and effort. Compared to the time of Artemis, EUFOR-MONUC cooperation had improved, but still was not perfect. As Gowan reports, 'frequent frustration over the lack of formal coordination structures' occurred and '(i)rritations arose over issues such as sharing documents'. Most importantly, cooperation in the field suffered from 'the fact that the two missions generated independent threat assessments – creating differences over precisely when deterrent action was necessary.'[80]

With respect to the EUFOR Chad operation, cooperation and planning between the EUFOR and UN planners had reportedly become smoother by this time. This was facilitated not least by the military leadership's temporary presence at the department of Peacekeeping Operations and the Department of Field Support in New York, which allowed for a good exchange of information and the application of lessons learned, despite the tight timeframe. Officers acquired some understanding of the working of UN headquarters and a joint concept of operations could be achieved. Reportedly, this was instructive when the operation faced challenges during deployment in the field, since 'MINURCAT military leadership knew who within the bureaucracy could resolve issues most quickly'.[81]

In contrast to the EU's Artemis operation in 2003, the EU operation in Chad was mandated simultaneously with the UN police mission, with detailed instructions concerning their respective duties and coordination structures. As Gowan noted, '(t)his implied a shared strategic vision between the EU and the UN'. But in reality the planning process allegedly was not harmonious, and was *de facto* realized in a disconnected manner, not least since '(t)he linkage between decision-making in the Security Council and the EU's General Affairs and External Relations Council (GAERC) is uncertain'.[82] After all, EUFOR Chad was meant to safeguard the build-up process of MINURCAT, which proved difficult and could only be accomplished thanks to the readiness of EU and its member states to 're-hat' EUFOR troops in March 2009. Without the re-hatting of EU troops, the bridging concept was bound to fail, and the operation's takeover by troops from other countries only happened slowly over the course of 2009. A lesson learned, accordingly, was that 'early definitive commitment of the follow-on force seems key' for its success.[83]

Another area of marked difference between the EU and UN exists in the realm of support and logistics. As Kuehne reports, the UN has developed a rather systematic and well entrenched approach to both over the decades, while the EU procedures are less streamlined. This factor hampered inter-organizational cooperation regarding operation Artemis when the EU requested the use of UN DPKO logistics assets. This did not match with UN procedures. Similar problems were also reported for the initial phase of EUFOR deployment in Congo 2006, though, according to the technical agreement between both organizations, this time MONUC was explicitly in charge of providing support to EUFOR. Moreover, different working methods also exist in the area of financing and are another factor which sometimes strains cooperation; whereas UN peacekeeping operations are fully funded from the assessed peacekeeping budget, the ESDP funding mechanisms are more complicated.[84]

In sum, evidence for procedural obstacles is abundant. There are contradictory procedures concerning planning, financing and logistics of operations, incompatible decision-making procedures, and lack of knowledge about the practices of the other organization. This hampers cooperation and may well become a factor undermining the effectiveness of ESDP operations in support of the UN. Regarding the impact of this cluster of factors on the success of inter-organizational cooperation, Kuehne is right in writing: 'Increasingly mission personnel is more busy coping with these structures than with the task they are primarily deployed for – managing and solving conflict!'[85]

Conclusions: The Impact of 'Strategic Culture' on EU–UN Cooperation Problems

Analysis of the factors supposedly accounting for the problems of inter-organizational cooperation allowed for the generation of many different causal factors – first and foremost material factors, such as the interests and preferences of EU member states, and institutional factors, related to 1. internal EU structures and 2. procedural differences between the EU and the UN in conflict and crisis management operations. But what about 'strategic culture', the relative significance of which for influencing inter-organizational cooperation has been the core research interest of this analysis?

This analysis is based on core primary sources available from the EU and UN and on the pertinent secondary literature on EU–UN cooperation in the security realm. Only a handful of original research analyses are available, and most of the vast body of literature on this topic relates back to these few first-hand accounts. Otherwise, most studies are citing each other when it comes to the question of providing evidence to the allegedly observed empirical 'facts & figures'.

Moreover, in most analyses strategic culture or related analytical concepts do not matter explicitly, maybe due to a lack of awareness or due to prejudgement that strategic culture may not be a viable concept. Only four authors used the term 'culture', with some variation:

- Martinelli identifies 'different institutional cultures informing Council and Commission interventions in crisis areas have been troubling the EU peacebuilding

efforts'. According to her, institutional culture became 'visible in different conceptions of purpose and modalities concerning' EU security efforts.[86]
- Kuehne found that 'the culture, institutions and procedures for planning a field mission are very different'.[87]
- According to Helly, EUFOR Chad was 'an important experience and highly instructive', facilitating a 'multicultural learning process' and possibly creating 'an embryonic European military culture'.[88]
- Moreover, Tardy's categories of cooperation constraints entail 'structural/cultural constraints' compounding institutional structures and 'crisis management cultures and procedures', but not explicitly referring to 'strategic culture' either.[89]

Thus, instead of referring explicitly to SC, existing analyses point to some sort of 'institutional culture', 'military culture' or 'culture' in general without any immediately obvious specific understanding of these terms. However, this marginal reference to the impact of 'cultural factors' on inter-organizational cooperation is not necessarily evidence that the factor is insignificant.

Thus the question remains: What about strategic culture? Can it be found hidden as sub-text in the information base used here? Coming back to the concept of SC as conceptualized by Johnston used in this analysis, how do the factors empirically influencing inter-organizational cooperation between the EU and the UN in the realm of conflict and crisis management relate to Johnston's concept of strategic culture, that is, actors' assumptions about 1. the origins and role of war in human affairs, 2. the nature of the adversary and the risks and threats challenging security, 3. the efficacy of force and the conditions under which force is useful and 4. the efficacy of different available strategic options?

In view of the elaborations on the strategic culture of both organizations, it comes as no surprise that empirically criteria 1 and 2 do not matter in this regard. If the EU and the UN disagreed in this respect, they would probably not cooperate in the field at all. Concerning criteria 3 and 4, however, we might come to more substantial conclusions. Different assumptions about the efficacy of force may be considered as one component influencing the variations in EU reactions to UN requests for ESDP operations in support of UN conflict management. EU reactions were different, ranging from general approvals, as in the cases investigated here, to outright refusal to engage at all, as in the case of the UN request to send an ESDP operation into the Kuvi region (RD Congo) in 2008. However, without more detailed information on the line of arguments during the decision-making process within the EU, it will be hard to come up with a substantive claim that SC was indeed the explanatory factor, or study what this factor's relative significance was in concert with the various 'material' and 'institutional factors' which have evidently played a role. The declared readiness to engage and the actual delay in most deployments, as well as the negative decision in the Kuvi case, are most likely driven by EU MS cost-benefit calculations and, based on these, member states' divergent positions and preferences.

Moreover, evidence has been provided that many and various hampering factors relate to institutional structures. Institutional factors mostly seem to mirror divergent

MS positions based on 'material factors'. And most of the time it seems that EU structures like the well-known traditional 'three-pillar' institutional setup and the respective decision-making procedures within the EU (sometimes summarized as problems of 'multi-level governance') are far from conducive to overcoming internal cooperation problems and reaching consensus. What has been identified as one of the features of EU SC, that is, the norm of policy 'coherence' across the policy fields and institutions involved, very often underlines the empirically manifest differences between promises made and promises kept. Thus, if 'coherence' is not taken as a manifest result of internal policy-making, but as a cultural norm supposedly guiding policy-making, it is not so much the norm and thus 'strategic culture' hampering cooperation, but the lack thereof in political practice. However, a deviation from the norm does not render a social norm *per se* non-existent, but rather just a weak norm.

If the factor of strategic culture is moreover supposed to be about concepts of efficacy of different available strategies (criterion 4), it might be interpreted to be about 1. *what* to do in a given situation and 2. *how* to do it. Thus we might be inclined to describe some of the factors mentioned in the previous sub-section as 'procedural differences' as actually being about SC. Apparently, differences in rules and procedures concerning planning processes, decision-making rules and chain of commands, as well as financing and logistics, become more important the closer both organizations are to planning and implementing a given conflict or crisis management operation. But once again it becomes an awkward business to ascribe deficiencies of information exchange and consultations, differences regarding the issue of *how* to do the planning in Brussels or New York, and the implementation practices on the ground unequivocally to SC. Why shouldn't organizational egoism (for example, the EU deploying their forces without properly informing the UN) be ascribed to an organization's interest in fostering its own power rather than the other's, and thus pertain to the category of material factors. Or why shouldn't the fact that EU member states are more interested in giving the EU an edge over the UN, rather than the other way round, be ascribed to institutional or material factors in terms of political cost-benefit calculations rather than SC?[90]

In so far as these procedural differences and conflicts between the EU and the UN are based on different traditions and ingrained habits and operational reflexes incorporated in some sort of 'standard operational procedure', it may be justified to ascribe some impact to cultural factors. But perhaps these are indeed more appropriately addressed as institutional, organizational or bureaucratic cultures than actually as *strategic* culture. Thus, in conclusion, the relative significance of SC for inter-organizational cooperation between the EU and the UN in the realm of conflict and crisis management – as far as evidence could be provided in this analysis – is comparatively marginal.

Nevertheless, these summarized findings seem to correspond to the intermediate hypotheses formulated at the end of section 2. Accordingly, the conceptual similarities of both organizations' SC are supposedly not allowing for a great deal of influence on inter-organizational cooperation. Likewise, this study could not find evidence for the expectation which qualified the basic hypothesis and became the second expectation, that is, the assumption that both organizations might be evolving in opposite directions. If so, SC should become more significant over time. Empirical proof of this expectation requires further investigation.

NOTES

1. European Council, 'A Secure Europe in a Better World. European Security Strategy 2003', http://ue.eu.int/uedocs/cmsUpload/78367.pdf (accessed on 10 April 2007).
2. See Council of the European Union, 'Joint Declaration on UN-EU Co-operation in Crisis Management', 2003, http://www.consilium.europa.eu/uedocs/cmsUpload/st12730.en03.pdf (accessed 10 January 2011); Council of the European Union, 'Council Conclusions on the CSDP', 2010, http://www.consilium.europa.eu/uedocs/cms_data/docs/pressdata/en/esdp/114737.pdf (accessed 10 January 2011).
3. For details see United Nations Security Council, *Update Report. UN Co-Operation with Regional and Subregional Organisations in the Maintenance of International Peace and Security* (New York: United Nations, 2010); Council of the European Union, 'Joint Declaration' (note 2); European Council, 'EU–UN Co-operation in Military Crisis Management Operations Elements of Implementation of the EU–UN Joint Declaration, Adopted by the European Council (17-18 June 2004)', http://www.consilium.europa.eu/uedocs/cmsUpload/EU-UN%20cooperation%20in%20Military%20Crisis%20Management%20Operations.pdf (accessed 20 January 2011); Thierry Tardy, 'United Nations - European Union Relations in Crisis Management', International Forum for the Challenges of Peace Operations, CERI Science Po, 2008, pp. 4–7.
4. See United Nations, *Improving Lives. Results of the Partnership between the United Nations and the European Union in 2009* (Brussels: United Nations, 2010), http://www.EU-UN.europa.eu/documents/en/100607_Improving_Lives_2009.pdf (accessed 14 January 2011), p. 12; Tardy, 'United Nations – European Union Relations in Crisis Management' (note 3), pp. 3–4.
5. See Alastair Iain Johnston, 'Thinking about Strategic Culture', *International Security*, Vol. 19, No. 4 (1995), pp. 32–64. For a literature review see also Darryl Howlett, 'Strategic Culture: Reviewing Recent Literature', *Strategic Insights*, Vol. IV, No. 10 (October 2005), http://www.nps.edu/Academics/centers/ccc/publications/OnlineJournal/2005/Oct/howlettOct05.html (accessed 3 December 2010).
6. For an analysis of the opposite impact-dimension – that is, from the practice of cooperation on EU policy-making, though not framed in terms of SC – see Philippe Adriaenssens, 'Rapprochement between the EU and the UN: History and Balance of Intersecting Political Cultures', *European Foreign Affairs Review*, Vol. 13, No. 1 (2008), pp. 53–72.
7. For a rare theoretical, neo-institutional approach (though referring to the UN, the EU and NATO in the Balkan wars) see Rafael Biermann, 'Towards a Theory of Inter-organizational Networking', *The Review of International Organizations*, Vol. 3, No. 2 (2008), pp. 151–177.
8. See Paul Cornish and Geoffrey Edwards, 'The Strategic Culture of the European Union: A Progress Report', *International Affairs*, Vol. 81, No. 4 (2005), pp. 801–20; Adrian Hyde-Price, 'European Security, Strategic Culture, and the Use of Force', *European Security*, Vol. 13, No. 4 (2004), pp. 323–43; Vasilis Margaras, *Common Security and Defence Policy and the Lisbon Treaty Fudge: No Common Strategic Culture, No Major Progress* (Brussels: CEPS, 2010), p. 1, p. 6; Richard Gowan, 'The Strategic Context: Peacekeeping in Crisis 2006–08', *International Peacekeeping* Vol. 15, No. 4 (2008), pp. 453–69; Espen Barth Eide, et al., *Report on Integrated Missions: Practical Perspectives and Recommendations. Independent Study for the Expanded UN ECHA Core Group* (Oslo: Norwegian Institute for International Affairs, 2005), p. 20.
9. See Asle Toje, *America, the EU and Strategic Culture* (New York: Routledge, 2008), pp. 147–148; Christoph O. Meyer, *The Quest for a European Strategic Culture: Changing Norms on Security and Defence in the European Union* (Basingstoke: Palgrave Macmillan, 2006), pp. 163, 169; Peter van Ham, 'Europe's Strategic Culture and the Relevance of War', *Oxford Journal on Good Governance*, Vol. 2, No. 1 (2005), pp. 39–44; James Rogers, 'From "Civilian Power" to "Global Power": Explicating the European Union's Grand Strategy through the Articulation of Discourse Theory', *Journal of Common Market Studies*, Vol. 47, No. 4 (2009), pp. 831–862; Ian Manners, 'Normative Power Europe Reconsidered: Beyond the Crossroads', *Journal of European Public Policy*, Vol. 13, No. 2 (2006), pp. 182–199 (Manners is not explicitly referring to any concept of SC); Michael Barnett and Martha Finnemore, *Rules for the World. International Organizations in Global Politics* (Ithaca: Cornell University Press, 2004), pp. 3–9, 122–129, 130–135, 154–155.

10. See Alvaro de Vasconcelos, 'The European Security Strategy 2003–2008. Building on Common Interests', Paris: European Union Institute for Security Studies (ISS), ISS Report No. 05, 2009, pp. 17–24.
11. As pertinent documents for the EU the following are analysed: European Council, 'A Secure Europe in a Better World. European Security Strategy 2003' (note 1); European Council, 'Report on the Implementation of the European Security Strategy. Providing Security in a Changing World', 2008, http://www.consilium.europa.eu/ueDocs/cms_Data/docs/pressdata/EN/reports/104630.pdf (accessed 11 December 2010); Council of the European Union, 'Draft European Union Programme for the Prevention of Violent Conflicts', 2008, http://www.consilium.europa.eu/ueDocs/cms_Data/docs/pressdata/en/misc/09537-r1.en1.html (accessed on 21 December 2010); Council of the European Union, 'Civil Military Co-ordination', 2003, http://register.consilium.eu.int/pdf/en/03/st14/st14457.en03.pdf (accessed 14 January 2011). For the UN these documents were chosen: United Nations, 'An Agenda for Peace. Preventive Diplomacy, Peacemaking and Peace-keeping', 1992, http://www.un.org/Docs/SG/agpeace.html (accessed 28 January 2011); United Nations, 'Report of the Panel on United Nations Peace Operations ("Brahimi Report")', 2000, http://www.un.org/peace/reports/peace_operations/ (accessed 15 January 2011); United Nations, 'Integrated Missions Planning Process (IMPP)', 2006, http://www.undg.org/docs/9907/IMPP-Revised-Guidelines-130606.pdf (accessed 15 January 2011); United Nations, 'A More Secure World: Our Shared Responsibility. Report of the High-level Panel on Threats, Challenges and Change', 2004, http://www.un.org/secureworld/report2.pdf (accessed 16 January.2011); United Nations, 'United Nations Peacekeeping Operations. Principles and Guidelines ("Capstone Doctrine")', 2008, http://pbpu.unlb.org/pbps/Library/Capstone_Doctrine_ENG.pdf (accessed 15 January 2011).
12. European Council, 'European Security Strategy' (note 1), p. 1; Council of the European Union, 'Programme for Prevention' (note 11), p. 2.
13. See also Vasconcelos, 'The European Security Strategy 2003–2008' (note 10), p. 17.
14. United Nations, 'An Agenda for Peace' (note 11), paras.13, 19, 80.
15. European Council, 'European Security Strategy' (note 1), pp. 9–10; European Council, 'Report' (note 11), p. 2; United Nations, 'An Agenda for Peace' (note 11), paras.15, 19, 81, 82.
16. European Council, 'European Security Strategy' (note 1), pp. 3–5; United Nations, 'An Agenda for Peace' (note 11), para.8.
17. European Council, 'Report' (note 11), p. 1; United Nations, 'An Agenda for Peace' (note 11), para.11; United Nations, 'A More Secure World' (note 11), para.1.
18. Council of the European Union, 'Programme for Prevention' (note 11), pp. 2–3, p. 5; in the EU's own definition, a crisis is 'a situation deteriorating into violence' (*Ibid.*, p. 3); United Nations, 'An Agenda for Peace' (note 11), para.15.
19. European Council, 'European Security Strategy' (note 1), p. 7; see also Vasconcelos, 'The European Security Strategy 2003–2008' (note 10), pp. 17–18.
20. See European Council, 'European Security Strategy' (note 1), p. 12; European Council, 'Report' (note 11), pp. 9–10.
21. United Nations, 'A More Secure World' (note 11), para.4; United Nations, 'Brahimi Report', pp. VIII-X; United Nations, 'Capstone Doctrine' (note 11), p. 35.
22. See European Council, 'European Security Strategy' (note 1), pp. 10–1; European Council, 'Report' (note 11), p. 9; Vasconcelos, 'The European Security Strategy 2003–2008' (note 10), p. 19.
23. United Nations, 'An Agenda for Peace' (note 11), paras.5, 13; United Nations, 'A More Secure World' (note 11), para.2.
24. United Nations, 'An Agenda for Peace' (note 11), para.20; United Nations, 'Capstone Doctrine' (note 11), p. 22, pp. 24–25.
25. See European Council, 'European Security Strategy' (note 1), pp. 9, 11–13; European Council, 'Report' (note 11), p. 2.
26. European Council, 'European Security Strategy' (note 1), pp. 9–11 (p. 9); Council of the European Union, 'Programme for Prevention' (note 11), p. 2; Council of the European Union, 'Civil Military Co-ordination' (note 11), p. 5.
27. United Nations, 'An Agenda for Peace' (note 11), paras.16, 60; United Nations, 'A more secure world' (note 11), para.272.
28. European Council, 'European Security Strategy' (note 1), p. 7, p. 11; European Council, 'Report' (note 11), p. 9; Council of the European Union, 'Programme for Prevention' (note 11), pp. 4–7.
29. United Nations, 'An Agenda for Peace (note 11)', paras.15, 23.
30. Council of the European Union, 'Programme for Prevention' (note 11), p. 4, p. 6.
31. Council of the European Union, 'Civil Military Co-ordination' (note 11), pp. 3–5.

32. United Nations, 'Brahimi Report' (note 11), p. XIV; United Nations, 'Integrated Missions' (note 11), pp. 24, 6; United Nations, 'Capstone Doctrine' (note 11), pp. 53–57.
33. See United Nations, 'Integrated Missions' (note 11), p. 23; United Nations, 'Brahimi Report' (note 11), p. XIII.
34. United Nations, 'Integrated Missions' (note 11), p. 7.
35. See Council of the European Union, 'Civil Military Co-ordination' (note 11), pp. 3–5; Council of the European Union, 'Joint Declaration' (note 3), p. 2. Some renowned experts seem to support this conclusion, though not framing it in terms of a common 'strategic culture'. See Jan Wouters, 'The United Nations and the European Union. Partners in Effective Multilateralism', Brugge, College of Europe, Department of EU International Relations and Diplomacy Studies, EU Diplomacy Papers, 2007, p. 4; Tardy, 'United Nations – European Union Relations in Crisis Management' (note 3), p. 4; Bastian Giegerich, 'European Military Crisis Management', *Studia Diplomatica*, Vol. LXII, No. 3 (2009), p. 40.
36. See Ham, 'Europe's Strategic Culture and the Relevance of War' (note 9), pp. 39–44; Rogers, 'From "Civilian Power" to "Global Power"', (note 9), pp. 831, 843–844; Barnett and Finnemore, *Rules for the World* (note 9), pp. 130–135, 154–155.
37. This selection covers only a limited number of EU–UN cooperations in conflict and crisis management and will not allow for general insights across all cases of inter-organizational cooperation in this field. For basic facts and figures see respective EU and UN homepages: http://www.consilium.europa.eu/showPage.aspx?id=268&lang=en (accessed on 15 February 2011); http://www.un.org/en/peacekeeping/operations/current.shtml (accessed on 15 December 2011). For a typology of EU–UN cooperation see Wibke Hansen, 'EU–UN Cooperation in Peace Operations: Chances, Concepts and Constraints', in Hans-Georg Ehrhart *et al.* (eds), *Die Europäische Union im 21. Jahrhundert* (VS Verlag für Sozialwissenschaften, 2007), pp. 242–45; Tardy, 'United Nations – European Union Relations in Crisis Management' (note 3), pp. 5–6.
38. See Damien Helly, 'The EU Military Operation in DR Congo (Artemis)', in Giovanni Grevi *et al.* (eds), *European Security and Defence Policy. The First Ten Years (1999–2009)* (Paris: European Union Institute for Security Studies [ISS], 2009), pp. 181–85; EU Presidency, 'The Situation in the Central African Region, Statement to the UN Security Council (24.11.)', 2003, http://www.europa-EU-UN.org/articles/en/article_3028_en.htm (accessed on 21 December 2011); Fernanda Faria, 'Crisis Management in Sub-Saharan Africa: The Role of the European Union', Occasional Papers No. 51, EUISS, Paris, 2004, pp. 43–44; Helly, 'The EU Military Operation' (note 38), 183–184; Richard Gowan, 'ESDP and the United Nations', in Grevi *et al.* (eds), *European Security and Defence Policy* (note 38), pp. 117–126; Damien Helly, 'The EU Military Operation in the Republic of Chad and in the Central African Republic (Operation EUFOR Tchad/ RCA)', in Grevi *et al.* (eds), *European Security and Defence Policy* (note 38), pp. 339–351; A. Sarjoh Bah (ed.), *Annual Review of Global Peace Operations. Center on International Cooperation (CIC)* (Boulder, CO: Lynne Rienner, 2009), pp. 36f. See also United Nations, 'Report of the Secretary General on the United Nations Mission in the Central African Republic and Chad', 2008, http://minurcat.unmissions.org/Portals/MINURCAT/SG%20Report%2012%20September%202008.pdf (accessed 15 January 2011).
39. See Hans-Georg Ehrhart, 'EUFOR RD Congo: A Preliminary Assessment', *European Security Review*, No. 32 (2007), pp. 9–10; Denis M. Tull, 'EUFOR RD Congo: A Success, But Not a Model', in Muriel Asseburg, *et al.* (eds), *The EU as a Strategic Actor in the Realm of Security and Defence* (Berlin: Stiftung Wissenschaft und Politik (SWP), 2009), p.52; Marta Martinelli, 'Implementing the ESDP in Africa: The Case of the Democratic Republic of Congo', in Michael Merlingen *et al.* (eds), *European Security and Defence Policy: An Implementation Perspective*, (London: Routledge, 2008), p. 125; Helly, 'The EU military operation in the Republic of Chad', pp. 348–9.
40. James Dobbins, 'Europe's Role in Nation-Building: From the Balkans to the Congo', Santa Monica, CA: RAND, 2008, 110-11; Faria, 'Crisis Management in Sub-Saharan Africa' (note 38), p. 47; Kees Homan, 'Operation Artemis in the Democratic Republic of Congo', in Andrea Ricci *et al.* (eds), *Faster and More United? The Debate about Europe's Crisis Response Capacity* (Luxembourg: Office for Official Publications of the European Communities, 2006), pp. 151–155.
41. Ehrhart, 'EUFOR RD Congo' (note 39), pp. 9–10; Claudia Major, 'The Military Operation EUFOR RD Congo 2006', in Giovanni Grevi *et al.* (eds), *The European Security Strategy 2003–2008. Building on Common Interests* (Paris: European Union Institute for Security Studies [ISS], 2009), pp. 318–321; Tull, 'EUFOR RD Congo' (note 39), p. 52; Martinelli, 'Implementing the ESDP in Africa' (note 39), p. 125.

42. Council of the European Union, 'Council Conclusions on operation EUFOR Tchad/RCA', 2008, http://register.consilium.europa.eu/pdf/en/08/st12/st12101.en08.pdf (accessed 22 February 2011); United Nations, 'Report of the Secretary General on the United Nations Mission' (note 38); Oxfam International: 'Mission Incomplete: Why Civilians Remain at Risk in Eastern Chad', Oxfam Briefing Paper 119/2008. See also Helly, 'The EU Military Operation in the Republic of Chad' (note 38), pp. 344–5, p. 350-1; Ehrhart, 'EUFOR RD Congo' (note 39), pp. 77-8.
43. Helly, 'The EU Military Operation' (note 38), p. 348; Bah (ed.), *Annual Review* (note 38), pp. 36–37.
44. Faria, 'Crisis Management in Sub-Saharan Africa' (note 38), p. 47.
45. Martinelli, 'Implementing the ESDP in Africa' (note 39), p. 118, p. 125; see also: Ståle Ulriksen *et al.*, 'Operation ARTEMIS: The Shape of Things to Come?', *International Peacekeeping*, Vol. 11, No. 3 (2004), pp. 508–525; Homan, 'Operation Artemis', (note 40, p. 154); Pierre-Antoine Braud, 'Implementing ESDP Operations in Africa', in Anne Deighton *et al.* (eds), *Securing Europe? Implementing the European Security Strategy* (Zürich: ETH, 2006), pp. 76–77.
46. See Martinelli, 'Implementing the ESDP in Africa' (note 39), p. 125.
47. Giegerich, 'European Military Crisis Management' (note 35), p. 41.
48. See Ehrhart, 'EUFOR RD Congo' (note 39), p. 10; Martinelli, 'Implementing the ESDP in Africa' (note 39), p. 123; Gowan, 'ESDP and the United Nations (note 38), p. 124.
49. For a similar but still different categorization of factors constraining inter-organizational cooperation see Tardy, 'United Nations – European Union Relations in Crisis Management' (note 3), pp. 7–13.
50. For details on the EU decision-making process in this realm see Winrich Kuehne, *How the EU Organizes and Conducts Peace Operations in Africa: EUFOR/MINURCAT* (Berlin: Center for International Peace Operations [ZIF], 2009), pp. 10–11.
51. See Helly, 'The EU Military Operation' (note 38), pp. 183–184; Helly, 'The EU Military Operation in the Republic of Chad' (note 38), p. 350; Kuehne, 'How the EU Organizes' (note 50), pp. 10–11.
52. See Gowan, 'ESDP and the United Nations' (note 38), p. 125.
53. See Martinelli, 'Implementing the ESDP in Africa' (note 39), pp. 125–126; Gowan, 'ESDP and the United Nations' (note 38), p.125.
54. Tull, 'EUFOR RD Congo' (note 39), p. 48.
55. *Ibid.*, p. 49, p. 53; see Martinelli, 'Implementing the ESDP in Africa' (note 39), p. 122; Major, 'The Military Operation EUFOR RD Congo 2006' (note 41), pp. 315–316.
56. Martinelli, 'Implementing the ESDP in Africa' (note 39), p. 122; see Richard Gowan, 'The EU's Multiple Strategic Identities: European Security after Lebanon and the Congo', *Studia Diplomatica*, Vol. 60, No. 1 (2007), pp. 59–80.
57. See Helly, 'The EU Military Operation in the Republic of Chad' (note 38), pp. 340–341, 346–347; Alexander Mattelaer, 'The Strategic Planning of EU Military Operations – The Case of EUFOR TCHAD/RCA', IES Working Paper, 2008, pp. 18–19.
58. See Helly, 'The EU Military Operation in the Republic of Chad' (note 38), p. 349.
59. Gowan, 'ESDP and the United Nations' (note 38), p. 120.
60. See Helly, 'The EU Military Operation' (note 38), pp. 184-185; Braud, 'Implementing ESDP Operations in Africa' (note 45), p. 77; Homan, 'Operation Artemis' (note 40), p. 154.
61. Martinelli, 'Implementing the ESDP in Africa' (note 39), p. 125.
62. See Braud, 'Implementing ESDP Operations in Africa' (note 45), pp. 76–77; Gowan, 'ESDP and the United Nations' (note 38), p. 125.
63. See Helly, 'The EU Military Operation', (note 38) pp. 184–185; Braud, 'Implementing ESDP Operations in Africa' (note 45), p. 77; Homan, 'Operation Artemis' (note 40), p. 154.
64. See Faria, 'Crisis Management in Sub-Saharan Africa' (note 38), pp. 44–45, 47; Homan, 'Operation Artemis' (note 40), pp. 151–155.
65. Gowan, 'ESDP and the United Nations' (note 38), p. 122; Major, 'The Military Operation EUFOR RD Congo 2006' (note 41), p. 316.
66. Gowan, 'The EU's Multiple Strategic Identities' (note 56), pp. 68, 75.
67. Giegerich, 'European Military Crisis Management' (note 35), p. 41.
68. Kuehne, 'How the EU Organizes' (note 50), p. 10.
69. See Tull, 'EUFOR RD Congo' (note 39), pp. 47–48; Major, 'The Military Operation EUFOR RD Congo 2006' (note 41), p. 316.
70. See Dobbins, 'Europe's Role in Nation-Building' (note 40), pp. 110–111.
71. Helly, 'The EU Military Operation in the Republic of Chad' (note 38), pp. 347–348.
72. See Braud, 'Implementing ESDP Operations in Africa' (note 45), pp. 76–77.
73. Martinelli, 'Implementing the ESDP in Africa' (note 39), p. 123. See for a similar argument, though relating to the Balkan wars, Biermann, 'Towards a Theory' (note 7), p. 158.

74. Gowan, 'ESDP and the United Nations' (note 38), p. 125.
75. *Ibid.*
76. See Braud, 'Implementing ESDP Operations in Africa' (note 45), pp. 76–77.
77. Kuehne, 'How the EU Organizes' (note 50), p. 12.
78. See Ehrhart, 'EUFOR RD Congo' (note 39), p. 11; Martinelli, 'Implementing the ESDP in Africa' (note 39), p. 123.
79. Kuehne, 'How the EU Organizes' (note 50), p. 11.
80. Gowan, 'The EU's Multiple Strategic Identities' (note 38), p. 79, Major, 'The Military Operation EUFOR RD Congo 2006' (note 41), p. 317.
81. Benjamin C. Tortolani (ed.), *Annual Review of Global Peace Operations*, (New York: Center on International Cooperation [CIC], 2010), pp. 40–41.
82. See Gowan, 'ESDP and the United Nations' (note 38), p. 122; see also Helly, 'The EU Military Operation in the Republic of Chad' (note 38), p. 348.
83. Helly, 'The EU Military Operation in the Republic of Chad' (note 38), pp. 344–345, 348.
84. See Kuehne, 'How the EU Organizes' (note 50), p. 11; Braud, 'Implementing ESDP Operations in Africa' (note 45), pp. 76–77; Homan, 'Operation Artemis' (note 40), p. 154; Major, 'The Military Operation EUFOR RD Congo 2006' (note 41), p. 314, p. 318; Helly, 'The EU Military Operation' (note 38), pp. 184–185.
85. Kuehne, 'How the EU Organizes' (note 50), pp. 10–11.
86. Martinelli, 'Implementing the ESDP in Africa' (note 39), p. 123.
87. Kuehne, 'How the EU Organizes' (note 50), pp. 10–11.
88. Helly, 'The EU Military Operation in the Republic of Chad' (note 39), pp. 348–349.
89. Tardy, 'United Nations - European Union Relations in Crisis Management' (note 3), p. 11.
90. *Ibid.*, p. 8.

Overlap or Opposition? EU and NATO's Strategic (Sub-)Culture

BENJAMIN ZYLA

With the Cold War's end, the debate on the future of Europe's security policy has largely centred on three issues: 1) strengthening the European Union's security and defence policy; 2) generating more military capabilities; and 3) facilitating intra-institutional cooperation between the security institutions in Europe.[1] Here, we will focus on the third dimension and examine more closely the inter-institutional relationship between the two leading security organizations in Europe, namely the North Atlantic Treaty Organization (NATO) and the European Union (EU).

The history of NATO–EU relations is complex and deeply embedded in the two security actors' role-finding process in the aftermath of the end of the Cold War. More precisely, at the heart of that quest for organizational identity is NATO's search for a security role for its European members. While the European Union member states were an integral part of American grand strategy during the Cold War, they acquired an increasingly autonomous standing and role in European security in the post-Cold War era. Beginning with the Maastricht Treaty the European Union began to think about not only its place and role in the world but also the appropriate means by which to carry out such roles (such as the Petersberg Tasks).

Much ink has already been spilled tracing the evolution of the relationship between the two organizations.[2] In the 1990s, it was particularly cultivated by the George H. Bush administration, which requested that Europe share a greater slice of the Atlantic burden[3] and increase its contribution to regional security in Europe by way of creating a European Security and Defence Identity (ESDI).[4] This arrangement under ESDI took place inside NATO and essentially allowed European forces to borrow American military assets to conduct crisis management missions in Europe's immediate neighborhood. In turn, US forces in Europe benefited from this arrangement by being freed from some of their non-Article 5 responsibilities.

The ESDI principle was formally agreed upon at the NATO Council in Berlin in 1996, and became known as the 'Berlin-Plus' agreement. Negotiations on the complicated and contested details of the agreement lasted until December 2002 where an institutionalized and strategic partnership between the two organizations was finalized.[5] In light of the crisis in the Balkans and the explicit American discontent about Europe's weakening military capabilities, the St Malo Summit in 1999 set in motion the creation of an autonomous EU security and defence policy (ESDP) outside of NATO.[6] While the summit established the European Union as an independent global actor, it immediately raised conceptual and practical questions about future relations between the EU and NATO. At the kernel of the dispute rests the involvement of non-EU NATO members (such as Turkey and Norway) in intra-European security affairs, as the Berlin-Plus arrangement offered no venue for those states to be fully involved in such. It also left the 'right of first refusal' principle of NATO largely unspecified.

To be sure, this historical account is not new at all.[7] Moreover, the body of literature is mostly descriptive rather than analytical, and only recently have researchers begun to explore the relationship between the two organizations by bringing the issue into the realm of the discipline of international relations.[8]

Against this backdrop, it is therefore hardly sensible, and possibly even redundant, to write another piece that traces the complex and interwoven relationship between the two organizations. Rather than studying their material overlaps I take a different approach to studying strategic cultures and examine the ideational structures that affect the institutions' social behaviour, as well as their behaviour toward each other. Inspired by the concept of a strategic culture[9] I conceptualize strategic cultures as elite expressions of strategic beliefs, values, and norms. The objective of this research article then is twofold: first, to tease out how structures of meaning in the form of norms, values, and beliefs have affected the behaviour of those two organizations toward each other; and second, to introduce a new exploratory argument of a subcultural relationship of the two organizations that can help explain their attitudinal divergences.

In order to make my argument, I will unpack the prevalent strategic cultures of the European Union and the North Atlantic Treaty Organization into their normative, ideational, and behavioural components. In so doing, I will cluster them according to 1. the meanings they assign to future challenges and threats; 2. the behavioural prepositions of how to respond to those threats; and 3. the preferred modes of international cooperation.

I provide two arguments. First, there is a significant normative overlap between the two institutions, especially with regard to future challenges and threats, as well as the role of third parties and international organizations. Yet there exists an elementary difference in terms of the values the institutions attach to the use of force, the sanctioned range and type of missions, and the resources justified to carry them out. Because of the limitations regarding the scope and length of this study, the empirical section can only provide a snapshot of potentially larger ideational forces at play. Second, by building on of Gabriel Almond and Sidney Verba's works on political culture, I argue that the best way to map out the social world and to make sense of the ideational divergences of the two organizations is to conceptualize NATO's strategic culture as a subculture of the European Union. That is to say that NATO's strategic culture in the 1990s has become a subcultural trait of shared and distinctive sets of values, norms, and beliefs that are different from those held at the EU level.[10] This section of the paper should be understood as a bold exploratory attempt to better conceptualize the attitudinal divergence of the two organizations under the cultural framework.

The article starts by briefly outlining the methodology used for the empirical part. What follows is a historical review of the concept of strategic culture. This will help us to appreciate the salience of the concept as well as the contribution that this article makes to the literature. In the third section, I define the concept of norms before explaining the nexus between a strategic culture and a security strategy/strategic document. The empirical part concentrates on an examination of the three normative clusters as mentioned above. The fourth section explores ways of conceptually explaining the attitudinal divergence of the two organizations by introducing the concept of subcultures to the study of EU–NATO relations. This section should be understood as an exploratory undertaking to explain the institutional overlap.

Methodology

Before we compare the European Union's and NATO's strategic culture across their normative and behavioural values, it is important to elucidate the methodologies employed in this study. To reiterate, the objective of this study is to tease out how structures of meaning in the form of norms, values, and beliefs affected those two organizations' behaviour towards each other between 2003 and 2010.[11] The principal challenge thus lies in how to delineate those organizations' strategic cultures and measure their non-material variables without running a tautological argument. Such tautology occurs if one compounds inferences from behaviour into the analysis, which amalgamates the dependent and the independent variable.[12] This is precisely why the empirical analysis concentrates on primary rather than secondary sources, as the latter mostly describe certain behaviours of the two organizations. Put differently, in order to avoid such inference I study normative, ideational, and behavioural components of security cultures rather than the behaviour of those organizations. As noted, these attitudinal structures are expressed by the political elite in the form of strategic documents like a security strategy (in the case of the EU)[13] or the strategic concept (in the case of NATO). Put simply, we will examine written rhetoric expressed in strategic documents.[14]

Studying elite expressions of values, norms, and beliefs of national security has a number of advantages. To start with, elite political cultures are easier to describe and measure[15] than, for example, public opinion polls, which are usually too elaborative to reveal specific underlying cultural mindsets on security issues. Second, attitudinal structures held by elite policy makers are assumed to possess sophisticated political belief systems that are more coherent than those of ordinary individuals.[16] Third, those elites hold primary responsibility for formulating the security policies of the organizations in question, and thus show a great deal of influence in key decisions on values, beliefs, and norms of international security.

I rely on the interpretive variant of the content analysis method[17] to gain access to the attitudinal structures of those organizations' strategic cultures while being fully aware that such a narrow analysis can only provide a snapshot picture in a specific given time and of a potentially much larger trend.[18] Hence, there is no claim for comprehensiveness in this study; nor is the claim made that the two organizations' cultures have developed over time. I am particularly interested in three clusters (or categories) of normative attitudes: 1. the nature and interpretation of threats, 2. accepted ways and methods to address these threats, and 3. values attached to international organizations.[19] The first examines the extent and degree to which threats endanger social agents, as well as the ways in which they are interpreted and used to justify security behaviour. The second category of normative attitudes focuses on accepted social practices regarding how to address these threats, including the application of civilian and military resources of state power. What are the organizations' attitudes towards the use of force? Under which conditions, if at all, should it be used? The final category examines the values that both the EU and NATO attach to international cooperation and international law, and how such practices, if at all, should be conditioned by international rules and norms.

It should, however, be noted that there is an imbalance in comparing the EU and NATO's security strategy. One major difference, of course, is their size and thus the scope and extent of detailing they provide. The NATO document is much more extensive and elaborative than its European counterpart. A second difference is that both strategies can only be seen as the lowest common denominator of the national security values and beliefs held by the member states.[20] For example, most of the EU member states as well as Canada and the United States maintain a national security strategy – and thus a national strategic culture – that should be noted as an addition to the EU strategy.

Concepts

The Strategic Culture Concept

Reviewing the history as well as the ontological underpinnings of the strategic culture concept helps us to appreciate the origins and theoretical refinements of this approach over time. The literature, broadly speaking, clusters the scholarship on strategic cultures into four 'generations'.[21] Haglund, Norheim-Martinsen, and Rynning superbly discussed the first three in the theoretical section earlier in this volume; thus there is no need for me to repeat the historical evolution of the concept here, nor to trace the evolution of the literature in each of the three generations. Rather, I simply state that this paper builds on the fourth generation's scholarship of sociological studies of strategic cultures. Specifically, it provides a comparative analysis of strategic cultures and attempts to tease out hidden cultural logics.[22]

This scholarship began to emerge in the early 1990s and questioned the ontological assumptions of the earlier generations. Inspired by the evolving constructivist school of international relations, scholars began to theorize about identity formations and norms that were shaped by the interplay of history, tradition, and culture. A strategic culture was conceived as an independent or intervening variable that affects the security behaviour of social agents.[23] It is conceived as a metaconcept that goes beyond representing a singular process of cause and effect, reflects a national identity ('who we are') and normatively informs 'what it is that we do' or 'should do'.[24] Above all, constructivists held that national identities and interests were not a by-product of the international system; they are socially constructed and shaped by practices of interaction among social actors.

Following this line of thinking implies two things: first, societies rather than external structures shape and define the identities, interests, and capacities of social agents. Second, societies contain normative elements that require interpretation and understanding.[25] Social actors reproduce norms and structure by reflexively basing their actions on their acquired knowledge, habits, and routines.[26] Transmitted to the domain of security studies, strategic culture approaches charge that individual state interests are constructed in the 'patterns of perceptions about a country's role in international politics as well as in the use of military force towards achieving political ends'.[27] It is precisely in this sense that strategic cultures are able to provide an insight into the 'reasons' behind international agents' actions.[28] In short, constructivism has enabled scholars to examine more closely the cultural and social contexts in which international actors operate.

Norms

Definitions of strategic cultures, as David Haglund's essay in this volume reminds us, are diffuse and inconsistently used in the literature. One way of operationalizing them, however, is to unpack the expression of a strategic culture into normative, ideational, and behavioural components. Put differently, this is to say that normative structures are part of a state's strategic culture. This in turn implies that their analysis can provide meanings of the two organizations' social reality. Norms are defined as 'intersubjective beliefs about the social and natural world that define actors, their situations, and the possibilities of action'.[29] They are social facts that set standards of appropriate behaviour, express the agents' identities, and in this sense have a prescriptive element regarding how things ought to be in the world.[30] Norms also help social agents to situate themselves in relation to other social actors, and to interpret these actors' interests and actions.[31]

Cultural studies have shown that in contrast to material conditions, norms are the least volatile components of a political and thus strategic culture.[32] They are deeply ingrained, identity-derived collective expectations of what is appropriate behaviour for social agents.[33] This, in turn, implies two things: first, a strategic culture is unique to each organization; second, because of their complex and interrelated integral components, they could not be replicated elsewhere. Also, as John Duffield has found, they are resistant towards change precisely because they are widely shared among societal groups, whereas competitive proposals still have to convince a critical societal mass.[34] The second reason why strategic cultures are difficult to change is because it is generally difficult to establish the falsity of a claim, norm, or value. Only dramatic historical events or traumatic national experiences can function as a catalyst for changing strategic cultures.[35] However, even in those exceptional circumstances, states are most likely to rely on a pre-existing *Weltanschauung* (national world views) as guidance for their security behaviour(s).

The Nexus Between a Strategic Document and a Strategic Culture

John Duffield has found that institutional sources of normative predispositions of security are 'likely to reside in the central government organs charged with the formulation and execution of policy'.[36] Political elites, he argues, are the primary holders of such normative structures, and embody a 'negotiated reality' of societal predispositions. In that sense, political elites function as the gatekeepers of societal norms, beliefs and values regarding national security issues. They aggregate and then replicate them back into society.

Political scientists defined elites as those 'who in any society rank toward the top of the (presumably closely intercorrelated) dimensions of interest, involvement, and influence in politics'.[37] While being the 'spokespersons' of individual members of society, they function as an aggregate panel that accumulates diverse sets of norms, beliefs, and values of civil society on issues related to national security. Those elites hold the expertise to aggregate those norms and then 'process' and 'translate' them for society by means of a publicly accessible language. In so doing, elites 'homogenize' norms that are vaguely expressed and shared by members of society, and make them available and understandable. This process of norm aggregation and expression is completed by engaging in political discourses such as writing policy documents like white papers, policy memos, or security strategies. In turn, because a national security strategy is rooted in the beliefs, attitudes, and value systems of society as well as in societal interpretations of social reality[38] the European Union's Security Strategy (ESS) and NATO's new strategic document can both be conceptualized as outcomes of the bargaining and negotiation processes of nationally held strategic beliefs, values, norms and ideas of security.[39] Specifically, those two documents outline elite normative predispositions about the values and meanings assigned to security threats and scenarios, including broadly cast justifications for government action and practices. As Neumann and Henrikki remind us, security documents converse about fundamental philosophical questions of the meanings of life and the relationships between the self and others.[40] It is in this sense that strategic documents contain information about the processes by which social actors learn from their peers. They also show a relational component to other social actors as well as a dynamic interplay between discourse and practice defined as socially recognized forms of activity and learning.[41] Martha Finnemore and Kathryn Sikking remind us that '[w]e only know what is appropriate by reference to the judgments of a community or society.'[42]

To be sure, strategic guidance papers like the European Security Strategy or the NATO strategic document are elite political documents that aim to provide normative and evaluative signposts for social actors on a range of issues, including transnational risks and threats, strategies, and concepts. They prescribe behavioural attitudes and activities, and often are designed to either create or maintain political unity among its constituent parts. This is particularly true for the EU and NATO. Strategic documents thus serve three functions: 1. they express an elite consensus held by the respective member states on issues of security and defence; 2. they provide a basis for planning and guiding military and non-military activities in international politics; and finally, 3. because they determine relations to other social actors, they can be perceived as an instrument of public policy.

Empirical Evidence

Using Alexander Wendt's definition of norms from above, this section discusses and compares the intersubjective beliefs that the European Union and NATO hold about the social and natural world in terms of anticipated threats and challenges, mandates, and roles of third parties and international organizations.

Interpretation and Meanings of Future Challenges and Threats

In the European Security Strategy, terrorism and the proliferation of weapons of mass destruction (WMD) are listed as 'potentially the greatest threat to our security'[43]. Other threats are believed to stem from regional conflicts, such as those in the Middle East, Bosnia, the Caucasus, and the Mediterranean;[44] failed and failing states (such as Somalia and Afghanistan);[45] and organized crime in the form of cross-border trafficking of drugs, women, illegal migrants and weapons, or more recently piracy.[46] This laundry list of threats was augmented in the 2008 document by soft security issues like energy security, cyber security, and climate change. Such an extensive list of potential threats provides a strong indication that the new security environment is believed to be populated by military *and* non-military threats.

It is important to note, however, that the European Security Strategy identified terrorism as a strategic threat.[47] It is recognized as a complex phenomenon that is ingrained in European societies and has multiple causes: '... These include the pressures of modernization, cultural, social and political crisis, and the alienation of young people living in foreign societies.'[48] Thus, it is hardly surprising that the ESS deduces global rather than regional solutions from this perception.

Unlike its predecessors in 1999 and 1991, NATO's 2010 strategic document does not envision future 'threat scenarios' or grand threats that the alliance should prepare for. Rather, like the European Security Strategy it lists a broad range of military and non-military threats. The first is conventional force. A number of non-EU countries, for example, are in the process of updating their conventional force capabilities by proliferating ballistic missiles.[49] Second, threats to Euro-Atlantic security continue to result from the proliferation of nuclear weapons and their technology, as well as other weapons of mass destruction.[50] Third, terrorism and extremist groups are considered a threat to the security of the alliance. Fourth, regional instabilities and conflicts that are the result of radical extremism, terrorism, or illegal activities like drug trafficking and human smuggling are believed to endanger the security of the alliance. Those sources of conflict often have a transnational character and thus can easily spread beyond national boundaries and into one of the member states. Fifth – and this may come as a surprise to some NATO observers – allies perceive cyber attacks[51] as a threat that could inflict significant damage on, for example, NATO's collective infrastructure.[52] Explicit listing of this non-military threat is not only a novelty in the history of the alliance; it also reveals the high normative meanings that NATO assigns to non-military threats. Other non-military threats could result from damage to transit ways or communication installations, as well as environmental pollution, climate change, and water scarcity.[53] In sum, NATO's list of threats shows a lack of specificity and thus can be interpreted as a catalogue of global risks rather than genuine security threats.

Behavioural Norms in Response to Threats

The European Security Strategy explicitly expresses a normative aspiration to make the world a better place. This implies an activist interpretation of security.[54] By recalling the norm of fostering pan-European integration, the ESS lays strong meanings on

Europe as a region and vows to export its success by creating prosperity and peace for the immediate European neighbourhood.[55] This approach has become known as the European Neighbourhood Policy (ENP), which has created a strong normative framework that guides relations with other social agents.[56] While stability in the rest of the world is important, stability at home in Europe is pivotal and perceived as a precondition for the EU's role as a global actor. It is thus hardly surprising that the ESS does not spend much time discussing how to best project its military capabilities.[57] Above all, the project of European Union integration was inspired by the application of soft rather than hard power. Thus, the EU's behavioural benchmark is the peaceful integration of Europe and the values that have accompanied this process.[58]

The European codes of conduct sanction the use of force, making it permissible only in an act of self-defence.[59] Pre-emptive or preventative military behaviours that are carried out without the explicit endorsement of the UN Security Council are considered illegitimate and prohibited at all times. The use of force is justified in exceptional circumstances only, as the very last resort of European statecraft after all sources of diplomacy and negotiation have been exhausted.[60] Behind these normative principles is a strong aversion to using military force as a means to achieve political objectives.[61] Instead, the EU sees itself as a nation-builder that helps to restore governments and foster democracies in places like the Balkans, Afghanistan, or the Democratic Republic of Congo (DRC).[62] Those normative predispositions are succinctly constituted by the so-called Petersberg Tasks that inadvertently made the European Union an active global actor in the domains of peacekeeping, peacemaking, and providing humanitarian assistance. In other words, it is precisely these Petersberg principles that provide constitutive norms of accepted behaviour and limit the scope and extent of the EU's role as a global actor.[63]

At the same time, the European Security Strategy acknowledges that the new security environment after 11 September, as well as increasing degrees of globalization, have transformed the ways in which states and organizations respond to threats. The first line of European defence lies no longer at home, but abroad.[64] Such strategic belief highlights the value attached to forward security engagements – that is, addressing threats and risks away from the home territory and before they become a liability at home. Moreover, by positing that 'none of the new threats is purely military' indicates that conflict prevention – that is, preventative rather than reactive engagement – is considered more effective than coercive force in addressing those threats. Transnational conflicts should be addressed by using a range of tools and instruments such as sanctions, export controls or asset freezing, as well as political and economic engagements. Crisis management also requires resources in policing, the rule of law, strengthening civilian administration, negotiation and consultation[65] and foreign aid.[66] This implies that the EU considers peace-building and poverty reduction essential approaches to global crisis management. Those behavioural values and beliefs reveal a strong indication that the EU's security elite champions a comprehensive definition of security[67] that is aimed at long-term engagements and lasting stabilization.

Spreading European values of peace, order, and good governance as well as respect for human and humanitarian rights and solidarity are considered complementary normative elements of the EU's global engagement: 'Spreading good governance, supporting social and political reform, dealing with corruption and abuse of power, establishing the rule of law and protecting human rights are the best means of strengthening the international order.'[68] Norm violators or states that categorically reject those norms should be partially engaged in international forums rather than being marginalized.

NATO's new strategic document, on the other hand, starts off by mapping out the alliance's particularistic role in 'ensuring our common defence and security' and ensuring that 'the Alliance remains an unparalleled community of freedom, peace, security and shared values'.[69] This gives meaning to the very specific and selective role in the defence of its members' territory and populations that NATO acquired through Article 5 of the Washington Treaty. It implies that unlike the European Union, NATO perceives itself as a regionally confined military alliance with a primary reason d'état of ensuring the physical safety of its member states.[70] In addition, NATO envisions its playing an active role in four ways:[71] 1. to provide collective defence by means of defence and deterrence; 2. to be active in crisis management by using its vast array of military and civilian means that can be applied before, during, and after conflicts;[72] 3. to enhance its own security through cooperative security partnerships with other international organizations, regimes and countries; and 4. to engage in crisis and conflict management by employing a mix of political, civilian, and military means.[73] Nonetheless, provision of defence and deterrence are considered the two most pivotal behavioural norms in response to the most imminent threats. The acceptable means by which these mandates are carried out include a mix of highly mobile and robust conventional and nuclear force capabilities.

The Role and Significance of Third Parties and Other International Organizations

In light of the threat perceptions and values attached to security, the ESS assigns a pivotal value to the United Nations' role in managing international peace and security, as well as fostering multilateralism. Indeed, the United Nations stands at the 'apex of the international system', and the European Union has made it a priority to seek a mandate from the Security Council for its actions abroad.[74] International alliances (such as NATO) and strategic partnerships with countries like Canada, China, India, and Japan or regional organizations like ASEAN, SAARS, and the African Union are also assigned vital importance in the EU's role as a global actor. To be sure, the EU's attitudinal structures towards international institutions go beyond and above the security domain and reference, for example, the World Trade Organization (WTO) or the International Monetary Fund (IMF). They reveal a strategic thinking in terms of *interlocking institutions*, which refers to conditions whereby international institutions experience a functional overlap in a rather narrowly defined situational context. Such overlap is evaluated positively as it reinforces a complex set of strategic objectives that cannot be mastered by one organization alone.[75]

Against this backdrop, it is hardly surprising that the European Union stresses the value of acting in concert with others as its foremost normative foreign policy principle. Above all, it is believed to be the vehicle that ensures Europe's security and prosperity.[76] Thus multilateralism has become a concept with a strong normative connotation in the European Union discourse. It reveals attitudinal structures that see international organizations as independent social actors in international politics that help to: 1. manage global threats and pockets of insecurity; 2. promote security in the EU's neighbourhood; and 3. create an internationally based order of effective multilateralism and cooperation among states that are guided by sources of international law. Put differently, the EU seeks to create a multilateral system of global governance that is based on a rules-based international order and the aspiration to develop a 'stronger international society'.[77]

The North Atlantic Treaty Organization perceives itself as a unique community of states that stands for values like freedom, liberty, human rights, and the rule of law. The new strategic document stresses that the alliance is committed to upholding and abiding by the principles laid out in the UN Charter, and accepts the Security Council as the primary institution that upholds international peace and security.[78] This means that the normative spaces provided for the United Nations in both the European Union and NATO's strategic document are nearly identical. Also, both organizations see themselves as holding a global mandate. For its part, NATO pledges to work closely with the UN and perceives its role as subordinate to the UN. It also seeks to expand its network of multilateral contacts[79] by partnering with other international organizations and states like Russia and Australia, believing that this helps NATO to defend and spread its liberal democratic values as well as promoting cooperation, dialogue and mutual respect. The list of potential cooperation partners is non-exhaustive, implying that all states and institutions could potentially be collaborators and partners.

However, the partnership with the European Union is assigned particular importance. The strategic concept notes that '... the EU is a unique and essential partner for NATO'.[80] Cooperation with the European Union is said to foster security in Europe and around the world, although it is recognized that dialogue between the two institutions is in need of improvement to reduce rivalries and redundancies among their members.[81] This statement, however, is somewhat contradictory to NATO's explicit endorsement of a stronger European security and defence policy under the Lisbon Treaty, because it creates a Union that increasingly competes with NATO in the areas of foreign, security, and defence policy. Thus it is difficult to be convinced that NATO's new strategic concept values a strategic partnership between the two organizations that is based on the principles of complementary and mutual reinforcing roles. More convincing seems the argument that NATO and the European Union stand in competition with one another for resources, influence, and roles abroad. It thus appears that NATO's perception of itself as an autonomous security institution in Europe is less clear than the EU's perception of itself both globally and in relation to NATO. In the EU's mind, NATO is but one organization with which a strategic partnership should be sought. Moreover, its role perceptions in global politics go far beyond NATO's rather limited focus on defence issues. In contrast to NATO, the European Union clearly anticipates a comprehensive global role for itself.

Summary of Empirical Analysis

It is useful at this point to summarize the empirical findings from above. It is remarkable to observe that both the European Union and the North Atlantic Treaty

Organization have almost identical normative values and interpretations of future challenges and threats and the role of third parties and international organizations. To be sure, there are nuances in those interpretations and meanings, but they are subtle and, in the grander picture of things and especially with regard to inferring conclusions about the nature of strategic cultures, of little consequence or importance. One of those nuanced differences is, for example, that NATO continues to see conventional forces as a vital threat to its security, whereas the European Union does not even mention such a threat and thus does not assign any meaning to it. Another subtle difference is that NATO aspires to become a 'hub' in international security policy that allows other international organizations and states to functionally coordinate their efforts with those of the alliance. The EU does not envision such a role for itself and its list of organizations with which it wishes to cooperate is slightly more extensive and diversified. To reiterate, these are subtle rather than obvious inconsistencies of normative predispositions.

One stark difference in the attitudinal structures of the two organizations, however, appears when comparing the two organizations' behavioural norms in response to future challenges and threats. Here, we speak not of nuanced but rather of elementary normative differences, especially in terms of the values attached to the use of force, the sanctioned type and range of missions, and the sets of resources justified to employ them. On the EU side, the list of threats reveals a comprehensive definition of security that allows the application of a wide range of resources by way of combining military and civilian assets for global crisis management operations, including foreign aid and economic assistance, as well as strengthening capabilities in areas such as policing, the rule of law, or security sector reform. The first line of European Union defence and security is allegedly abroad, and halting potential conflicts before they can become a vital security threat to its member states becomes a primary policy objective. In other words, the European Union believes that global conflicts are pertinent and require an activist interpretation of security as well as a whole range of government resources to address them, including economic assistance and foreign aid.[82]

The EU's role as a global actor is further defined and guided by the principles laid out in the Petersberg Tasks, which set the types of missions as well as the normative standards by which the EU's engagement in international security affairs is justified. However, by holding the Petersberg tasks as normative benchmarks for its role as a global actor, the European Union demonstrates that it increasingly operates in competition with NATO.[83] In addition, because of its comprehensive line-up of civilian and military capabilities it shows that it is better equipped and resourced to address the modern security threats. By making use of the Berlin-Plus agreement and gaining assured access to NATO's military assets, the European Union is now at least partially able to functionally replace NATO militarily and push back NATO's role in areas where the EU holds expertise and a comparative advantage.[84] The European Union therefore expresses not only cooperative but also competitive traits that directly compete with those of NATO.

NATO, on the other hand, has a much more regionally confined mandate, which is to provide collective defence for its member states. Its first line of defence is at home, and thus it has a very particularistic role in international security governance. Its raison d'état precisely results from maintaining the relevance of Article 5.[85] While the alliance aspires eventually to be able to concurrently deploy civilian and military resources in its operations, it clearly lacks such civilian capabilities at this moment in time.[86] Only the European Union maintains comprehensive assets that could potentially augment NATO's superior military capabilities. It can be said therefore that NATO needs a 'Berlin-Plus in reverse' agreement to fulfil its civilian responsibilities. In short, NATO defines itself as a regionally confined military alliance that provides collective defence for its member states. In contrast, the EU foresees a broader and more active role for itself in international security affairs that goes far beyond military engagements.

How to Interpret such Normative Overlap and Divergence?

While these empirical findings may be satisfactory to some, they nonetheless call for further explanation and analysis. How can we explain such attitudinal overlapping of two security organizations in Europe?[87]

One way to conceptually explain such attitudinal overlap and divergence is to conceive the EU's strategic culture as a set of sufficiently shared norms among all European Union member states. In this sense, EU norms are the least common and contentious denominator of the belief systems held EU-wide. Defining the EU's strategic culture in this way leaves out all those controversial attitudes and issues in which there is no EU-wide agreement. This is a reasonable expectation given that 21 of NATO's 28 members are concurrent members of the EU. However, while this may appear to be a convincing proposition at first sight, it does not explain the variation of attitudinal structures with regard to the behavioural norms in response to threats as discussed above.

Instead, I suggest that a more convincing, yet still preliminary and exploratory, conceptual argument to explain this cultural overlap as well as the empirical findings above is to cast the European Union and NATO's strategic cultures in terms of a subcultural relationship. Because of its rather limited and regionally focused scope of providing collective security in Europe, NATO's strategic culture can be seen as a subculture of the EU's strategic culture.

The concept of subculture is not novel in the social sciences and humanities. It helps us to map the social world and to make sense of social behaviours.[88] In the most general terms, a subculture is an explanatory device that refers to a subset of cultural traits or a group of social actors that share distinctive sets of values, beliefs, norms, and behaviours that differ from those held by the larger society or group.[89] In this sense, members of subcultures are parts of the mainstream society that have developed unique beliefs, norms, and values and associate with one another more personally than with members of other groups,[90] and are an analytical and descriptive vehicle through which to explain social actions and change.

Alfred Lee is credited with the first use of the term in the field of sociology and anthropology.[91] Inspired by sociological thinking about cultures, the concept of subcultures was introduced into the field of political science by Gabriel Almond and

Sidney Verba in their seminal work on comparative political cultures.[92] It is used as an analytical framework to study patterns of political cultures and to describe persistent and significant differences in political or organizational orientations. A group of individuals in society may, for example, be oriented towards pursuing a particular set of political objectives and outputs but remain positively oriented towards the existing political structure.

Such conceptualization of subcultural relations holds some currency for our case study of the North Atlantic Treaty Organization and European Union. In particular, the two organizations' attitudinal and normative divergence of envisioned missions and mandates could be explained by a particular set of subcultural (NATO) values and attitudes that are part of a much broader EU strategic culture.[93] More precisely, the EU's normative predispositions and attitudinal structures provide the broader cultural and normative frame of which NATO's strategic culture has become part. From the empirical discussion above, it is also apparent that NATO's strategic culture is more particularistic and narrower than the EU's. For example, many conflicts and crises increasingly require the use of civilian crisis management capabilities as well as a combination of diplomatic and economic instruments and resources. The application of the so-called 3D concept in Afghanistan has in particular shown that the military component of the commitment is only one of many. Afghanistan also showed the limitations that a military alliance can encounter in a multidimensional conflict. In strategic culture terms, narrow military strategies have demonstrated the limitations of NATO's engagements in Afghanistan and underlined the absence of an overarching political strategy. NATO is particularly ill-equipped to apply the full spectrum of civilian crisis management capabilities given the fact that it is a military alliance.[94] It does not possess nor have access to civilian resources to the extent the European Union does. In order to make use of such capabilities, NATO has to ask its European members to provide for such complements. Following this line of thought makes the alliance's strategic culture a subculture within the EU's strategic culture – that is, an integral yet subordinate part of the EU's strategic culture – while maintaining an orientation towards the dominant European Union culture. In that sense, as Komarovsky and Sargent remind us, subcultures 'constitute relatively cohesive social systems. They are worlds within the larger world or our national culture'[95], and provide new resources of identity and difference among international institutions. Above all, it shows that subcultures exercise agency, and were formed within the context of a dominant culture.[96]

In addition, the conceptualization of NATO's strategic culture as a subculture provides the social causation that helps to explain a number of interrelated issues and phenomena: we should understand those arguments as preliminary and exploratory rather than fully developed attempts to explain the cultural overlap of the two institutions. To start with, the conceptualization of NATO as a subcultural entity of a much broader political European culture is consistent with the importance assigned to Article 5 in the new strategic concept. The principle of collective defence continues to be of paramount importance for the alliance (as well as for the development of the EU's foreign policy) precisely because it provides a very focused and limited military role for NATO that ensures the territorial integrity of its member states. This allows the EU's Common Security and Defence Policy (CSDP) to neglect this collective defence responsibility and to concentrate on other aspects and non-military aspects of security. Put differently, the principle of collective defence remains the core normative responsibility of NATO while, in contrast, the European Union pursues more of a collective security role.[97] Such division of labour in EU security affairs reassures NATO's member states that the alliance is primarily an inward-looking organization with a regional rather than a global mandate. It also portrays NATO as a non-threatening organization in the European Union security environment.[98]

Second, critics may point out that one of NATO's most central objectives is to provide a political forum that facilitates policy exchange and debates across the Atlantic. While such portrayal is undoubtedly true, it does not conflict with the subcultural model. Above all, it is wrong to assume that NATO represents the full embodiment of European Union-American relations. This relationship extends far beyond the military domain and covers issues in domains such as energy, business, culture, justice, and health.[99] In other words, the domain of security is only a small component of a much more broad and extensive European Union-American relationship.

Third, a subcultural relationship between the European Union and NATO helps to explain why the European Union sees conflict and tension with Russia beyond the security and defence domain. More specifically, the European Union perceives the challenges resulting from Central and Eastern Europe in the framework of a neighbourhood policy (ENP). The fact that Russia's distrust of NATO has not, interestingly enough, hampered its relations with the EU implies that 'the EU clearly provides a security policy agenda that Russia regards as more pragmatic and less confrontational than NATO's'.[100] In other words, the EU is seen as an international actor with which Russia shares more preferences than it does with NATO.[101]

Fourth, building on the analysis of the EU's crisis management operations since 2003 (for discussion see earlier essays in this volume), it is apparent that the European Union runs twice as many civilian than military operations. This underlines not only the EU's predisposition towards civilian crisis management capabilities but also its value judgments and commitment to managing such crises. More specifically, out of the total 24 operations deployed by the EU so far, only 7.5, or 31.2 per cent, were of a military nature.[102] The vast majority of those missions (16.5, or 68.7 per cent) can be counted as civilian operations. More interesting, perhaps, is the fact that only a very small fraction of those 7.5 military operations made use of the Berlin-Plus arrangements. Operation Concordia in Macedonia was the first ever mission that took place under the Berlin-Plus banner, followed by Operation Althea in Bosnia and Herzegovina. Above all, it is noteworthy that the EU's operations are of small scale and usually follow those conducted by NATO. An example of this is Operation Althea which, as Charles Pentland noted in his article, continues to pursue the objectives set by its predecessor NATO, primarily in the areas of deterring threats to security and the population, security sector reform, police training, and fighting organized crime. This supports the subcultural conception of the relationship between the European Union and NATO, especially as the latter organization pursues a much more particularistic role in international crisis management.

Conclusion

This article examined the ideational structures of the European Union and NATO that affect both institutions' social behaviour (and their behaviour towards each other). The analysis was inspired by constructivist scholarship on strategic cultures, which were conceptualized as an elite expression of strategic beliefs, values, and norms. Norms were defined as 'intersubjective beliefs about the social and natural world'. The aim of the research article was to tease out how structures of meaning in the form of norms, values, and beliefs have affected those two organizations' behaviour towards each other. In order to gain access to the EU and NATO's attitudinal structures in the empirical section, their strategic cultures were unpacked into normative, ideational, and behavioural components and clustered according to 1. the meanings they assign to future challenges and threats; 2. the behavioural prepositions of how to respond to those threats; and 3. the preferred modes of international cooperation.

I argued that there is a significant overlap between the two institutions' attitudinal structures, especially with regard to the meanings and values they attach to future threats and the role of third parties and other international organizations. I also argued that there exists an elementary cultural difference in terms of the values attached to the use of force, the sanctioned range and type of missions, and the resources justified to carry them out. The ongoing NATO air strikes against the Libyan regime of Muammar Gaddafi are a case in point where NATO and not the European Union was able to agree on a military campaign.

I then started to explore a conceptual argument that could explain the attitudinal divergence of the two institutions, proposing to conceptualize NATO's strategic culture as a subculture of the EU's strategic culture. That is to say that NATO's strategic culture has acquired a subcultural trait of shared and distinctive sets of values, norms, and beliefs that are different from those held at the European Union level. Generally speaking, a subculture is an explanatory device that refers to social actors that share distinctive sets of values, beliefs, norms, and behaviours that differ from those held by the larger society or group. With this logic applied to the EU-NATO relationship, I showed that while NATO's strategic culture assigns the highest value to the principle of collective defence (Article 5), the EU's attitudinal structures are much broader and resemble a thinking of collective security. To be sure, this conceptualization of a subcultural relationship between the European Union and NATO should be seen as a provisional exploratory argument that could potentially allow us a more in-depth view of the inter-institutional relationship between the two most pivotal security organizations in Europe, going beyond their shared and contested material capabilities and assets. At the same time, I am aware that such argument cannot be fully developed here due to space limitations, and thus should be understood as an attempt to explore an alternative conceptual explanation. It should also be noted that the empirical section was only able to provide a snapshot of potentially larger ideational forces at play, which undoubtedly poses the limitations of this analysis.

However, as the literature on strategic culture reminds us, in comparison to material conditions, political cultures are rather stable.[103] They change only very slowly, and usually after experiencing seminal historical events that have an enduring effect on societies. Put differently, political cultures change very slowly, if at all, and such alteration will take place under the condition of dramatic national events that require nationally held beliefs, values, and norms to be revisited, such as the end of the Cold War in 1990 and the ethnic conflict in the former Yugoslavia that left most European countries helplessly watching history unfold without having the physical capability, readiness, or ability to intervene. Such events had a lasting effect on the development of attitudinal structures of the EU as well as NATO and their overlapping roles in international crisis management. Against this historical perspective, it seems unlikely that other seminal historical events will unfold in the near future that could potentially alter the security strategies of the two organizations.

ACKNOWLEDGEMENTS

I would like to thank the Social Sciences and Humanities Research Council of Canada (SSHRC) and the Centre for International Relations, Queen's University (Canada) for their generous support. I am particularly grateful to Peter Schmidt, Srdjan Vucetic, Elke Winter, Frédéric Merand, Gregory Liedtke, and three anonymous reviewers for their comments. All errors, of course, remain mine.

NOTES

1. Asle Toje, 'The EU, NATO and European Defence: A Slow Train Coming', Occasional Paper, European Union Institute for Security Studies, Paris, 2008.
2. This literature is vast. See, for example, Hans-Christian Hagman, *European Crisis Management and Defence: The Search for Capabilities* (Oxford: Oxford University Press, 2002); Bernhard May, May-Britt Stumbaum, and German Council on Foreign Relations (eds), *NATO versus EU?: Security Strategies for Europe* (Berlin: German Council on Foreign Relations, 2005); Antonio Missiroli, 'EU–NATO Cooperation in Crisis Management: No Turkish Delight for ESDP', *Security Dialogue*, Vol. 33, No. 1 (2002), pp. 9–26; Sten Rynning, 'Why Not NATO? Military Planning in the European Union', *Journal of Strategic Studies*, Vol. 26, No. 1 (2003), pp. 52–72; David S. Yost, *NATO and International Organizations*, vol. 3, Forum Paper (Rome: NATO Defense College, 2007).
3. See, for example, 'Sharing (Which?) NATO Burdens', *The New York Times*, 16 June 1988, A26; Andrew Bennett, Joseph Lepgold, and Danny Unger, *Friends in Need: Burden Sharing in the Persian Gulf War*, 1st edn (New York: St. Martin's Press, 1997); Christopher Coker, *Shifting into Neutral?: Burden Sharing in the Western Alliance in the 1990's*, 1st edn (London and Washington, DC: Brassey's, 1990); Rosemary Fiscarelli, 'Europe is Grabbing The Spoils of Peace', *The New York Times*, 9 March 1990; Peter Kent Forster and Stephen J. Cimbala, *The US, NATO and Military Burden-sharing* (London, New York: Frank Cass, 2005); Michael R. Gordon, 'U.S. War Game in West Germany to Be Cut Back', *The New York Times*, 14 December 1989, A23; Josef Joffe, *The Limited Partnership: Europe, the United States, and the Burdens of Alliance* (Cambridge, MA: Ballinger Pub. Co., 1987); Josef Joffe, 'The Trans-Atlantic Numbers Game', *The New York Times*, 18 May 1988, A31.
4. G. Wyn Rees, *The US-EU Security Relationship: The Tensions between a European and a Global Agenda* (Basingstoke and New York: Palgrave Macmillan, 2011).
5. Jean-Yves Haine, 'From Laeken to Copenhagen: European Defence. Core Documents Volume III', Chaillot Paper, EU-ISS, Paris, 2003, especially pp. 178–180.
6. Jolyon Howorth and John Keeler (eds), *Defending Europe: The EU, NATO and the Quest for European Autonomy* (New York: Palgrave, 2003); Martin Reichard, *The EU–NATO Relationship: A Legal and Political Perspective* (Aldershot: Ashgate, 2006).
7. See House of Commons of the United Kingdom Defence Committee, 'The Future of NATO and European Defence: Ninth Report of Session 2007–08', (London: Stationery Office); M.I. Clausson (ed.), *NATO: Status, Relations, and Decision-Making* (New York: Novinka Books, 2007); *NATO–EU Cooperation in Post-Conflict Reconstruction*, NDC Occasional Paper No. 15, NATO Defense

College, Rome, 2006; Atlantic Council of the United States, 'Transatlantic Transformation: Building a NATO–EU Security Architecture', Policy Paper, Atlantic Council of the United States, Washington, DC, 2006; Centre for European Reform, *A European Way of War* (London: Centre for European Reform, 2004).
8. See Stephanie C. Hofmann, 'Why Institutional Overlap Matters: CSDP in the European Security Architecture', *Journal of Common Market Studies*, 49, No. 1 (2010), pp. 101–120.
9. In studying these two security strategies and not the policies and practices surrounding or following them, it is acknowledged that this approach inevitably sets the limitations of this essay. However, space limitations do not allow a detailed examination of the two organizations' security policies and practices over time. We will also refrain from analysing the behaviour of states as it risks producing tautological arguments as to how strategic culture has influenced the behaviour of states or groups of states.
10. I hereby indirectly acknowledge that NATO had established the dominant security culture in the Cold War – qua practice so to speak – and the emergence of an autonomous European Union in the 1990s has questioned and altered this situation.
11. The purpose here is not to make a historical argument nor to show how their respective strategic cultures have evolved over time.
12. The danger of tautological inference is explicitly noted, for example, in Joel D. Aberbach, Robert D. Putnam, and Bert A. Rockman, *Bureaucrats and Politicians in Western Democracies* (Cambridge, MA: Harvard University Press, 1981), pp. 30–31; Gabriel A. Almond and Sidney Verba, *The Civic Culture: Political Attitudes and Democracy in Five Nations* (Princeton, NJ: Princeton University Press, 1965), p. 50; Thomas U. Berger, 'Norms, Identity, and National Security in Germany and Japan', in Peter J. Katzenstein (ed.) *The Culture of National Security: Norms and Identity in World Politics*, (New York: Columbia University Press, 1996), p. 328; Charles Kupchan, *The Vulnerability of Empire* (Ithaca, NY: Cornell University Press, 1994), pp. 26–27; Jeffrey Legro, *Cooperation under Fire: Anglo-German Restraint during World War II* (Ithaca, NY: Cornell University Press, 1995), p. 30.
13. In the case of the EU, I will also include a 2008 Report by the European Council on the implementation of the ESS, which is an update of the 2004 ESS.
14. For a related approach see Ronald R. Krebs and Patrick T. Jackson, 'Twisting Tongues and Twisting Arms: The Power of Political Rhetoric', *European Journal of International Relations*, Vol. 13, No. 1 (2007), pp. 35–66.
15. John S. Duffield, *World Power Forsaken: Political Culture, International Institutions, and German Security Policy after Unification* (Stanford, CA: Stanford University Press, 1998), p. 33.
16. Kupchan, *The Vulnerability of Empire* (note 12), p. 43; Robert D. Putnam, 'Studying Elite Political Culture: The Case of "Ideology"', *American Political Science Review*, Vol. 65, No. 3 (1971), p. 652.
17. Some have called this approach 'discourse analysis'.
18. I very much acknowledge here that NATO of the 1990s and NATO in the 2000s are very much different organizations. Indeed, NATO has undergone a significant process of internal transformation, and also adapted to the new situational environment that presented itself. However, space limitations here do not allow me to fully discuss and engage in such long-term trend analysis – that is, changes of strategic cultures over time.
19. Inspiration for these clusters came from Christoph Meyer, 'Convergence towards a European Strategic Culture? A Constructivist Framework for Explaining Changing Norms', *European Journal of International Relations*, Vol. 11, No. 4 (2005), pp. 523–549.
20. Indeed, I assume that both the EU and NATO are sovereign and autonomous social actors that act independently of their member states. A counterargument is provided by Peter Schmidt in this volume.
21. It should be noted though that not all scholars agree with this clustering. For a different approach see Alastair Iain Johnston, *Cultural Realism: Strategic Culture and Grand Strategy in Chinese History* (Princeton, NJ: Princeton University Press, 1995), pp. 5–22.
22. This point was made by Sarah M. Corse and Marian A. Robinson, 'Cross-cultural Measurement and New Conceptions of Culture: Measuring Cultural Capacities in Japanese and American Preschools', *Poetics*, Vol. 22, No. 4 (1994), pp. 313–325.
23. Duffield, *World Power Forsaken* (note 15); Theo Farrell and Terry Terriff, *The Sources of Military Change: Culture, Politics, Technology* (Boulder, CO: Lynne Rienner Publishers, 2002); Colin Gray, 'Strategic Culture as Context: The First Generation of Theory Strikes Back', *Review of International Studies*, Vol. 25, No. 1 (1999), pp. 49–69; Peter J. Katzenstein, *The Culture of National Security: Norms and Identity in World Politics* (New York: Columbia University Press, 1996).

24. Ronald L. Jepperson and Ann Swidler, 'What Properties of Culture do we Measure?' *Poetics*, Vol. 22, No. 4 (1994), p. 360.
25. John Gerard Ruggie, 'Continuity and Transformation in the World Polity: Towards a Neo-realist Synthesis', *World Politics*, Vol. 35, No. 2 (1983), pp. 261–285. John Gerard Ruggie, 'What Makes the World Hang Together? Neo-utilitarianism and the Social Constructivist Challenge', *International Organization*, Vol. 52, No. 4 (1998), pp. 855–885.
26. Alexander Wendt, *Social Theory of International Politics* (Cambridge and New York: Cambridge University Press, 1999). To be sure, constructivists do not negate the influence that material factors can have on social actions.
27. Iver B. Newmann and Hennikki Heikka, 'Grand Strategy, Strategic Culture, Practice: The Social Roots of Nordic Defence', *Cooperation and Conflict*, Vol. 40, Nos. 5–23 (2005), p. 6.
28. Martha Finnemore, *The Purpose of Intervention: Changing Beliefs about the Use of Force* (Ithaca, NY: Cornell University Press, 2003), p. 15.
29. Alexander Wendt, 'Constructing International Politics', *International Security*, Vol. 20, No. 1 (1995), pp. 73–74. I am fully aware that the literature further delineates between constitutive and regulative norms. This distinction, however, is not relevant here. For a discussion see John R. Searle, *The Construction of Social Reality* (New York: Free Press, 1995), p. 28.
30. Katzenstein, *The Culture of National Security* (note 23), p. 19; see also Finnemore, *The Purpose of Intervention* (note 28), p. 22; Audie Klotz, 'Norms Reconstituting Interests: Global Racial Equality and U.S. Sanctions Against South Africa', *International Organization*, Vol. 49, No. 3 (2005), pp. 451–478; Audie Klotz, *Norms in International Relations: The Struggle Against Apartheid* (Ithaca, NY: Cornell University Press, 1995); Martha Finnemore and Kathryn Sikkink, 'International Norm Dynamics and Political Change', *International Organization*, Vol. 52, No. 4 (1998), p. 892.
31. However, this paper's purpose is not to discuss the norm evolutions of those two organizations. Consequently, I will not analyse the processes of 'norm emergence', 'norm cascade', and 'norm internalization' as described by Finnemore and Sikkink, 'International Norm Dynamics' (note 30), pp. 887–917.
32. See David Elkins and Richard E.B. Simeon, 'A Cause in Search of Its Effect, or What Does Political Culture Explain?', *Comparative Politics*, Vol. 11, No. 2 (1979), p. 130; Lucian W. Pye, 'Culture and Political Science: Problems in the Evaluation of the Concept of Political Culture', in Louis Schneider and Charles M. Bonjean (eds), *The Idea of Culture in the Social Sciences* (Cambridge: Cambridge University Press, 1973), pp. 65–67.
33. Berger, 'Norms, Identity, and National Security in Germany and Japan', (note 12), p. 329; Harry Eckstein, 'Culturalist Theory of Political Change', *American Political Science Review*, Vol. 82, No. 3 (1998), p. 790.
34. Duffield, *World Power Forsaken* (note 15), p. 24.
35. *Ibid.* An alternative proposition was put forward by Legro, who noted that bureaucratic organizational cultures could influence the strategic culture of states. See Jeffrey Legro, 'Culture and Preferences in the International Cooperation Two-Step', *American Political Science Review*, Vol. 90, No. 1 (1996), p. 120.
36. Duffield, *World Power Forsaken* (note 15), p. 29.
37. Putnam, 'Studying Elite Political Culture' (note 16), p. 651.
38. Duffield, *World Power Forsaken* (note 15), p. 23; see also Berger, 'Norms, Identity, and National Security in Germany and Japan' (note 12); Elkins and Simeon, 'A Cause in Search of Its Effect' (note 32). This point, however, is debated in the literature. While Meyer finds that a EU security culture is emerging, Giegerich disagrees with such an assessment. See Bastian Giegerich, *European Security and Strategic Culture: National Responses to the EU's Security and Defence Policy* (Baden-Baden: Nomos, 2006); Christoph O. Meyer, *The Quest for a European Strategic Culture: Changing Norms on Security and Defence in the European Union* (New York: Palgrave Macmillan, 2006). I acknowledge that there are methodological inconsistencies in comparing two state-based security strategies with that of a supranational organization. However, since the making of Europe's foreign and defence policy still remains highly intergovernmental as opposed to supranational, this approach appears to be justified.
39. It is in this sense that my conceptualization of culture is inherently interactionist and provides the means through which actors construct meanings in given situations.
40. Iver B. Neumann and Hennikki Heikka, 'Grand Strategy, Strategic Culture, Practice' (note 27), p. 7.
41. Barry Barnes, 'Practice as Collective Action', in Theodore R. Schatzki, K. Knorr-Cetina, and Eike von Savigny (eds), *The Practice Turn in Contemporary Theory* (New York: Routledge, 2001), p. 19.
42. Finnemore and Sikkink, 'International Norm Dynamics and Political Change', (note 30), pp. 891–892.

43. European Council, 'A Secure Europe in A Better World: European Security Strategy', (Brussels: European Council, 2003) p. 3.
44. *Ibid.* pp. 3–4, 7; European Council, 'Report on the Implementation of the European Security Strategy: Providing Security in a Changing World', S407/08(2008), p. 1.
45. European Council, 'European Security Strategy' (ESS) (note 43), p. 4.
46. *Ibid.* p. 4. For a discussion of this see Jolyon Howorth, 'Beyond NATO? The European Security and Defence Project', in John Baylis and Jon Roper (eds), *The United States and Europe: Beyond the Neo-Conservative Divide?*, (New York: Routledge, 2006), pp. 117–118.
47. Nicole Gnesotto, *European Defence: A Proposal for a White Paper* (Paris: European Union Institute for Security Studies, 2004), p. 26.
48. European Council, 'European Security Strategy' (ESS) (note 43), p. 4; European Council, 'Implementation of the European Security Strategy' (note 44).
49. North Atlantic Council, *Strategic Concept: For the Defence and Security of the Members of the North Atlantic Treaty Organization, Adopted by the Heads of State and Government in Lisbon* (Brussels: NATO Office of Information and Press, 2010), points 7 and 8. The obvious countries are Iran and North Korea.
50. *Ibid.*, point 9.
51. RAND has warned NATO about this threat for nearly a decade. See F. Ronfeldt, *The Emergence of Noopolitik: Toward an American Information Strategy* (Santa Monica, CA: RAND, 1999); John Arquilla and David F. Ronfeld (eds), *Networks and Netwars: The Future of Terror, Crime, and Militancy* (Santa Monica, CA: RAND, 2001). See also Melissa E. Hathaway, 'Toward a Closer Digital Alliance', *SAIS Review*, Vol. XXX, No. 2 (2010), pp. 21–31.
52. North Atlantic Council, *Strategic Concept* (note 49), point 12.
53. *Ibid.*, points 13 and 15.
54. See also Pascal Vennesson, 'Europe's Grand Strategy: The Search for a Postmodern Realism', in Nicola Casarini and Constanza Musu (eds), *European Foreign Policy in an Evolving International System* (New York: Palgrave Macmillan, 2007), p. 18.
55. European Council, 'A Secure Europe in A Better World' (note 43), p. 7. For further analysis of this notion see Justin Vaisse, 'Transformational Diplomacy', Chaillot Paper, EU Institute for Security Studies, Paris, 2007. On the EU neighbourhood policy see, for example, Vennesson, 'Europe's Grand Strategy' (note 54), pp. 18–19; F. Algieri and Arnold Kammel, 'In Search of Structure: The EU's Foreign Policy Strategy against the Background of a Missing Global Order', *European View*, Vol. 8, No. 2 (2008), p. 289; Stefan Gänzle and Alan G. Sens, *The Changing Politics of European Security: Europe Alone?* (Basingstoke: Palgrave Macmillan, 2007).
56. European Council, 'Implementation of the European Security Strategy' (note 44).
57. The EU also does not defend its moral principles of liberty or democracy with the use of force. See also Christoph Meyer, 'Convergence towards a European Strategic Culture? A Constructivist Framework for Explaining Changing Norms', *European Journal of International Relations*, Vol. 11, No. 4 (2005), pp. 523–549.
58. Albert Bressand, 'Between Kant and Machiavelli: EU Foreign Policy Priorities in the 2010s', *International Affairs*, Vol. 87, No. 1 (2011), pp. 59–85, pp. 59–85.
59. European Council, 'European Security Strategy' (note 43), p. 7.
60. Sven Bernhard Gareis, 'Sicherheitspolitik zwischen "Mars und Venus"? Die Sicherheitsstrategien der USA und der EU im Vergleich,' in Johannes Varwick (ed.), *Die Beziehungen zwischen NATO und EU: Partnerschaft, Konkurrenz, Rivalitaet?* (Opladen: Verlag Barbara Buderich, 2005), p. 88; Kenneth Keulman, 'European Security and Defence Policy: The EU's Search for a Strategic Role', in Janet Adamski, Mary Troy Johnson, and Christina M. Schweiss (eds), *Old Europe, New Security: Evolution for a Complex World* (Aldershot: Ashgate Publishing Limited, 2006), p. 52.
61. This may be explainable by pointing out that the ESS was written in 2003 *in response* to the NSS.
62. European council, 'European Security Strategy' (ESS) (Note 43), p. 9.
63. See, for example, Volker Heise and Peter Schmidt, 'NATO und EU: Auf dem Weg zu einer strategischen Partnerschaft?', in Thomas Jäger, Alexander Höse, and Kai Oppermann (eds), *Transatlantische Beziehungen: Sicherheit, Wirtschaft, Öffentlichkeit*, ed. Thomas Jäger, Alexander Höse, and Kai Oppermann (Wiesbaden: VS Verlag, 2005).
64. European Council, 'European Security Strategy' (ESS) (note 43), p. 9.
65. 2385th European Council meeting, General Affairs, 19-20.XI.2001, Brussels, 19–20 November 2001.
66. European Council, 'Implementation of the European Security Strategy' (note 44), pp. 4, 9.

67. Emil J. Kirchner and James Sperling, 'The New Security Threats in Europe', *European Foreign Affairs Review*, Vol. 7, No. 4 (2002), pp. 423–452.
68. European Council, 'European Security Strategy' (ESS) (note 43), p. 10.
69. North Atlantic Council, *Strategic Concept* (note 49), preface.
70. It should be noted t that NATO's member states from Central and Eastern Europe have pushed the alliance particularly hard for reassurance that self-defence is still the central objective of the alliance. See, for example, *NATO 2020: Assured Security; Dynamic Engagement* (Brussels: North Atlantic Treaty Organization [NATO], 2010); David Yost, 'NATO's Evolving Purposes and the Next Strategic Concept', *International Affairs*, Vol. 86, No. 2 (2010), pp 489–522; 'Fewer Dragons, More Snakes: NATO is About to Adopt a New Strategic Concept. Can it Keep Pace with the Way the World is Changing?', *The Economist*, 11 November 2010; Linas Linkevicius, 'Reset With Russia, but With Reassurance', *The New York Times*, 9 September 2010.
71. North Atlantic Council, *Strategic Concept* (note 49), preface, point 4 a.–c.
72. However, it needs to be pointed out that NATO is a military alliance that holds very limited civilian crisis management capabilities. See Natalia Touzovskaia, 'EU-NATO Relations: How Close to "Strategic Partnership"?', *European Security*, Vol. 15, No. 3 (2006), pp. 235–258.
73. *Ibid.*, points 20–22. NATO's role in civilian crisis management is particularly idealistic as it currently possesses only very limited civilian crisis management capabilities to be deployed.
74. 2385th European Council meeting, General Affairs, 19-20.XI.2001, Brussels, 19–20 November 2001: 2, 9.
75. NATO's management of the strategic vacuum left behind by the withdrawal of the Soviet Union in the aftermath of the fall of the Berlin Wall in 1989 is a case in point. For a discussion see Ingo Peters, 'The OSCE, NATO and the EU within the "Network of Interlocking European Security Institutions": Hierarchization, Flexibilization, Marginalization', in *OSCE Yearbook 2003* (Hamburg: Institute for Peace Research and Security Policy at the University of Hamburg, 2004); Uwe Nerlich, 'Das Zusammenwirken multilateraler Institutionen: Neue Optionen für kollektive Verteidigung und internationale Friedensmissionen', in Bernard von Plate (ed.), *Europa auf dem Wege zur kollektiven Sicherheit?* (Baden-Baden: Nomos, 1994); Michael Cox, 'Whatever Happened to the 'New World Order?', *Critique*, Vol. 25, No. 1 (1997), pp. 85–96.
76. 'European Security Strategy' (ESS) (note 43), p. 9.
77. *Ibid.* p. 9.
78. North Atlantic Council, *Strategic Concept* (note 49), point 2.
79. On the notion of multilateralism as an issue in transatlantic affairs see John van Oudenaren, 'What is Multilateral?', *Policy Review*, Vol. 117, February/March (2003), pp. 33–47; John van Oudenaren, 'Transatlantic Bipolarity and the End of Multilateralism,' *Political Science Quarterly*, Vol. 120, No. 1 (2005), pp. 1–32.
80. North Atlantic Council, *Strategic Concept* (note 49), point 32.
81. See Jolyon Howorth and John T.S. Keeler (eds), *Defending Europe: The EU, NATO and the Quest for European Autonomy* (Basingstoke: Palgrave MacMillan, 2003).
82. Based on the latest OECD data, the EU is the world's leading provider of official development assistance (US$45 billion of a total US$128 billion). See http://stats.oecd.org/index.aspx?DatasetCode=REF_TOTALODA (accessed 2 February 2010).
83. A similar argument was made by Heise and Schmidt, 'NATO und EU' (note 63).
84. See Hans van Santen and Arnout Molenaar, 'EU-NAVO-samenwerking: tijd voor transformatie', *Internationale Spectator*, Vol. 62, No. 6 (2008), pp. 343–348.
85. States from CEE in particular insisted on this principle at NATO's Lisbon Summit in 2010.
86. For a greater discussion see Arnold Kammel and Benjamin Zyla, 'Looking for a "Berlin-Plus in Reverse"? NATO in Search of a New Strategic Concept', *Orbis*, Fall (2011), pp. 1–14.
87. This section should be seen as taking exploratory steps to further explain inter-institutional relationships.
88. See, for example, Ken Gelder and Sarah Thornton, *The Subcultures Reader* (London and New York: Routledge, 1997), p. 1. The concept has its origins in the fields of sociology and anthropology; elements of it can be found in the classical sociological tradition ranging from Karl Marx and Emile Durkheim to Max Weber and Talcott Parssons.
89. Shyon Baumann, 'Culture and Culture Change,' in Lorne Teppermann and James Curtis (eds), *Principles of Sociology: Canadian Perspectives* (Don Mills, Ont.: Oxford University Press, 2009), pp. 35–36.
90. To be sure, a subculture should not be confused with countercultures that strongly and vehemently reject dominant societal beliefs and norms. For a discussion see J. Milton Yinger, *Countercultures: The Promise*

and Peril of a World Turned Upside Down (New York: Free Press, 1982); J. Milton Yinger, 'Contraculture and Subculture,' *American Sociological Review*, Vol. 25, No. 5 (1960), pp. 625–635.

91. Alfred McClung Lee, 'Levels of Culture as Levels of Social Generalization,' *American Sociological Review*, Vol. 10, No. 4 (1945), pp. 125–143. See also M. Gordon, 'The Concept of Sub-culture and its Application', *Social Forces* (1947).
92. Almond and Verba, *The Civic Culture* (note 12), pp. 27–31. For a country-specific application of the concept see, for example, Justin Massie, 'Regional Strategic Subcultures? Canadians and the Use of Force in Afghanistan and Iraq', *Canadian Foreign Policy*, Vol. 14, No. 2 (2008), pp. 19–48.
93. This, however, is not to say that the EU only holds one subculture; indeed, it can have many and varying subcultures at the same time.
94. Alvaro de Vasconcelos, 'Introduction: Why an EU Perspective on the NATO Strategic Concept Matters', in *What do Europeans want from NATO?* (Paris: European Union Institute for Security Studies, 2010), p. 7.
95. M. Komarowsky and S. Sargent, 'Research into Subcultural Influences upon Personality,' in S. Sargent and M. Smith, *Culture and Personality* (New York: The Viking Fund, 1949).
96. For a discussion of subcultures emerging from either within or from outside of the context of a dominant culture see David Downes, *The Delinquent Solution: A Study in Subcultural Theory* (London: Routledge, 1966), pp. 8–12.
97. For the notion that the EU should adapt a unique way or war see Centre for European Reform, *A European Way of War* (note 7).
98. For an account of an embryonic division of labour between the EU and NATO see Richard G. Whitman, 'NATO, the EU and ESDP: An Emerging Division of Labour?', *Contemporary Security Policy*, Vol. 25, No. 3 (2004), pp. 430–451.
99. For an interesting discussion see Rebecca Steffenson, *Managing EU–US Relations: Actors, Institutions and the New Transatlantic Agenda* (Manchester and New York: Manchester University Press, 2005); Nikos Kotzias and Petros El Liakouras, *EU–US Relations: Repairing the Transatlantic Rift* (New York: Palgrave Macmillan, 2006); Elias G. Carayannis, Dimitris G. Assimakopoulos, and Masayuki Kondo, *Innovation Networks and Knowledge Clusters: Findings and Insights from the US, EU and Japan* (Basingstoke and New York: Palgrave Macmillan, 2008); Natividad Fernández Sola and Michael Smith, *Perceptions and Policy in Transatlantic Relations: Prospective Visions from the US and Europe* (Abingdon and New York: Routledge, 2009).
100. Teija Tiilikainen, 'The EU, NATO and Russia', in *What do Europeans want from NATO?* (note 94), p. 22.
101. On the notion of preferences see Andrew Moravcsik, 'Preferences and Power in the European Community: A Liberal Intergovernmentalist Approach', *Journal of Common Market Studies*, Vol. 31, No. 4 (1993), pp. 473–524; Andrew Moravcsik, 'Taking Preferences Seriously: A Liberal Theory of International Politics', *International Organization*, Vol. 51, No. 4 (1997), pp. 513–533.
102. This number may appear to be confusing, but the EU's own accounting places the mission in support of the African Union in Darfur as half civilian and half military. See http://www.consilium.europa.eu/showPage.aspx?id=268&lang=en (accessed 24 March 2011).
103. Berger, 'Norms, Identity, and National Security in Germany and Japan', (note 12), p. 326; Legro, *Cooperation under Fire* (note 12), pp. 22–25; Arendt Lijphart, 'The Structure of Inference,' in Gabriel A. Almond and Sidney Verba (eds), *The Civic Culture: Political Attitudes and Democracy in Five Nations* (Boston: Little Brown, 1980), p. 42; Harry Eckstein, 'A Culturalist Theory of Political Change', *American Political Science Review*, Vol. 82, No. 3 (1988), p. 792.

Index

Page numbers in **Bold** represent illustrations.

Afghanistan: EUPOL 58
Africa: CSDP, and 57–8; EU civilian operations 121–41; EU operations in 46
African security challenges 123–6; economic failure 124; former colonial powers, and 125; nature of problems 123–4
African Union: civil-military mission in support 129–31
Albright, Madeleine 45
Almond, Gabriel 26, 195
AMIS 129–30
anarchy: nature of 55
Andres, Giovanni 16
Annan, Kofi 85, 88, 106
APSA 131
Artemis 85–9, 169, 172–3
Ashton, Catherine 61–2
Astaire, Fred 11

Balkan miltary missions 68–83
Barcelona Report 108–9
barrack yard syndrome 92–3
behaviour: culture, and 36
Berlin-Plus agreement 184
Biscop, Sven 43–4
Bush, George H. 184

Calleo, David P. 60
Campbell, David; *Writing Security* 38
caricatures of culture 36
Carr, E.H. 54
Center for Contemporary Conflict 84
civilian crisis management: development 144–55
civilian CSDP in Brussels 133–7; ESS, and 134–5; Finland, and 134; institutionalizing civilian component 136–7; political pressure 134–6; responsive concept 134–6; Sweden, and 134
civilian missions in DR Congo and Guinea-Bissau 127–9
civilian operations 121–41; activists among EU member states 133; Africa, in 121–41; assessing 131–3; civil- military approach 132; development of EU foreign and security policy, and 138; experience 132; mixed record 131; mode of intervention 138; performance 137–8; political system, and 132; rational choices 126–33; strategic culture, and 121
classical realism 52–67; dualism, and 54; emphasis on politics 53–4
CMCO 136, 167
CMPD 136
Cold War 20, ESS, and 40–1
Colson, Charles W. 24
Common Foreign and Security Policy 68
Common Security and Defence Policy (CSDP) 1,2, 52–67, Africa, and 57–8, America, differences with 115; Brusselization process 114; classical realist assessment and critique 52–67; constructivist argument 59; crisis 114–15; crisis of legitimacy 115; current format 100; endorsement of military operations 104; failure of 102; German power, and 57; Headline Goal 58; limited power, as 56–9; operational activity 57; origin 100; preservation of restraint in Europe, and 63; prudence, as 59–62; Rafah mission 58; Russia-Georgia war, and

INDEX

58; transatlantic dialogue, and 63; world order, and 63
conceptual conumdrum 13–15
constructivists 20–1
core concepts: definition 11
Cornish, Paul 70
Cotonou Agreement 124
CPCC 135
culture; meaning 15–16; re-emergence in security studies 18–20

Darfur 110
Democratic Republic of Congo 84–98; EU's military involvement in 84–98; France, and 85–6; Germany, and 86–7
Desch, Michael: culturalists, and 21
Dessler, David 21
Duffield, John 188
Duke, Simon 87

Edwards, Geoffrey 70
effective multilateralism 9
elites: definition 189
ENP 191
Erklaren 19
ESDP 34,35; constructive ambiguity 39; origins 144–5; overview of missions 71–2; Franco-British partnering, and 62–3
ethnicity 16
EU Balkan military missions 68–83; coherence 79; coordination 79; effective multilateralism 79; EU as civilian power 79; EU as recognised global player 79–80; geographic setting 78–9; objectives 78; security threats, and 78; tracing strategic culture 68–83
EUFOR Althea 75–7; authority of 76–7; international agencies, and 77; role 77; success of 77
EUFOR CHAD 99–129; Buria 107; concept 111; contradiction 114; cost 114; Deby, President, and 112–13; environment 112; France as Kingmaker 112; impact 113; logistics 111; military staff 104; nature of 99; RFC, and 112–13; UN approval 110–11
EUFOR Libya 72
EUFOR RD Congo 89–92, 127–8, 169; barrack yard syndrome 92–3; collective good 92; Germany, and 89–90, 91–3; Kinshasa 127; push by influential EU member 90
EULEX Kosovo **152**-5
EUPAT **151**-2
EUPM **145**-8
EUPOL: Afganistan 58
EUPOL Proxima **148**-50
EU strategic culture in formation 157
European Security Strategy 1, 34, 35, 69–70 adoption of 142–3; ambition of 101–2; Cold War, and 40–1; comprehensive notion of security 43; core European values, and 42; Key elements 39; military force, and 42; nature of 71; original rationale 42; purpose 39; rationale 41; reconciliatory motive 43; regional organizations, support for 125; restoring order 42; revision 39; self-assessment 124; strategic narrative, as 40–2; traditional security strategy, and 43
EU SSR Guinea-Bissau 128–9
EU strategic culture 34–51, 68–83; comprehensiveness 88; 'games' 94–5; preferences 93–4
EU-UN cooperation 168–76; Artemis 169, 172–3; collective action problems 170–3; conflicting procedures of organizations 174–6; hurdles for policy coordination 173–4; institutional factors 173–6; member states' interests amd preferences 170–3; military capabilities 170–3; strategic culture, impact of 176–9
European Union: Africa operations in 46; assertiveness 46; battle groups 1; conflict and crisis management 161–83; constraints of being global actor 6; cooperation with UN 161–83; cooperative approach 166; emergent role 70; export of regional integration model 125; flexibility principle 8,9; fundamental premises 164; future for strategic culture 121; global player, as 70; international cooperation, and 55; international society, and 164–5; legitimacy 103; liberal internationalist agenda 104; multi-level character of decision-making 8; nationalism, and 52; nature of 142; non-military power, as 44; power political perspective 52–3; preventive approach 166; role in world 9; security actor, as 1; security,

INDEX

and 165; strategic culture 164–8; strategic culture concept, and 45; strategic options 165; system of preferences 8; two-level character in defence affairs 91; use of force, and 165

Farrel, Theo; strategic culture, on 101
France; Democratic Republic of Congo, and 85–6
Freedman, Lawrence; culture, on 37–8
Freeman, Edward 16
French Afrika Corps 107–8
FYROM 73–5

Gaddafi, Muammar 1
Gaddis, John Lewis 15
GAERC 175
Geertz, Clifford: culture, on 16–17
Germany: Democratic Republic of Congo, and 86–7; EUFOR Rd Congo, and 89–90, 91–3
Gilpin, Robert 55
globalization; impact of 165
grand strategy: definition 101
Grant, Charles 70
Gray, Colin 3, 13, 18–19, 22, 34, 36, 100
Guehenno, Jean –Marie 87

Haglund, David: strategic culture research 4
Haine, Jean Y: Chad operation, on 5
Heikka, Henrikki: strategic culture, on 37
historical sociology 22–3
Hoffmann, Stanley 55
human security 108–9
humanitarian operations 107
Hyde-Price, Adrian 41

identity 24
IFOR 75
Iraq crisis 44

JAES 131
Johnston, Alastair Iain; culture, on 17–18; strategic culture, on 162

Kagan, Robert: strategic culture, on 17
Kammel, Arnold: CSDP civilian missions, on 5
Kissinger, Henry 55, 59–60
Kuvi region 177

Lantis, Jeffrey 13
Lee, Alfred 195
Libya 1; NATO intervention 27
Longhurst, Kerry: strategic culture, on 37
Loriaux, Michael 62

MAD strategy 35
metaphor 25–7
Michel, Louis 173
MINURCAT 175
modal personality 25
Moravcik, Andrew 94
Morgenthau, Hans 61
multilateral Caesarism 93
myth 25–7

national character 23
NATO: Europeanisation 105–6; Libya, intervention in 27; military force, and 7; revison of strategic concept 68
Nato-EU relations 184; behavioural norms in response to threats 190–2; content analysis method 186; elite expressions 186; empirical evidence 189–90; evolution 184; international organizations 192–3; interpretation of normative overlap and divergence 195–7; methodology 186–7; normative overlap 185; political cultures 198–9; strategic culture 184; summary of empirical analysis 193–5; third parties 192–3; threats, range of 190
neoclassical realism 22
Neumann, Iver B: strategic culture, on 37
new history 16
nexus between strategic document and strategic culture 188–9
Niebuhr, Reinhold 61
Nixon, Richard 24
Norheim-Martinsen, Per; strategic culture, on 4
norms 188
nuclear weapons: strategic culture, and 69

Operation Allied Harmony 73–4
Operation Althea 197
Operation Amber Fox 73
Operation Concordia 73–5, 197; authority 74; scale 74; success of 74–5
Ortega, Martin 38

INDEX

path dependence 23
Pentland, Charles; EU forces in Balkans, on 4
Perrin du Lac, Francois Marie 11–12, 23–4
Peters, Ingo: EU/UN relationship, on 6
Petersberg Tasks 102–3, 194
Pierson, Paul; path dependence, on 23
political culture 26
politics: classical realism, and 53–4; nature of 63
power: meta-concept, as 14
Posen, Barry: CSDP, on 56
Praline summit 106

Rafah mission 58
realism: dissatisfaction with 28
Recamp Programme 108
Rose, Gideon: neologists, on 22
Rummel, Reinhardt: CSDP civilian missions, on 5
Russia-Georgia war 58
Rynning, Sten: strategic culture on 4

Saint-Malo process 102–3; 105; 184–5
Sarkozy, President 39
Schlesinger, Arthur Jr. 24
Schmidt, Peter: Europe's Congo missions, on 5
Schmitt, Carl 54
science: culture, and 20–2
security culture as strategic culture 11–33
SFOR 75–6
Snyder, Jack 3, 69; strategic culture, on 35
Stability Pact For Central and Eastern Europe 44
Sterling-Folker, Jennifer 60
strategic: meaning 15
strategic culture as explanatory factor **163**
strategic culture concept 187–8
strategic cultures 1–2; cognition, as 25–7; context, as 22–5; definition 15–18; dynamic interplay 46; elasticity 2; key variables 142; literature 2–3, 13; scholarship 2–3; system of preferences, as 84
strategic narratives 38
symbolism 25–7; political culture, and 26–7

Tardieu, Andre 12
Taylor, Edward B. 16
trajectory of strategic culture paradigm 2–4
Treaty of Lisbon 68

United Nations 161–83; comprehensiveness 166; conflict and crisis management 161–83; cooperation with EU 161–83; cooperative approach 166; EU, and 161–83; international society, and 164–5; operational guidelines 167; preventive approach 166; security, and 165; strategic culture 6–7, 164–8; use of force, and 165; war, use of term 164
United States: European unification project, and 60; foreign and security policy 105–67
UNPREDEP 73
UNPROFOR 73, 75
UN Secretary General: role of 88–9
US National Security Strategy 40

Van Ham, Peter 41
Van Rompuy, Herman 61–2
Verba, Sidney 196
Verstehen 19
Von Ranke, Leopold 16

Waever, Ole; Europe as security community, on 37
Waltz, Kenneth: bipolarity, on 20
weapons of mass destruction (WMD) 13
Weldon, W.T. 14–15
Wendt, Alexander 36–7
Western Balkans 142–60; analysis of missions 143; coherence of EU actions 156–7; EU civilian crisis management 142–60; geography 156; parameters to detect strategic culture 155–7; rapid reation to crises 156; whole of governmant approach 156
Wilde, Oscar 13

Zyla, Benjamin: EU and NATO, on 6

www.routledge.com/9780415695671

Related titles from Routledge

European 'Security' Governance

Edited by George Christou and Stuart Croft

This book argues that we can understand and explain the EU as a security and peace actor through a framework of an updated and deepened concept of security governance. It elaborates and develops on the current literature on security governance in order to provide a more theoretically driven analysis of the EU in security. A theoretical framework is constructed with the objective of creating a conversation between these two literatures and the utility of such a framework is demonstrated through its application to the geospatial dimensions of EU security as well as specific cases studies in varied fields of EU security.

This book was originally published as a special issue of *European Security*.

George Christou is Associate Professor in European Politics, Department of Politics and International Studies, University of Warwick, Coventry, UK.

Stuart Croft is Professor of International Security, Department of Politics and International Studies, University of Warwick, Coventry, UK.

December 2011: 246 x 174: 208pp
Hb: 978-0-415-69567-1
£80 / $125

For more information and to order a copy visit
www.routledge.com/9780415695671

Available from all good bookshops

www.routledge.com/9780415688833

Related titles from Routledge

Reconceptualising Arms Control
Controlling the Means of Violence
Edited by Neil Cooper and David Mutimer

This book examines issues surrounding sovereignty, geopolitics, nuclear disarmament, securitization of space, technological developments, human rights, the clearance of landmines, the regulation of small arms and the control of the black market for arms and nuclear secrets. The book discusses terrorism with reference to the case of the suicide attacks in Beirut in 1983 and how the Obama administration is orientating its posture on nuclear arms.

This book was published as a special issue of *Contemporary Security Policy*.

Neil Cooper is Senior Lecturer in International Relations and Security Studies in the Division of Peace Studies, at the University of Bradford.

David Mutimer is Deputy Director of the Centre for International and Security Studies and Associate Professor of Political Science at York University.

November 2011: 234 x 156: 280pp
Hb: 978-0-415-68883-3
£85 / $145

For more information and to order a copy visit
www.routledge.com/9780415688833

Available from all good bookshops